AF817952

Tourism and Sustainable Development in China

Modern China Series

Tourism and Sustainable Development in China

Guo Yan

North American Business Press

Tourism and Sustainable Development in China

Copyright © 2025 by North American Business Press, Inc.

ISBN: 978-1-948915-36-6

All rights reserved. No part of this book may be reproduced or transmitted in any form or by any means, electronic or mechanical, including photocopying, recording, or by an information storage and retrieval system - except by a reviewer who may quote brief passages in a review to be printed in a magazine or newspaper - without permission in writing from the publisher.

North American Business Press
Atlanta, Georgia
Miami, Florida
New York, New York
Toronto, Canada

FIRST PRINTING, 2025

About Modern China Series

As one of the oldest civilized regions globally, China has emerged as a "new world" because it embraces its essence and heritage and links them to viable economic strategies. In the last 25 years, China has made tremendous strides. The country and its people have every right to take pride in these accomplishments. Many Chinese leaders and intellectuals anticipate continuing growth with these successes. Furthermore, China's plans and strategies are often based on this premise.

The U.S. has tremendous interest in the Chinese economy and business environment. China has emerged as a global superpower, and scholars and business people in the U.S. are keenly interested in learning how this will affect them and do business with China. In response to growing interest from international and Asian scholars, North American Business Press is pleased to announce our Modern China Series (MCS) books. It is the first book series about modern China in the U.S., garnering tremendous interest in the U.S. and worldwide. With our first book reaching stores in September 2011, this initiative develops relationships between NABP and Chinese scholars. They desire to promote their academic and applied business writings to the rest of the world.

We have had an overwhelming demand for the Modern China Series from authors who would like to publish in the series and people who would like to read the books. The books have been viewed by thousands of people from the U.S. and the rest of the world. There are currently ten books published in the series, and we have a couple of dozen books that we are considering for the series.

We have published books on several areas revolving around the Chinese business environment. We have a few that focus on the best practices in marketing in China; some are compared to "best practices" in doing business in China, and a few are on the outlook of the Chinese economy. The market for the Modern China Series is enormous. There are tens of thousands of scholars who are keenly interested in the continued growth of the Chinese economy and the implications that it will have on the business world. Even more significant are the millions of business people interested in the impact that China will continue to have on the global economy. It is difficult to pinpoint the exact demand for the series, but it Is enormous.

We have big plans to grow the Modern China Series. It can be one of the most significant economic/business series ever produced. We are very selective with the books we will add to the collection, but we encourage scholars who think they have unique and exciting perspectives on China to submit their book manuscripts. From the readers' perspective, we are committed to producing high-quality books regularly, so readers should expect a steady stream of insightful books to come out for many years.

This initiative is headed by Dr. Robert Tian, a renowned researcher and academic. He spearheads our efforts to partner with foreign authors and administer the day-to-day operations of this series. Dr. Tian, the Vice-President of North American Business Press and Editor of this series, spends much of his time in Beijing, Shanghai, and other Chinese cities, focusing on developing and managing our interests with authors and universities. Below is the list of the books we have published:

Enterprise Strategy: New Horizon, authored by Zhang Xiuyu
Governance of Private Enterprises in Modern China, authored by Zhong Qin
The Art of War and Enterprise Strategy Management, authored by Fu Shouzhi
Marketing Issues in Modern China, edited by Robert Guang Tian et al.
The Footprints of the Academician, authored by Fu Zhouzhi
Marketing and Economics in Modern China (I) edited by Xiaoguang Qi et al.
Marketing and Economics in Modern China (II) edited by Wang Tianjin et al.
An Islamic Heritage in China, authored by Ma Zhanming
China Environmental Anthropology authored by Wang Tianjin, Tian Guang, and Ma Jianfu
Can China Rule the New World? Authored by Tian Guang and Chen Gang

Critiques on Pan-marketization authored by Li Cunlin, Liu Hongfei, and Tian Guang

Economic and Business Anthropology in China, edited by Xiaoguang Qi and Tian Guang

China-Mongolia Economic Corridor authored by Eerdun Taoketao, Zhang Zhe, Wang Gang, and Wei Lisi

Anthropology of Chinese Foodways authored by Tian Guang and Chen Gang

Urbanization of Rural China, authored by Li Taohong

Child Rearing in Rural China by Jiang Youchun and Yang Yunyi

Belt and Road vs. China and World by Tian Guang and Chen Gang

Modernization of China by Tian Guang, Luo Kanglong and Chen Qian

Abnormal School Behaviors: China vs. South Korea by Yu Yanyan

China in Xi Jinping Era by Shu Xiaohui, Li Yangkuo and Tian Guang

Shi Zhengyi and Chinese Ethnological Economics by Tian Guang and Zhong Ni

Decoding Entrepreneurial Vision by Fan Xiaoping

Huaihua International Inland Port by Shu Xiaohui, Hou Tengteng and Tian Guang

Tourism and Sustainable Development in China by Guo Yan

Table of Contents

Preface

This book, Tourism and Sustainable Development in China, is the culmination of years of research conducted during my doctoral studies at the Faculty of Business, Economics, and Accountancy, Universiti Malaysia Sabah. It explores the intricate relationship between tourism and poverty alleviation in China, with a particular focus on how tourism policies can help reduce poverty while contributing to sustainable development. The research behind this book examines the intersection of tourism, poverty, and sustainability, offering fresh insights into how well-designed tourism initiatives can drive economic, social-cultural and environmental transformation in underserved communities.

The motivation behind this book stems from the urgent need to address the gaps in empirical evidence and theoretical frameworks that currently hinder a comprehensive understanding of tourism's potential in sustainable development, particularly within the context of China's Tourism-Assisting the Poor Policies (TAPPs). As global recognition grows regarding tourism's role as a catalyst for reducing poverty, there remains a distinct lack of insight into how government interventions can effectively channel tourism benefits to those who are most in need—especially within developing countries, where pro-poor tourism policies often adopt a neo-liberal approach.

Poverty is a complex and multi-dimensional challenge that intersects with various Sustainable Development Goals (SDGs). However, when assessing China's progress in fulfilling SDG1—ending poverty in all its forms everywhere—the focus has largely been limited to the poverty line, neglecting a more holistic view of the broader impacts of tourism on sustainable development. This oversight prompted me to embark on this project, driven by a deep conviction that tourism's potential as a tool for sustainable development extends beyond economic gains to also include the creation of lasting, transformative change for marginalized communities.

This book aims to fill these gaps by critically examining the sustainability of TAPPs and their implications for the development of impoverished regions. Through an exploration of tourism's role in poverty eradication, I hope to offer a nuanced perspective on how policy interventions, government support, and community engagement can shape tourism in a way that prioritizes the needs of the poor while contributing to the broader SDGs. My goal is to provide both theoretical insights and practical implications for policymakers, scholars, and practitioners interested in the intersection of tourism, poverty reduction, and sustainable development.

The inspiration for this book stemmed from a series of observations and experiences during my academic and field research in China, where I witnessed firsthand both the potential and challenges of tourism in driving economic, social, cultural, and environmental changes, particularly in impoverished rural areas. The research process involved extensive engagement with rural communities, policymakers, and tourism practitioners, coupled with a critical review of existing literature and policy documents. Through these efforts, I sought to identify the key factors that influence the effectiveness of TAPPs and the ways in which these policies can be made more inclusive, equitable, and sustainable.

It is my hope that this book will serve as a valuable resource for a diverse audience, including scholars, policymakers, and anyone interested in understanding the complexities of tourism's potential to contribute to achieving SDG1 and the broader SDGs. I aim to foster a deeper appreciation for the multifaceted role tourism plays in sustainable development, encouraging readers to think critically about the policies and strategies that can ensure tourism serves as a force for good in both the short and long term.

Ultimately, Tourism and Sustainable Development in China is not just a book about tourism; it is about the broader aspirations of creating a more just, inclusive, and sustainable world. Through this work, I invite readers to join me on a journey of discovery, analysis, and reflection as we explore the role of tourism in promoting sustainable development in one of the world's most dynamic and rapidly evolving regions.

Acknowledgment

I would like to express my sincere gratitude to all those who have contributed to the successful completion of this book, which is based on my doctoral thesis.

First and foremost, I would like to extend my sincere thanks to my supervisor, Prof. Dr. Awangku Hassanal Bahar Pengiran Bagul from the Faculty of Business, Economics, and Accountancy at Universiti Malaysia Sabah. His expert guidance, unwavering support, and valuable insights have been essential throughout my research journey. I am truly grateful for his mentorship and encouragement.

I would also like to express my heartfelt appreciation to the three reviewers who provided invaluable input and suggestions to improve this work. Prof. Dr. Hairul Nizam Ismail of Universiti Teknologi Malaysia, Dr. Tini Maizura Mohtar, and Dr. Izyanti Awang Razli from Universiti Malaysia Sabah have all offered constructive comments that greatly enhanced the manuscript.

In addition, I would like to thank Prof. Dr. Robert Guangtian and the entire team at North American Business Press for their dedicated efforts in publishing this book. Their professionalism and commitment to this project have been instrumental in bringing this work to fruition.

Lastly, I am thankful for the support of my family, friends, and colleagues, whose encouragement has been invaluable during this journey.

Thank you all for your contributions to this work.

Foreword

Harnessing Tourism for Sustainable Development

Prof. Dr. Awangku Hassanal Bahar
Pengiran Bagul

Faculty of Business, Economics and Accountancy
Universiti Malaysia Sabah

The quest to eradicate poverty stands as one of the most pressing global challenges, and it is enshrined as Sustainable Development Goal 1 (SDG1) in the United Nations Agenda (2030 Agenda) for Sustainable Development. Yet, the role of tourism in this grand endeavor remains a subject of considerable debate. While tourism undeniably offers opportunities for economic growth, the pathways through which it can contribute to poverty alleviation have been underexplored, particularly in terms of empirical evidence and theoretical frameworks. This book, emerging from a groundbreaking doctoral dissertation, tackles these gaps head-on by investigating the relationship between tourism, poverty reduction, and sustainable development within the context of China's Tourism-Assisting the Poor Policies (TAPPs).

The Chinese government's recognition of tourism as a vehicle for poverty alleviation through TAPPs stands as a testament to its commitment to using all available tools to combat poverty. This work explores the complexities of government-driven tourism policies, particularly in impoverished areas, and provides valuable insights into the effectiveness of TAPPs. What sets this study apart is its multi-dimensional approach, extending beyond the conventional economic measures of poverty to consider social, cultural, and environmental factors—each intricately connected with other SDGs.

Through a rigorous mixed-methods approach, the author provides a comprehensive analysis of TAPPs' sustainability, policy instruments, and their impacts on both economic development and multi-dimensional poverty reduction. The use of advanced analytical tools, such as the Computable General Equilibrium (CGE) model and the Alkire-Frost Multi-Dimensional Poverty Index, allows for an empirical understanding of how tourism can generate economic growth that benefits the poor, directly challenging traditional neo-liberal approaches. Not only does the study examine the direct effects of tourism on poverty reduction, but it also uncovers the broader impacts of TAPPs on the sustainable development of destinations. This is an important contribution to the growing body of literature that seeks to understand how tourism policies can be more inclusive and sustainable.

The author's work underscores the importance of aligning tourism strategies with sustainability principles—economic, social, and cultural—while showing that government interventions can play a pivotal role in steering the benefits of tourism toward the poor. The findings suggest that the success of TAPPs lies in their holistic approach, focusing on long-term goals rather than short-term economic gain. This is critical in fostering a tourism model that not only alleviates poverty but also builds resilient communities.

This book represents a significant advancement in our understanding of pro-poor tourism (PPT), government policy, and sustainable development. It will be of great interest to scholars, policymakers, and practitioners in the fields of tourism, sustainable development, and poverty reduction. Moreover, it offers novel conceptual insights that extend beyond the specific case of China, providing a framework for applying these lessons globally.

As the world continues its fight against poverty, this study provides essential evidence that tourism can, indeed, be a powerful force for good—when guided by sustainable, inclusive policies. I am confident that this book will make a lasting impact on the field and inspire further research into the potential of tourism to support the achievement of SDG1 and beyond.

Chapter 1
Introduction: Tourism for Sustainable Development

This chapter briefly explains the research background and the problems that motivated this study to be conducted. Research questions and research objectives also will be explained in this chapter before the significance of the study is outlined. The researcher also briefly describes the definition of key terms used in this research at the end of this chapter.

Introduction

Poverty has always been a recurring and tricky problem that hinders the sustainable development of the whole world, especially in many developing countries. The global extreme poverty elimination progress has been reversed for the first time in over 20 years due to the devastating disaster caused by Covid-19 in 2020 (World Bank, 2020). Poverty elimination has been the central mission of some influential world organizations such as the World Bank and the United Nations. In 2013, the World Bank declared its two primary goals: to eradicate chronic extreme poverty by 2030; and to promote shared prosperity, defined in terms of economic growth of the poorest segments of society (Renwick, 2016). The United Nations also put poverty elimination on the top agenda of the 2030 Sustainable Development Goals (Griggs et. al., 2013). Besides these international organizations, the government is an essential stakeholder in poverty alleviation (Qin et. al., 2019). The Chinese government has been combating poverty since founding of the People's Republic of China in 1949. Thanks to more than 40 years of reform and opening up, the Chinese government finally ended absolute poverty after delisting the remaining 832 impoverished counties in 2020, ten years ahead of the schedule set by the World Bank and the United Nations (Xinhua, 2020).

Since mass tourism developed in the 1950s, the world has witnessed tourism's contribution to poverty alleviation in many developing countries. Since the 1980s, tourism has gradually become one of the significant poverty alleviations means the Chinese government relies on. Chinese tourism plays its role in reducing poverty under the guidance of Chinese Tourism-Assisting the Poor Policies (TAPPs) issued by the government. Tourism has contributed 20%-30% to the fulfilment of the country's 2020 absolute poverty eradication goal. Chinese absolute poverty eradication is mainly measured through the economic poverty line. However, scholars argue that economic growth brought by tourism does not naturally back up poverty alleviation (Chok et. al., 2007; Wattanakuljarus & Coxhead, 2008) due to the unequal distribution of economic benefits (Truong, Hall & Gary, 2014). Besides, tourism as a poverty alleviation tool is criticized for its adverse impacts on destinations' natural environment and social and cultural development (Mowforth & Munt, 2009; Gascón, 2015; Teng et. al., 2021), which impedes the sustainable development of destinations required by the SDGs.

Therefore, this study investigated the government's role in strengthening the tourism-poverty link and sustainable development through pro-poor tourism policies. Chinese TAPPs are a typical example of understanding the government's intervention in distributing tourism economic benefits for the poor and sustainable development through policy formulation and implementation. As is indicated by the sustainable development paradigm, poverty should not be limited to an economic dimension but a multi-dimensional issue (Holden, 2013; Mitchell & Ashley, 2010; Alkire & Shen, 2017). Stakeholders' perception of TAPPs' impacts on the sustainable development of poverty-stricken areas could reveal how multi-dimensional poverty is alleviated in a sustainable way through pro-poor tourism policies.

Background of the Study

During the past decades, tourism as a means for developing countries to escape the restriction of underdevelopment has been widely recognized (UNWTO & UNCTAD, 2001; Goodwin, 2008; Mowforth & Munt, 2015), particularly for earning foreign exchanges and creating new jobs (Sinclair, 1998; UNCTAD, 2017; King, 2018; Folarin & Adeniyi, 2020). Since PPT (pro-poor tourism) was proposed in 1999, tourism's role in poverty alleviation has drawn wide attention from tourism practitioners and researchers. Some aid organizations have devoted funds to developing community-based tourism to alleviate poverty (Harrison & Schipani, 2007; Hummel & Duim, 2012). Many developing countries launched tourism-based projects, policies, and strategies to reduce poverty (Zhao & Ritchie, 2007; Slocum & Backman, 2011).

The persuasive statistics have indicated tourism as an active economic booster for governments' poverty alleviation strategies, particularly in some Asian and African countries (Scheyvens & Hughes, 2019) such as Lao PDR (Harrison & Schipani, 2007), Vietnam (Truong et. al., 2014) and sub-Saharan African countries (Folarin & Adeniyi, 2020) including Tanzania (Slocum & Backman; 2011) and Kenya (Job & Paesler, 2013). However, Croes (2014) and Kim et. al. (2016) argued that tourism contributes most to poor people with lower income levels. Croes (2014) found that tourism does not systematically affect absolute poverty alleviation in developing countries. Mahadevan and Suardi (2017), after comparing 13 tourism-dependent countries, found that tourism growth neither narrows income inequality nor reduces the poor population. The poor local farmers in Western Uganda were less involved in the local tourism value chain than local intermediary suppliers, undermining tourism's role as a pro-poor tool (Adiyia & Vanneste, 2018). Therefore, whether tourism benefits have been distributed to the poorest remains an intense debate among the international academic community (Truong et. al., 2014; Adiyia & Vanneste, 2018).

"To end poverty, protect the planet and ensure prosperity for all" by 2030 is listed on the UN Agenda (2030 Agenda) for Sustainable Development. The UN expected tourism to increase economic benefits to developing countries with abundant tourism resources while maintaining the sustainable use of the natural resource, marine resources and promoting environmental conservation, employment generation and local culture and products. Empirical evidence has shown that tourism has been less sustainable than ever globally (Hall, 2011; Rutty, Gössling, Scott, & Hall, 2015; Scott, Hall, & Gössling, 2016; Scott, Gössling, Hall, & Peeters, 2016). Scheyvens (2019) even doubted if tourism could be a pivotal driver to eliminate poverty worldwide as required by SDGs.

Despite the world's controversy regarding tourism's contribution to SDGs, tourism in China has played an essential role in the national initiative to eliminate absolute poverty (Qin et. al., 2019) owing to the TAPPs implemented by the Chinese Central Government. The Chinese government aimed to lift 12 million people out of poverty through tourism from 2016 to 2020 (CNTA, 2017). China National Observation Report on Rural Tourism Poverty Alleviation shows that by the first half year of 2019, the rural tourism income averaged 1.432 million yuan, an increase of 38.4% year-on-year, in the 13 poverty alleviation monitoring villages (documented poor villages) in China's deeply impoverished "three regions" (Tibet, the four prefectures of Hotan, Aksu, Kashgar and Kizilsu in southern Xinjiang, and the ethnic Tibetan areas in Sichuan, Yunnan, Gansu and Qinghai) and the "three prefectures" (Liangshan Yi Autonomous Prefecture in Sichuan, Nyjiang Lisu Autonomous Prefecture in Yunnan and Linxia Hui Autonomous Prefecture in Gansu). The rate of tourism's contribution to the Chinese absolute poverty eradication goal in 2020 reaches 20% - 30%, despite the different contribution rates in different stages. In order to explore how Chinese pro-poor tourism contributes to sustainable development, it is essential to look back at the path of world tourism and sustainable development, Chinese tourism development stages, Chinese anti-poverty initiative and Chinese tourism-assisting the poor stages.

World Tourism and Sustainable Development

Tourism stands as one of the largest global industries, interconnecting with numerous key sectors of the world economy (Fennell, 2020). As a major player in the global economic landscape, tourism serves as a significant creator of wealth and a vital contributor to economic expansion and progress (Garau-Vadell et al., 2018). It plays a pivotal role in the economies of many localities and nations, and its contribution to world trade continues to expand (Hunter, 1995). Over the past fifty years, global tourism has witnessed a notable average annual growth rate of 6.6%, with international tourist arrivals experiencing a substantial surge from 25.2 million in 1950 to 972.68 million in 2010 (Fennell, 2020). From 2010 to 2019, the number of international tourists rose from 972.68 million to 1462.27 million, with an average annual increase of approximately 5% (see Figure 1-1). Unfortunately, the international tourist arrivales declined sharply by 72.2% in 2020 from 2019 due to the pandemic outbreak.

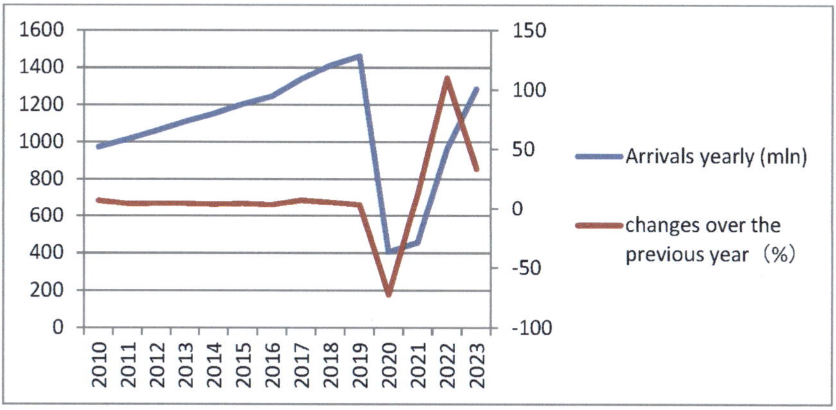

Figure 1-1 International tourist arrivals and changes (2010-2023)

Source:https://www.unwto.org/tourism-data/global-and-regional-tourism-performance

In 2023, international tourism rebounded significantly, reaching 88% of pre-pandemic levels, driven by robust pent-up demand. Globally, approximately 1,286 million international tourists (overnight visitors) were tallied, marking a 34% surge from 2022, equivalent to 325 million more tourists (see Figure 1-1). Notably, the Middle East spearheaded the recovery among regions, surpassing pre-pandemic levels with a 22% increase in arrivals and a 23% rise in receipts compared to 2019, as depicted in Figure 1-2. Europe saw tourist arrivals and receipts reach 94% and 97% of pre-pandemic levels in 2023, respectively, while Africa and the Americas attained 96% and 83%, and 90% and 74% in terms of arrivals and receipts. Asia and the Pacific exhibited a more gradual recovery, reaching 65% and 36% of pre-pandemic levels since the beginning of 2023. Following a robust resurgence in 2023, international tourism is anticipated to fully recover pre-pandemic levels by 2024, with initial forecasts suggesting a 2% growth over 2019 levels in international tourist arrivals. The positive sentiment towards the sector is reflected in the latest UN Tourism Confidence Index survey, where 67% of tourism professionals anticipate better or much better prospects for 2024 compared to 2023. The anticipated unleashing of remaining pent-up demand, enhanced air connectivity, and a stronger revival of Asian markets and destinations are poised to bolster a complete recovery by the conclusion of 2024 (UNWTO, 2024).

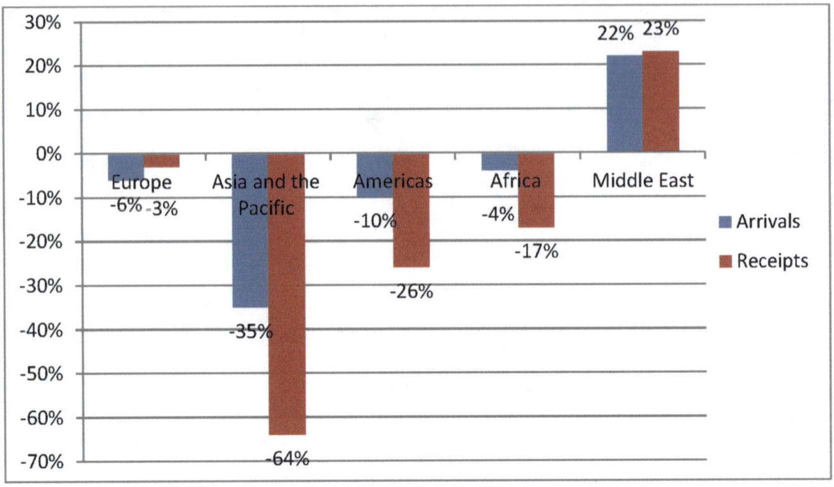

Figure 1-2 Changes of international tourism 2023 over 2019

Source: https://www.unwto.org/tourism-data/un-tourism-tourism-dashboard

The rise of worldwide tourism has coincided with the broadening of travel markets and a proliferation of tourism spots. In 1950, Europe and the Americas dominated as the top five travel destinations, commanding 71% of the global travel market (Fennell, 2020). However, by 2002, their share dwindled to just 35%, highlighting the emergence of accessible destinations in Africa, Asia, the Middle East, and the Pacific Rim, including many developing nations. Over the past seven decades, global tourism has seen substantial growth as an economic sector, playing a significant role in the economic advancement of numerous countries.

The potential of tourism development to foster sustainable growth stems from various distinctive features of the tourism industry (UNWTO, 2002). Initially, tourism offers a chance for economic diversification, especially in regions with limited export alternatives. Tourists are drawn to distant locales rich in cultural, wildlife, and scenic assets. These assets often constitute the cultural and natural heritage of developing nations, presenting an avenue for income generation by preserving heritage values. Unlike other export sectors, tourism involves consumers traveling to the exporting country, enabling lower-income households to engage in exporting by selling goods and services to foreign visitors. Additionally, tourism is labor intensive, creating opportunities for small-scale employment and advancing gender equality. Furthermore, there are indirect advantages for impoverished communities, such as improved market access for remote areas through the development of transportation, infrastructure, and communication networks. Nonetheless, travel is highly sensitive to income fluctuations and has a significant carbon footprint, posing sustainability challenges for the tourism sector (Lenzen et al., 2018).

Concerns regarding environmental issues emerged in tourism studies at a time when global consciousness about the environmental repercussions of human actions was expanding. In 1972, alongside the publication of "The Limits to Growth" (Meadows et al., 2018), which underscored apprehensions regarding the consequences of exponential economic and population expansion in a world with finite resources, the United Nations Conference on the Human Environment convened in Stockholm. Notably, this year also marked the iconic Blue Marble photograph of Earth, taken by the Apollo 17 spacecraft crew (Höhler, 2015, p. 10). This image, depicting the planet shrouded in the darkness of space, swiftly became emblematic of Earth's fragility and susceptibility.

The idea of sustainable tourism development emerged as a response to the prevalence of mass tourism, characterized by the involvement of large numbers of individuals often participating in structured or packaged tours. Over the past fifty years, mass tourism has experienced a significant surge. Since 1950, international arrivals have surged at an average annual rate exceeding 25%, with many of these journeys encompassing mass tourism activities (UNWTO, 2020). While data on the extent of domestic mass tourism are limited, mass tourism endeavors dominate the global tourism landscape. While mass tourism contributes to benefits for host nations, such as income and job creation, it also presents challenges such as economic leakage (where tourism revenue flows out of the host country) and economic dependency (where developing nations rely on wealthier countries for tourists, imports, and investments) (Conway & Timms, 2010; Peeters, 2012). Mass tourism is linked to numerous adverse environmental and social effects (Liu, 2003; Peeters, 2012; Conway & Timms, 2010; Fennell, 2020). Sustainable tourism development has been advocated as a conceptual framework to address many of these economic, environmental, and social concerns.

Sustainable tourism development is envisioned as a method of managing all resources to fulfill economic, social, and aesthetic requirements while preserving cultural integrity, vital ecological processes, biodiversity, and life support systems (Inskeep, 1991, p. 461). Hunter (1995) contends that sustainable tourism development should, both in the short and long term, cater to the needs and desires of the local host community by enhancing living standards and quality of life, meet the demands of tourists and the tourism industry to attract them continually, and safeguard the environmental resource base for tourism, which includes natural, built, and cultural elements, to accomplish the aforementioned goals (Hunter, 1995, p. 156).

Some scholarly works have recognized the ambiguity surrounding the notion of sustainable tourism development. This ambiguity has led to advocacy for fundamentally divergent approaches to tourism development, potentially intensifying existing conflicts between conservation and development ideologies (Garrod & Fyall, 2018; Hunter, 1995; Liu, 2003; McKercher, 1993b). Comparable critiques have been directed at the concept of sustainable development, which has been characterized as a paradoxical term encompassing a broad spectrum of interpretations (Daly, 1990) and being "defined in such a manner as to be either morally objectionable or logically unnecessary" (Beckerman, 1994, p. 192). Sharpley (2000) proposes that within tourism literature, there has been a consistent and fundamental inability to establish a theoretical connection between sustainable tourism and its foundational paradigm, sustainable development.

Hunter (1995) contends that practical approaches aimed at implementing sustainable tourism overlook key aspects integral to the broader concept of sustainable development and may even undermine its core principles. He suggests that conventional sustainable tourism practices focus primarily on safeguarding immediate resources necessary for tourism growth, disregarding broader concerns such as air pollution, congestion, invasive species, and diminishing oil reserves within the larger tourism ecosystem. The prevailing model of sustainable tourism development is portrayed as inward-looking, centered on tourism, and engaged in resource competition with other industries (McKercher, 1993a). Hunter (1995, p. 156) advocates for an alternative perspective termed the "extraparochial" paradigm, which reconceptualizes sustainable tourism development in relation to its contribution to holistic sustainable development objectives. This alternative paradigm would reassess the extent, magnitude, and sectoral dynamics of resource utilization issues associated with tourism.

Despite the ambiguity surrounding the concept of sustainable tourism development, the United Nations World Tourism Organization (UNWTO) (2024) observed that guidelines and management practices for sustainable tourism development are relevant across all types of tourism and destinations, encompassing both mass tourism and various niche segments. The principles of sustainability encompass the environmental, economic, and socio-cultural facets of tourism development, necessitating a delicate equilibrium among these dimensions to ensure its enduring viability. Additionally, the UNWTO has affirmed its commitment to promoting responsible, sustainable, and universally accessible tourism aligned with the overarching goals of the Agenda (2030 Agenda) for Sustainable Development and the Sustainable Development Goals (SDGs).

Hence, it's evident that tourism is a multifaceted aspect tied to sustainable development, encompassing social, cultural, and economic dimensions. Nonetheless, the available data on tourism, along with the current international statistical standards guiding its measurement, predominantly emphasize the economic aspect. There's a necessity to broaden the scope of tourism statistics to include the social and environmental aspects, while also reevaluating the economic assessment of tourism through a sustainability perspective.

The Measuring the Sustainability of Tourism (MST) program, led by the UNWTO in collaboration with the United Nations Statistics Division (UNSD) and key nations, along with support from organizations like the International Labor Organization (ILO), seeks to establish a globally accepted framework for assessing the impacts and interconnections of tourism on the economy, society, and environment, at both national and subnational levels. Serving as a tangible example of surpassing reliance on GDP, MST aids in generating dependable, internationally comparable data in countries regarding the sustainability performance of both nations and specific tourism destinations. By August 2020, the UNWTO had released the inaugural volume of MST pilot studies dedicated to measuring tourism sustainability. These pilot studies encompassed 11 countries: Austria, Canada, Fiji, Germany, Italy, Mexico, Netherlands, Philippines, Saudi Arabia, Sweden, and Thailand (Table 1-1).

Table 1-1 Pilot studies on tourism's contribution to sustainable development

Pilot country	Pilot program	Key findings
Austria	A pilot study that culminated in a Master-plan in Tourism	Economic dimension: 7.3% of total GDP (2018-2019). Environmental dimension: 1.15% of total Austrian final energy consumption (2017). Social dimension: Tourism perception index amounted to 78 points on a scale from 0 to 100 (2020).
Fiji	A roadmap to measuring the sustainability of tourism	Economic dimension: To focus on tourist accommodation industry. Environmental dimension: To collect data on water, electricity and land use by tourism industries.
Germany	A new "Tourism-Sustainability Satellite Account" (TSSA)	Economic dimension: Labor productivity in tourism is about 1/3 lower compared to the overall share of the German economy (2016). Environmental dimension: Energy-use in tourism accounted for 3.7% of the German economy; tourism-related greenhouse gas (GHG) emissions accounted for 4.5% of total emissions of the German economy (2016); Social dimension: Men-women pay gap in tourism lower than the whole economy; share of employment with low wages in tourism industries twice as high as the whole economy.
Italy	Measuring the impact of tourism-related air emissions	Economic dimension: Tourism consumption accounted for 5.2% of the total economy output (as of 2015). Environmental dimension: Tourism generated 16.4 % of total air emissions of ground level ozone, 15.5 % for acidification and 5.9% for GHGs and required 5.5 % of total use of energy products by economic activities; energy use and GHG emissions generated by tourism 12% higher than the whole economy (2018).
Mexico	Identifying areas of	Economic dimension: The

Pilot country	Pilot program	Key findings
	influence for measuring the sustainability of tourism	Establishment Directories for tourism activities linked to the economic activities of Protected Natural Areas and archaeological sites, facilitating data reproduction in line with updated Economic Censuses and Maps of Land Use.
Philippines	Estimating water and energy consumption in tourism	Economic dimension: Tourism employment accounted for 13.5% of the total employment and tourism's contribution to GDP was 12.7% (2019); Environmental dimension: Total energy and water consumption of domestic tourism more than tripled during 2012-2019; Domestic tourism consumed 78% of water and energy for transport services and 18% for accommodation and food and beverage (2019); Inbound tourism was responsible for 24 % of the water and energy consumption of internal tourism, while domestic tourism accounted for 76 % (2019).
Samoa	An extended Tourism Satellite Account (TSA) pilot exercise	Economic dimension: Direct Tourism Contribution to GDP was 12.5%, tourism employment accounting for 21.5%, tourism income the second largest foreign exchange earner (2015-2017). Environmental dimension: Tourism uses 11.5 % of water resources and 10% of electricity (2016-2017).
Saudi Arabia	Estimating the environmental effects of tourism	Environmental dimension: 86% of total domestic tourists travel by private cars, consuming 324.8 million liters of fuel, 2,480 million Kwh of electricity, and 23.6 million m3 of water and producing 83,817 tons of CO2 (2017).
Sweden	A method for estimating GHG emissions in tourism	Economic dimension: Input-output analysis of tourism's indirect impacts on employment increased by 50% than the TSA results (2018).

Pilot country	Pilot program	Key findings
		Environmental dimension: travel is the primary contributor to greenhouse gas emissions, representing over 60 % of total GHG emissions (2018).
Thailand	A regional pilot that resulted in a National TSA-SEEA System of Accounts	Environmental dimension: Preliminary Tourism Water, Energy, GHG and Solid Waste Accounts for Thailand (2017) have been compiled for the possible computation of the expenditure of government on natural resources and environment activities contributing to tourism.
Vietnam	Land-based pollution in the Quang Ninh province	Economic dimension: Tourism contributed 11% to the regional GDP in Quang Ninh province (2018-2019). Environmental dimension: waste water from tourist boats accounted for 30% of water pollution load from the local population. But the wastewater from tourism-related activities was still smaller than coal mining and rice production (2018-2019).

Source: World Tourism Organization. 2020, Experiences from Pilot Studies in Measuring the Sustainability of Tourism-A Synopsis for Policy Makers, UNWTO, Madrid, DOI: https://doi.org/10.18111/9789284424047.

The primary findings from the aforementioned pilot studies highlighted that the economic and environmental effects of tourism on sustainable development were the primary concerns that were evident and quantifiable in most nations. Among the 11 pilot studies, nine provided data or observed various economic indicators related to tourism, including its contribution to GDP, labor productivity within the tourism sector, tourist spending, and the impact of tourism on employment at the national or regional level. Tourism emerged as a significant contributor to GDP in the Philippines, Samoa, and Vietnam, with its contribution surpassing 10%, notably higher than the global average. In Germany, tourism's labor productivity accounted for approximately 30% of the overall economy. Moreover, tourism was recognized as a major source of employment in the Philippines, where the tourism employment rate constituted 13.5% of total employment. In Sweden, the indirect employment impacts of tourism, as revealed through input-output analysis, were even 50% higher than the results obtained from TSA data in 2018.

In addition to examining various economic indicators, these pilot studies addressed the environmental effects of tourism primarily through metrics such as energy and fuel consumption, water and electricity usage, land utilization, greenhouse gas emissions, wastewater, and solid waste generation. Nearly all of the pilot studies demonstrated that tourism significantly contributed to energy and resource consumption, as well as being a major source of pollution and greenhouse gas emissions. Regarding the social impact of tourism, only Austria conducted a survey in 2020 to gauge the perceptions of resident populations. This survey encompassed personal opinions about tourism in Austria, overall impressions of tourism, the perceived importance of tourism for Austria, and individual identification with tourism in Austria. The perception index among the Austrian population scored 78 on a scale of 0 to 100, indicating relatively positive social sustainability impacts attributed to tourism in Austria.

After the initial release of 11 pilot studies, the UN revised five existing pilots and introduced seven new MST pilots to further enhance the development of the MST framework (refer to Table 1-2). These updated pilots shed light on the shifts in tourism's impact on sustainable development amid the Covid-19 pandemic. For instance, Austria and Fiji experienced significant declines in tourism's contribution to GDP and employment due to the pandemic. Concerning the environmental sustainability of tourism, Austria saw an uptick in the utilization of renewable energy, potentially mitigating the negative environmental effects of tourism. Italy pinpointed cars as the primary source of pollutant emissions from tourism activities. Additionally, Mexico and Sweden demonstrated advancements in implementing MST pilots by exploring data applicability and innovating research methodologies.

Table 1-2 Updated findings of existing pilots and new pilots on tourism's impacts on sustainable development

Existing pilots	Pilot program	Updated findings
Austria	Austria monitors its Tourism Master Plan with MST-based indicators	Economic dimension: Tourism's contribution to GDP decreased by 3.3% in 2020 and 3.5% in 2021 compared with 2019 due to the pandemic. Environmental dimension: 1.3% of total Austrian final energy consumption (2019); The share of renewable energy sources in accommodation and restaurant amounted to 54%, 5% more than two years before (2017). Social dimension: Tourism perception index (2021) remained the same as that in 2020.
Fiji	Advancing the implementation of the roadmap on MST	Economic dimension: Average tourism contribution to GDP for the period 2016–2020 stood at 10.2%. 2020 showed a drastic decline as a result of impacts of the pandemic. Total tourism employment showed an increasing trend in the years 2016 to 2019. Investment in terms of tourism gross fixed capital formation (TGFCF) for period 2016–2019 witnessed an average growth of 6.4%. Environmental dimension: Water, energy and waste data was collected but not linked to specific tourism industries.
Italy	Tourism and road transport emissions	Environmental dimension: The car is the vehicle that contributes predominantly to all emissions of pollutants with values that vary in 2019, between 70.8% of PM2.5 and 94.9% of VOCs. the greatest contribution to atmospheric

		pollutants is from campers, caravans and vans which mainly affect PM2.5 (26.2%) and NOx (18.6%) emissions.
Mexico	Scaling up the status of MST pilot to a national project	Under the leadership of the Instituto Nacional de Estadísticay Geografía – INEGI and the national tourism administration, Mexico has confirmed the possibility to link the work of MST with the Ecosystem Accounting and that the work of the Ecosystem Accounting can feed the MST project.
Sweden	An experimental method to measure environmental pressures from tourism consumption	Economic dimension: Previous research was further elaborated by using the PRINCE-model, which allows for more detailed and accurate data on the input needed throughout the whole value chain of imported goods consumed by visitors in Sweden. Environmental dimension: During the period 2015–2019, total consumption-based emissions from tourism decreased by 7%.
New pilots	**Pilot program**	**Key findings**
Costa Rica	Estimating the economic contribution of nature-based tourism	Economic dimension: Nature-based tourism increased by 21% from 2017 to 2018. It represented 1.2% of the GDP in 2017 and 1.4% in 2018.
Indonesia	Environmental impacts of tourism in marine areas	Economic dimension: Marine tourism is the third largest generator of employment. It has the second lowest labour productivity and proportion of intermediate consumption in output. It uses the second fewest natural inputs. Environmental dimension:

		2,03% of the total wastewater from marine tourism flows untreated to the ocean. The remaining of the total wastewater is treated in septic tanks (97.97%).
New Zealand	Measuring the contribution of tourism to greenhouse gas emissions	Economic and environmental dimensions: Tourism's contribution to GDP, employment from tourism and emissions from tourism,– all decreased sharply in 2020 due to New Zealand's COVID-19 travel restrictions.
South Africa	An experimental method to value nature-based tourism	Social dimension: Savanna and grassland biomes in South Africa contributed greatly to nature-based tourism value which increased by 50% from 2005 to 2011. But the spread of nature-based tourism value was not evenly distributed across different municipalities.
Spain,Canary Islands	Setting the focus on the micro-destination scale	Economic dimension: The number of visitors to 47 micro-destinations in Canary Islands dropped by 58.3% in 2021 over the previous year due to the pandemic. The annual Survey of Tourism Data at the micro-destination scale from 2009 to 2021 provided 16 different indicators related to the tourism supply side. Social and environmental dimensions: There are research projects underway on social and environmental data.
Uganda	Integrating biodiversity and tourism accounts	Economic dimension: Tourist visits and expenditure across the 12 wild-life protected areas in Uganda increased substantially during 2011-2019. Tourism activities could deliver livelihood opportunities and

		facilitate poverty alleviation. Environmental dimension: The Uganda wildlife-watching tourism maintained good natural condition.
Arab countries	A proposed roadmap for MST	Economic dimension: Only a few countries have developed TSA for measuring the economic impacts of Tourism. Social and environmental dimensions: a considerable gap in data availability, especially for social and environmental measures related to tourism.

Source: World Tourism Organization. 2022, measuring the sustainability of tourism – learning from pilots, UNWTO, Madrid, DOI: https://doi.org/10.18111/9789284424061.

Differing from the existing pilot studies which primarily focus on the sustainability of the broader tourism sector, the new pilot initiatives shift their attention towards the interplay between eco-tourism and sustainable development. Echoing the findings of previous studies, the additional pilots conducted in Costa Rica, Indonesia, and Uganda highlighted a notable surge in nature-based and marine tourism, showcasing their substantial contributions to GDP, employment, and poverty reduction before the onset of the pandemic. Conversely, New Zealand and the Canary Islands of Spain witnessed a steep decline in tourism's economic impact in 2021, attributed to the stringent Covid-19 travel measures. While most previous cases underscored tourism's significant consumption of energy, water, and electricity, along with its role as a primary emitter of pollutants, Indonesia presented fresh evidence indicating that its marine tourism sector exhibits comparatively lower labor productivity and intermediate consumption in output, as well as utilizing fewer natural resources. Additionally, a mere 2.03% of the total wastewater generated from marine tourism remains untreated, with the bulk being appropriately treated in septic tanks (97.97%).

Undoubtedly, implementing pilot programs for MST proves to be a valuable strategy for garnering agreement on critical measurement concerns within the MST framework. These endeavors demonstrate the feasibility of uniformly measuring the entire spectrum of factors that constitute tourism sustainability under a unified framework. Consequently, MST has received formal endorsement from the UN as the designated instrument for generating indicators to monitor global tourism within the SDGs. However, despite its recognized significance, MST pilot initiatives encounter obstacles stemming from insufficient financial resources, support, or engagement from the policy sphere, as well as challenges related to coordination among various agencies, methodological direction, and technical expertise.

According to the findings from MST surveys conducted in Arab countries, there exists a notable level of awareness among stakeholders in the tourism sector regarding the significance of sustainable tourism as a driver for development. However, it's observed that only a minority of countries have implemented Tourism Satellite Accounts (TSAs) to gauge the economic impacts of tourism. This underscores a substantial gap in data availability, particularly concerning social and environmental indicators associated with tourism. Additionally, the noteworthy role played by Chinese tourism in aiding the government's achievement of its 2020 target for absolute poverty alleviation suggests that pro-poor tourism holds considerable promise for advancing SDG1 and its interconnected goals. MST initiatives, exemplified by those in Uganda, have demonstrated that tourism could offer opportunities for livelihood enhancement and contribute to poverty alleviation. Despite these insights, MST pilots have yet to delve into exploring the nexus between Chinese pro-poor tourism and sustainable development. To gain a deeper understanding of this relationship, it becomes imperative to examine the various stages of Chinese tourism development in the subsequent section.

Chinese Tourism Development

Chinese tourism has mainly experienced four stages of development since the People's Republic of China (PRC) was founded in 1949 (a map of the PRC is provided in Figure 1-3). Chinese tourism development closely follows the government's economic and social system reform, especially China's reform and opening-up initiative launched in 1978. Therefore, the four stages of tourism development are: tourism developed for political reception (1949-1978), tourism developed for earning foreign exchanges (1979-1991), Chinese mass tourism (1992-

2011) and quality tourism (2012-present) (Liu & Ji, 2017; Hu & Huang, 2019; Cheng, Yang, Chen & Liu, 2020).

a. Political Reception Period (1949-1978)

During the 29 years from the founding of the PRC to the launch of the reform and opening-up, the Chinese tourism industry, though without characteristics of modern industry, witnessed its initial development on a tiny scale. During the early years of the founding of the PRC, the calamity-ridden Chinese nation got stuck in economic poverty and cultural blankness after about a century's fight against the twofold repression by imperialism and feudalism marked by the First Opium War in 1840. The backward economic and social conditions between 1949 and 1978 posed significant difficulties for tourism development. Despite these limited conditions, tourism started its initial development by receiving foreign politicians as its primary mission to expand political influence and enhance friendships with foreign countries. According to the "Suggestions on the Travel Permits for Diplomats" issued by the China Ministry of Foreign Affairs in 1955, foreign diplomatic officials are only allowed to travel in specified areas with their diplomatic cards or passports registered by the China Ministry of Foreign Affairs. Besides, the Overseas Chinese Service Agency, the first travel agency of the PRC, was established in October 1949 to receive overseas Chinese who return to China to visit relatives and friends (Chen et. al., 2020).

Later in October 1964, the China National Travel and Tourism Administration Bureau was set up to directly manage and run the international travel agencies, marking that the Chinese tourism industry stepped on the track of standardized development. In 1965, international tourists in China hit a peak of 12,877 since the founding of the PRC. Unfortunately, tourism development was hindered by the ten-year upheaval caused by the Chinese political movement - the Great Proletarian Cultural Revolution, launched in 1966. It was not until 1976, when Premier Zhou En'lai announced tourism recovery at the national tourism work conference, that tourism returned to normal. From 1949 to 1976, Chinese tourism received about 50,000 international tourists. The establishment of international tourism agencies and the national tourism administration authority laid a foundation for the gradual improvement and rigorous growth of the tourism industry after the reform and opening up (Chen et. al., 2020).

Figure 1-3 Map of the PRC showing major cities and administrative regions 2006-2023

Source: https://www.map-of-china.org/

b. Foreign Exchanges Earning Period (1979-1991)

Tourism has been taken as one of the primary sources for earning foreign exchanges in many developing countries. In the 1970s-1990s, the shortage of foreign exchanges was one of the major problems China faced. With the launch of the reform and opening-up initiative in 1978, the market economy mechanism was introduced into the planned economy system, unveiling the market-oriented reform and development of the tourism industry. Since then, tourism's role has shifted from political reception to economic construction. As tourism gained experience in serving foreign guests while receiving foreign politicians, it naturally became a primary means for the Chinese government to alleviate the foreign exchange shortage during the reform and opening-up situation.

The national tourism work conference at Beidaihe in 1979 proposed that all provincial capital cities should build at least one international hotel that could accommodate foreign tourists. This policy drove the construction of reception facilities for inbound tourism. In 1985, the State Council put forward the guidelines for the joint development of tourism by the central and local governments, enterprises and individuals to step up the construction of tourism infrastructure. In 1986, tourism was proposed by the Chinese government as an essential tool for economic construction and foreign exchange generation. In the seventh five-year plan (1985-1990), the Chinese central government directly invested 2.5 billion yuan for tourism infrastructure construction and improvement. As of 1991, there were 21,130 international tourist hotels, 321,100 guest rooms, and 619,500 beds, which were 15.5, 21.4, and 20.6 times the number in 1977.

The opening of Chinese tourism and improvement of infrastructure facilities promoted the steady increase of international tourists and inbound tourism revenue. Figure 1-4 shows that the number of international tourists rose from 4,203,900 in 1979 to 33,349,800 in 1991 and the foreign exchange income from inbound tourism increased from 0.449 billion US dollars in 1979 to 2.845 billion US dollars in 1991, representing a growth rate of 693% and 411%. In 1984, the number of inbound tourists and inbound tourism revenue broke 10 million and 1 billion US dollars respectively. This remarkable achievement was obtained owing to the reform of tourism system in response to the "Decision on Economic System Reform" made by the Third Plenary Session of the Twelfth CPC Central Committee.

Later in 1985, tourism was for the first time included in the national economic and social development program - the seventh five-year plan (1985-1990). The international tourist arrivals and inbound tourism revenue declined slightly in 1989 due to a small scale political turmoil. However, the inbound tourists during 1985-1990 totaled 133,379,700, creating a foreign exchange income of 10.968 billion US dollars. By the end of 1991, there were 4,980 tourism enterprises and institutions throughout the country. It is easily concluded that during 1979-1991, Chinese tourism's economic benefits were greatly improved with better reception conditions, laying a solid foundation for the market-oriented reform and development of tourism industrialization (Wei & Zeng, 2018).

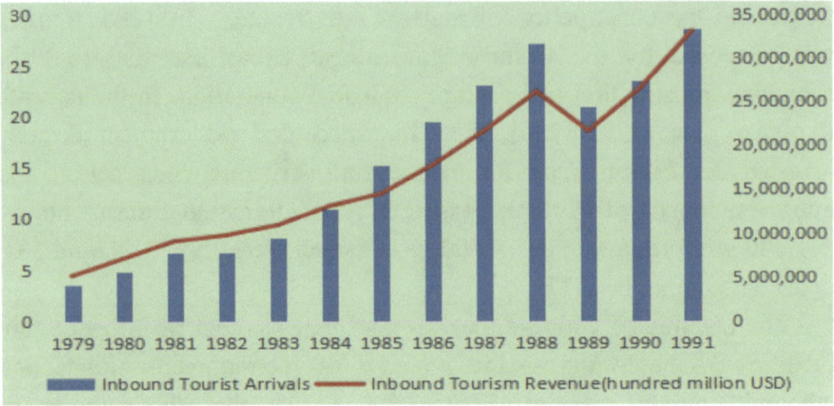

Figure 1-4 Inbound tourist arrivals and tourism revenue during 1979 -1991
Source: China Tourism Statistical Yearbook 1992

c. Chinese Mass Tourism Period (1992-2011)

After more than ten years of initial reform and opening up, the Chinese people's income increased and their living standards improved, making tourism a popular leisure activity that domestic residents could enjoy. The per capita disposable income of urban residents witnessed about a 7- times growth from 332 yuan in 1978 to 2143 yuan in 1991. In order to expand this achievement, Deng Xiaoping proposed accelerating the reform and opened up his speech on the Southern Tour in 1992. The target of establishing the socialist market economy system set by the 14th National Congress of the Communist Party of China in 1992 created a favorable environment for the further market-oriented development of the tourism industry. Under this circumstance, domestic tourism is recommended to be included in the national economic and social development plan in the "Opinions on Actively Developing Domestic Tourism Industry" issued by the National Tourism Administration in 1993 (Chen et. al., 2020).

Promoting tourism supply and demand became part of the government's goal in the mass tourism period. In 1992, the State Council approved the establishment of 11 national tourist resorts in the “Notice on the Trial Establishment of National Tourism Resorts.” In 2001, the "Notice of the State Council on Further Accelerating the Development of Tourism Industry" proposed diversifying tourism products further and vigorously developing ecological and urban tourism. In order to stimulate residents' demand for domestic tourism, the State Council reset the Schedule for National Holidays and Anniversaries in 1999, which created golden weeks for tourism, especially the Labour Day Holiday in May and National Day Holiday in October. In 2008, the "Regulations on Paid Annual Leave for Employees" was issued to release residents' potential for tourism consumption further. Figure 1-5 shows that domestic arrivals and domestic tourism consumption increased smoothly from 1994 to 2003 with the establishment of the tourism market reform system, except for a slight decrease in 2003 due to the SARS epidemic, which lasted only several months.

Thanks to the improvement of the tourism market reform system, the number of domestic tourists broke 1,000 million in 2004, and domestic tourism consumption exceeded 1 trillion yuan in 2009 when tourism was designated as the national strategic pillar industry by the State Council. By 2011, the total number of domestic tourists was 2.641 billion, and the total domestic tourism revenue was 1.93 trillion yuan, 8.8 times and 96 times that of 1991 respectively. Besides, in 1997, the Chinese outbound tourism market was officially opened by implementing "Interim Measures for of Chinese Citizens' Travel Abroad at Their Expenses". It can be seen from Figure 1-6 that the number of outbound tourists increased steadily from 20.222 million in 2003 to 70.25 million in 2011. However, the number is significantly smaller than that of inbound tourists, which grew from 91.66 million in 2003 to 135.42 million in 2011. It's easily found that, since the Chinese mass tourism period, domestic tourism, inbound tourism and outbound tourism have become three pillars of the tourism market, indicating that the Chinese tourism industry system has been established.

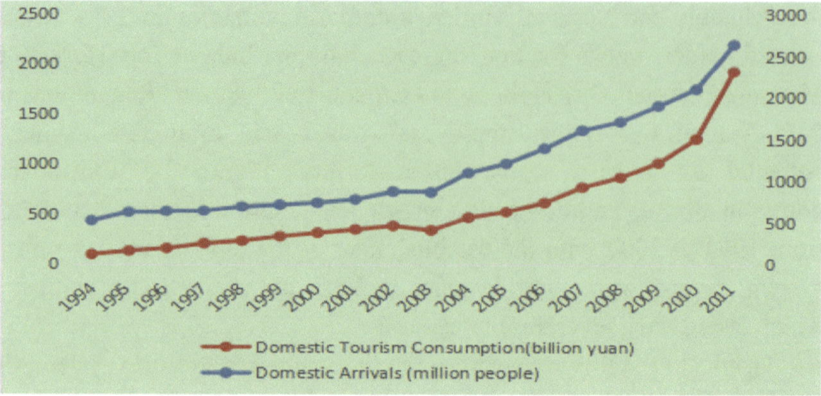

Figure 1-5 Domestic tourism consumption and tourist arrivals during 1994-2011
Source: China Tourism Statistical Yearbook 2012

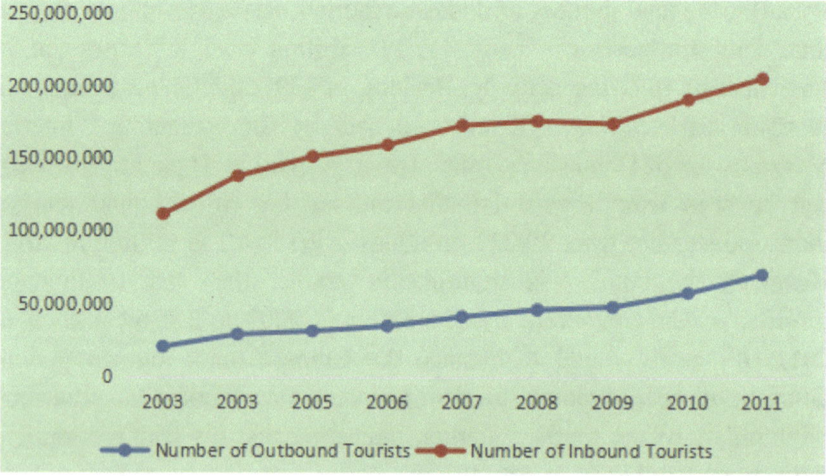

Figure 1-6 The number of outbound tourists and inbound tourists during 2003-2011
Source: China Tourism Statistical Yearbook 2012

d. Period of Quality Tourism (2012-Present)

After more than ten years of rapid development, the Chinese tourism industry shifted its focus from quantity to quality per the "Outline for the Development of Tourism Quality (2013-2020)" issued in 2012. This outline proposes building the tourism industry into a modern service industry for people's well-being and satisfaction. The Chinese tourism industry pursued its integrated development pattern to meet tourists' diverse demands and improve their experience of tourism services. In

2013, the "National Tourism and Leisure Outline (2013-2020)" proposed "tourism +", which advocated the integration of tourism with sports, agriculture, culture, education and other industries.

The "Thirteenth Five-Year (2016-2020) Plan for National Tourism Informatization" issued by the National Tourism Administration further highlighted the application of information technologies such as the Internet, artificial intelligence, computer simulation, big data and so on tourism. In the "Outline on Building China's Strength in Transportation", the State Council stressed the improvement of transportation facilities for tourism development. In 2016, tourism was at the top of the "Chinese Happiness Industries" list, including sports, health, education and training and elderly care related to people's quality of life and well-being. The merger of the Ministry of Culture and the National Tourism Administration into the Ministry of Culture and Tourism in 2018 showed the government's resolution to improve the quality of tourism services and products for people's well-being through the coordinated efforts of different industries.

The national tourism authority issued the "Guidelines on Development of All-for-one Tourism Demonstration Zones" in 2017 to promote integrated development patterns in the tourism industry. The idea of "all-for-one" tourism was first created in 2015. It was included in the 2017 Chinese government Work Report to achieve co-construction and sharing and promote the coordinated development of the economy and society by reorganizing tourism resources in tourist destinations (Xinhua, 2020). The demonstration zones must have high governance standards, extensive tourism products and services and active public participation.

Under the guidance of the "tourism +" and "all-for-one" tourism policies, the Chinese tourism industry enjoyed high-quality development with the further boom of the domestic tourism market. Figure 1-7 demonstrates that annual tourism revenue and tourism's contribution rate to GDP increased from 2012 to 2019, except for the sharp decrease in 2020 due to the Covid-19 pandemic. The annual tourism revenue increased from 2.59 trillion yuan in 2012 to 6.63 trillion yuan in 2019, representing a growth rate of 156%. In 2017, domestic tourists broke 5 billion for the first time, creating revenue of 4.57 trillion yuan which accounted for 84.63% of the annual tourism revenue. In addition, tourism's contribution to GDP witnessed rapid growth from 2012 to 2014 and remained steady increase from 2014 to 2019. The average contribution rate to GDP during 2012-2019 exceeds 10%, higher than tourism's average contribution to global GDP, which remains below 10% (WTTC, 2019). The global overall competitiveness ranking of Chinese tourism rose from 32 in 2011 to 13 in 2019.

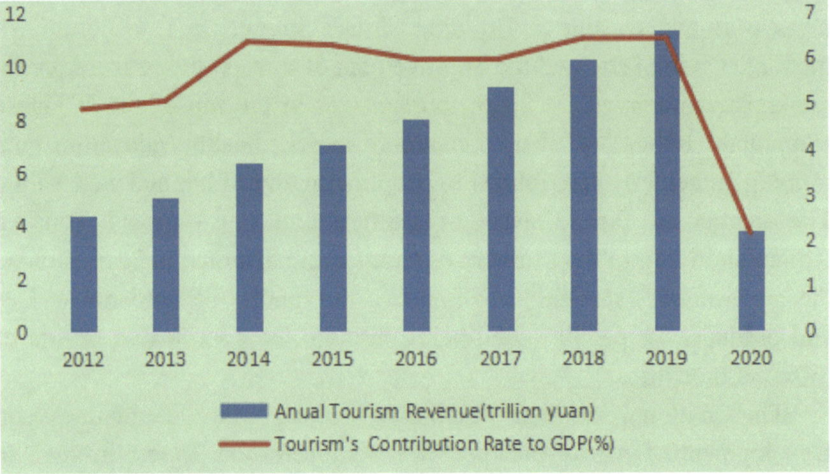

Figure 1-7 Annual Tourism Revenue and Tourism's Contribution Rate to GDP during 2012-2020

Source: China Tourism Statistical Yearbook 2021

This section revealed that tourism in the PRC developed in line with government goals under the national social and economic development conditions and plans. During the first 28 years of the founding of the PRC, tourism acted as a means for strengthening friendships with foreign countries and expanding the country's political impacts in the international community. Since the reform and opening-up in the late 1970s, tourism has gradually grown into a modern industry in response to the market and government's interaction for the market economy's development, always on a mission to improve people's well-being.

As the PRC was founded from ruins, poverty has always been the biggest problem hindering people's satisfaction and happiness. In order to realize Chinese people's common prosperity, the government has always been devoted to reducing poverty by implementing anti-poverty programs in which tourism plays a more and more important role. In order to understand how Chinese tourism development contributes to poverty alleviation, it's necessary to overview China's anti-poverty initiative in different periods in the next section.

Chinese Anti-poverty Initiative

When the Chinese government initiated poverty alleviation remains a controversy in the academic community. Some scholars argue that the Chinese poverty alleviation initiative could be dated back to 1949 when the new China was founded from the war-torn mess. In fact, during 1949-1977, the government focused on overcoming the political and economic difficulties of the whole country. No specific national policies were issued to tackle poverty which was believed to be naturally removed as long as political and economic problems were solved. As the living standards of the whole population were rather low during this period, the government only morally aided those individuals and families who lost the ability to work or were temporarily in poverty due to force majeure or unfavorable external conditions.

Therefore, many scholars agreed that the anti-poverty initiative was officially revealed after the reform and opening up in 1978. Since then, the Chinese government has carried out a series of policies on large-scale poverty alleviation (Liu et. al., 2019), guiding the market-oriented reform and development of tourism's contribution to reducing poverty. Based on the targets of the government's poverty alleviation policies, the anti-poverty initiative was generally considered to have experienced four stages: poor region-targeted period (1978-1985), poor county-targeted period (1986-2000), poor village-targeted period (2001-2012) and poor household-targeted period (2013-2020) (Table 1-3).

Table 1-3 Chinese anti-poverty stages and main features

Stages	Poor-region targeted period (1978-1985)	Poor county-targeted period (1986-2000)	Poor village-targeted period (2001-2012)	Poor household-targeted period (2013-2020)
Work Mechanism	Multi-departmental collaboration	Mainly responsible by provincial governments	Responsible by provincial governments and	Jointly responsible by secretaries of CPC

			Implemented by county governments	committees at provincial, municipal, county, township and village levels
Motivations	Rural system reform and rapid economic growth	Organized and planned large-scale poverty alleviation development	Sustainable poverty alleviation development	Anti-poverty governance by the Central Government
Major Strategies	Food and clothing relief; Special subsidy for agriculture development and work relief especially in the poor western region	Central government's special subsidy and collaboration of Eastern and Western Regions to solve the clothing and food problem in poor counties	Implementation of western development strategy; Improvement of living and production conditions in poor villages; Minimum basic living guarantee for poor villagers	Boosting economy to provide more job opportunities for the poor; Relocating the poor from inhospitable areas; shaking off poverty through compensations for economic losses associated with reducing ecological damage and getting eco-jobs; Improving education in impoverished areas; providing subsistence allowances for those unable to shake off poverty through their

				own efforts alone
Typical Policies	Three Western Regions (Dingxi and Hexi in Gansu and Xihaigu in Ningxia) Poverty Alleviation and Development Plan (1982)	The Eighth Seven-Year Poverty Alleviation Plan (1994-2000)	Outline of China's Rural Poverty Alleviation and Development (2001-2010)	Strategy of Targeted Poverty Alleviation (2013-2020)

Source: The China State Council Information Office. 2021. Poverty Alleviation: China's Experience and Contribution, http://pk.china-embassy.gov.cn/eng/zt/2356800/202104/P020210911658013307874.pdf

a. Poor Region-Targeted Period (1978-1985)

In the initial period of reform and opening-up (1978-1985), China was confronted by the problem of a largely impoverished population of 250 million in rural areas in 1978 (based on the 1978 poverty line of 100 yuan per capita). As Deng Xiaoping, head of the second generation of the CPC Central Committee, declared that socialism meant eliminating poverty, major reforms were initiated in the universally poor rural areas involving the integration of cooperative management and household contract management, the distribution system for agricultural products and the development of township enterprises. These efforts aimed to inspire the farmers' enthusiasm by clarifying the most basic production relations and increasing the overall income of rural areas.

Based on the rural system reform, the Central Government set the subsidy for the development of the most backward regions in 1980. Facing the shortage of food and clothing in poor rural areas, from 1980 to 1984, the central government allocated more than 30 billion yuan to guarantee food and clothing supply for poor farmers. In 1982, a special plan for poverty alleviation and development in the three most impoverished contiguous areas (Hexi Region and Dingxi Region in Gansu Province and the mountainous region in southern Ningxia Hui Autonomous Region) was issued to boost their agricultural development.

Known as a groundbreaking project in China's poverty alleviation efforts, this initiative involved 47 counties, cities and districts, setting a precedent in poor region-targeted poverty alleviation. Through the collaborative efforts of various government departments, the reform-driven poverty alleviation initiative yielded remarkable achievement, reducing the number of the poor in rural areas from 250 million in 1978 to 125 million in 1985.

b. Poor County-Targeted Period (1986- 2000)

The reform-driven poverty alleviation in poor regions yielded visible progress in poverty reduction in rural areas. In 1986, the Chinese central government established the first national poverty alleviation authority - the State Council Leadership Group for Economic Development in Poor Areas, renamed the State Council Leadership Group for Poverty Alleviation and Development in 1993. In this period, poverty had evolved from a widespread problem into one afflicting particular groups and populations, mainly distributed in 18 poverty-stricken areas, old revolutionary areas, minority areas, remote areas and extremely poor areas.

The national poverty alleviation authority took counties with a relatively high proportion of the poor as the basic target unites the special poverty alleviation plan. From 1986 to 1993, 331 counties were designated as poverty-stricken counties. By 1988, 370 counties across the country were designated provincial poverty-stricken counties. The central government arranged special poverty alleviation funds (mainly including special poverty alleviation loans, work-for-work relief and financial development funds) to support the 331 nationally designated poverty-stricken counties. From 1986 to 1993, the central government provided 46.72 billion yuan in poverty alleviation funds, of which special loans were 24.9 billion yuan, work-for-work funds were 8.9 billion yuan, and fiscal development funds were 12.92 billion yuan.

In 1994, the State Council launched the Eighth Seven-Year Poverty Alleviation Plan (1994-2000), China's first-ever national poverty alleviation program with definite goals, targets, measures and deadlines. It committed to ensuring that the basic needs of 80 million impoverished rural residents would be met in the seven years from 1994 to 2000. In 1996, the central authorities held the National Conference on Development-driven Poverty Alleviation, further clarifying the steadfast commitment to the goal of being able to provide adequate food and clothing for the impoverished people by the end of the 20th century and confirming the shift from relief-based poverty alleviation to development-driven poverty alleviation. Thanks to the implementation of this national poverty alleviation plan, by the end of 2000, the impoverished population in rural areas had been reduced to 32.09 million and the incidence of poverty down to 3.5%, based on the poverty alleviation standard at the time. However, the government remained the dominant stakeholder in poverty alleviation work, still following the concept of relief-based poverty alleviation. Under this concept, poverty alleviation is more like blood transfusion than constructing a hematopoietic mechanism with poor people's least participation in removing poverty through self-development.

c. Poor Village-Targeted Period (2001-2012)

Despite the significant progress in more than two decades of relief-dominated poverty alleviation, some rural residents in poverty-stricken villages still suffered from shortage of food and clothing. In order to guarantee the basic living needs of poor rural villagers, the central government issued the "Outline of China's Rural Poverty Alleviation and Development (2001-2010) at the beginning of the new century. This policy made major adjustments to the focus and targets of poverty alleviation work. 150,000 impoverished villages and 592 counties, mainly in central and western regions, were listed as key targets, covering 80% of the poor population. State strategy of regional development was implemented, such as developing western China, revitalizing old industrial bases in the northeast, and stimulating the rise of the central region. This strategy promoted coordinated development between regions and between rural and urban areas. In 2011, the central government announced the full launch of the battle against poverty, especially in 14 contiguous destitute areas. Another 240 counties were added to the previous list of 592 national poverty-stricken counties.

Unlike the passive relief-dominated poverty alleviation, more attention was paid to encouraging villagers' full participation in poverty alleviation efforts in this period. All "No. 1 central documents" during 2004-2012 focused on various flexible measures of providing more aid and reducing farmers' burden to increase their income and back up the implementation of the Western Development Strategy. "No. 1 central document" is the first policy statement released by China's central authorities each year and is seen as an indicator of policy priorities. A whole range of efforts was directed at business development, the training and transfer of rural labour, poverty alleviation through relocation, and relocation to develop the eco-economy. The minimum living guarantee system was set up to ensure the basic survival rights of poor farmers.

As a result, the impoverished rural population had been reduced to 26.88 million, and the incidence of poverty had fallen to 2.8% by the end of 2010, based on the 2010 poverty line of 1274 yuan a year. In 2011, the poverty line was raised to 2,300 yuan a year, which was about USD 0.98 a day based on the average exchange rate of yuan to USD in 2011, getting closer to the international poverty line of USD 1.25 a day in 2011. Under the adjusted poverty line, the poor population increased to 122 million. In order to accelerate poverty alleviation, the Outline of Development-driven Poverty Alleviation in Rural Areas (2011-2020) was issued, marking that China's poverty alleviation effort started to move from its primary mission of meeting the basic needs of the poor to a new stage of development-driven poverty alleviation in an eco-friendly way.

d. Poor Household-Targeted Period (2013-2020)

The Chinese government vowed to realize the CPC first centenary goal of building a moderately prosperous society in all respects after the 18th CPC National Congress in 2012. Extreme poverty elimination has been regarded as one of the most critical indexes for this achievement. The battle against extreme poverty has entered the toughest stage since 2013 as Chinese President Xi Jinping promised, "No single poor area or single poor person should be left behind in achieving this goal". The CPC set the goals that by 2020, it would help all the rural population out of poverty as defined by the existing standard, raise all impoverished counties out of poverty, and eliminate poverty over entire regions. It's essential to raise rural living standards of those of impoverished villagers to achieve initial prosperity in the countryside. Therefore, President Xi Jinping first proposed the poor household targeted poverty alleviation in 2013 on his inspection tour of a poverty-stricken ethnic minority village - Shibadong Village, in the west of Central China's Hunan Province.

The targeted poverty alleviation strategy was fully implemented in 2015 when the central government formulated the "Decision on Winning the Tough Battle for Poverty Alleviation". This policy specified the connotation and concrete measures of targeted poverty alleviation. It was clearly defined that based on the accurate identification of truly poor individuals and households, tailored measures should be taken to relieve these impoverished people and families out of poverty through appropriate arrangement of projects, allocation of subsidies and dispatch of poverty alleviation officials and talents to create achievements as planned. Five concrete measures were taken to carry out the targeted poverty alleviation strategy involving industrial development, relocation, education, ecological compensation and social security.

Under the guidance of these rigorous measures, during the poor household-targeted period, all 832 registered impoverished counties formulated industrial plans to boost economic development and agricultural production and provide more job opportunities for the poor. More than 96 million registered people moved into over 2.66 million newly constructed houses. About 200,000 students who dropped out of school due to poverty returned to school. More than 8 million students from poor families who failed to continue their studies or got employed after finishing high school received vocational education for free. Over 1.1 million registered people were employed as ecological forest rangers. These measures directly lifted a total of 3 million out of poverty. Since 2016, 19.36 million registered people have been included in the subsistence allowance, support and relief system. With the successful implementation of the targeted poverty alleviation strategy, the 2020 extreme poverty elimination goal was achieved as scheduled based on the raised poverty line 4,000 yuan a year or USD 1.59 a day (based on the average exchange rate of yuan to USD in 2020), very close to the updated international poverty line of USD 1.9 a day.

Motivated by the progress of reform and opening-up and the significance of poverty eradication to the Chinese government's mission of realizing the common prosperity of the people, the Chinese four periods of government-led anti-poverty initiatives featured the evolution from relief-based poverty alleviation to development-driven poverty alleviation strategies. In line with the national economic and social development plans and poverty alleviation outlines, poverty alleviation objects shifted from generally poor regions and counties to more accurately identified poor villages and households. During the first two periods before 2000, the central government and relevant departments were mainly responsible for the poverty relief work. In the new century, under the leadership of the central government, local governments and departments from the provincial, municipal, county, township, and even village levels are more and more involved in the sustainable development of poor regions and enhancing poor populations' capabilities and skills of shaking off poverty. These experiences demonstrated China's practical and down-to-earth approach to battling poverty, representing a poverty eradication track that accommodated the country's realities while reflecting unique Chinese characteristics.

Tourism-Assisting the Poor Stages

Tourism is one of the leading industries that have promoted the sustainable development of poverty-stricken areas and drawn the wide participation of poor people and other social forces in poverty alleviation in China. This section overviews the stages of the tourism-assisting the poor initiative (TAP) in tourism development and the national poverty alleviation programs.

According to the "World Tourism Development Report 2018-Global Pro-poor Tourism and Demands of the Times" released by the World Tourism Alliance and China Tourism Research Institute in 2018, China's TAP mainly experienced four stages: the early exploration period (1984-1996), the preliminary development period (1997-2004), the rapid improvement period (2005-2012) and the targeted and efficient period (since 2013). Table 1-4 shows that the four development stages of TAP closely followed China's national economic and social development strategies of reform and opening up, western development, rural tourism, and targeted poverty alleviation.

Table 1-4 Chinese anti-poverty stages, Chinese TAP stages and Chinese tourism stages

Chinese anti-poverty stages	Chinese TAP stages	Chinese tourism stages
Poor region- targeted period (1978-1985)	Early exploration period (1984-1996)	Foreign exchanges earning period (1979-1991)

Poor county -targeted period (1986-2000)	Initial development period (1997-2004)	Chinese mass tourism period (1992-2011)
Poor village-targeted period (2001-2012)	Rapid development period (2005-2012)	
Poor household-targeted period (2013-2020)	Targeted and efficient period (2013-2020)	Quality tourism period (since 2012)

Source: The World Tourism Alliance and China Tourism Research Institute. 2018. World Tourism Development Report 2018-Global Pro-poor Tourism and Demands of the Times, https://www.sohu.com/a/256265710_395870

TAPPs served as the guideline of China's TAP initiative and the government's most powerful weapon in anti-poverty work, which “ensures tourism growth contributes to poverty reduction" (Ashley et. al., 2001). During 1984-2020, the Chinese Central Government and its ministries released 64 TAPPs targeted or directly related to poverty alleviation through tourism, which yielded remarkable achievements in different stages of the TAP initiative. TAP achievements in different stages and locations varied due to local governments' responses and strategies under TAPPs. For example, tourism is part of the development strategies in both Yunnan and Guizhou in western China. However, Guizhou’s relatively small-scale tourism industry, mainly distributed in poor areas and mostly participated by poor households, contributed more to poverty alleviation than the large-scale tourism in Yunnan, whose tourism's economic results benefit little the poor (Donaldson, 2007). TAPPs in the targeted period contributed the greatest poverty alleviation, especially by cultivating and encouraging local small tourism enterprises (STEs) (Liang & Bao, 2018). However, Chinese tourism development has caused environmental degradation in some regions, including poor regions (Teng et. al., 2021).

The formulation and implementation effects of Chinese TAPPs were the main factors underpinning governmental power and influence in China’s TAP initiative. The attainment of China's 2020 poverty alleviation goal does not represent the end of China's battle against poverty, as the Chinese government realized that relative poverty remains a long-lasting task of this biggest developing country globally. Therefore, China has advanced rural revitalization to promote the sustainable development of rural areas inhabited by the most relatively poor population. Thanks to China’s successful control of Covid-19, tourism remains an effective driver for rural revitalization. In order to get recovered from the devastating disaster caused by the Covid-19, the tourism industry should be transformed into a more sustainable sector (Everingham et. al., 2020; Prideaux, 2020; Haywood, 2020), which urges the optimization of TAPPs in response to the country's rural revitalization strategy in the post-pandemic era.

Problem Statement

As is overviewed previously, during the first 30 years of new China, the country remained relatively closed off to international tourism due to political isolation and domestic priorities. China's interest in opening up to tourism emerged in the late 1970s and early 1980s, in line with the national economic reform and opening up policy. The Chinese government recognized tourism as a potential source of foreign exchange earnings and economic development, significantly reducing the largely impoverished population throughout different regions of the country. In addition to focusing on inbound tourism, since the 1990s, the government has also prioritized the development of domestic tourism. This was driven by factors such as rising disposable income, urbanization, and a growing middle class eager to explore their own country. The government launched campaigns to promote domestic travel and infrastructure development to support tourism within China. In order to maximize tourism's contribution to the country's poverty alleviation goal, the government has directed tourism's benefits to poor regions, counties, villages and households in different TAP stages under TAPPs. The government has utilized tourism as a major tool for absolute poverty elimination and the ongoing rural revitalization.

The outbreak of the COVID-19 pandemic in 2020 has caused unprecedented damage to various economic sectors (Amankwah-Amoah et. al., 2021; Bartik et. al., 2020). It is estimated to have reversed the target global extreme poverty rate of 7.9% to the global poverty rate of 9.2% in 2017. The pandemic caused the most significant defeat in the struggle against world poverty since World War II. The setback has significantly and long-lastingly changed the trajectory of poverty reduction, making the world deviate from the target of ending severe poverty by 2030 (World Bank, 2022). This pandemic disaster has posed the deepest crisis to the world tourism industry in history (Cavanagh et. al., 2020). The estimated economic contribution of tourism in 2021 (measured in terms of tourist direct gross domestic product) was US$ 1.9 trillion, up from US$ 1.6 trillion in 2020 but still much below the US$ 3.5 trillion pre-pandemic value (UNWTO, 2022). Amid the great recession of international tourism, the pandemic impact on domestic tourism is uneven in space and time (Hall et. al., 2020). Owing to people's perceived lower infection risks in rural areas, rural tourism has become domestic tourists' favourite choice for leisure. Therefore, rural tourism in some countries like France and Czechia enjoys increased consumption by domestic tourists (Seraphin & Dosquet, 2020; Stastna et. al., 2020), though other countries like Portugal still suffer the adverse pandemic impacts on rural tourism (Silva, 2022).

As some scholars argued that the pandemic also provided opportunities for rural tourism development (Stastna et. al., 2020; Polukhina et. al., 2021), Chinese rural tourism has become one of the major rural sectors that recovered rapidly from the pandemic owing to the Chinese government's anti-pandemic success. According to the China Ministry of Culture and Tourism, the number of tourists and total income of rural tourism in July and August 2020 recovered to more than 90 per cent of the same period in previous years. From January to August 2020, a total of 1.207 billion trips to rural areas were made across the country, creating total revenue of 592.5 billion yuan (about $86.7 billion). About 94.5 per cent of the business in rural tourism has returned to operation, hiring 10.61 million employees (CMCT, 2021).

Rural tourism has been taken as an important tool for poverty alleviation by the Chinese government since the early 21st century. Being one of the most promising sectors for the development of domestic tourism in the post-pandemic era (Polukhina et. al., 2021), rural tourism has the potential to play a positive role in achieving the SDGs, especially in rural areas both in China and the world if it is well managed (UNWTO & UNDP, 2017). Improved management is one of the crucial keys to avoiding tourism's negative impacts on sustainable development (Herrera-Couldo & Herrera-Couldo, 2016; Imon, 2017). Amid the world's debates on tourism's potential to end poverty, governmental power and influence have emerged as a new research trend to boost the effective and justified implementation of the PPT program (Spenceley &

Meyer, 2012). Tourism policies in many countries are criticized for having overemphasized economic growth (Mai & Smiths, 2015; Anderson et. al., 2018), which results in tourism's negative impacts on the natural environment, social and cultural development of destinations (Mowforth & Munt, 2009; Gascón, 2015; Teng et. al., 2021).

As a main stakeholder of TAP, the Chinese government has played a leading role in promoting tourism as an effective means to improve poor people's livelihood. Tourism's significant role in realizing the Chinese 2020 promise to eliminate absolute poverty positively reflected tourism's potential to achieve SDG1 in developing countries. This achievement, mainly assessed through the economic poverty line, represents tourism's contribution to economic development in poor areas. When China entered the post-poverty era, relative poverty became the focus of the government's anti-poverty campaign. The Chinese government has decided to pursue the balanced development of society, culture, economy and environment in the relatively poor areas in line with China's 14th Five-Year Plan and Vision 2035, which confirms the country's high quality and sustainable growth. Tourism has been listed as the government's long-term means to curb relative poverty.

As China is implementing its rural revitalization strategy to promote the sustainable prosperity of rural areas, the role of TAPPs must be transferred from an economic booster to a sustainable development guide for relatively poor rural areas. Under this new circumstance, poverty in China is more inclined to be a multi-dimensional issue relating to the three pillars of sustainability. Therefore, in order to optimize TAPPs for sustainable rural revitalization, it's worthwhile for this study to explore the Chinese government's efforts to increase tourism's contribution to SDG1-led SDGs through pro-poor policy formulation and implementation, the mechanism of channeling tourism's economic benefits to the poor by TAPPs and TAP stakeholders' perception of TAPPs' impacts on reducing multi- dimensional poverty under the sustainable development paradigm.

Research Questions

This study focuses on a holistic and deep understanding of how Chinese TAPPs impact poverty alleviation from the policy formulation and implementation process, TAPPs' role in channeling tourism's benefits to the poor and TAPPs' contribution to multi-dimensional poverty alleviation under the sustainable development paradigm. The researcher develops the following questions:

(1) What TAPPs' sustainability values and targets are highlighted in different TAP stages to ensure tourism's benefits to sustainable development in poor areas?
(2) What mix of policy tools are used to realize TAPPs' sustainability values and goals?
(3) How does tourism growth affect the economic sustainability of the poor under the guidance of TAPPs?
(4) How do Chinese TAPPs contribute to reducing multi-dimensional poverty under a sustainable development paradigm?
(5) How do TAP stakeholders perceive TAPPs' impacts on the sustainable development of TAP destinations?

Research Objectives

This study investigates how Chinese TAPPs affect poverty alleviation under the sustainable development paradigm from policy formulation and implementation, tourism's economic benefits to the poor and TAP stakeholders' perception of TAPPs' impacts on multi-dimensional poverty reduction. Therefore, in order to achieve the aim of this study, the researcher has set the following research objectives:

(1) To identify sustainability value orientations and policy targets of TAPPs in different TAP stages;
(2) To investigate the combinations of policy tools used to realize TAPPs sustainability values and targets;
(3) To examine consumption-driven and investment-led tourism growth's impacts on the economic sustainability of the poor under the guidance of TAPPs;
(4) To investigate TAPPs' contribution to reducing multi-dimensional poverty under the sustainable development paradigm;
(5) To explore TAP stakeholders' perceptions of TAPPs' impacts on the sustainable development of TAP destinations.

The research results are expected to provide a holistic and deeper understanding of how Chinese TAPPs contribute to China's achievement of SDG1-led SDGs by exploring the mechanism of channeling tourism's benefits to the poor through the match of policy orientations, policy targets and policy tool mixes. In addition, the study is hoped to provide an understanding of the strength of the tourism-poverty link. And finally, this study is hoped to explore tourism's role in advancing SDG1-led SDGs by revealing TAP stakeholders' perception of TAPPs' contribution to multi-dimensional poverty alleviation under the sustainable development paradigm so that recommendations and suggestions on optimizing TAPPs for sustainable rural revitalization could be proposed.

Significance of the Study

Tourism has been recognized as a tool for poverty alleviation, especially in many developing countries. However, tourism growth could benefit the poor remains a challenge for many countries striving to achieve SDG1 (Scheyvens, 2019). Despite the pandemic, the recovery of domestic tourism, especially rural tourism in China, provides opportunities for consolidating the achievement of SDG1 in 2020 and facilitating rural revitalization. This study is worth conducting for several reasons:

Theoretical Contribution

Since there has been a long-existing debate on whether tourism could be an effective tool for reducing poverty, this study is expected to enrich the literature on the tourism-poverty link by investigating whether tourism's income could be distributed to the poor based on the CGE analysis of the economic impacts of pro-poor tourism policies. Besides, this study is crucial to expand the literature on the government's approach to strengthening the tourism-poverty relationship by exploring how tourism's contribution to poverty elimination could be made by formulating and implementing pro-poor tourism policies. The novelty of this study is to make a theoretical contribution to development theories by exploring the model for improving the sustainability of the government-led pro-poor tourism through the content analysis of TAPPs documents, MPI analysis of TAPPs' impacts on the multi-dimensional poverty under the sustainable paradigm and Chinese TAP stakeholders' perceptions of TAPPs' impacts on the sustainable development at TAP destinations.

Pro-poor Tourism Policy Formulation and Implementation

Many developing countries have taken tourism as a prioritized means for achieving SDG1. As for practical contribution, this study could act as the basis of reference for the governments of developing countries in mapping out the strategies and policies to increase tourism's contribution to poverty alleviation by listing poverty alleviation instead of tourism growth as a primary pro-poor tourism policy goal with due attention to the sustainable development of destinations. Besides, since the Chinese government hasn't stopped its efforts to curb relative poverty by initiating a rural revitalization strategy, this study could also provide a reference for governments at all levels to improve the sustainability of TAPPs so that the sustainable development of rural areas in line with SDGs could be promoted and consolidated.

Definition of Key Terms, Terminology, and Concepts

Poverty

Poverty is a universal but contested concept worldwide with different overlapping meanings depending on the subject area or discourse (Gordon et. al., 1999). In China, poverty is usually defined and measured based on the Chinese situation and in line with the definitions adopted by some influential international organizations such as the World Bank or the United Nations. Poverty in China has traditionally been defined in terms of income. People who do not have enough money to meet their food requirements or their basic needs have been identified as poor. The headcount ratio is the most widely used indicator in policymaking. As the headcount ratio is criticized for being insensitive to the distribution of income among the poor, Anand and Sen (1997), Bourguignon and Chakravarty (2003), Atkinson (2003) and Alkire and Foster (2011) all argue that poverty is multi-dimensional and should be measured in the multi-dimensional perspective. After China fulfilled SDG1 in 2020, multi-dimensional poverty, assessed through a multi-dimensional poverty index (World Bank, 2016), could be a dominant poverty approach to monitor relative poverty (Alkire & Fang, 2019).

Pro-poor Tourism (PPT)

Pro-Poor Tourism (PPT), first proposed by the UK's Department for International Development (DFID) in 1999, is the notion that shows a direct correlation between tourism and poverty alleviation. PPT is described by DFID as tourism that brings in net revenues for the underprivileged. In pro-poor tourism reports commissioned by DFID, Ashley, Roe, and Goodwin (2001) provided a precise definition of PPT as a tourist sector approach that “generates net benefits for the poor and ensures that growth contributes to poverty reduction”. This definition is frequently referenced in tourism literature (Truong et. al., 2014; Revira et. al., 2019; Gonzo, 2023). "Net" means that, from the standpoint of low-income individuals, PPT's advantages exceed its disadvantages. A variety of stakeholders, including the government, the underprivileged, the private sector, and civil society, are involved in PPT's policies that improve benefits to the poor, with the primary goal being to unlock opportunities for the poor (Ashley et. al., 2001).

Tourism-Assisting the Poor (TAP)

“Tourism-Assisting the Poor” (TAP) is a Chinese term for pro-poor tourism to highlight the introduction and adaptation of the concepts and principles of PPT and ST-EP to China. It is suggested that TAP in China has been generally defined as a tourism-induced poverty reduction strategy led by the government and oriented by the market. TAP aims to lift the poor from poverty by transforming the unique and abundant tourism resources in poverty-stricken rural areas into marketable tourist products and services. It targets creating benefits for local communities, particularly the poor, and contributes to local poverty reduction while sustaining regional economic development and environmental conservation (Zeng & Ryan, 2012). In this study, TAPPs (tourism-assisting the poor policies) will be used as the Chinese characteristic PPT policy concept to refer to policies for any tourism poverty alleviation strategy or program initiated by the Chinese government under the market-oriented mechanism with sustainable poverty alleviation as the central task.

Computable General Equilibrium (CGE)

The computable general equilibrium (CGE) model has increasingly been used in tourism research, useful for modeling industry-wide effects, inter-industry effects and national or regional impacts of major economic changes, including tourism-related changes. They could also provide welfare estimates (Dixon & Parmenter, 1996). They incorporate an input-output framework that links all industries, foreign exchange markets, and consumer and government spending behavior and reflect the macro-parameters of the economy. Recent uses of CGE modeling in tourism have involved the assessment of the economic impacts of government policies (Blake & Sinclair, 2003) and; the economic impacts of changes in inbound tourism (Dwyer et. al., 2003, 2006; Sugiyarto et. al., 2003; Narayan, 2004) and economic impacts of special events (Li, Blake & Cooper, 2011; Dwyer et. al., 2005).

Sustainability

Sustainability has been widely discussed in the literature of scientific, social and economic disciplines (Mauri, 2020) and even emerged as an independent academic discipline in the new century (Kates et. al., 2001). The United Nations promoted the application of sustainability globally by proposing sustainable development in the 1980s and initiating Sustainable Development Goals (2015-2030). Tourism is one industry closely associated with sustainability (World Travel and Tourism Council, 1998; Mauri, 2020). Sustainable tourism, which directly associates tourism and sustainable development, has become a prominent research focus and attracted concerns from different stakeholders in developed and developing countries (Chan, 2010; Bramwell & Lane, 2011). In order to recover from the devastating disasters caused by the Covid-19, the tourism industry should be transformed into a more sustainable sector (Everingham et. al., 2020; Prideaux, 2020; Haywood, 2020).

Rural Revitalization Strategy

The rural revitalization strategy was first implemented during the 19th National Congress of the Communist Party of China in 2017 and has been repeatedly stressed by the Chinese leadership since then. The strategy aims to build rural areas with thriving businesses, pleasant living environments, social etiquette and civility, effective governance, and prosperity. Since rural areas are the main battlefield for the Chinese poverty alleviation program, they remain the target areas where the achievement of SDG1 in 2020 should be consolidated, and relative poverty should be curbed. Rural tourism has been regarded as a major means for boosting rural businesses in the implementation process of rural revitalization strategy.

Policy Values, Targets and Tools

Policy values are the basis of policy goals and policy problems, functioning as motivators of government action and the basis of policy choice (Stewart, 2009, p. 14). The values-based approach provides a perspective for a better understanding of whether and how TAPPs have balanced sustainable development in poor areas. Policy targets, representing the policy values, are the goals, requirements and results expected to be achieved by policy implementation. It is an integral policy element and prerequisite for implementing the policy. Policy targets are realized through policy tools. Policy tools or instruments are ”a set of techniques by which governmental authorities wield their power in attempting to ensure support and affect or prevent social change” (Vedung, 1998, p. 21), ”an identifiable method through which collective action is structured to address a public problem” (Salamon, 2002, p. 19) or the means governments use “to deliberately affect the nature, types, quantities and distribution of the goods and services provided in a society" (Howlett, 2000, p. 415).

Conclusion

This chapter presents the introduction to introduce the reader to the context of conducting this research, the research problem, questions and objectives aimed to be solved throughout this study, and key terms used in this study. The next chapter will review literature related to major poverty concepts, theories of development, tourism forms for poverty alleviation, government's roles, power and policy effects in PPT and sustainable tourism policy to lay the basis for identifying the research gap.

Chapter 2
Literature Review

Introduction

This chapter mainly aimed to review past research on exploring the tourism-poverty link from a policy perspective. The first section begins with conceptualising and measuring poverty, including absolute and relative poverty, capability and multi-dimensional poverty and social exclusion. In order to understand poverty alleviation through tourism development, the second section reviewed the literature on development theories, tourism forms related to poverty alleviation, the critique and assessment of the tourism-poverty relief link, the roles, power of government in pro-poor tourism and policy effects and sustainable tourism policy. Finally, the literature was analysed to identify the gaps within the literature to locate the present study.

Defining and Measuring Poverty

Defining poverty clearly (Holden, 2013) is vital to assess the impacts of Chinese Tourism-Assisting the Poor Policies (TAPPs) on poverty reduction. Poverty definition has always been debated due to different technical and theoretical assumptions for social-political reasons in different countries, regions, and destinations (Ajakaiey & Adeyeye, 2001; Misturelli & Heffernan, 2010; Mansur et. al., 2013; Mansur et. al., 2017). Absolute and relative poverty are the most general poverty concepts recognised by the government, non-governmental organisations (NGOs), and the academic community worldwide (Sen, 1983; Wang et. al., 2020). Among various approaches to measure poverty, the most effective are the standard money-metric, multi-dimensional, and social exclusion approaches. The three approaches have demonstrated poverty concepts' political and ideological nature, thus dominating global development agendas such as MDGs and SDGs over time (Fischer, 2019).

Absolute vs. Relative Poverty

The concept of absolute poverty could be dated back to Rowntree (1901), who first defined "poverty is not having the financial resources necessary to support a person at the subsistence level of food, shelter, clothing and other necessities". The United Nations defined absolute poverty as “a condition characterised by severe deprivation of basic human needs, including food, safe drinking water, sanitation facilities, health, shelter, education and information.” (UN, 1995, p. 57). The lack of basic living needs is the key feature of absolute poverty (Begovic et. al., 2007; Streeten, 1984). However, it is challenging to identify essential needs because they could be interpreted differently in different societies and cultures (Begovic et. al., 2007), making poverty a phenomenon intermingled with economic factors and values of different countries and cultures (Mowafi, 2004). In addition, the basic needs in any specific society will change as the living conditions improve (Seers, 1969).

Therefore, Townsend (1979) suggested understanding poverty from relative deprivation by stating that “the term is understood objectively rather than subjectively. Individuals, families and groups in the population could be said to be in poverty when they lack the resources to obtain the types of diet, participate in the activities and have the living conditions and amenities which are customary, or at least widely encouraged or approved, in the society to which they belong” (Townsend, 1979, p. 31).

Oppenheim (1996) further noted that poverty in a specific society refers to material, social and emotional scarcity, with lower expenditure on food and clothing than average. Foster (1998) proposes that relative poverty measurement should be based on comparing demanded resources. If the resources of individuals or families do not reach the poverty line (set against the reference group), they should be considered impoverished. Relative poverty is not concerned with “some absolute basket of goods” but the minimum standard of living accepted by a given society (Mowafi, 2004; Gordon, 2006).

Absolute poverty and relative poverty are usually assessed through the poverty line. Up to the 1960s, income and employment were believed to be effective economic means to reduce poverty. Since then, the standard money-metric measures, which are indirect measures based on income or expenditure measured in units of money, have become the primary approach to measuring poverty, primarily through GDP per capita growth. Throughout the 1960s-1980s, per capita GDP was the major poverty indicator. Absolute poverty lines aim to have constant real value. For example, according to the World Bank (WB) and the International Monetary Fund (IMF), extremely poor people are those who earn less than US$1, US$1.25 or US$1.99 per day (Ajakaiye & Adeyeye, 2001; Akindola, 2009; Sachs, 2005; World Bank, 2016). The international poverty line once dominated some developed countries such as the USA and remained popular in most developing countries owing to the convenience of comparison and measurement (Chen & Ravallion, 2013).

However, Wagle (2002) argued that the international poverty line is "too crude, unrealistic and misleading" without consideration of the differences in family size, socio-cultural and physical needs prices and locations in different countries. In addition, income is one instead of the only factor that determines the multi-dimensional nature of poverty (Ashley et. al., 2001; Karnani, 2007; Kotler et. al., 2006; Akindola, 2009; Bourguignon & Chakravarty, 2003; Mestrum, 2006; Mowforth & Munt, 2009; Novak, 1995). People above the international poverty line might suffer from bad environmental quality, illness or limited political freedom (Akindola, 2009; Flik & Praag, 1991). Since the mid-1960s, some countries have witnessed a widened gap in equality between the poor and non-poor groups despite the per capita income growth (Kotler et. al., 2006).

By contrast, the relative poverty line or national poverty line is set at a constant proportion, usually one-half of the country or year-specific mean (or median) income (Sachs, 2005; Atkinson, 2003; Nolan, 2007). Relatively poor people are those who earn less than the median income in a given society or the mean national income (Sachs, 2005; Wagle, 2002) or fail to meet the living standards acceptable to the society in which they live (Ajakaiye & Adeyeye, 2001; Cutler, 1984; Sen, 1983). The relative poverty line is a dominant poverty measurement in Western European countries. Like the absolute poverty line, income is the dominant factor in the relative poverty line for technical reasons and perceived objectivity (Sumner, 2007). Nevertheless, the different economic levels and living standards make it difficult to poverty comparison across countries and societies. Income growth might only sometimes lead to a decrease in the relatively poor population (Flik & Praag, 1991). The living conditions of people just slightly below or above the poverty line might not differ significantly (Akindola, 2009; Novak, 1995). So using the income poverty line based on a money-metric approach could not adequately evaluate absolute or relative poverty (Novak, 1995).

Capability Poverty and Multi-dimensional Poverty

The inadequacy of money-metric measurement was perceived when Seers (1969) suggested that the economic measures should have retreated from the centrality of poverty evaluation. Maxwell (1999) further focused on non-monetary poverty, particularly regarding isolation, dis-empowerment, vulnerability, and lack of voice and representation (Ajakaiye & Adeyeye, 2001). The poverty noted in the 1980 WDR (World Development Report) was also expanded from income to other aspects such as nutrition, education and health (World Bank, 1980:32). These efforts to shift the poverty debate gradually led to the formation of capability poverty measurement "Human Development Indices" issued by the UNDP (the United Nations Development Program) in 1990. Capability poverty refers to the deprivation of opportunities through which people can fully develop their potential to achieve the balanced formation and use of basic capabilities to improve knowledge, nutrition, health and income (UNDP, 1990).

The 1998 Nobel winner Sen further provided a theoretical basis for this poverty concept through his capability approach. Unlike the consumption-oriented economic measures represented by the proxy of income-per-capita GDP, the capability approach focuses on "the process of enlarging people's choices" (UNDP, 1990). What people could do or be for freedom is essential to the well-being defined in this approach (Saigaran et. al., 2015). Sen's well-being indicators are both economic and non-economic, with more comprehensive ranges than those covered in the UNDP Human Development Indices (Sumner, 2007). Nevertheless, Wagle (2008) argued that capability poverty measurement fails to reveal why people with similar capabilities may suffer from different degrees of poverty. It also needs to be clarified what constitutes capabilities and how to measure them correctly (Laderchi et. al., 2003).

Thanks to Sen's contribution to broadening the poverty measurements, since the 2000s, the multi-dimensional nature has been identified and recognised by many scholars (e.g. Blank, 2003; Bourguignon & Chakravarty, 2003; Holden, 2013; Mestrum, 2006; Misturelli & Heffernan, 2010; Mitchell & Ashley, 2010; Novak, 1995; Sumner, 2007), thereby the multi-dimensional poverty was proposed. The multi-dimensional approach, which builds off the entitlement, capability and human development approaches, has improved the money-metric approach by introducing indicators beyond per capita GDP or income.

UNDP (2010) defined the multi-dimensional approach as "a measure of serious deprivations in the dimensions of health, education and living standards that combines the number of deprived and the intensity of their deprivation" (UNDP, 2010, p. 26). This approach recognises that income and other aspects of poverty are equally important for human development. It demonstrates a significant change in the conceptualisation of poverty from a reductionist approach that limits poverty to income or several needs to a generalist approach that recognises poverty as a multi-dimensional phenomenon.

Economic measures are gradually decentralised or equally important to non-economic measures in capability and multi-dimensional poverty. However, policymakers assume that economic indicators are more objective and rigorous. Naturally economic measures remained at the top among indicators in MDGs (Millennium Development Goals), the HDIs, and the PRSPs (Poverty Reduction Strategy Papers), SDGs (Sustainable Development Goals). Thus, multi-dimensional measures still need to resolve the problems relating to money-metric poverty lines fundamentally but might also increase confusion and arbitrariness in selecting and defining those composite indicators (Fischer, 2019). The Alkire-Foster Multi-Dimensional Poverty Index (AF methodology), first developed by Alkire and Foster (2007) and adopted by the UNDP in 2010, was believed to have partly solved these problems. Unlike the human development index (HDI) which focuses on measuring the poverty of the group, MPI could measure the poverty of individuals, becoming one of the most widely used methods to measure multi-dimensional poverty worldwide.

First launched in 2010, the global Multi-dimensional Poverty Index (MPI) is an important international resource that measures acute multi-dimensional poverty in over 100 developing countries and is vital in advancing SDG1 (Alkire et. al., 2022). With AF methodology, the changes in multi-dimensional poverty in 34 countries and 338 sub-national regions as well as 80 of 107 countries, including China, were calculated and analysed under the global MPI by Alkire, Roche and Vaz (2017) and Alkire, Kovesdi, Scharlin-Pettee and Pinilla Roncancio (2020). The applicability of AF methodology worldwide owes to the fact that this approach is a general framework for measuring multi-dimensional poverty since many key decisions are left to use. Users have the flexibility to determine the selection of dimensions, dimensional cutoffs, dimensional weights, and poverty cutoffs.

In recent years, most developing countries witnessed a decline in overall MPI, destitution and severity levels (Alkire et. al., 2022). Using Uganda household survey data (2002, 2007), Levine et. al. (2012) found a reduction in the national multi-dimensional poverty index (MPI) for Uganda using the methodology outlined by Alkire and Foster (2007). Alkire and Seth (2015) found a significant decrease in all dimensions of India's multi-dimensional poverty between 1999 and 2006. However, this reduction has not been uniform across all regions, castes, or religions. Mitra (2017) further concluded that Muslims are less poor than Hindus in India by calculating multi-dimensional poverty in 16 major states with AF methodology (2011), contrary to conclusions based on an income-based approach. Dehury and Mohanty (2017) and Kanungo et. al. (2019) also proposed that MPI was an effective tool to help the Indian government improve the most deprived environmental conditions of people experiencing poverty by increasing public health investment. The MPI evaluation in Iran revealed that culture, environment and security were the most neglected measures for poverty alleviation (Torabi Kahlan, Navvabpour, & Bidarbakht Nia, 2022).

You (2013), Alkire and Shen (2017) and Alkire and Fang (2018) measured China's multi-dimensional poverty with MPI using different data sources such as China Health and Nutrition Survey (CHNS) and China Family Panel Studies (CFPS). They all identified the mismatch between China's MPI and income poverty ratio. Yu (2013) reported the mismatch between multi-dimensional poverty and income poverty in most provinces in China, which could explain the mismatch between these two in the whole country. The mismatch also reflected the unevenness of the reduction of multi-dimensional poverty and income poverty reduction in different provinces and regions of China, similar to India, whose multi-dimensional poverty reduction was not uniform across all regions, castes, or religions (Alkire and Seth, 2015). Both Alkire and Shen (2017) and Alkire and Fang (2018) reported the high deprivation levels of "years of schooling" and "cooking fuels" in China. As China eradicated its absolute poverty in 2020, it is necessary to formulate a novel MPI standard to realise the SDGs 2030 (Zhao et. al., 2022).

The disaggregated analysis is an integral part of the MPI evaluation. The multi-dimensional poor groups could be divided by ethnicity, age, rural and urban areas, gender of household head and household register etc. (Alkire & Shen, 2017; Alkire & Fang, 2018; Alkire & Kovesdi, 2020; Alkire, Kanagaratnam, & Suppa, 2021; 2022; Rogan, 2016). Similar findings were concluded on MPI results of rural and urban area groups that the rural population has higher MPI, destitution and severity levels than the rural population. Alkire and Shen (2017) further noted that, from 2010 to 2014, the MPI levels of rural hukou (rural household register) in China declined significantly with China's migration action. In Indonesia, the agricultural sector population had higher MPI and poverty intensity than the non-agricultural sector population (Amalia & Kadir, 2016). In Malaysia, the indigenous people in rural areas are more impoverished than those in urban and suburban areas (Saifullah, 2022). These studies also noted that the rural-urban gap in most countries worldwide is narrowing with the overall MPI reduction.

Social Exclusion

Another major non-monetary poverty concept is social exclusion, frequently used in official documents of the UK and Europe and the world academic community. This concept was first coined by Réné Lenoir (1974) in his book Les Exclus, referring to the situation where people are excluded for being unable to work due to physical or mental disabilities. The Council of the European Communities (1975) defined low-income people as "individuals or families whose resources are so small as to exclude them from the minimum acceptable way of life of the member state in which they live." It has easily concluded that social exclusion was originally a cause of poverty. Burchardt et. al. (1999) further noted that social exclusion is usually defined as a dimension of social deprivation in multi-dimensional concepts or social processes that lead to poverty. It is one aspect of capability deprivation and instrumentally causes further diverse capability failures (Sen, 2000, p. 5).

The most outstanding contribution of this concept is its dealing with social relations, which is also the focus of capability poverty (Sen, 2000) and the relative deprivation (Townsend, 1979). Therefore, Sen (2000) argues that social exclusion has been implicit in many approaches and is an adjunct to different poverty approaches. These definitions also imply that social exclusion is worth attention only if it results in poverty (Gore & Figueiredo, 1997, p. 10), despite that some scholars argue that social exclusion is more than poverty (Atkinson, 2003; Daly, 2010). Since the 1990s, social exclusion has become a keyword in poverty studies and an antithesis of social inclusion promoted by the World Bank and the global development agendas in the 21st century (Fischer, 2019). It has been taken as one of the main ways of defining and measuring poverty (Laderchi et. al., 2003).

The assessment of social exclusion depends on its conceptualisation. In the established literature, the interpretation of this concept follows three types: the lack of participation in social institutions (Duffy, 1995; Paugam & Russell, 2000), the denial or non-realisation of rights of citizenship (Room, 1995; Klasen, 2002) and increase in the distance among population groups (Bossert et. al., 2007). Some scholars suggested establishing measures of social exclusion in these conceptualisation approaches (Bradshaw et. al., 2000; Tsakloglou and Papadopoulos, 2002). For example, as social exclusion deals with people's capability failures in participation, Tsakloglou and Papadopoulos (2002) proposed an index of social exclusion based on the distribution of an individual welfare indicator. They set a threshold to identify people with a high risk of deprivation. Nevertheless, establishing the threshold is arbitrary, and the theoretical foundations of these measures often need to be clarified (Bossert, Chakravarty, & Ambrosio, 2019).

Poverty as a multi-dimensional phenomenon could be defined and measured in many ways (Lok Dessallien, 1999). No universal poverty concepts or approaches are accepted by the academics, governments and organisations involved in anti-poverty policymaking. Absolute poverty, relative poverty, capability poverty, multi-dimensional poverty and social exclusion are the most influential poverty concepts adopted by governments, international organisations, regional organisations, and global development agendas. The distinction and overlapping of these concepts affirm and reflect the complex nature of the multifaceted poverty phenomenon.

Poverty measurement relies on the identification of poverty's nature and causes. The standard money-metric, multi-dimensional, and social exclusion approaches are the three most dominant measurement approaches that demonstrate the fundamentally political and ideological nature (Fischer, 2019) of the above popular poverty concepts. With the development of the world's anti-poverty initiatives in different countries, the multi-dimensional nature of poverty has been recognised with the decentralisation of economic factors in poverty measurement and equal attention to non-economic measurements. However, scholars' debates emphasise the arbitrariness of choosing economic and non-economic indicators. MPI developed by Alkire-Foster has been proven to have partly solved this problem.

The Chinese government’s initiative to end absolute poverty by 2020 is mainly measured through a money-metric approach. The National Bureau of Statistics of China (NBS) calculated the minimum costs for satisfying people’s basic survival needs as an absolute income poverty line. Existing academic studies that analyse poverty in China have used income or expenditure as key indicators for estimating China's poverty trends and levels (Appleton, Song, & Xia, 2010; Goh, Luo, & Zhu, 2009; Meng, Gregory & Wang, 2005; Park & Wang, 2001; Zhang, Xu, Zhou, Zhang, & Xie, 2014). Despite fulfilling China's absolute poverty elimination goal, tackling relative poverty will be a long-term task. Relative poverty line and multi-dimensional poverty have attracted the most concern from some poverty policy researchers of the Chinese State Council represented by Li and Xu (2018), Sun and Li (2019), as well as many scholars, such as Jiang et. al. (2019), He and Lou (2020).

Understanding Poverty Alleviation through Tourism Development

Since the middle of the 20th century, many countries consider tourism an effective developmental growth pole to boost economic development (Sharpley, 2015). Development is a multi-dimensional process that could yield positive results in economic growth, national institutions, and poverty reduction (Todaro & Smith, 2011). Scholars' views on the tourism-poverty link have evolved from tourism as a modernisation strategy for newly independent Third World countries to earn foreign exchange during the 1950s and 1960s to that poor people and non-Western countries benefit little from tourism growth in the 1970s and 1980s to tourism as a tool for poverty alleviation since 1990s (Scheyvens, 2007). The evolution of tourism's role in poverty alleviation follows the paradigms of development thought. In order to properly explore how Chinese TAPPs affect the fulfillment of SDG1, it is necessary to understand the theories of development and different tourism forms related to poverty alleviation under these theories.

Theories of Development

There are five main development paradigms: modernisation (1950-1960s), international dependency (1960-1970s), economic neoliberalism of markets (1970-1980s), alternative development (the 1980s) and sustainable development (since the 1990s) (Sharpley, 2000; Dadwal, 2018; Manzoor et. al., 2019).

a. Modernisation Theory

Known as the first development paradigm most popular in the late 19th till the mid-20th century (Sharpley, 2000), modernisation is an endogenous process which realises the potential for development in all societies (Hettne, 1990: 61). With economic growth the central premise, modernisation is believed to transform societies from the traditional stage to mass consumption (Rostow, 1960). It is used by theorists as a social indicator for economic development (Manzoor et. al., 2019), which "trickles down" or diffuses benefits through "growth impulses" or "poles of growth" (Perroux, 1955) to the grassroots, especially in the form of vast employment opportunities. Influenced by this paradigm, tourism is mainly a modernisation tool for economic development, employment and income generation (Holden et. al., 2011; Scheyvens, 2007). Since the 1950s, international tourism has become an essential form of mass consumption or growth pole (Mishra et. al., 2011), generating benefits that could trickle down to the poor population (Truong et. al., 2014).

b. Dependency Theory

Another development paradigm dominant in the academic community in the late 1960s and 1970s is the dependency theory. This theory focuses on the reliance of less developed or poor countries on the developed or rich countries, particularly in economic development. Dos Santos (1970) explains that the dependency theory depicts:

"a conditioning situation in which the economies of one group of countries are conditioned by the development and expansion of others. A relationship of interdependence between two or more economies ... becomes a dependent relationship when some countries could expand only as a reflection of the expansion of the dominant countries" (Dos Santos, 1970, p. 231).

The inequalities between the rich and the poor countries (Willis, 2011) or "historical patterns of colonialism and dependency (Lea, 2006) are also reflected in the international tourism (Sharepley, 2000). Since the 1970s, foreign direct investment (FDI) has been seen as a means to stimulate stagnating economies, and investment in tourism added a possible dimension attracting foreign exchange. However, tourism was associated with enclave development, dependence on foreign capital, growing socio-economic inequality, and high economic leakages. Tourism undermined local cultures, social networks, and traditional livelihoods (Milne & Ateljevic, 2001; Holden et. al., 2011; Scheyvens, 2007; Truong et. al., 2014). Therefore, international tourism's potential for underdeveloped countries' economic and social progress is limited and" the political framework of their existence has to be drastically revamped" (Baran, 1963).

c. Neoliberalism

In response to the criticism of the dependency theory, the voices for establishing the new international economic order became stronger in the 1970s. Neoliberalism became a representative development paradigm in the 1980s. Neoliberalism was embedded in the neo-classical economic theory, which suggested that liberalised international trade could positively affect export-led economic development (Ingham, 1995: 334). It advocates development relying on the free market or market liberalisation, the privatisation of state enterprises and the most minor government intervention. Rather than narrow the gap between the poor and rich countries, neoliberalism further intensifies the inequality between developing and developed countries.

Neoliberalism is often described as the ideology of the market and private interests as opposed to state intervention. Although neoliberalism conveys an ideology and propaganda, it is fundamentally a new social order in which the power and income of the upper fractions of the ruling classes - the wealthiest persons - was re-established after a setback. We denote as 'finance' this upper capitalist class and the financial institutions through which its power is enforced. Although the conditions for the structural crisis were gradually superseded, most of the world economy remained plagued by slow growth and unemployment, and inequality increased tremendously. This was the cost of a successful restoration of the income and wealth of the wealthiest. (Duménil & Lévy, 2005, p. 9).

Under the guidance of neoliberalism, the World Bank and the International Monetary Fund (IMF) and their Structural Adjustment Lending (SAL) Programs only offered loans to those countries whose economic and social structures were neo-liberal (Mosley & Toye, 1988). As SAL has significantly reduced the influence of the state and highlighted the importance of the private sector, tourism in developing countries has to enhance its relationship with Western Transnational Companies (TNCs) for better development opportunities (Dieke, 1995). In the neo-liberal tourism development pattern, hotel chains could play a significant role in attracting foreign investment. Capitals from the private tourism sectors could boost the local and national economies when they are used to improve infrastructure construction in scenic areas. However, the reduction of state participation in tourism has led to decreased spending on health, education, safety, environmental protection and other public services, as well as the welfare programs that benefit the grassroots and the poor (Sharpely & Telfer, 2015). In addition, the state would not interfere with the distribution of tourism income and profits, which might cause higher leakages or intensify the exploitation of the poor countries and their poor population by the rich countries or elites (Chok et. al., 2007; Hall, 2007; Harrison, 2008; Gascón, 2015).

d. Alternative Development

Aside from the previous economic growth-based paradigms (Redclift, 1987), alternative development strives to deal with the relationship between humans and the environment that the economic growth-oriented development theories ignore. Streeten (1977) proposes that alternative development should stimulate grassroots endogenous capabilities to satisfy their own basic needs while fulfilling their potential to promote community development. This paradigm represents a broader resource-based and bottom-up approach, focusing on the grassroots role in community development as Schumacher (1974) proposes that "development does not start with goods; it starts with people and their education, organisation and discipline" (Schumacher, 1974, p. 140).

Besides, the environmental constraints to development or the need for "eco-development" (Redclift, 1987, p. 34) are recognised as the focus of equal importance to grassroots contribution to alternative development. Thus, this development paradigm arouses community residents' environmental concerns in their efforts to improve community development. Tourism's link to alternative development is manifested in the alternative tourism popular in the 1980s. Alternative tourism is regarded as "a new style in North-South relations" (Dernoi, 1981), which follows the environmental harmony (Budowski, 1976; Farrell & McLellan, 1987), self-reliance and fundamental requirements of alternative development.

e. Sustainable Development

As development theories experienced the evolution from the narrower economic growth-centred paradigms to the broader alternative development approach concerning the environment-development relationship, sustainable development has become a long dominant global development strategy since the late 1980s (Sharpely, 2000; Olawumi & Chan, 2018). Two reports that attracted worldwide attention to sustainable development are the Brundtland Report outlining "Our Common Future" (WCED ,1987) and IUCN's "Caring for the Earth" (IUCN, 1991).

Once believed as the mixture or combination of development theory and environmental sustainability (Manzoor et. al., 2019), sustainable development is now conceptualised as a multi-dimensional (Slimane, 2012), integrated (Sartori et. al., 2014) approach based on the principles of sustainability (Dovers & Handmer, 1992), aiming to seek the balance between preserving the ecosystem and meeting human needs (Olawumi & Chan, 2018). Sustainability and sustainable development are often used interchangeably (Norton, 2005). However, sustainable development is more of a collective societal process that involves multiple stakeholders with differing salience levels and powers, and sustainability focuses more on preventing the depletion of natural resources, biodiversity conservation, and ecological integrity (Axelsson et. al., 2011; Parrotta et. al., 2006). The sustainable development currently represents a holistic paradigm with environmental, social and economic sustainability as its three pillars.

Tourism is linked to sustainable development through sustainable tourism when the World Tourism Organization (WTO) introduced the concept of Sustainable Tourism Development in 1993. The Charter for Sustainable Tourism jointly issued by the UNESCO, UNEP and WTO in 1995 in Spain further made sustainable development a guideline for tourism development (Hall, 2011; Castellani & Sala, 2010). The connotation of sustainable tourism has been expanded from the initial focus on environmental issues to the overall balanced development of society, the environment and the economy (Torres-Delgado & Palomeque, 2012). The relationship between different stakeholders should be coordinated and balanced in sustainable tourism development (Guo et. al., 2019). Women and marginalised groups could get employment opportunities as the tourism industry has the potential to contribute to sustainable development, particularly by job creation (Cukier, 2002).

As poverty elimination was included in the UN Millennium Development Goals and UN Sustainable Development Goals, tourism intended to become more involved in reducing poverty through community tourism, sustainable tourism for eliminating poverty program (ST-EP) and pro-poor tourism, which called for efforts to guarantee the equitable flow of tourism benefits to different stakeholders, especially the poor grassroots. As an essential stakeholder of tourism forms to reduce poverty, the government could play a vital role in influencing the distribution of tourism income and sustainable development of the poverty-stricken areas through policy formulation and implementation (Sofield, 2003; Mowforth & Munt, 2009).

Though some developing countries such as Lao PDR and Vietnam issued some tourism policies related to poverty alleviation, poverty reduction is secondary to tourism development (Harrison & Schipani, 2007; Truong et. al., 2014). Mahadevan and Suardi (2017), after comparing 13 tourism-dependent countries, found that tourism growth neither narrows income inequality nor reduces the poor population. Many governments still need to put growth on the top agenda and make realistic and unsustainable projections for tourist numbers and revenue growth. Despite these constraints, the Chinese government-led tourism assisting the poor initiative under sustainable development guidance significantly contributed to the country's fulfilment of SDG1. However, the government or state's power has not been adequately appreciated in research on tourism (Coles & Church, 2007). Little attention has been paid to formulating policies and governance behaviours in sustainable tourism development (Guo et. al., 2019).

Besides, Sustainable development is a significant concern for tourism policymakers and researchers in the field (Hall, 2019). The UN General Assembly have endorsed some agreements recognising tourism's role in promoting global sustainable development, including the Agenda (2030 Agenda) and its Sustainable Development Goals (SDGs) (UN, 2015). The United Nations 70th General Assembly designated 2017 the International Year of Sustainable Tourism for Development (UNTWO & UNDP, 2017). If not founded on sustainability principles, tourism development could hinder social welfare and economic growth (Richards & Hall, 2003; Coccossis & Mexa, 2004). In order to recover from the devastating disasters caused by the Covid-19, the tourism industry should be transformed into a more sustainable sector (Chirisa et. al., 2020; Prideaux, 2020; Haywood, 2020). However, sustainability has not been universally conceptualised as it could be influenced by local environmental, social, and economic contexts that need more attention to be paid to some specific sectors over others (Twining-Ward & Butler, 2002).

The global sustainability rationale accepted among most tourism academics and practitioners is the three pillars of sustainability. This rationale requires the tourism development pattern that could create the most social and economic benefits while preserving the culture and environment at tourist destinations (Swarbrooke, 1998; Purvis et. al.,2019; Niavis et. al., 2019). Nevertheless, there needs to be a complete consensus on the precise definition of tourism sustainability because such a broad approach leaves room for different interpretations (Jovicic, 2014). The complicated nature of sustainability poses a challenge to measuring tourism sustainability. Various tourism sustainability assessment approaches tend to be arbitrary and non-systematic (Vukadin et. al., 2020; Rasoolimanesh et. al., 2020; Asmelash & Kumar, 2019), and there is a lack of clear sector-specific guidance on how to measure environmental and socio-cultural sustainability (Agyeiwaah, McKercher, & Suntikul, 2017; Torres-Delgado & Saarinen, 2014).

A case study is the most popular research method for Chinese scholars (eg. Jiang, 2009; Tian et. al., 2020; Li et. al., 2021 etc.) to assess the tourism sustainability at the local level. They mainly focus on a single sustainability dimension, such as the evaluation of tourism eco-sustainability in Lijiang County (Jiang, 2009) tourism environmental sustainability in Hubei Province (Tian et. al., 2020) and China water national parks (Li et. al., 2021), tourism social sustainability in Hong Kong (Qiu Zhang et. al., 2017) and tourism cultural sustainability in Pingyao ancient city (Weng et. al., 2019). The tourism sustainability measurements from different dimensions are relatively few except for comparing historic buildings and sites sustainability between China and the UK based on the three pillar sustainability framework (Ren & Han, 2018).

Therefore, this book is expected to enrich the sustainable development paradigm by identifying the match of Chinese TAPPs value orientations, policy targets and policy tools, which could be used to explain how the Chinese government ensures tourism's positive role in achieving SDG1. The assessments of TAPPs' impacts on sustainable multi-dimensional poverty reduction and TAP stakeholders' perception of TAPPs' contribution to sustainable development of TAP destinations add empirical evidence for applying sustainable development theory in poverty alleviation through tourism.

Tourism Forms Related to Poverty Alleviation

Throughout the evolution of development theories, tourism's contribution to poverty reduction has been reflected in different forms of poverty alleviation-related tourism, mainly ranging from mass tourism, alternative tourism, eco-tourism, community-based tourism, sustainable tourism and pro-poor tourism.

a. Mass Tourism

Mass tourism is a form of tourism involving large numbers of tourists (Fink, 1970) who consume highly standardised and inflexible all-inclusive tour packages (Higgins-Desbiolles, 2006; Poon, 1993) provided by all-inclusive tour companies. Emerging at the end of the Second World War, it was regarded as the panacea for economic problems in less developed countries and regions (Butler, 1990) by bringing a substantial amount of foreign currency to host communities, job opportunities, backward linkages with agriculture and improving poor people's life quality through funding basic facilities, education, and training (De Kadt, 1979).

However, other scholars criticise that the growth of mass tourism has resulted in damaged socio-cultural environments, destruction of pristine beaches, untouched forests and local culture, inequitable distribution of material profits, leakages, new diseases, extreme poverty, prostitution in developing countries (McLaren, 2003; Mowforth & Munt, 2009; Lansing, & de Vries, 2007; Poon, 1993) and the third world countries' dependence on foreign assistance (Toh, Khan, & Ng, 1997). Mass tourism's social, cultural, and environmental impacts sometimes outweigh its economic benefits (Marson, 2011). In addition, mass tourism is insufficient to alleviate poverty in a reasonable period, and the allocation of physical benefits to the poor and less poor groups in society requires due attention (De Kadt, 1979).

b. Alternative Tourism

Alternative tourism became a buzzword in the 1980s (Butler, 1990) as an approach to reducing the negative impacts of mass tourism on the host environment and communities (Cater, 1993; Higgins-Desbiolles, 2006). It is the type of tourism which "is consistent with natural, social, and community values and which allows both hosts and guests to enjoy positive and worthwhile interaction and shared experiences" (Eadington

& Smith, 1992 p. 3), a means that "promotes a just form of travel between members of different communities. It seeks to achieve mutual understanding, solidarity and equality among participants" (Holden, 1984). Alternative tourism could create almost the same socio-economic benefits as the mass tourism to the host destinations and communities (Dernoi, 1981). Since its operations are usually small-scale, owned and run by local people rather than multi-national tourism companies that develop the mass tourism, alternative tourism could further avoid the mass tourism's leakages and retain higher profits for local people (Cater, 1993).

However, Butler (1990) argues that alternative tourism could not settle all problems caused by mass tourism and is not the alternative to all forms of tourism. It might cause as severe social and environmental problems as mass tourism because alternative tourism explores vulnerable and untouched destinations for tourists to enjoy the wild nature and learning about indigenous cultures (Burns & Holden, 1995; Bramwell, 2004). Besides, if the small scale is not proper, it may decrease revenues, reduce employment and lower the living standards of local communities (Butler, 1990; Wheeler, 1992). Therefore, Scheyvens (2002) questioned if alternative tourism indicated a significant change in approach to tourism or if it was "just a new name for an old product".

c. Eco-tourism

As an alternative to mass tourism, eco-tourism emerged in the 1980s (Orams, 1995). For tourists, eco-tourism means "travelling to relatively undisturbed and uncontaminated areas with the specific objective of admiring, studying, and enjoying the scenery and its wild plants and animals, as well as any existing cultural features (both past and present) found in these areas" (Ceballos-Lascurain, 1988). Ziffer (1989) further gave a multi-dimensional and comprehensive definition, noting the eco-tourists' financial contribution to nature conservation and the economic well-being of the local people by paying for their experience of enjoying the natural history of the undeveloped areas, non-consumptive use of wildlife and natural resources and residents, communities' participation in planning, establishing and managing their eco- tourist sites and land. Eco-tourism has been expected to protect vulnerable resources and threatened areas while benefiting local people (Cater, 1993; Khan, 1997). However, monetary benefits are aimed at promoting environmental protection or advocating sustainable activities (Neto, 2003; Ryel, 1991; Stronza & Gordillo, 2008) and benefits for local people are secondary only.

Though local communities' participation is the key to the success of eco-tourism (Pengiran Bagul et. al., 2011), local communities are excluded from benefit distribution if eco-tourism is driven for business purposes (Scheyvens, 1999). Even when eco-tourism generates economic income for local communities, it does not necessarily alleviate poverty (Neto, 2003). The eco-tourists consume enormous amounts of natural resources, just like any other tourists (McLaren, 2003), which may destroy wild areas and local socio-cultural environments, thus degrading residents' life quality (Wilkinson & Pratiwi, 1995).

d. Sustainable Tourism

Sustainable tourism is expected to be an alternative approach to addressing the adverse effects of tourism and maintaining its long-term viability (Liu, 2003). In line with "sustainable development" proposed by the World Commission on Environment and Development, sustainable tourism considers its current and future economic, social and environmental impacts, reducing the tension of complex interactions between visitors, the industry, the environment and host communities (Bramwell & Lane, 1993; UNWTO, 2005: 12).

The conceptualisation of sustainable tourism has broadened from environmental to economic, social, cultural and political issues such as climate change, poverty alleviation, power and equity in society, urbanisation and political globalisation (Bramwell et. al., 2008; Mowforth & Munt, 2015). Among them, poverty alleviation has been listed as SDG1 of the UN Sustainable Development Goals (SDGs) 2015-2030. Scheyvens (2018) suggested that the sustainable tourism research focus should be shifted beyond tourism's contribution to economic growth, an increase of job opportunities and income, to consideration of sociopolitical aspects of poverty and structural inequalities that hinder people's development due to the multi-dimensional nature of poverty.

International organisations and the academic community have recognised tourism's positive role in accelerating the attainment of SDGs. If effectively managed, tourism may promote social, economic, environmental advancement and hasten the achievement of the SDGs such as poverty eradication (SDG 1), gender equality (SDG 5), environment protection (SDG 7, SDG 13 and SDG14), decent work and economic growth (SDG 8), responsible consumption and production (SDG 12) (Rasoolimanesh et. al., 2020; Scheyvens, 2018; Trupp & Dolezal, 2020; Birendra et. al., 2021).

It has easily found that tourism could contribute to achieving many interconnected SDGs, not just limited to SDG1. According to Scheyvens and Hughes (2019), the tourism industry should support marginalised groups like women and low-income people. Without proper planning, tourism developments in their communities may significantly worsen women's personal, social, economic, and environmental circumstances (Boluk, 2019). The cooperation between stakeholders is vital to maximise tourism's potential to SDGs (WTO & UNDP, 2017; Hall, 2019; Movono & Hughes, 2020).

However, too few tourism scholars were engaging with the challenges identified by SDGs, the Paris Agreement and other global initiatives (Bramwell et. al., 2017), including SDG1. In practice, UNWTO (2002, 2004) initiated the Sustainable Tourism for Eliminating Poverty program (ST-EP) on a mission to reduce poverty through socially, economically and ecologically sustainable tourism development. However, sustainable tourism programs prefer to fund mainstream tourist destinations in developed countries (Ashley et. al., 2001). Therefore, impoverished people, especially in LDCs, seldom benefit from sustainable tourism or ST-EP.

Another tourism form rooted in sustainable tourism is ethical tourism originated from the British government's ethical trading initiative in 2000 (Weeden, 2002; Rimoldi, 2005). Though it follows the major principles of sustainable tourism (Weeden, 2002), ethical tourism depends on tourists' willingness to spend money on products and services provided by tourism enterprises to improve tourism workers' working conditions and fair wages. Therefore, usually taken as tourism enterprises' competitive advantage, it has limited capacity to create economic benefits to host destinations (Butler & Clark, 1992) and plays a subtle role in reducing poverty.

e. Community-based Tourism

Since the 1990s, community-based tourism (CBT) has become a research focus related to poverty alleviation in LEDCs (Spencely & Meyer, 2012). World Wildlife Fund (WWF) (2001) defines CBT as tourism whose development and management are substantially controlled by the community and most benefits are retained within the community. Community control and profit distribution are the most widely accepted CBT definitions (Mowforth et. al., 2008; Trejos & Chiang, 2009), which could ensure an equitable flow of benefits to all tourism stakeholders (Saayman et. al., 2015). Goh (2015) found that CBT in East Malaysia plays an active role in poverty alleviation and natural conservation participated by local communities. Sher et. al. (2015) further concluded that community attachment and community involvement have significantly affected locals' support for sustainable tourism. Giampiccoli and Saayman (2016) even suggested that CBT principles and practice should be promoted as a just and re-distributive tourism development approach.

However, the community seldom manages or operates CBT because it is funded by donor agencies and non-governmental organisations in South America and Asia (Harrison & Schipani, 2007; Häusler, 2008; Hoque, 2020) or organised groups (Trejos & Chiang, 2009). In addition, power imbalances between CBT stakeholders (Jamal & Getz, 1995) cause the inequity of participating in the decision-making process. The poorest groups are most possibly excluded from CBT control or profits distribution (Truong et. al., 2014). Besides, the CBT programs controlled by the community could fail if the decision is not well-informed (Blackstock, 2005) or if CBT management teams have a poor understanding of tourism planning, development, management or marketing etc. (Spenceley, 2008). Even though Kibicho (2008) proved that local communities could be empowered to control the development process of small-scale CBT programs and enjoy equitable benefits, poverty alleviation is not the focus of communities (Ashley et. al., 2001). Local communities benefit little from tourism in some developing countries because they have no power to control how tourism is developed (Mowforth & Munt, 2003; Li & Hunter, 2015).

f. Pro-poor Tourism

The first concept that establishes the direct relationship between tourism and poverty alleviation is Pro-Poor Tourism (PPT), proposed by the UK's Department for International Development (DFID) in 1999. DFID defined PPT as tourism that generates net profits for the poor. Commissioned by DFID, Ashley, Roe and Goodwin (2001) delivered pro-poor tourism reports where they further clearly defined PPT as an approach to the tourism industry that "generates net benefits for the poor and ensures that growth contributes to poverty reduction". This definition has often been cited in the tourism literature (Truong et. al., 2014; Revira et. al., 2019; Gonzo, 2023). The word "net" indicates that PPT's benefits outweigh the costs from the perspective of low-income people. With the core aim to unlock opportunities for the poor, PPT focuses on strategies that enhance benefits to the poor, involving a range of stakeholders such as the government, poor people, the private sector, and civil society (Ashley et. al., 2001).

Harrison (2008), Butler et. al. (2013) and Medina-Muñoz et. al. (2016) discussed and summarised six key features of PPT as follows: incorporating the poor into capitalist markets by increasing job and entrepreneurial opportunities and collective benefits; providing education and training so that they could take up these opportunities; promoting participation and cooperation of different stakeholders such as the poor, government and private sectors etc.; distributing benefits the poor and non-poor locally; applying to any tourism or programs at the regional or national level as long as tourism's benefits could accrue to the poor and depending on existing tourism structures and markets.

Based on these features, studies specifically explored some significant factors involved in PPT such as community engagement and empowerment, cultural preservation and heritage management, sustainable resource management, policy governance and frameworks, partnerships and collaboration. Though community-based tourism might not benefit the poor, Ashley and Roe (2017) emphasized the importance of involving local communities in PPT planning, development, and decision-making processes. If properly designed, community-based PPT initiatives could empower local residents especially women economically and socially (Scheyvens and Momsen, 2019). Besides the economic and social benefits to the impoverished individuals, PPT stresses the preservation of cultural heritage and traditions as a means of promoting sustainable tourism development (Richards, 2019; Lor et. al., 2019; Zandi, 2020).

Additionally, environmental sustainability is a key consideration PPT initiatives. Researchers (eg. Mowforth and Munt, 2009; Patrick, 2019; Vinodan et. al., 2022) have examined strategies for promoting responsible PPT practices, minimizing negative environmental impacts, and supporting the conservation of natural resources. The effectiveness of pro-poor tourism interventions depends on supportive policy and governance frameworks at various levels. Studies have analyzed policy mechanisms, regulatory frameworks, and institutional arrangements that facilitate or hinder the implementation of pro-poor tourism strategies (Ashley et. al., 2001; Garrod and Fyall, 2018; Rivera and Tuazon, 2019; Chipfuva, 2021; Gonzo, 2023). Collaboration among stakeholders, including government agencies, NGOs, private sector actors, and local communities, is crucial for the success of PPT initiatives. Researches have explored the dynamics of partnerships, the role of social networks, and the importance of building trust and mutual understanding among diverse stakeholders to achieve sustainable and inclusive tourism development (Adiyia and Vanneste, 2018; Yu et. al., 2019; Geoffrey et. al., 2021; Abate, 2022).

Mitchell and Ashley (2010) further noted that PPT has three impacts on the poor: direct, secondary, and dynamic. PPT has become the latest in a long line of terms and types to attract attention, funding and energy within the tourism industry (Mowforth & Munt, 2015) and enjoys wider popularity than ST-EP in many developing countries like China. However, social sustainability, environmental sustainability, and economic growth stressed by ST-EP are all necessary for the success of the PPT initiative in developing countries such as environmentally vulnerable and economically dependent small island states (Scheyvens & Momsen, 2008).

The evolution of different forms of poverty alleviation-related tourism worldwide shows that ST-EP and PPT are the most influential concepts directly related to poverty alleviation through tourism. Zeng and Ryan (2012) translated the Chinese term "fu pin lv you" for pro-poor tourism into 'tourism-assisting the poor' (TAP) to highlight the introduction and adaptation of the concepts and principles of PPT and ST-EP to China. It is suggested that TAP in China has been generally defined as a tourism-induced poverty reduction strategy led by the government and oriented by the market to lift the poor out of poverty by transforming the unique and abundant tourism resources in poverty-stricken rural areas into marketable tourist products and services. It targets creating benefits for local communities, particularly the poor and contributes to local poverty reduction while sustaining regional economic development and environmental conservation (Zeng & Ryan, 2012). In this study, TAP will be used as a Chinese characteristic PPT concept to refer to any tourism poverty alleviation strategy or program initiated by the Chinese government under the market-oriented mechanism with sustainable poverty alleviation as the central task.

Tourism-poverty Relief Link: Critique and Assessment

The idea of linking tourism to poverty alleviation could be traced back to the 1970s (Harrison, 2008). Tourism has been perceived as an opportunity for impoverished communities because of its labour-intensive nature and reliance on natural and cultural capital, among the few resources poor communities tend to possess (Ashley and Roe, 2003). The developmental discourse of tourism is particularly influential in developing countries, where tourism is treated almost like a panacea of poverty (Ezeuduji, 2015; Zeng & Ryan, 2012). Under this context emerged PPT, which is widely questioned conceptually and substantively (Harrison, 2008; Butler, 2012; Turong et. al., 2014; Lo et. al., 2019).

Table 2-1: Critical focuses and positive evidences of PPT

Main critical focuses	Authors	Main positive evidences and arguments	Authors
Tourism Intensifying poverty under Neo- liberal process	Harrison (2008); Hall (2007); Chok et. al. (2007); Gascón (2015); Scheyvens (2007); Brohman (1996); Tourism Concern (2004) Mbaiwa and Darkoh, (2009). Mowforth and Munt (2009) ; Akama (1996, 2004); Britton (1982); Oppermann and Chon (1997)	Tourism's contribution to economic development of LDCs	Ashley and Mitchell (2007); Belisle (1983, 1984); Meyer (2007); Momsen (1996); Torres (2002, 2003); Kirsten and Rogerson (2002); UNCTAD (2013, 2017)
Tourism not the best choice for poverty alleviation	Farrell and Twining-Ward (2005); Suntikul et. al. (2009)	Tourism's contribution to social development of LDCs	Anker (1998); Scheyvens (2002); Rao and Chen(2018)

Tourism's economic benefits distribution not pro-poor	Spenceley and Goodwin (2007); King and Dinkoksung (2014);Truong, Hall, and Garry (2014); Xi and Zhang (2016); Lo et. al.(2018); Gascón (2015); Ashley et. al.(2000); Saffu et. al. (2008); Park et. al. (2012); Zhao et. al. (2011)	Tourism's contribution to nature conservation of LDCs	Sarinen (2009); Spenceley (2008); Scheyvens (2018)

It could be seen from Table 2-1 that critiques of PPT come into three focal points. First, PPT tacitly follows a neo-liberal approach to development and tries to harness rather than challenge the existing capitalistic international tourism system, attempting to alleviate poverty by embedding impoverished communities within the neo-liberal processes of globalisation and commodification (Hall, 2007; Harrison, 2008). As such, PPT may eke out a few resources for small, selected groups of the poor (or relatively poor) in destination areas (Harrison, 2008), making local populations vulnerable to labour exploitation and further enhancing poverty rather than alleviating it (Chok et. al., 2007). In particular, whereas the host communities always bear tourism's social and environmental costs, the economic benefits could mainly be distributed among outside investors, the state, and local elites (Gascón, 2015).

Several studies warned that tourism could increase inequalities (Scheyvens, 2002, 2007), increase dependency on outward-orientated growth (Brohman, 1996), exploit the workforce (Tourism Concern, 2004), lead to the displacement of communities (Akama, 1996, 2004; Mowforth & Munt, 2009) and contribute to conflict over scarce resources (Mbaiwa & Darkoh, 2009). A key concern has been that the global structures of the tourism industry made it impossible for LDCs to reap the benefits from tourism development (Scheyvens, 2009) because "leakages" were exceptionally high in this industry (e.g. Britton, 1982; Oppermann & Chon, 1997). Therefore, the political nature of PPT further strengthens the existing world order, making it even more challenging to transition to post-capitalist political-economic systems.

The second line of critique argues that tourism is often not the best choice for poverty alleviation. Tourism is a highly competitive industry, and it could be difficult or financially risky for the poor to participate in tourism without adequate support and knowledge transfer. Furthermore, the seasonality of tourism means that income generated from PPT could be more stable (Farrell & Twining-Ward, 2005). Also, because tourism is a destination-based activity, the applicability of PPT depends on the possession of certain tourism assets, such as natural or cultural resources, as well as the adequacy of infrastructure to support tourism, and therefore, may not be suitable for all impoverished areas (Suntikul et. al., 2009).

Third and central to the present analysis is the distribution of economic benefits. Spenceley and Goodwin (2007), who studied the impact of PPT in and around Kruger National Park in South Africa, found that PPT has little tangible impact on most people living in populated rural communities. However, the impact is substantial for the few people who directly participate. King and Dinkoksung (2014) investigated a village in Thailand's Isan region and found that participation is limited to the few villagers with entrepreneurial skills. Adiyia and Vanneste (2018) also found poor farmers needed help in getting involved in the local tourism value chain in Western Uganda. Truong et. al. (2014) studied Sapa, Vietnam and identified the lack of capital and foreign language proficiency as the main barriers to participation in PPT. Xi and Zhang (2016) and Lo et. al. (2018) found that PPT caused differentiation within the previously homogeneous community, with direct participants in tourism activities enjoying a better quality of life than indirect participants and non-participants.

This line of critique suggests that the benefits of PPT are often limited to a small part of the community that is considered elite, whereas the whole community shares the cost of tourism development (King & Dinkoksung, 2014). Consequently, most poor people fail to gain from PPT and lose in absolute terms (Gascón, 2015). Several factors have been identified as influencing participation of the poor in tourism. Financial and human capital is critical inputs for small-scale tourism operations (Ashley et. al., 2000; Saffu et. al., 2008). Social capital has also been found to correlate with participation in tourism by establishing tourism businesses (Park et. al., 2012; Zhao et. al., 2011). As noted by many scholars, there needs to be more empirical evidence on the link between tourism development and poverty alleviation (Chok et. al., 2007; Goodwin, 2009; Truong et. al., 2014; Winters et. al., 2013; Yang, 2015).

Despite these critiques, some positive evidence and arguments indicate that leakages were not necessarily higher in tourism than in other industries (Page, 1999; Roe et. al., 2004), and that tourism could contribute to GDP growth and poverty alleviation (Donaldson, 2007; Li et. al., 2018; Qin et. al., 2019), employment and income generation (Ashley & Mitchell, 2007; UNCTAD, 2013, 2017; Folarin & Adeniyi, 2020), gender equality (Anker, 1998; Scheyvens, 2002; Knight & Cottrell, 2016; Scheyvens & Hughes, 2019; Boluk, 2019), education and knowledge exchange (Ashley et. al., 2001; Knight & Cottrell, 2016; Rao & Chen, 2018; Qin et. al., 2019), inter- sectoral linkages (Belisle,1984; Torres & Momsen, 2004; Torres 2002; 2003; Meyer, 2007; Goodwin, 2008), entrepreneurship and small, medium and micro-enterprise (SMME) development (Kirsten & Rogerson, 2002), and nature conservation (Saarinen et. al., 2009; Spenceley, 2008). However, the literature needs more empirical evidence of the extent of this link (Mitchell & Ashley, 2010; Goodwin, 2007; Jamieson et. al., 2004). Even though the potential mechanisms through which tourism could alleviate poverty are well established, the magnitude of these links still needs to be established. For example, Mitchell and Ashley (2007) identified three primary pathways through which tourism impacts poverty: direct effects, secondary effects and dynamic effects.

A more concerted effort needs to be made to quantify the tourism-poverty link. As Table 2-2 shows, Winters et. al. (2013) argued that the tourism-poverty relief links exist. The critical point is to identify under what conditions the link could be the strongest. Input-output (IO) models and social accounting matrices (SAMs) are recommended as the two most basic models for mapping the economy-wide effects of tourism. However, their limitation is that they need to respond to price and wage changes which do exist in tourism and related industries.

Computable general equilibrium (CGE) models could avoid these limitations and adequately assess the role of tourism by examining how changes in tourism receipts are transmitted through an economy, allowing an estimate of the influence of tourism on employment and earnings (Winters et. al.,2013). CGE analysis could produce precise numerical estimates of the change of tourism expenditure's direct, indirect and induced impacts on related industries and sectors in economy tourism (Wickramasinghe & Naranpanawa, 2022). In the late 1980s, the Centre for International Economics (CIE) and the Industries Assistance Commission (IAC) in Australia pioneered the application of CGE modelling in tourism analysis. Since the late 1990s, researchers inside and outside Australia have become more interested in tourism CGE analysis. These researches mainly focused on assessing the impacts of tourism demand and tourism policy, the impact of mega events on tourism and the economy, the impact of tourism on the environment and natural resources and the distributional effect of tourism.

The impacts of tourism demand and policies have received the most academic attention (Wickramasinghe & Naranpanawa, 2022). Zhou et. al. (1997) are the first authors outside Australia to do both I-O and CGE analyses on the economic effects of a decline in tourism demand in Hawaii. The study found that a 10 % decline in visitor expenditures reduced output in tourism sectors but affected less in non-tourism sectors. Besides, the I-O model overestimates the economic effects of the decline in tourism demand. However, the CGE analysis has advantages over the I-O model in assessing this impact because it could consider resource movements between sectors in the face of changing prices.

With different CGE models, researchers made a detailed analysis of tourism's impacts on the overall economy (Adams and Parmenter, 1999; Dwyer et. al.,2003; Taylor et. al., 2003; Narayan, 2004; Rossouw & Saayman, 2011; Meng, 2014; Gul, 2015; Pratt, 2015; Matilainen et. al., 2016; Ivanov & Webster, 2007); Dutch disease effects (Forsyth & Dwyer, 2014; Inchausti-Sintes, 2015; Pham et. al., 2015; Dwyer et. al., 2016); income elasticity (Inchausti-Sintes et. al., 2020); tourism productivity (Dwyer et. al., 2007; Blake et. al., 2006; Inchausti-Sintes et. al., 2021); tourism quality (Inchausti-Sintes, 2020) and labour migration (Forsyth et. al., 2012; Konan, 2011). The impacts of various tourism and its related policies were investigated such as the effects of tourism tax policies (Gooroochurn & Sinclair, 2005; Ihalanayake, 2012; Ihalanayake, 2013; Mahadevan et. al., 2017); tourism investment policies (Banerjee et. al., 2019); tourism moratoria or opening up for tourism (Chen & Yang, 2010; Inchausti-Sintes & Voltes-Dorta, 2021) and carbon tax policies (Dwyer et. al., 2012; Meng & Pham, 2017; Zhang & Zhang, 2018, 2019).

The impacts of mega events are a second concern of tourism CGE modellers. Based on the estimation of mega events' impacts on tourism demand, CGE models are used to simulate the economic effect of the change in tourism demand. Some studies experiment with these effects in different scenarios, such as big, medium, and low changes in tourism spending. Most widely discussed mega-events by tourism CGE researchers are sports and tourism-related events (Blake, 2009; Li et. al., 2011; Allan et. al., 2017; Li et. al., 2017), terrorism (Adams et. al., 2001; Blake & Sinclair, 2003), health-related shocks such as foot and mouth disease outbreak (Blake et. al., 2003), SARS epidemic (Yang & Chen, 2009; Dwyer et. al., 2006) and Covid-19 (Deriu et. al., 2022).

Studies on how tourism affects the environment and natural resources are becoming more popular as people become more conscious of the environmental issues brought on by economic growth and the spread of tourism. CGE modellers evaluated tourism's impacts on natural resources and carbon emission (Roson & Sartori, 2014; Sun & Pratt, 2014; Gilliland et. al., 2020), climate change (Berrittella et. al., 2006; Pham et. al., 2010) and sea level rise (Bigano et. al., 2008). However, the CGE literature appears to be underrepresented in terms of economic evaluations of the effects of the environment and climate change on the tourism sector.

The study of tourism's distributional effects is a major initiative to assess tourism-poverty links with CGE models. If poor households are properly recognized among household categories in the SAMs, it is possible to for CGE models to determine whether jobs and wage gains go to poor households. The link between poverty and tourism could thus be determined with CGE analysis (Winters et. al., 2013). Undoubtedly, CGE has become one of the most suitable methods for exploring the tourism-poverty links, especially the distributional effects.

Some CGE analyses demonstrate tourism’s minor effects on poor people’s benefits. Wattanakuljarus (2006) and Wattanakuljarus and Coxhead (2008), through standard CGE analysis, explored Thailand's inbound tourism expansion on income levels of four groups of households. It's found that the growth of inbound tourism demand in Thailand raised aggregate household income. However, the richest gained more benefits from tourism revenues than the poorest in both agricultural and non-agricultural sectors, thus worsening the income distribution. The two studies concluded that the Thailand government's policy of promoting international tourism program is not pro-poor. Saayman et. al. (2012) also reveals that inbound tourist expenditure in South Africa benefits little to the poor in the short run. Nevertheless, the study suggests focusing on improving the labour market and human resources development to strengthen the tourism-poverty link.

Other CGE studies reveal tourism's positive role in poverty alleviation. Blake (2008) examined the Brazil's tourism-poverty relationship based on a 54-sector CGE model. The model incorporates price, earnings and government, regarded as the three channels influencing the distribution of income of four groups of households. Findings showed that tourism growth was positive for all income groups, including poor households. However, the lowest income households benefited less than the higher income groups. Based on these results, it was suggested that the government should employ more unskilled people, initiate more pro-poor programs, and reduce income inequality through redistribution.

Mahadevan et. al. (2017) found that Indonesia's domestic and inbound tourism growth reduced poverty but widened income gaps between the poor and the rich. The income inequality might be addressed by more targeted policies for touristic and non-touristic areas. Through the multiregional CGE model for Belize, Banerjee et. al. (2018) found that tourism investment decreased the poverty headcount despite a small increase in income inequality because poor people lacked skills for the new positions in the investments. Using the dynamic CGE model combined with Foster-Greer-Thorbecke (FGT) index for Kenya, Njoya and Seetaram (2018) demonstrate that tourism expansion enables poorer households to move closer to the poverty line, significantly reducing poverty gap and poverty severity.

The applications of CGE model in Chinese tourism research mainly involved the impacts of economic policies such as appraisal of the "opening up to Mainland Chinese tourist arrivals" policy on Taiwan (Chen & Yang, 2010), whether inbound tourism backed up the supply-side structural reform policy (Li et. al., 2019), the impacts of climate change policies such as economic impacts of the carbon tax on Chinese tourism industry (Zhang & Zhang, 2018, 2019), short-run effects of an Emissions Trading Scheme (ETS) and two auxiliary policies on the

Chinese tourism industry (Meng et. al., 2019); the impacts of shocks such as the magnitude of the economic impact of the economic slowdown on China's tourism (Li et. al.,2010), the economic contribution of tourism generated by the Beijing Olympics 2008 (Li et. al., 2011), tourism implications of the SARS epidemic in Taiwan (Yang & Chen, 2009).

Macroeconomic time-series data is used to assess tourism's long-term dynamic effects on development, not specifically on poverty alleviation. Most research finds that tourism is positive on economic growth, especially in some developing countries such as African countries (Fayissa et. al., 2008), Latin American countries (Fayissa et. al., 2009), and Pacific Island countries (Narayan et. al., 2010). Some scholars used this method to assess tourism's impact on poverty reduction. Using data from Nicaragua, Croes and Vanegas (2008) found a causal link between tourism and economic expansion and poverty reduction as measured by the poverty headcount. Deller (2010) used a spatial analysis to examine the impact of tourism and recreation activities on rural poverty. Xu (2016) examined the link between tourism and poverty and the conditions that shape this link in Latin America with panel quartile regression analysis.

Besides IO and SAM, Chinese scholars prefer to use Data Envelopment Analysis (Deng, 2015), Grey Correlation Analysis, Geographical Weighted Regression model (Ding, 2018), Hierarchical Fuzzy Comprehensive Evaluation model (Chen, 2019) and AHP Fuzzy Comprehensive Evaluation model (Yu, 2022) to assess TAP effects in poverty-stricken regions. Most of these evaluations on TAP effects indicate that Chinese tourism's CGE, which has been widely taken as a tool for economic and policy analysis in international trade, environment and energy, is seldom used in Chinese tourism research (Liu & Ji, 2017).

Table 2-2 Past studies on quantifying tourism's impacts on poverty alleviation

Studies	**Methods**	**Findings**
Winters et. al. (2013) Assessing the role of tourism in poverty alleviation: A research agenda	Theoretical paper	IO and SAMs are basic methods for assessing the economic effects of tourism on the poor but price and wage

Studies	Methods	Findings
		changes are not included. CGE overcomes these limitations.
Taylor et. al. (2003) The Economics of Eco-Tourism: A Galapagos Island Economy-wide Perspective; Taylor et. al. (2009) Ecotourism and Economic Growth in the Galapagos: An Island Economy-wide Analysis	CGE	Tourism leads economic growth and increase of residents' income in Galapagos.
Blake et. al. (2008) Tourism and poverty relief	CGE	Tourism's effects on all income groups are positive but low income groups get the least benefits from tourism.
Wattanakuljarus and Coxhead (2008) Is Tourism-based Development Good for the Poor?: A general equilibrium analysis for Thailand	CGE	Tourism raises aggregate household income but worsens the inequality between the rich and the poor.
Pratt (2015) The economic impact of tourism in SIDS	IO analysis, linkage analysis , CGE	Tourism generates economic activities but income left in the destinations is very small
Mahadevan et. al. (2016) Regional impacts of tourism-led growth on poverty and income inequality: a dynamic general equilibrium analysis for Indonesia	CGE	Tourism leads to poverty reduction and an increase in income inequality in both rural and urban regions in Indonesia.
Fayissa et. al. (2008) Impact of Tourism on Economic Growth Development in Africa	Panel data analysis	Tourism contributes significantly to GDP and economic growth of Sub-Saharan African countries.
Narayan et. al. (2010) Tourism and Economic Growth: A Panel Data Analysis for Pacific Island Countries	Panel data analysis	Tourism's contribution to economic growth in

Studies	**Methods**	**Findings**
		Fiji, Tonga, the Solomon Islands and Papua New Guinea grows.
Croes and Vanegas (2008). Cointegration and causality between tourism and poverty reduction	Co-integration and causality tests	Tourism could play a positive role in reducing poverty by allocating public and private resources to tourism development.
Deller (2010) Rural Poverty, Tourism and Spatial Heterogeneity	Geographically Weighted Regression	Tourism and recreation play a small role in explaining changes in poverty rates.
Xu (2016) A Panel Quartile Regression Analysis of Tourism Effects on Poverty Alleviation	Panel Quartile Regression Analysis	Tourism development contributes more to GDP growth than poverty alleviation
Zhang (2016) Research on Tourism Poverty Alleviation Model and Poverty Alleviation Effect —Analysis of survey data based on poor areas in Hainan Province	Data Envelopment Analysis	TAP in China contributed more significantly to low income residents.
Pang (2019) Grey Correlation Analysis of Rural Tourism Poverty Alleviation and Tourism Income in Longnan City	Grey Correlation Analysis	There is strong correlation between tourism revenue growth and increase of poor rural residents' income in Longnan, China.
Ding (2018) Analysis on the Heterogeneity of TAP Effect in Wuling Mountain Area	Geographical Weighted Regression	Scenic areas of different levels in Wuling Mountain Area have different impacts on income increase of poor rural residents.
Chen (2019) Evaluation of TAP Effects in Wuling Mountain	Hierarchical Fuzzy	TAP has positive effects on social,

Studies	Methods	Findings
Concentrated Contiguous Destitute Area	Comprehensive Evaluation	economic and environmental development of Wuling Mountain concentrated contiguous destitute area.
Yu (2022). AHP Evaluation of Chongqing Rural Tourism Poverty Alleviation and E-Commerce Poverty Alleviation Integration Development Strategy	AHP Fuzzy Comprehensive Evaluation	The integration degrees of TAP and e-commerce industry varied in different areas of Chongqing.

Government in PPT: Roles, Power and Policy Effects

Government is one of PPT's major stakeholders, joined by local communities, non-government organisations (NGOs), international development organisations (IDOs), the private sector and the poor people (Chok et. al., 2007; Phi et. al., 2016; Tolkach et. al., 2012). Government is pivotal in controlling, planning and directing tourism growth (Mowforth & Munt, 2015). Liu et. al. (2020) noted that in China, the central and local governments play different roles in rural tourism development. The role of governments in tourism is an outcome of their tourism policy formulation and implementation (Hall, 1994). Therefore, the study of governments' policies for PPT will help understand the roles and ideologies of governments in poverty alleviation through tourism.

However, under the guidance of neo-liberalism, which tends toward free-market capitalism and away from government spending, regulation, and public ownership, the general tourism literature has scarcely discussed the politics of tourism (Dredge & Jenkins, 2007; Hall, 1994, 2008, 2011). Government approaches and strategies for reducing poverty in tourism are not the core of national tourism strategies in many LDCs, including South Asia (Lemma, 2014) and Africa (Folarin & Adeniyi, 2020).Therefore, researchers pay more attention to community-based tourism (CBT)'s role and impacts on poverty alleviation (e.g. Wearing & McDonald, 2002; Harrison & Schipani, 2007; Manyara & Jones, 2007; Bramwell, 2010; Choi & Murray, 2010; Stone & Stone, 2011; Marx, 2011; Phommavong & Sorensson, 2014; Amir et. al., 2015; Giampiccoli,

A. & Saayman, 2017), NGOs and ISOs' funding and participation in PPT projects (Harrison & Schipani, 2007; Harrison, 2008). Spenceley and Meyer (2012) found that the literature explored PPT politics from broader structural conditions and power relations between the global tourism industry and local communities. Hall and Brown (2006), for example, question the potential of PPT by asking, "Does PPT simply offer another route by which economic imperialism, through tourism, may extend its tentacles, or is it an appropriately liberating and remunerative option?"

During the new century, governments realised that tourism could bring more benefits if development took a form in which state governance focused on national interests (Clancy, 1999; Potter, 1993). The neo-liberal orthodoxy was challenged by a renewed focus on the state's role (Sofield, 2003). It became clear that inequalities between developed and developing countries were increasing and that liberalising economies did not automatically lead to enhanced economic growth (Scheyvens, 2011). A "new poverty" agenda was increasingly focusing on enhancing the role of the state and on the importance of strong institutions, governance, and more effectively targeting poverty and vulnerability.

Researchers became interested in detailed studies of systems, processes, places and interactions between people in order to understand how power influences the actions of stakeholders and the link between tourism and poverty (e.g. Burns, 2004; Higgins-Desbiolles, 2006; Schilcher, 2007; Teo & Li, 2003). These studies have embraced the complexity of tourism and moved away from a reductionist approach that sees tourism either as a force for good or as a force for evil. Rather than viewing tourism as an industry aligned to neo-liberal thinking, tourism was perceived as a powerful social force that must be better understood to connect it more effectively to development agendas beyond purely economic considerations.

Table 2-3 shows that governments' policies to strengthen tourism's role in poverty alleviation have increasingly attracted scholars' interest in recent years. Lemma (2014), based on the overview of six countries' poverty reduction policies of national tourism strategies in South Asia, found that links between poverty reduction and tourism have been recognised, whereas actionable strategies must be made explicitly.

Community-based tourism approach, enterprise support, and sustainable tourism are the main PPT methods that concern governments' policies and strategies, yielding positive effects. Tourism as a contributor to poverty alleviation has been emphasised in Lao PDR's National Growth and Poverty Eradication Strategy and National Tourism Strategy, which focus on proper planning for pro-poor tourism. Among different PPT forms, eco-tourism in rural areas is prioritised by the Lao government's policy thanks to the government's successful cooperation with NGOs (Harrison & Schipani, 2007).

Based on the investigation of Vietnam's tourism policy evolution with a policymaking model, Truong (2013) found that the government has been actively involved in tourism as an operator/entrepreneur, regulator, planner, promoter, coordinator, and educator who adopted the neo-liberal approach in tourism policies, making poverty alleviation secondary to tourism growth. In the pro-poor tourism framework for Zimbabwe proposed by Chipfuva (2021), government was a main though not a leading actor to implement the pro-poor rural tourism initiative. Similar to Chipfuva (2021), Gonzo (2023) recognized government as an important stakeholder within the broader framework of inclusive community development through pro-poor tourism. With the system Generalised Method of Moments (GMM) estimation technique, Folarin and Adeniyi (2020) assessed the effects of the pro-poor tourism policies of Sub-Saharan African (SSA) countries and found that policies targeted at increasing the attractiveness and awareness of the existing SSA tourism sites have considerable poverty reduction potential.

Unlike most neo-liberalism-oriented PPTs, the Chinese government implemented its tourism-assisting the poor (TAP) initiative with the top-down approach (Dai et. al., 2012). In response to President Xi's new guidelines on targeted poverty alleviation (Li et. al., 2021), Chinese TAPPs put poverty reduction on the top agenda, especially after 2015, lowering the poverty rate dramatically and creating substantial benefits for the poor population in several areas. Chinese TAPPs actively responded to the common prosperity and well-off society ideology (Xin, 2018), closely following the pace of the national poverty alleviation strategy, and strived to accurately drive the construction of a well-off society in an all-round way. First put forward by Comrade Mao Zedong (Boer & Boer, 2021), the idea of common prosperity idea laid the basis for the reform and opening strategy, the theory of poverty alleviation and development, the scientific concept of development and the idea of targeted poverty alleviation proposed by the following generations of leaders (Xi, 2017). "A well-off society" was first proposed by Comrade Deng Xiaoping. Constructing a well-off society in an all-round way was formally proposed in the report of the 18th CPC National Congress in 2012. Building a moderately prosperous society in an all-round way was the phased goal of common prosperity (Xigen, 2019).

Under the guidance of the Chinese central government's common prosperity and well-off society ideology, Chinese TAPPs impacted the poor. Through semi-structured interviews, Qin et. al. (2019) analysed China's adapted PPT policies' economic, socio-cultural and environmental impacts on the poor in three National Poverty Alleviation Tourism Pilot Zones in northern China. Since pro-poor tourism is both an opportunity-dependent and an opportunity-generating process (Knight, 2018), poor people's lack of capabilities and skills in participating in the pro-poor tourism projects is one of the main barriers to draw the maximum benefits from tourism (Park & Ondicho, 2017). Therefore, the Chinese government is a leader in promoting cross-group knowledge transfer to capacity-building of impoverished populations to enhance their capability to catch the PPT opportunities (Rao & Chen, 2018). An increasing number of Chinese migrant workers tended to return home to seize entrepreneurship and work opportunities (Yang et. al., 2021), which could be provided by targeted poverty alleviation and rural revitalisation through tourism.

Table 2-3 Main studies on governments' PPT policies

Studies	**Status of PPT policies**	**Policy impacts on poverty alleviation**	**Methods**
Lemma, A (2014) Tourism for Poverty Reduction in South Asia	Not the core part of national tourism policies in South Asian countries	Limited impacts on poverty alleviation without actionable strategies.	desk-based literature review
Harrison and Schipani (2007). Lao tourism and	Emphasized by the Lao PDR's National Growth	Significant contribution to poverty	Interview

poverty alleviation: Community-based tourism and the private sector	and Poverty Eradication Strategy and National Tourism Strategy	alleviation especially in rural areas.	
Truong, V. D. (2013). Tourism policy development in Vietnam: a pro-poor perspective	Secondary to tourism development policies	Limited poverty alleviation effects due to the government's neo- liberal approach	Policy analysis
Folarin and Adeniyi (2019) Does tourism reduce poverty in sub- Saharan African countries	Targeting at enhancing attraction of destinations rather than alleviating poverty	Considerable poverty alleviation potential	System Generalized Method of Moments
Qin et. al. (2019). Perceived impacts of the poverty alleviation tourism policy on the poor in China.	Leading position in Chinese national poverty alleviation and tourism policies especially after 2015	An effective way to reduce poverty and increase incomes among the poor	Semi-structured Interview
Rao and Chen (2018) Cross-group knowledge transfer and capacity-building for the poor: a case study of tourism targeted poverty alleviation in Guangdong province, China.	Active role in enhancing the poor's skills participating in tourism in Guangdong, China	Assisting the poor to catch PPT opportunities.	semi-structured interviews, informal interviews, on-site observations, tourists survey and secondary data collection

The differences of Chinese TAPPs from neo-liberal PPT policies could be further understood by identifying the policy values, targets and use of policy instruments, which represent the typical policy analysis framework. Public policy is what governments choose to do or not to do (Dye, 2005: 1), indicating that the process of policy formulation and implementation is the "the authoritative allocation of value" (Easton, 1965). Policy values could be defined as "the valued ends embodied in, and implemented through, the collective choices we make through policy processes" (Stewart, 2009:14). Stewart (2009) first drew out the dichotomous nature of some general policy values. It's believed that a value is only identifiable through its opposite, for example, growth or greenness. Reconciling the conflict between employment, output and environmental issues manifested by this values pair is the challenge the sustainable development policies should respond to (Stewart, 2009:146).

As the linkage between policy formulation and implementation, policy instruments realise policy values and achieve policy targets (Eliadis, Hill, & Howlett, 2005; Ali, 2013; Howlett, M. 2020; Guo, 2020). It provides a proper perspective to understand TAPPs' role in strengthening the tourism-poverty link and promoting sustainable development of poor areas in China. Capano, Priton and Vicentini (2020) argued that an instrument-based approach could better enlighten the nature of policy dynamics and help policymakers make more effective decisions. The understanding of instrument and mix dynamics over time needs to be deepened through more empirical studies (Howlett, Mukherjee, & Woo, 2018; Capano & Howlett, 2020).

Policy instrument analysis is a fundamental and major subject throughout the history of policy sciences. The research on this subject could be dated back to 1950-1980, when Lowi and other scholars developed classifications and theories on policy instruments (Capano & Howlett, 2020). Since then, extensive agreements on what policy instruments are have been reached. They are defined as "a set of techniques by which governmental authorities wield their power in attempting to ensure support and affect or prevent social change" (Vedung, 1998: pp. 21), "an identifiable method through which collective action is structured to address a public problem" (Salamon, 2002: pp. 19) or the means governments use "to deliberately affect the nature, types, quantities and distribution of the goods and services provided in a society" (Howlett, 2000: pp. 415). These definitions agree that policy tools are governance techniques through which government pursue their policy targets (Ali, 2013; Capano & Howlett, 2020).

The achievement of policy targets depends on properly choosing policy instruments (Flanagan et. al., 2011). The selection of individual and mix of instruments from the "toolbox" usually starts from the classification of policy tools, which could help policymakers know the characteristics of instruments and their applicability to the context (Eliadis et. al., 2005; Howlett & Ramesh, 1993). There are substantial policy instrument typologies in general or specific fields. Salamon, Vedung, Schneider, Ingram and Hood are the most frequently cited policy instrument typology scholars (Acciai & Capano, 2021). Since "any given policy tool is a package that contains a number of different elements" (Salamon, 2000, p. 43), Salamon (2002) proposed that policy instruments have four dimensions of coerciveness, directness, automaticity, and visibility. The classifications of Vedung (1998) and Doern and Phidd (1983) are coercion-based, with the former including regulative, economic, and informational instruments and the latter identifying five instruments. Based on behavioural assumptions, Schneider and Ingram (1990) classified policy tools into authority, incentive, and capacity, symbolic and hortatory and learning instruments.

Besides these popular general typologies, Rothwell (1985) divided government policy instruments into demand, supply, and environmental tools. This typology stresses the policy impact on practical work (Yue et. al., 2020). It is widely used in some specific areas, including technology and innovation (Bergek & Norrman, 2015; Lin et. al., 2017), energy (Huang et. al., 2018; Zhou et. al., 2020), human resource (Zhang et. al., 2019), health care (Yue et. al., 2020) especially in the Chinese context. These authors agreed that Rothwell's typology emphasises policy tools selected to address public problems and achieve policy goals. The selection and implementation of tools are determined by their characteristics and affected by the environment and background. Chinese TAPPs evolve with the application of different policy instrument mix for the achievement of TAP goals in different stages. Therefore, this classification provides a useful framework for our research of investigating the match of policy instruments and TAP goals over time to explore how tourism develop into a major poverty alleviation means in China under the guidance of TAPPs.

Sustainable Tourism Policy

Sustainable tourism policy is an established part of tourism policy research (Hall, 2011). There are six themes usually discussed by scholars: the concept of sustainability in tourism policy, sustainable tourism policy implementation, stakeholders, sustainable tourism and climate policy, sustainable tourism indicators and planning and the role of sustainable tourism policy (Guo et. al., 2019). Case studies from the United Kingdom, Germany, China, Malta and Turkey reflect the state interventions that affect tourism sustainability in destinations (Bramwell & Lane, 2011), especially through policy implementation.

Due to the ambiguous definition of sustainability, many countries' policies are criticised for overemphasising economic growth (Mai & Smiths, 2015; Anderson et. al., 2018). In order to scientifically formulate sustainable tourism policies, it's necessary to develop indicators for guiding sustainable tourism planning (Blancas et. al., 2010). Some scholars constructed various indicator systems with various methods for better sustainable tourism planning (eg. Castellani & Sala, 2010; Blancas et. al. 2011; Tanguay et. al., 2013; Fernandez-Tabales et. al., 2017).

It’s very difficult to implement sustainable tourism policies, which is not a merely technical problem but involved with political, cultural, economic, social and human psychological changes (Guo, 2019). If the sustainable tourism is not treated holistically (Andersen et. al., 2018), sustainable goals in sustainable tourism policies might conflict other goals in a regulatory framework (Cao, 2015). Most nations struggle to incorporate sustainable tourism into their public policies (Brendehaug et. al., 2017).

The Chinese government guided the sustainable tourism development through its sustainable development strategy. China launched a sustainable development strategy in the 1990s (Zhang & Wen, 2008; Wang & Chang, 2014). In 1997, the 15th National Congress of the Communist Party of China positioned the sustainable development strategy as one of the national economic development strategies. This strategy was further developed by the scientific development concept put forward by the 16th National Congress of the Communist Party of China in 2002. Good ecological environment was regarded as one of the most important goals of building a well-off society in the report of the 17th

National Congress of the Communist Party of China in 2007. The concept of "green development" proposed by the Fifth Plenary Session of the 18th Central Committee in 2015 further inherited and updated the concept of sustainable development, integrating "green development" into the entire process of targeted poverty alleviation, thus forming the concept of "green poverty alleviation" (Qin & Zhang, 2022; Guo & Liu, 2022), which laid the basis for sustainable tourism policy formulation and implementation in China. Nevertheless, tourism growth in some Chinese regions is still criticised for causing environmental degradation (Teng et. al., 2021).

Different sustainable tourism policy stakeholders have different understandings of the tourism sustainability based on their interests (Jackie Ong & Smiths, 2014; Wesley & Pforr, 2010; Truong et. al., 2014), leading to the gap between policy development and policy implementation. In some countries, national tourism policies target sustainable development. However, government officials are more concerned about economic development from tourism growth, resulting in the inconsistency between the priorities of government officials and the gorals of sustainable tourism policies (Yüksel et. al., 2012). The complicated power dynamics among multiple stakeholders influence the controversy over sustainable tourist development in many destinations (Wesley & Pforr, 2010). The lack of public participation and discussion of sustainability in existing programs makes planning difficult to implement effectively (Simão & Partidário, 2012). Vellecco and Mancino (2010) concluded that lack of shared responsibility makes it difficult to execute sustainable tourism policies.

The sustainable tourism policy impact measurement is quite rare in the academic literature due to the unsuccessful development and implementation of sustainable tourism policies. It's in very recent years especially after the outbreak of the Covid-19 that few scholars start to pay attention to measuring impacts of sustainable tourism policy. Petrevska et. al. (2020) examined policy enablers' perception of sustainable tourism policies' impacts on sustainable development in tourist destinations in Serbia under the three pillars of sustainability. It's found that policy enablers consider socio-cultural impacts as the most important for achieving sustainability when developing tourist destinations. The study proved that Serbia's tourist sites must reform their growth strategies and plans.

Haibo et. al. (2020) reviewed publications and statistics on China's tourism policy impacts on economic and environmental sustainability between 1980's and 2019. They found that China's efforts to lead the world in tourist destinations have had a severe impact on the environment, which has a knock-on effect on the economy and society at large. On the other hand, China, as a major member of the United Nations, has adopted sustainable development principles in the modern era to support environmental protection. However, there is a lot of work to do. As one of the countries that rely on tourism as a pillar industry, Malaysia initiated sustainable tourism policies in the 1990s. Using partial least square structural equation modeling, Khan et. al. (2021) proposed that sustainable tourism policy, destination management, and destination social responsibility significantly impact sustainable tourism development. Additionally, destination social responsibility partially mediates the relationship between sustainable tourism policy, destination management, and sustainable tourist growth.

No consensus has been reached on which indicator system is more effective for tourism sustainability and who should be responsible for reducing tourism's negative impact on the environment or equality of sustainable tourism policies (Miller, 2001). Sustainable tourism policies encourage the balanced development of environment, economy and society of destinations. Scholars even argue that sustainable tourism policies should face the tourism challenges posed by climate change (Gossling et. al., 2012; Moyle et. al., 2014). Most of these policies only respond to part of sustainable development principles and goals with employment and labour (Baum, 2018), whereas poverty alleviation is rarely considered. Academic researches centre on policies' impact on tourism sustainability with little attention to the process of formulating policies and governance behaviours in tourism sustainable development (Guo et. al., 2019).

Literature Review Analysis

The literature review mainly discusses dominant concepts and measurements of poverty, development theories and tourism forms related to poverty alleviation, critique and assessment of tourism-poverty relief link and government roles in PPT and sustainable tourism policy. The most influential poverty concepts and measurement approaches tend to reveal the multifaceted nature of poverty, involving the shift from income focus to equal attention to economic and non-economic factors. Absolute poverty and money metric approach are widely used in most developing countries like China to eradicate extreme poverty. In contrast, some wealthy countries, such as European countries, mostly adopt relative poverty and other concepts and approaches. The subjectivity in selecting the poverty measurement indicators has been widely debated by the scholars, which, however, could be partly avoided by MPI developed by Alkire and Foster (2011).

Poverty alleviation is a problem of human development. The focuses of development theories have shifted from the narrower economic growth in the 1950s to the broader alternative development approach concerning the environment-development relationship in the 1980s and finally to holistic and multi-dimensional sustainable development since the late 1980s. Poverty measurements are more diversified and multi-dimensional with the evolution of development theories. Under sustainable development, poverty has become a multi-dimensional issue involving economic, social, cultural and environmental sectors. After China accomplishes SDG1 in 2020, mainly measured by the narrower economic poverty line, the government is implementing Rural Revitalization Strategy to reinforce the SDG1 achievement and realise sustainable development in relatively poor rural areas. The relative poverty in China after 2020 should be measured through the multi-dimensional approach instead of the only economic poverty line. Through MPI analysis and TAP stakeholders' perceptions, this study will evaluate TAPPs' impacts on multi-dimensional poverty under the sustainable development paradigm.

The review of various tourism forms linked with poverty reduction revealed that PPT, ST-EP, and TAP are three dominant concepts directly related to poverty alleviation through tourism. TAP is the Chinese characteristic PPT, combining the ideology of PPT's creating net benefits for the poor and ST-EP's eliminating poverty by sustaining tourism development. PPT is criticised for widening the gap between developing and developed countries by following the neo-liberalism approach, which resulted in its limited applicability in poverty reduction and accessibility of few benefits to the poor. Government is the main actor in the PPT's stakeholder network, whereas its roles are limited under the guidance of neoliberalism. That is why the research on PPT politics focuses on the unfair distribution of PPT benefits between developed and developing countries with little attention to government behaviours in PPT policy formulation and implementation.

Amid the criticism and controversy on the neo- liberalism's influence on PPT, the role of government in directing more PPT's net benefits to the poor has increasingly been recognised thanks to the significant results achieved by some developing countries' PPT initiatives, including China's TAP initiative led by the government. PPT policies as a major tool for the government to participate in poverty reduction through tourism have been studied mainly from perspectives of the status of poverty reduction in tourism policy, PPT methods and forms supported by the government, government's roles in PPT-related policymaking process, effects and impacts of PPT policies. These researches are few and must be broadened and deepened systematically and holistically. In particular, there lacks understandings of how poverty alleviation focused government pro-poor tourism strategies channel tourism benefits to the poor.

Literature started to have a general introduction of Chinese TAPPs, the government's efforts to empower the poor and the poor people's perception of TAPPs' effects, which could to some extend reveal Chinese characteristic PPT experience. However, little concerted effort has been made to quantify the tourism-poverty link. Some quantitative research proved that tourism has driven the economic growth and household income increase but benefited little to the poorest. Among the few quantitative approaches to quantifying tourism-poverty link, CGE has its advantages in revealing whether tourism income is distributed to the poor through PPT policies. Nevertheless, it is seldom used to quantify the tourism-poverty link under Chinese Tourism-Assisting the Poor Policies. It's obvious that there is insufficient empirical evidence on the tourism-poverty link.

Besides, PPT policies in many developing countries are criticised for paying too much attention to economic growth but ignoring the sustainable development of destinations. Though scholars have widely researched sustainable tourism policies, agreements have yet to be reached on the concept of sustainability and sustainable tourism indicators. Furthermore, sustainable tourism policies only respond to some sustainable development goals with rare attention to poverty alleviation. The theoretical underpinnings for tourism's role in promoting SDG1-led SGDs need to be further explored.

Therefore, with the combined use of quantitative and qualitative methods, this study will assess the impacts of China's TAPPs on SDG1 involving economic and non-economic factors under the sustainable development paradigm. The match of Chinese TAPPs' value orientation, policy targets and policy tool mix will be investigated to help the academic community and governments devoted to achieving SDGs understand how TAPPs have gradually made tourism a leading poverty relief tool since 1980's. Then the mechanism of how TAPPs have directed tourism's benefits to the poor will be investigated by quantifying the tourism-poverty link in implementing TAPPs. Besides the economic impact analysis, MPI developed by Alkire and Foster (2011) will be modified according to the sustainability dimensions identified in Chinese TAPPs documents to assess TAP's contribution to the alleviation of multi-dimensional poverty in TAP destinations. Further, semi-structured interviews will be conducted to investigate TAPPs' impacts on the sustainable development of TAP destinations perceived by the TAP stakeholders. Finally, the study will explore the conceptual model of TAPPs' impacts on the sustainable development of TAP destinations to offer some implications for optimizing TAPPs for sustainable rural revitalization in China and maximizing tourism's potential to advance SDGs in other developing countries.

Conclusion

Since TAP is, in essence, a problem of human development through tourism, this chapter, based on the overview of poverty concepts and measurements, reviews development theories and different tourism forms related to poverty alleviation. After China fulfils the goal of eliminating absolute poverty in 2020, the long-existing relative poverty problem tends to be a multi-dimensional issue. The Chinese government's leading role in TAP through TAPPs has made tourism a major tool in poverty alleviation. This chapter further overviews poverty critique and assessment of tourism-poverty relief links and roles of government in PPT and sustainable tourism policy. Based on the analysis of these reviews, this chapter finally identified knowledge gap, empirical evidence gap and theoretical gap for this research to fill. The knowledge gap lies in the lack of an in-depth understanding about how poverty alleviation focused government pro-poor tourism strategies channel tourism benefits to the poor. Moreover, there is insufficient empirical evidence on the tourism-poverty link. Besides, the theoretical underpinnings for tourism's role in promoting SDG1-led SGDs need to be further explored. The following chapter will explain how to collect and analyse the data to achieve research objectives for filling these gaps.

Chapter 3
Research Methodology

Introduction

This chapter specifically introduces the research methodology used in this study for data collection and analysis, including research philosophy, research approaches, time horizon, data collection and data analysis with mixed methods, and the way to establish trustworthiness is elaborated further in this chapter.

Research Process

Research methodology involves researchers' attitudes to and understanding of their research and the strategies selected to answer research questions (Greener, 2008). Since research is a process of people discovering things systematically, the Saunders Research Onion is proposed to demonstrate the progression of stages through which a research methodology could be designed (Saunders et. al., 2016). With its flexible adaptability to various contexts, the research onion becomes a valuable and effective model for designing a methodology (Bryman, 2012). Therefore, in order to answer the research questions proposed, this study follows Sanders Research Onion for choosing the suitable research methodology. Like peeling an onion, this study chooses its methodology from the outer layer to the inner layer (Saunders et. al., 2016). Figure 3.1 shows six layers in the onion, each describing a more detailed stage of the research process (Saunders et. al., 2019).

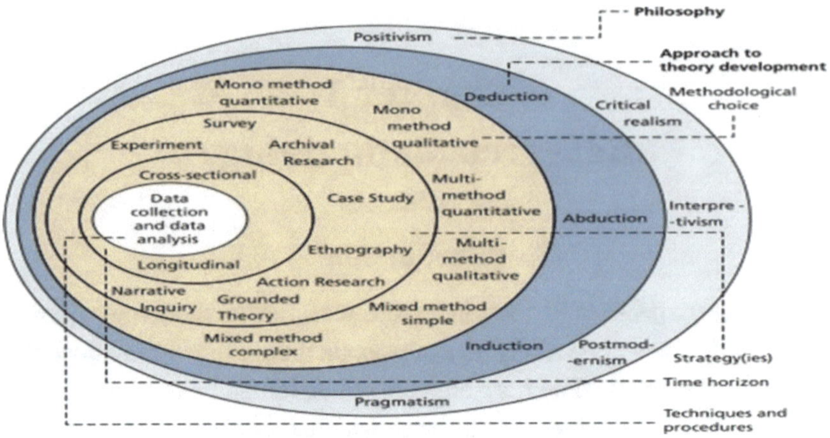

Figure 3-1 Research onion

Source: Saunders, M., Lewis, P., and Thornhill, A. 2019. Research Methods for Business Students. New York: Pearson Education Limited. (p.130)

Like peeling an onion, this study chooses its methodology from the outer layer to the inner layer (Saunders et. al., 2016). After identifying the research philosophy and approach to theory development, the researcher develops the research design of this study, including methodological choice, research strategies, and time horizon. The techniques and procedures for data collection and data analysis are demonstrated in the innermost layer. The research onion of this study is shown below in Figure 3.2, with six layers describing a more detailed stage of the research process (Saunders et. al., 2019).

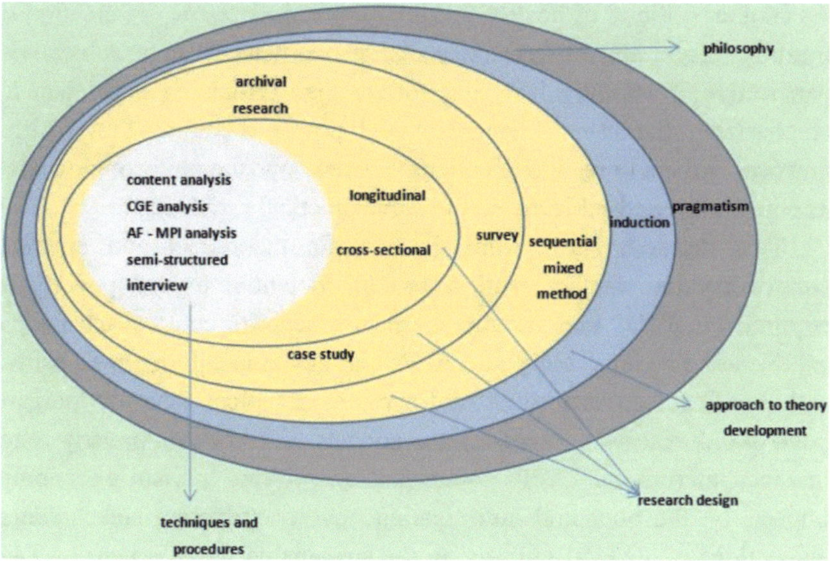

Figure 3-2 Research onion of this study

Research Philosophy

The outermost layer of the research onion is research philosophy. It represents a system of fundamental beliefs and assumptions about the world we are researching (Abdelhakim, 2021; Saunders et. al., 2019). These assumptions and beliefs inevitably shape how researchers understand research questions and underpin the choice of research methods, strategies, data collection techniques and analysis procedures (Crotty, 1998; Saunders et. al., 2019). Among various types of basic assumptions at different research stages (Burrell & Morgan, 2016), three types of fundamental assumptions are the most prominent, including ontology about the study of realities, epistemology dealing with what is and how researchers get the proper knowledge and axiology about the extent and ways researchers' values influence the research process.

Based on these basic assumptions, Saunders et. al. (2019) proposed five major philosophies: positivism, critical realism, interpretivism, postmodernism and pragmatism for business and management research (Figure 3.1). Positivism focuses on obtaining detailed and accurate knowledge and producing law-like generalizations from an observable social reality like natural science. Unlike direct realism, which supports positivism, critical realism intends to explain what we see and experience.

As another critique of positivism, interpretivism stresses the creation of meanings from the observable social phenomena from a subjectivist perspective. Postmodernism goes further than criticizing positivism by emphasizing the role of language and power relations. Pragmatism, however, strives to reconcile various or even opposite philosophies, such as objectivism and subjectivism, to solve practical problems.

This research starts from the world's theoretical and practical controversy on whether tourism has the potential to end poverty as required by SDG1 and whether tourism's benefits could reach people experiencing poverty. Chinese TAPPs that have made tourism a positive and significant poverty relief tool serve as a typical case for tourism-poverty link research. Assessing the impacts of TAPPs on poverty relief involves interpreting TAPPs documents, quantifying tourism's economic impacts on the poor and investigating poverty reduction stakeholders' perceptions of TAPPs' impacts on the sustainable development of TAP destinations.

Therefore, the philosophy of this research is not limited to any extreme assumption but reconciles objectivism and subjectivism, facts and values embraced by pragmatism. Ontologically, TAPPs' impacts on poverty reduction are practical consequences of the Chinese government's value orientations, targets, formulation and implementation of TAPPS policies, and stakeholders' involvement in TAP initiatives. Epistemologically this research strives to explore the government's influence on enhancing the tourism-poverty link through PPT policies in the Chinese context by investigating the match of TAPPS value, targets and policy tool mix that ensure tourism's benefits to the poor, finding out the condition under which the tourism-poverty link is the greatest and analyzing stakeholders' perceptions of TAPPs' impacts on the sustainable development of TAP destinations. Axiologically, the researcher of this study intends to add empirical evidence to the tourism-poverty link and explore the mechanism that ensures tourism's benefits to people with low incomes through the government's PPT policies. In addition, the research findings and analysis results are of implications for China to promote sustainable rural revitalization through tourism and for developing countries to improve tourism's contribution to achieving SDG1 and related SDGs.

Approach to Theory Development

The use of theory is usually involved explicitly or non-explicitly in a research project design where testing or building a theory is a core question. In the research onion, the layer next to the research philosophy is an approach to theory development. This process helps the researcher figure out how theories are used. There are three approaches to the reasoning research adopts: deduction, induction and abduction (Figure 3.1). The deductive approach is used to test a theory. In contrast, the inductive approach aims to generate or build a theory. The abductive approach is adopted to generate a new or modify an existing theory by observing and testing a "surprising fact" (Kennedy & Thornberg, 2018).

PPT is an issue of sustainable human development through tourism. As stated in the literature review, PPT reflects the multi-dimensional approach or philosophy of sustainable development, which results in people experiencing poverty obtaining more net benefits from tourism, including short-term or long-term economic, social or environmental benefits (Ashley et. al., 2000; Chok et. al., 2007). However, the academic community has always doubted whether tourism has the potential to eradicate poverty and criticized PPT policies' overemphasis on economic growth. The lack of empirical evidence of the tourism-poverty links and PPT's contribution n to the sustainable development of poor areas hinders the research and practice of PPT's role in poverty reduction in developing nations. Therefore, this study follows the inductive approach (Figure 3.2) to explore the mechanism of how Chinese TAPPs ensure tourism's benefits to the impoverished people and whether tourism contributes to reducing the multi-dimensional poverty of TAP destinations under the sustainable development paradigm.

Research Design

A research design is an overall plan of a research project. In the research onion, the process of a research design is demonstrated by the three layers of methodological choice, strategies and time horizon shown in Figure 3.1. The selection of these three layers in building up the research design is influenced by the above-peeled two outer layers of research philosophy and approach to theory development.

Methodological Choice

The first step of the research design is to choose research methods among mono-quantitative, mono-qualitative, multi-quantitative, multi-qualitative, and mixed methods. In business and management research, multiple methods are usually adopted since they are likely to overcome the weaknesses of using mono methods and offer diversified approaches to investigating, analyzing and interpreting research issues (Bryman, 2006).

In formulating a coherent research design, the methodological choice should align with research philosophies and approaches to theory development. Mixed methods research, which is the branch of multiple methods research, combines the use of quantitative and qualitative data collection techniques and analytical procedures. According to Saunders et. al. (2019), pragmatism and induction usually influence mixed methods designs (Figure 3.3) and range from simple and concurrent forms to more complex and sequential forms. Pragmatists advocate that research methods should be selected to address practical problems. Mixed methods are most possibly used unless a practical problem can be solved with one particular method.

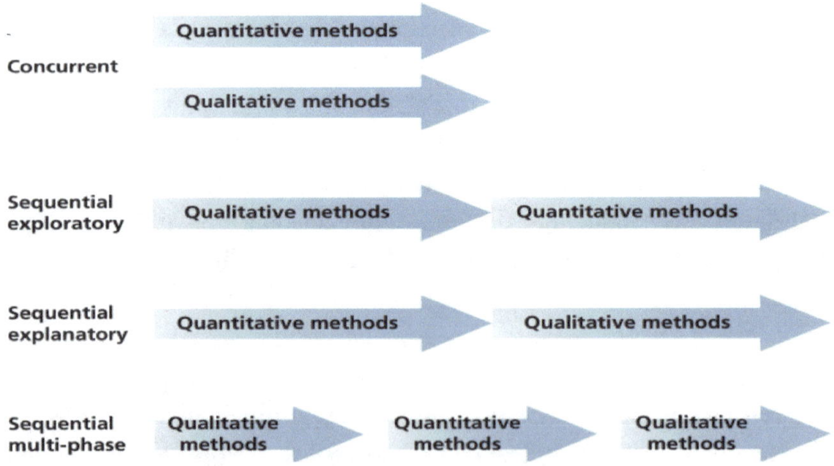

Figure 3-3 Mixed methods research designs

Source: Saunders, M., Lewis, P., and Thornhill, A. 2016. Research Methods for Business Students. New York: Pearson Education Limited.(p.170)

The assessment of TAPPs' impacts on poverty relief is based on pragmatism and inductive analysis. Objective and subjective analysis is involved in understanding the mechanism of how Chinese TAPPs ensure tourism's benefits to the sustainable development of the poor areas and TAPPs' impacts on the multi-dimensional poverty reduction under the sustainable development paradigm. It is almost impossible to carry out a comprehensive assessment of TAPPs' impacts with any mono method. Therefore, as shown in Figure 3.4, this study chooses sequential mixed methods in different data collection and analysis stages to generate complementary findings to address the research problems.

In the first stage, a qualitative method was used to identify the sustainability values, targets and policy tool mix reflected in the TAPPs documents. Then, a quantitative method was adopted to assess TAPPs' role in channeling tourism's benefits to people experiencing poverty. In the final stage, a quantitative method was first used to evaluate TAPPs' impacts on reducing multi-dimensional poverty under the sustainable development paradigm. Next, a qualitative method was utilized to investigate TAP stakeholders' perceptions of TAPPs' impacts on the sustainable development of TAP destinations.

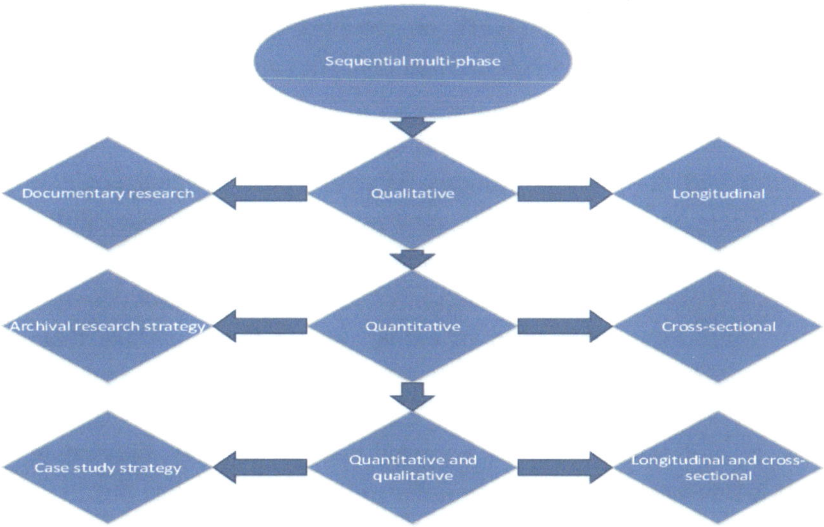

Figure 3-4 The mixed method research design of this study

a. Research Strategies

A research strategy is a plan of action for a researcher to answer research questions and a methodological link between research philosophy and choice of methods for data collection and analysis (Denzin & Lincoln, 2011). In the research onion, the choice of research strategies is in coherence with the research philosophies and methodological choice and guided by research questions. Among the strategies shown in Figure 3.1, experiment and survey are mainly linked to a quantitative research design. In contrast, ethnography, action research, grounded theory and narrative inquiry primarily relate to a qualitative research design. Case studies and archival and documentary research are more involved in qualitative, quantitative, or mixed designs.

Figure 3.4 shows that the documentary research strategy was used to identify the TAPPs value orientations, targets, and policy tool mixes reflected in policy documents. TAPPs documents issued by the Chinese central government and local governments could be searched through official government websites to ensure the quality and accessibility of TAPPs documents. Then the archival strategy was used to explore, explain, or describe the past or changes from the secondary data over time. Therefore, the archival research was adopted in the second stage to quantify the impacts of TAPPs on the poor and explore under what conditions the link between tourism and poverty is most significant in China.

A case study is the assessment of a single unit to establish its key features and draw generalizations (Bryman, 2012), which could offer insight into the specific nature of any example (Silverman, 2013). It could incorporate multiple cases or conclude a within-case (single-case) analysis. This strategy is advantageous in answering ‘what’, ‘why’ and ‘how’ questions, often used in explanatory and exploratory research (Beeton, 2005; Yin, 2014; Saunders et. al., 2016). Single case studies are suitable to the following contexts: firstly, they could be used to validate, critique, and extend a widely accepted theory; secondly, they could be used to analyse unique cases in order to gain new insights; thirdly, they could be used to analyse representative and typical issues in order to develop an understanding of similar events and objects; and fourthly, they could be used to conduct a longitudinal case study in order to reveal how the cases have changed over time (Yin, 2013).

This study chose a single case study, which could provide an opportunity to observe and analyze TAPPs' impacts on attaining multi-dimensional SDG1-led SDGs in a specific context. The case study sites were selected based on theoretical sampling (Su & Zhang, 2015). The single case study site selection criteria in this research (Table 3.1) were based on the TAP definition by Zeng and Ryan (2012) and the National Tourism-Assisting the Poor Demonstration Cases for Rural Revitalization compiled by the China Ministry of Culture and Tourism (CMCT, 2021).

Table 3-1 Case study site selection process

Typical poor areas (villages)	**The largest impoverished population among provinces with more than two million poor residents or poverty ratio exceeding 50%**	**Tourism revenue ranking top five or accounting for more than 50% of villagers' income**	**Local government-led TAP projects with poverty alleviation on the top agenda**	**Abundant in unique ethnic cultural and natural tourism resources**	**Local government's special measures on sustainable TAP promotion**	**Selection results**
Guizhou	Yes	Yes	Yes	Yes	Yes	Accepted
Yunnan	No	No	Yes	Yes	Yes	Rejected
Henan	No	No	Yes	No	Yes	Rejected
Guangxi	No	No	Yes	Yes	No	Rejected
Hunan	No	No	Yes	No	Yes	Rejected
Sichuan	No	No	Yes	No	Yes	Rejected
Gansu	No	No	Yes	No	Yes	Rejected
Anhui	No	No	Yes	No	No	Rejected
Shaanxi	No	No	Yes	No	No	Rejected
Hebei	No	No	Yes	No	No	Rejected

Jiangxi	No	No	Yes	No	Yes	Rejected
Hubei	No	No	Yes	No	No	Rejected
Shanxi	No	No	Yes	No	No	Rejected
Haohuahong Buyi Ethnic Village	No	Yes	Yes	Yes	No	Rejected
Shepeng Li and Miao Ethnic Village	No	Yes	Yes	Yes	No	Rejected
Xiaohewan Village	No	Yes	Yes	Yes	No	Rejected
Zhaoxing Dong Ethnic Village	Yes	Yes	Yes	Yes	Yes	Accepted
Longguang Village	No	Yes	Yes	Yes	No	Rejected
Yunshe Tujia Ethnic Village	No	Yes	Yes	Yes	No	Rejected

According to Table 3.1, Guizhou in southwest China is the only province that meets all TAP case study site selection criteria among the 13 Chinese provinces with more than two million impoverished residents. Table 3.2 demonstrates that the population of Guizhou's impoverished people ranks first among the provinces whose poor population exceeds two million in 2014 and 2015 with Guizhou's poverty ratio listed among the top five. Besides, Guizhou features unique karst landforms, mild weather and diversified ethnic culture. These characteristic resources have made tourism a vigorous tool for the local government to boost economic growth and reduce poverty since the 1980s when Guizhou first proposed the concept of TAP in China. Tourism's status as Guizhou's pillar industry was strengthened in the targeted and efficient TAP period. Table 3.2 reveals that Guizhou's annual tourism revenue increased from 288,000 million yuan in 2014 to more than 1.2 trillion yuan in 2019. The ranking of Guizhou's tourism revenue jumped from fifth in 2014 to first in 2019 among the 13 provinces with more than two million impoverished residents. It could be easily seen from Table 3.1 that the largest impoverished population and the highest ranking of tourism revenue are the two main factors that highlight Guizhou as the most representative TAP case study area for this study.

Zhaoxing Dong Ethnic Village was recognized as a typical TAP destination among six National TAP Demonstration Villages in Guizhou. Table 3.1 reveals that Zhaoxing Dong Ethnic Village is also the only TAP destination up to all TAP case study site selection criteria. The Zhaoxing village was distinguished from the other five villages in that the village once had the highest poverty ratio of 64% and the Zhaoxing local government issued special regulations on the sustainable development of TAP projects. Section two of chapter five overviewed the basic realitities and causes of poverty and pro-poor tourism development in Guizhou and Zhaoxing Dong Ethnic Village. These facts could further elaborate how the study area meets all criteria listed in Table 3.1.

Table 3-2 Chinese provinces with more than two million impoverished population (2014-2015) and their tourism revenue in 2014 and 2019

Province	**Impoverished population (mln)**		**Poverty ratio (%)**		**Annual tourism revenue (mln yuan)**	
	2014	**2015**	**2014**	**2015**	**2014**	**2019**
Guizhou	623	493	18.0	14.0	289,598	1,231,800
Yunnan	574	471	15.5	12.7	266,500	1,180,000
Henan	565	430	7.0	5.3	433,600	960,706
Guangxi	540	452	12.6	10.5	260,000	999,882
Hunan	532	464	9.3	8.1	300,000	976,200
Sichuan	509	381	7.3	5.5	489,100	1,159,432
Gansu	417	307	20.1	14.8	708,00	267,600
Anhui	371	309	6.9	5.7	343,00	851,000
Shaanxi	350	264	13.0	9.8	252,140	721,159
Hebei	320	299	5.6	5.2	256,149	931,336
Jiangxi	276	200	7.7	5.6	264,970	965,600
Hubei	271	384	6.6	9.4	375,286	692,738
Shanxi	269	231	11.1	9.5	284,651	802,692
Guizhou ranking	1`	1	4	4	5	1

Source: China Statistical Yearbook 2016, China Tourism Yearbook 2020

The case study in this research combined the use of quantitative and qualitative data. More specifically, the case study was divided into two stages. The first stage quantified TAPPs' impacts on multi-dimensional poverty under the sustainable paradigm in Guizhou Province. The second stage investigated how TAP stakeholders perceived TAPPs' impacts on the sustainable development of typical TAP destinations represented by Zhaoxing Dong Ethnic Village in Guizhou.

b. Time Horizon

The time horizon is an essential element in the research design. According to the research onion, if the study is a "snapshot" undertaken at a particular time, it is called cross-sectional research. It is called longitudinal research if it is a "diary" or representation of events over some time. This research is mainly a pragmatic, inductive and exploratory study of TAPPs' impacts on poverty alleviation through sequential multi-phase mixed methods. The use of research methods and research strategies varied in different stages of data collection and analysis, resulting in changes in time horizons. Figure 3.4 demonstrates that documentary research was longitudinal, with TAPPs documents between 1984-2020 investigated to identify the evolution logic of TAPPs sustainability values, targets and policy instruments. The archival data for quantifying the strength of the tourism-poverty link was cross-sectional, considering the data accessibility and analysis model. In the case study, the survey-based secondary data was longitudinal for observing the changes in TAPPs' impacts on multi-dimensional poverty under the sustainable development paradigm in the targeted and efficient TAP period. Besides, the investigation of TAP stakeholders' perception of TAPPs' impacts on the sustainable development of TAP destinations was cross-sectional.

Techniques and Procedures

The innermost and core layer of the research onion is techniques and procedures, the choice of which is dependent on the methodological approach used (Bryman, 2012). This layer explains the purposes and techniques of data collection and analysis. Based on the choice of research methodology and strategies, this research adopted content analysis of TAPPs document-based secondary data, CGE and AF-MPI analysis of survey-based secondary data and semi-structured interviews for the case study to answer the research questions proposed.

a. Content Analysis of TAPPs Documents

Policy values, targets and instruments are reflected in policy documents. As the Chinese central government intensified the reform and development of the tourism industry in 1984, tourism's contribution to poverty alleviation began to emerge. According to the "World Tourism Development Report 2018-Global Pro-poor Tourism and Demands of the Times" released by the World Tourism Alliance and China Tourism Research Institute in 2018, China's TAP has mainly experienced four stages: the early exploration period (1984-1996), the initial development period (1997-2004), the rapid improvement period (2005-2012) and the targeted and efficient period (2013-2020). Therefore, this study analysed the TAPPs documents between 1984-2020 issued by the Chinese Central Government, ministries and commissions to ensure the samples' reliability, typicality and authority.

This study used content analysis through text mining software Rost 6.0 and NVivo 11 in the investigation of TAPPs documents, aiming to have a systematic, objective and insightful analysis of how TAPPs ensure the sustainable development of poverty-stricken areas. With its concept first proposed by Berelson (1952), content analysis is an objective, quantitative and qualitative mass communication research method for analysing information disseminated through various media, including documents (Zhang et. al., 2019). It is usually carried out through six steps: research issues, sampling, analysis units defining, data classifying and encoding, reliability verification, data analysis and conclusions (Liu, 2014).

Content analysis has been widely used in policy analysis, including identifying historical changes in policy themes, the choice of policy tool mix and various policy research issues (He, 2018). It could help researchers perceive essential facts and development trends of policies through documents (Krippendorff, 2012). NVivo is used in this approach to analyse texts of TAPPs documents since the 1980s promulgated by the Chinese central government. The text coding is based on the Chinese TAP development stages framework- sustainability value orientation-policy tool. The policy value dimensions were set and adjusted through the word frequency software Rost 6.0 and the literature review. The choice of policy tools to achieve the TAP value and goals were investigated based on the Rothwell policy tool taxonomy. This analysis aims to identify the Chinese government's sustainability value orientations, goals and policy tool mix selection in TAPPs and their evolution logic and features, thus laying the basis of the TAPPs impacts assessment.

b. Computable General Equilibrium (CGE) Analysis of TAPPs Economic Impacts

The computable general equilibrium (CGE) models are used widely in the analysis of both policy effects and tourism economic effects, especially in developed-country academic settings. A standard computable general equilibrium model in GAMS developed by Lofgren, Harris, and Robinson (2001) is a static "standard" CGE model with features particularly applicable to developing countries. Funded by the International Food Policy Research Institute (IFPIR), the manual of standard computable general equilibrium (CGE) in GAMS was printed in 2002, which significantly promoted the application of the standard CGE. This research established China TAP CGE model from the IFPIR's standard CGE model based on the available data to capture country-specific and sector-specific detail, structure and parameter values.

China TAP CGE model was based on the updated version of the latest China Social accounting matrices (SAMs) 2017 to map the economy-wide effects of tourism by taking account of all income and all expenditures in tourism and other related institutions such as households and government concerning data from Chinese tourism database, Chinese Tourism Statistical Bulletin, Chinese Statistical Yearbook, China Fiscal Yearbook and Chinese General Social Survey (CGSS). This model explored the effects of TAPPs on poverty alleviation, emphasising factor income or income distributions, which was the leading indicator of extreme poverty alleviation. The TAPPs simulation experiment was conducted to find under what conditions the tourism-poverty link is the strongest, which was of reference to propose suggestions for TAPPs adjustment and optimisation to improve economic sustainability in relatively poor rural areas.

c. Alkrie-Foster (AF) Multi-Dimensional Poverty Index (MPI) Analysis of TAPPs' Impacts under Sustainable Development Dimensions

The income and basic needs concepts of poverty are characterised predominantly by quantitative indicators (Lok-Dessallien, 1999). MPI analysis and semi-structured interviews were adopted to assess TAPPs' impacts on reducing multi-dimensional poverty in TAP areas under the sustainable development paradigm. This study used the AF methodology proposed by Alkire and Foster (2011) due to its intuitive and policy-relevant properties (Alkire & Seth, 2015). The dimensions, indicators, deprivation thresholds and weights were mainly established according to the global MPI indicators by Alkire, Kanagaratnam and Suppa (2020) incorporated with the sustainability values and targets identified in TAPPs documents, thus generating AF-MPI indicators for this research. Data was collected from China Family Panel Studies (CFPS) in 2016 and 2018, during which the number of TAPPs issued by the central and local governments increased primarily. The data was complemented and compared with the Chinese General Social Survey (CGSS) of Renmin University of China and the available Poverty Monitoring Report of Rural China 2016 and 2018, including alleviation information in the case study area. The results were compared between 2016 and 2018 to explore the TAPPs' impacts on the local poor regarding economic and non-economic factors.

d. Semi-Structured Interview

Based on MPI analysis, semi-structured interviews further investigated TAP stakeholders' perceptions of TAPPs' impacts on the sustainable development of TAP destinations. A semi-structured interview is a popular technique for gathering qualitative data owing to its flexibility and versatility (Kallio et. al., 2016). It is a type of exploratory interview that is commonly used in social sciences, including tourism programs or policy evaluation (e.g. D'Anna et. al., 2016; Brendehaug et. al., 2014; Qin et. al., 2019; Wulandari & Firdausy, 2020; Da Silva'Farias & Figueiredo; Huynh et. al., 2022). This technique usually begins with an interview protocol consisting of open-ended questions asked of each participant (Burkard & Knox, 2014). It allows for discovery and gives space to follow topical trajectories as the conversation unfolds. Therefore, researchers could use semi-structured interviews to discover essential questions that could not be adequately addressed in a standard survey without more open-ended questions and extended probing (Madill, 2011).

This research adopted semi-structured interviews to explore TAP stakeholders' perceptions of how TAPPs impacted the achievement of SDG1-led SDGs at TAP destinations by realising TAPPs value and targets through the TAPPs mix, especially in the targeted and efficient period (since 2013). A stakeholder is defined as an individual, group, organization, or entity that has an interest or concern in a particular process, project, organization, or system (Freeman et. al., 2018). Based on this definition, TAP stakeholders could be defined as individuals, groups, organizations, or entities that are actively involved in or affected by tourism initiatives aimed at reducing poverty and promoting sustainable development among disadvantaged areas. Typical PPT stakeholders are local communities, government agencies, non-government organisations (NGOs), international development organisations (IDOs), the private sector and the poor people (Chok et. al., 2007; Phi et. al., 2016; Tolkach et. al., 2012; Abate, 2022). In China, the main TAP stakeholders include the government, enterprises, poor residents and non-poor residents (Qin et. al., 2019).

Therefore, in line with TAP stakeholder definition, typical PPT stakeholders and Chinese TAP practice, this study selected four major TAP stakeholder types: government officials, tourism entrepreneurs or staff, and poor and non-poor households. The government is responsible for planning and monitoring of TAP projects while enterprises and poor and non-poor residents implement TAP projects under the guidance of government's TAPPs. The semi-structured interview used snowball sampling to choose interviewees of these four types. Snowball sampling is one of the categories of purposive sampling, in which the researcher finds out from selected individuals other individuals that might be relevant to be included in the investigation (Oppong, 2013). Recommended by the university the researcher worked for, the research team initially selected local government officials working for TAP or TAP entrepreneurs who could better understand TAPPs' impacts on the sustainable development of poor areas. These selected interviewees also had a more comprehensive interpersonal network, which helped the researcher invite more cooperative respondents that meet the purposes of the interview.

Interview themes were derived from the content analysis results of TAPPs documents and AF-MPI analysis. The interviewers mainly used a digital voice recorder to record the interview, supplemented by the interviewers' written records of the main contents and research diaries. After being transferred into texts, the recording material was numbered along with researchers' written records and research diaries and imported into NVivo 11 for data coding and analysis. The coding framework was established concerning sustainable development theory and the TAPPs value- TAPPs target and TAPPs instruments identified in the content analysis. The interviews were completed when theoretical saturation was achieved. When no new information was found in the interviews, three more interviews were conducted to verify the conjectures; thus, the interview process was finished (Francis et. al., 2010).

Establishing Trustworthiness

Data quality issues are critical to the trustworthiness of quantitative and qualitative research, which ensures that the data could be collected and interpreted appropriately and accurately. Credibility, dependability and transferability are common data quality issues highlighted by many researchers, such as Bloomberg and Volpe (2012) and Saunders et. al. (2016).

a. Credibility

Credibility reflects on the accuracy and validity of research findings from the data collected. It is the parallel criterion to the internal validity of quantitative research, emphasising the match of research participants' socially constructed realities and intentions (Saunders et. al., 2016). It also refers to the logical match between research questions and methods chosen, data analysis appropriateness, and data interpretation validity (Bloomberg and Volpe, 2012). Among various techniques to ensure this match, triangulation is considered an effective technique to enhance the confidence of the findings through the confirmation of a proposition with more than one approach (Cox and Hassard, 2010), providing a more comprehensive picture of results than any single method could do (Tashakkori & Teddle, 2003).

The credibility of TAPPs documentary research through content analysis was mainly guaranteed through the proper sampling, semantic network analysis and NVivo coding test. This study selected the TAPPs documents issued by the Chinese Central Government authorities as samples to ensure the reliability, typicality and authority of sampling.

Documents included were mainly TAPPs enacted by the State Council, the Ministry of Culture and Tourism, the Ministry of Agriculture and Rural Affairs, the State Council Leading Group Office of Poverty Alleviation and Development and other relevant ministries and commissions. Policy documents were searched in the official websites of the above national authorities with the keywords of "poverty alleviation", " tourism assisting poverty alleviation", " rural tourism", "leisure agriculture", "targeted poverty alleviation", and "rural revitalisation". Then, the social and semantic network generation functions of the Chinese text mining tool ROST 6.0 was used to extract high-frequency words, filter meaningless words, extract line features, construct a network of co-occurring words, and finally generate semantic network TAPPs documents. High-frequency words such as "tourism" and "poverty alleviation" were at the network's core, proving that the data matched the research question. Finally, the selected samples were coded by the authors of this study with NVivo independently. The reliability of their coding results was tested through the NVivo coding comparison function.

The credibility of secondary data used for CGE analysis and AF-MPI analysis was ensured by comparing and complementing data from more than one source. The primary data for CGE analysis was a social accounting matrix which was compiled based on data from various sources such as the Input and Output Table, China Tax Yearbook, China Finance Yearbook, Capital Flow Statement, Balance of International Payments, Balance of the Household Column and so on (see Table 4.9). The data required by MPI analysis was mainly obtained from China Family Panel Studies (CFPS) provided by Peking University. The credibility of the CFPS was improved through comparison with other data sources, such as the Chinese General Social Survey (CGSS) of the Renmin University of China and the Poverty Monitoring Report of Rural China.

A high level of credibility could be achieved in the semi-structured interviews if they are conducted carefully using clarifying questions, probing meanings and exploring responses from various angles (Saunders et. al., 2016). Therefore, in order to increase the interpretation validity of the semi-structured interview, the researcher used the respondent validation method to confirm and justify the match of interpretation and interviewees' intentions. In other words, the researcher asked interviewees to confirm whether the data interpreted by the interviewer during or after the interview was consistent with their opinions and views on the issues investigated.

In addition, the researcher established credibility of the semi-structured interview by choosing government officials, tourism entrepreneurs or staff, and poor and non-poor households as suitable interviewees based on TAP stakeholder definition, typical PPT stakeholder network and Chinese TAP practice. The researcher established a good personal relationship with the initially sampled respondents who were government leaders or TAP entrepreneurs with good reputations in the local areas. These local elites could help the researcher find more cooperative respondents with good knowledge of TAP projects, diverse educational levels, occupations and ages. Besides, in order to ensure the accuracy of the interview texts and TAPPs documents for coding, all interview material and TAPPs texts in Chinese was first translated by the researcher and then proofread by Robert Tian, who is a Chinese American professor and the authors' colleague.

b. Dependability

The dependability of qualitative research is a parallel criterion to the reliability of quantitative research. It means that all the changes in the research are recorded to produce a dependable account of the emerging research focus that could be replicated in future studies in similar contexts. However, it is unrealistic or unnecessary to make qualitative research such as semi-structured interviews in this study repeatable because these interviews reflect reality at the time they were collected, in a situation which may be subject to change. However, the dependability of the content analysis of TAPPs documents and semi-structured interviews on TAP stakeholders' perceptions of TAPPs' impacts was ensured by explaining the details of the research design, the reasons underpinning the choice of strategy and methods, and how the data were obtained. Others could refer to this to help understand the study's processes and the research findings.

c. Transferability

The transferability of qualitative research is the parallel criterion to the external validity or generalisability of quantitative research. Indeed, the case study using semi-structured interviews in this study or content analysis of Chinese TAPPs documents could not be used to make statistical generalisations of the pro-poor tourism development throughout the world. However, the researcher offered a detailed description of how TAPPs evolved in different TAP stages, the demographic information, and setting of all participants as well as the saturation point of the semi-structured interview. This helped the reader judge the transferability of the study to another similar but non-identical setting (Patton, 1990) they are interested in. This is necessary as Schram (2003) noted that the rich and detailed information provided by qualitative research might apply to some broader context. The detailed description of content analysis of TAPPs documents and semi-structured interviews of TAP stakeholders' perceptions of TAPPs impacts in Guizhou may apply to some pro-poor tourism cases in developing countries.

Enhancing Reliability and Validity

Reliability and validity are vital to the quality of quantitative research. Reliability refers to replication and consistency. If an earlier research design could be replicated and generate the same findings, this research could be considered reliable. Reliability could be classified into internal reliability and external reliability. Internal reliability refers to ensuring consistency during a research project. As CGE and AF-MPI analysis in this study were both based on secondary data, the secondary data quality was crucial to enhance the internal consistency of the research. Comparing the data collected with other sources (Patton, 1999) could be an excellent way to deal with secondary data quality issues. Therefore, the data for the CGE model and AF -MPI were collected from and compared between more than one authoritative source, including government sources and the database sponsored by some leading universities such as China Family Panel Studies (CFPS) of Peking University and Chinese General Social Survey (CGSS) of the Renmin University of China.

Additionally, the researcher invited another researcher Liu skilled at running the software GAMS and SPSS to replicate all steps involved in these two research techniques to ensure the consistency of the quantitative research. External reliability could be achieved if the data collection techniques and analytic procedures in research could produce consistent findings if another researcher replicated them on another occasion. The researcher of this study elaborated on the whole procedure of TAP CGE and AF – MPI, including the data collection, model construction, choice of dimensions and indicators, data processing, and analysis to help other researchers have a thorough understanding of how to replicate the research design.

Besides reliability, validity is also a key to the quality of quantitative research. Validity also includes internal validity and external validity. Internal validity usually concerns whether the data represents the reality the research is measuring. Therefore, in the CGE and AF -MPI analysis, the data collection was guided by the research questions, objectives, and requirements of the CGE model and AF methodology. Since the tourism-poverty link is a highly complex phenomenon in different countries, it is challenging to achieve external validity, which concerns the statistical generalisation of research findings. Nevertheless, the details of the quantitative research were presented to help researchers in similar contexts judge whether the findings are valid.

Conclusion

This chapter illustrates the research methodology employed in this research based on Saunder's research onion model. After identifying the research philosophy and approach to theory development, the research design is formulated involving research methodological choice, research strategies, and time horizon. Based on the research design, techniques and procedures for data collection and analysis are elaborated. Finally, how to establish trustworthiness and enhance realibility and validity are further explained. The next chapter will present the process of data analysis.

Chapter 4
Sustainability of Chinese Pro-poor Tourism Policies

Introduction

As stated in previous chapters, the first three research objectives of this study are to identify the policy values and targets of the Tourism-Assisting the Poor Policies (TAPPs) in different TAP stages; to investigate the policy tools used to realize those values and targets; and to assess tourism's contribution to economic sustainability under TAPPs. According to the methodology design in chapter three, content analysis of TAPPs documents is conducted to explore TAPPs sustainability values, targets and the use of policy tool mix and find out how they match to strengthen the tourism-poverty nexus. Then a computable general equilibrium (CGE) analysis is used to examine consumption-driven and investment-led tourism growth's impacts on the economic sustainability of the poor under the guidance of TAPPs. This chapter reports the findings from the content analysis of TAPPs documents and the CGE analysis of how Chinese tourism development affects income distribution to the poor under TAPPs.

The first section describes the data for the content analysis. Sections two, three and four present the sustainability values, policy targets and instruments in the TAPPs documents. Section five of this chapter establishes the Chinese TAP CGE model by introducing tourism into the standard CGE model in GAMS developed by Lofgren, Harris, and Robinson (2001). Section six introduces the database of the Chinese TAP CGE model and parameters. Section seven presents simulations and results of tourism development. The last section concludes the policy analysis and CGE analysis. This chapter will guide and lay a solid foundation for the assessment of TAPPs' impacts on multi-dimensional poverty reduction under the sustainable development paradigm and the investigation of TAP stakeholders' perceptions of TAPPs' impacts on the sustainable development at TAP destinations in the next chapter.

Data of Content Analysis

As policy documents are the physical carrier of policies, policy documents have been a significant channel for understanding government behaviours in policy formulation and implementation (Wu, 1995; Featherston & O'Sullivan, 2017; Huang, 2018; Werdiningtyas et. al., 2020). The Chinese government's efforts to develop tourism into a leading means for poverty reduction are systematically and formally recorded in TAPP documents, laying the factual basis for TAPPs analysis. Policy documents include legislative documents, laws, bills, planning, notices, communiqués, bulletins, resolutions, speeches, outlines, decisions, proposals, agreements, research reports and other documents issued by the governmental authorities (Huang, 2018; Van Dijk, 1997). Besides these categories, TAPP documents in this study also include suggestions and "No.1 central document" issued by the Chinese central government (Table 4-1).

Table 4-1 Distribution of TAPPs documents (1984-2020)

TAP Stages	Text Quantity	Issuing Authorities	Policy Categories and Quantity
Early Exploration Period（1984-1996）	3	Office of the StateCouncil, National Tourism Administration, Central Committee of CPC, StateCouncil	Decision（1） Notice（1） Outline（1）
Initial Development Period（1997-2004）	2	State Council, National Tourism Administration, State Planning Commission, State Economic and Trade Commission、Ministry of Public Security、Ministry of Housing and Urban-rural Development, Ministry of Railways	Notice（2）

Rapid Development Period（2005-2012）	4	State Council, National Tourism Administration, Office of the Leading Group for Poverty Alleviation and Development of the State Council	Outline（1） Agreement（1） Proposal（2）
Targeted and Efficient Period（2013-2020）	55	Standing Committee of NPC, Central Committee of CPC, State Council and its 37 ministries, departments and directly affiliated institutions	Law（1） Proposal（4） Planning（4） Notice（14） Suggestion（24） “No. 1 central document”（5） Other documents（3）

Since the 1980s, the Chinese government has issued a series of TAPPs in different TAP stages. In the formulation process of TAPPs, the Chinese central government acts as the leader, always actively responding to local governments. Therefore, in order to ensure the authority, typicality and reliability of TAPP documents, this research chooses TAPP documents issued by the Chinese central government, ministries and commissions such as the State Council, the Ministry of Culture and Tourism, the Ministry of Agriculture and Rural Affairs, the State Council Leading Group Office of Poverty Alleviation and Development and other relevant ministries and commissions with TAPPs issued by the local governments excluded.

Policy texts were searched on the official websites of the above national authorities with the keywords "poverty alleviation", " tourism assisting poverty alleviation", “ rural tourism”, “leisure agriculture”, and "targeted poverty alleviation”. After removing policies unrelated to TAP, 64 policy documents were selected as the samples. The distribution of these TAPPs in different TAP stages is shown in Table 4-1.

Among the 64 samples, 55 policies were enacted during the TAP target and efficient period, accounting for 86% of the total samples. The two authorities always involved in formulating and issuing TAPPs in four stages are the State Council which is the highest administrative authority of the Central Government, and the National Tourism Administration, which is responsible for tourism planning and development and merged with the Ministry of Culture into the Ministry of Culture and Tourism in 2018. The Office of the Leading Group for Poverty Alleviation and Development of the State Council became one of the TAPPs issuing authorities during the rapid development period (2005-2012), indicating that tourism's role in poverty alleviation was increasingly recognized.

Further, in the targeted and efficient period (2013-2020), most departments, ministries and institutions directly affiliated with the State Council got engaged in the TAPPs formulation and implementation, marking tourism as one of the primary poverty areas alleviation tools by the government. In 64 TAPP documents, notices and suggestions are the most commonly used policy document categories, revealing the government's efforts not to mandate but guide tourism's contribution to poverty alleviation.

As was explained in chapter one, Chinese TAPPs represent typical public policies that comprise a series of value-based processes involving the realization of policy targets through a mix of instruments or means (Colebatch, 2002; May, 2012; Stewart, 2009). In order to understand whether and how TAPPs contribute to sustainable development through tourism in poverty-stricken areas, it's necessary for this section to investigate TAPPs' value orientations and policy targets on ensuring sustainable development in poor regions and what policy instruments were used to realize the sustainability values and goals.

In line with the research design of chapter three, the content analysis of TAPPs documents reflecting policy values, targets and tools will be made through Rost 6.0 and Nvivo 11. Rost 6.0 establishes the TAPPs documents semantic network to testify to the reliability of selected samples and facilitate the construction of policy values. Nvivo is typical qualitative analysis software that could encode structured and semi-structured policy texts. There are two most commonly used coding methods. The first is to establish the coding layers and nodes based on an analysis framework and then detail the coding through line-by-line reading. The second is the encoding procedures the grounded theory researchers follow: opening, spindle, and selective encoding (Holton, 2007).

This chapter uses the first coding method with the specific steps as follows:

(1) Analyzing the semantic network of selected samples with Rost 6.0 to verify the reliability of samples selected in the previous section; (2) Establishing sustainability values framework based on the text mining results and the modified TAPPs sustainability value dimensions; (3) Coding the samples based on the nodes established under the sustainability value analysis framework with Nvivo 11; (4) Quantifying and analyzing the coding results for conclusions; (5) Identifying TAPPs targets based on literature review, sustainability value analysis and semantic network analysis; (6) Proposes a theoretical framework of TAPPs targets-TAPPs instruments based on the Rothwell's policy tool taxonomy; (7) Coding samples based on the TAPPs targets-TAPPs instruments framework; (8) Quantifying and analyzing the coding results for exploring the match of policy values, targets and tools contained in the TAPPs documents to promote sustainable development in the impoverished areas.

Results of Exploring TAPPs Sustainability Values

Sustainability is a widely-discussed issue closely related to tourism through sustainable tourism. Poverty alleviation on the top of the agenda of 2030 SDGs is also an essential part of the conceptualization of sustainable tourism. China's TAP initiative led by the government targeted poverty reduction and sustainable development in impoverished areas. The Chinese government's leading role in TAP relies on formulating and implementing TAPPs. Teng et. al. (2021) found that tourism growth in some Chinese regions causes environmental degradation, especially CO_2 emissions. The poverty line mainly measures China's extreme poverty eradication. Does this indicate that Chinese TAPPs focus on tourism's contribution to the local economy boom instead of sustainability in TAP destinations? If not, what sustainability values are reflected in TAPPs throughout different TAP stages?

Semantic Network of TAPPs Documents

ROST is text mining software that could perform word segmentation, word frequency analysis and social and semantic network analysis of texts. This research mainly uses the social and semantic network generation functions of ROST to extract high-frequency words, filter meaningless words, extract line features, construct a network of co-occurring words, and finally generate semantic network TAPPs documents (Figure 4.1). It could be seen from Figure 4.1 that "tourism" is the word with the highest frequency in the samples, and other high-frequency words are "development", “assistance", “construction", "poverty alleviation", "poverty", "region", and "rural". The links between “rural areas”, “tourism”, and “poverty relief” were relatively intense, indicating that the selected research samples were closely related to TAP.

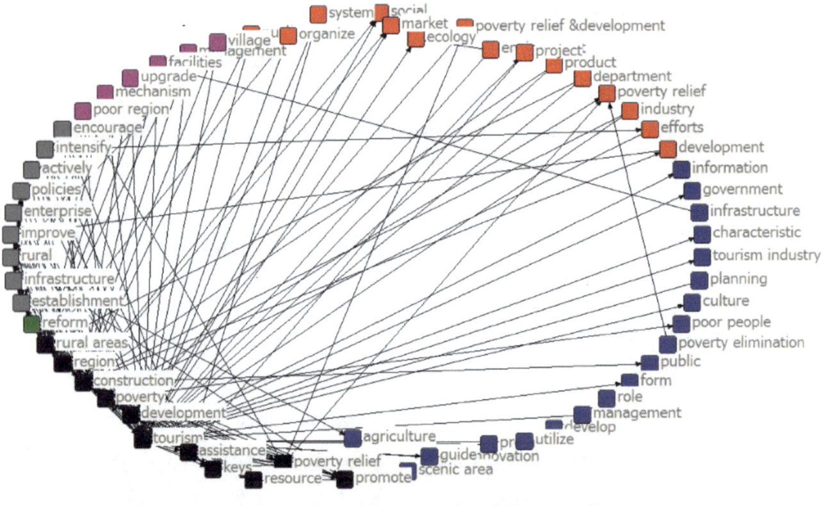

Figure 4-1 The semantic network of TAPPs documents

The high-frequency words “rural area”, “poverty”, and “region” implied that in China, rural areas and contiguous poor areas, which inhabited the largest poor population, were the main focuses of TAPPs. With the rapid growth of the tourism industry and the deepening of poverty alleviation strategies, the role of tourism in driving the economic and social development of poverty-stricken areas and rural areas has become increasingly prominent. It played an essential role in national strategies such as "Construction of a New Socialist Countryside",

"Construction of Beautiful Countryside", and "New Urbanization Construction". Therefore, "development" and "construction" were also located in the central area of the network.

Other high-frequency words related to TAP included "infrastructure", "improve", "resource", "key issue", "project", "mechanism", "policies", etc. These keywords showed that in the existing TAPPs, infrastructure construction and tourism resource development in poverty-stricken areas were key projects that the Chinese government implements TAP guaranteed by sound policies and mechanisms.

TAPPs Sustainability Value Dimensions

As the policy formulation and implementation process is "the authoritative allocation of value" (Easton, 1965), as early as in the 1940s, policy value was taken as a vital factor in policy analysis by Harold Lasswel, the founder of policy science. The task of identifying policy values is necessary as the public policy process is a rational and principled activity (Lasswell, 1948). However, positivism dominated policy research, especially in the 1970-the 1980s. The unobservable policy values did not become a valuable perspective for policy analysis until the 1990s when Yanow started to perceive the policy process as "a struggle for the determination of meanings" (Yanow, 1996, p. 19) in an interpretive way. Values are usually identified to frame policy problems in policy discussion and making (Rein & Schon, 1996). Administrative systems unconsciously adopt policy devices to avoid values conflicts (Thacher & Rein, 2004). Exploring the dominant social values in any nation might be a complicated task. However, it's easier to identify the values of public policies in specific sectors, such as health policy (Abbasi, 2018).

Though Stewart (2009) first proposed the dichotomous nature of some general policy values, the literature on poverty alleviation through sustainable tourism revealed that ST-EP has the most significant impact on China's TAP, focuses on the social, economic and ecological tourism development to avoid the tourism's negative impacts on poverty reduction. Sustainability value dimensions of Chinese TAPPs are not limited to growth and greenness but involve the three pillars of sustainability: economic, social and environmental sustainability (Mori & Christodoulou, 2012; Purvis et. al., 2018).

Therefore, the dimensions of sustainability values could be modified into economic, social, cultural, and environmental values in the Chinese TAP context, as shown in Figure 4.2. As the studies on the formation process of sustainable tourism policies are far from enough (Guo et. al., 2019), it's worthwhile for this study to identify the sustainability values of Chinese TAPPs from the modified sustainability value dimensions to find out how the Chinese government has mitigated the conflicts of economic, social and environmental values in TAPPs formulation.

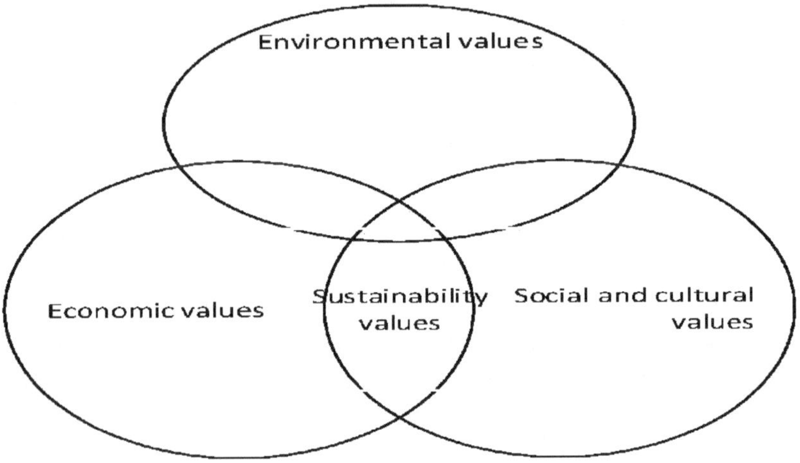

Figure 4-2 Sustainability value dimensions

Note: Adapted from typical sustainability intersecting circles model by Purvis et. al., (2018)

Regarding the most popular three pillars of sustainability dimensions among tourism scholars, this study sets up the TAPPs sustainability values model (Figure 4.2) based on the sustainability policy values pair proposed by Stewart (2009), Chinese TAP connotation and the typical three sustainability intersecting circles model (Purvis et. al., 2018). Since the high-frequency words in the semantic network of policy texts could reveal the core values of policies (Zhang et. al., 2019), the applicability of this value dimension model in the Chinese TAPPs analysis is testified through the TAPPs documents semantic network.

According to Figure 4.1, the network-centric words "tourism" and "development" have a close relationship with high-frequency words such as "rural", "poverty", "region", "enterprise", "resource", "market", and "agriculture ". It revealed that TAPPs guided market entities such as enterprises to explore tourism resources and boom their tourism market in rural and impoverished areas. In this way, employment and entrepreneurship were stimulated to increase the income of farmers and poor households and promote economic development in disadvantaged areas. The revitalization of rural and rural industries manifested the economic value orientation of TAPPs.

The co-occurrence of network-centric words and high-frequency words such as "public", "management", "infrastructure", "facilities", "social", and "culture" reflects that TAPPs paid attention to improving infrastructure facilities, social culture management and public service in rural and impoverished areas, indicating the social and cultural value orientation of TAPPs. The connection between the core words of the network and the high-frequency word "ecology" fully showed that the TAPPs attached importance to the protection of the ecological environment in rural and impoverished areas. It indicated that the ecological environment underpinned the sustainable development of the TAP program. Improving the rural habitat was the key to the national initiative of constructing beautiful villages. These focuses reflected the environmental value orientation of the TAPPs.

Establishment of TAPPs Values Framework

Based on the applicability of the TAPPs sustainability values dimension model, it's necessary to establish further the framework to identify the TAPPs sustainability values. Before generating the TAPPs documents semantic network, 172 words were obtained after filtering meaningless words and extracting high-frequency words. These 172 high-frequency words were then classified into three categories: economic values, social and cultural values and environmental values. Following the classification, keywords were refined through merging and adjustment to form the sub-categories of value dimensions. The formation process of the TAPPs values framework is shown in Table 4-2:

Table 4-2 TAPPs sustainability values framework formation process

Categories (Value Dimensions)	Sub-categories	Examples of High Frequency Words
Economic Values	Economic stimulation	Rural areas, countryside, poor, region, economic, development, investment, stimulate...
	Eliminating poverty and getting rich	Tourism, income, increase, poverty alleviation, farm products, projects, resource...
	Industry revitalization	Structure, quality, upgrading, strategy, industry, revitalization, economy, integration…
	Consumption promotion	Consumption, leisure, tourists, family, demand, tourism industry, promoting…
	Employment and entrepreneurship	Employment, entrepreneurship, professional, guide, enterprise, market...
Social and Cultural Values	Public service	Public, service, infrastructure, facility, medical service, transport, safety...
	Participation and cooperation	Farmers, poverty population, market, enterprise, participation, cooperation ...
	Governance under regulation and law	Regulation, mechanism, policy, improvement, supervision, problems, governance...
	Professional training	Professional, staff, talents, farmers, vocational, training, education...
	Reform and innovation	Policy, system, regulation, market, mechanism, reform, innovation...
	Cultural inheritance	Countryside, tourism, culture, heritage, project, protection, propagandize...
Environmental Values	Human habitat improvement	Rural village, habitat, environment, project, engineering, construction, infrastructure, facility, improvement...
	Upgrading scenic	Scenic area, tourist facility, project,

Categories (Value Dimensions)	Sub-categories	Examples of High Frequency Words
	areas	development, quality, improvement...
	Environmental protection	Ecological environment, protection, intensify, planning, management, guarantee...
	Washroom renovation	Rural tourism, scenic area, toilet, washroom, project, improvement, renovation...

TAPPs Documents Encoding

Establishing TAPPs sustainability values framework through semantic network analysis laid a foundation for identifying the value orientations of TAPPs. However, in order to understand the evolution characteristics and distribution of TAPPs values in different TAP stages, the TAPPs documents should be encoded through Nvivo11 to explore the content of policy values further. The 64 policy texts were classified and merged based on stages and imported into Nvivo11 for independent coding. Stages refer to the four TAP stages, including the early exploration, initial development, rapid improvement, and targeted and efficient periods. Economic, social, cultural, and environmental values were taken as parent nodes, and sub-categories of three value dimensions in the sustainability values framework were labelled as child nodes.

Finally, the imported policy texts were coded line by line semantically. The words, sentences or paragraphs reflecting the specific values of value dimensions were classified as references of child nodes. Thus the coding hierarchy of "stage-parent node - child node - reference point" was formed, as demonstrated by the example of the coding process in Table 4-3. Two coders completed the whole coding process independently, and a total of 951 codes were obtained. The coding reliability was tested through the Nvivo coding comparison function. The consistent percentage of the two coders was found to be 99.4%, indicating a high coding reliability.

Table 4-3 Coding process example

Code No.	Samples in TAP Stages	Parent Node	Child Node	Reference Point
1-2-3-2	TAPPs texts in early exploration period	Social and cultural values	Governance under regulation and law	Strengthen the supervision and administration of the tourism market in the areas of business, public security, taxation, and pricing; resolutely prohibit fraud, forced sale and other illegal phenomenon harmful to tourists.
2-2-5-2	TAPPs texts in initial development period	Social and cultural values	Reform and innovation	Encourage various economic forces to participate in TAP development and actively cultivate diversified stakeholders in TAP market.
3-3-3-10	TAPPs texts in rapid improvement period	Environmental values	Environmental protection	Support TAP participants to actively utilize new energy and new materials. Promote use of technologies for energy conservation, water conservation and emission reduction.
4-1-2-19	TAPPs texts in targeted and efficient period	Economic values	Eliminating poverty and getting rich	Help farmers get rid of poverty and become rich by exploring characteristic tourism resources in poverty-stricken areas, building beautiful villages and giving play to role of scenic areas in increasing poor households' income.

Structural Characteristics of TAPPs Sustainability Values

The distribution of codes under value dimensions and categories reveals the structural characteristics of the sustainability values of TAPPs. In Nvivo, 951 codes of TAPPs in the four stages were classified under the sustainability values framework. The sustainability value proportion chart (Figure 4.3) exhibits the obvious differences in the distribution of the three value dimensions in TAP stages. The frequency and proportion of codes under the value dimensions and categories in different stages and their overall distribution were calculated in Table 4-4.

Figure 4.3 showed that TAPPs sustainability value orientations in different TAP stages were dominated by the economic values and social and cultural values though the proportion of the latter declined gradually except for the initial development period. The proportion of economic value fluctuated throughout the four stages. Overall, environmental values occupied the lowest percentage, showing a linear growth trend. From the early exploration to the initial development period, the percentage of economic values dropped significantly despite the remarkable rise of the social and cultural values. The reference points of environmental values emerged in the initial development period. This indicated that, as tourism started to promote the economic development of poor areas, its negative effects on the environment, especially in scenic areas, started to attract the government's attention.

Therefore, in the initial development period, TAPPs managed to alleviate the conflict between economic development and environmental problems in the process of TAP by greatly increasing the proportion of social and cultural values. From the period of rapid improvement to the targeted and efficient period, the proportion of economic values gradually exceeded the proportion of social and cultural values. The environmental values experienced a steady increase though its proportion was still less than the other two dimensions. The distribution change of the three value dimensions implied that tourism became one of the important ways to eliminate absolute poverty in the government's poverty alleviation strategy in a more environmental-friendly way.

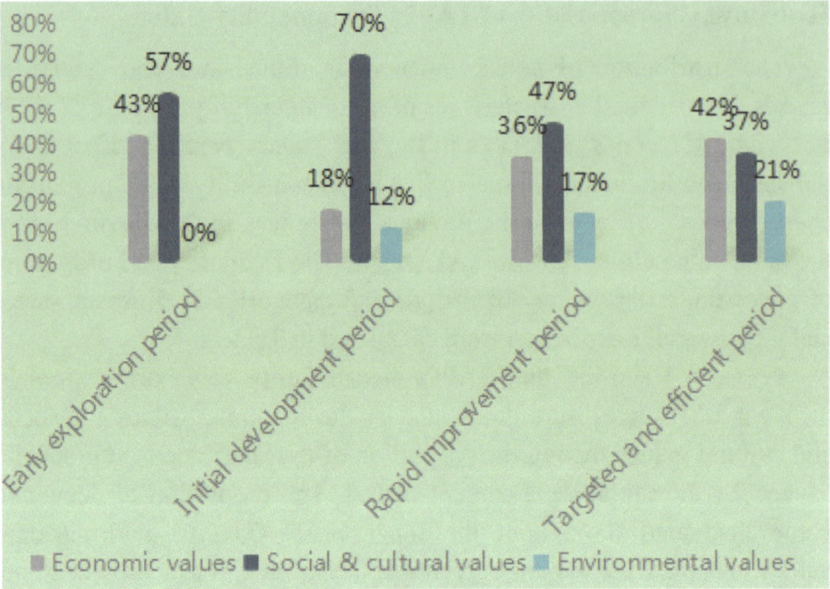

Figure 4-3 Distribution of sustainability values in Chinese TAPPs (1984-2020)

Table 4-4 Frequencies of TAPPs sustainability values in TAP stages

Value dimensions	**Value categories**	**Early exploration period**	**Initial development period**	**Rapid improvement period**	**Targeted efficient period**	**Total by category**	**Proportion by dimensions**
Economic values	Economic stimulation	4	4	2	91	101	39.9%
	Eliminating poverty and getting rich	0	2	16	92	110	
	Industry revitalization	3	2	6	38	49	
	Consumption promotion	1	2	7	63	73	
	Employment and entrepreneurship	1	0	4	41	46	
Total by period		9	10	35	325	375	

Value dimensions	Value categories	Early exploration period	Initial development period	Rapid improvement period	Targeted efficient period	Total by category	Proportion by dimensions
Social and cultural values	Public service	3	16	18	54	91	41%
	Participation and cooperation	1	4	11	90	106	
	Governance under regulation and law	4	6	6	36	52	
	Professional training	0	2	4	34	40	
	Reform and innovation	4	5	5	34	48	
	Cultural inheritance	0	5	2	46	53	
Total by period		12	38	46	294	390	
Environmental values	Human habitat improvement	0	0	3	52	55	19.1%
	Upgrading scenic areas	0	4	1	18	23	
	Environmental protection	0	2	11	67	80	
	Washroom renovation	0	0	1	23	24	
Total by period		0	6	16	160	182	
In total		21	54	97	779	951	

Based on the distribution of TAPPs sustainability values in different stages, the overall structure characteristics of TAPPs values were further analyzed according to the frequency of reference points in Table 4-4. The main features are as follows:

a. Social and Cultural Values and Economic Values Balance

The overall value structure of TAPPs highlighted the social and cultural values and economic values. According to the frequency of reference points aggregated by value dimensions in Nvivo, the frequency of social and cultural and economic values accounted for 80.9%. Table 4-4 shows that the number of reference points of six specific values under the social and cultural value dimension totalled 41%, only 1.1% higher than that of five specific values under the economic dimension. This slight difference implied the balanced proportion of social, cultural, and economic values in TAPPs. The balance owed to China’s strategy of “constructing material civilization and spiritual civilization and attaching equal importance to both" was implemented over four decades of the country's reform and opening-up in 1978. The Fifth Plenary Session of the 18th CPC Central Committee proposed the coordinated development of material and spiritual civilization in 2015. The strategy constituted the basic tasks of building a moderately prosperous society in all respects and was further elaborated in the 19th CPC National Congress report in 2017.

Chinese TAPPs actively responded to the strategy of balancing the spiritual civilization and material civilization by focusing on the tourism’s impacts on the economic, social and cultural development in poverty-stricken areas. In TAPPs, the advantages of abundant tourism resources were explored to drive tourists’ consumption and help poor households shake off poverty and get rich through increased employment and income. In this way, the status of tourism in China's poverty alleviation program was largely promoted. Besides the importance of economic values, the TAPPs realized social and cultural values by investing in infrastructure, education, culture, health and other public services in poor areas. Various measures were taken to stimulate the enthusiasm of local governments, social forces and impoverished people's participation in TAP. The mechanism that hindered TAP was reformed. Laws and regulations were improved to guarantee tourists and operators’ benefits, preserve and inherit traditional culture. Professional training was intensified to enhance the skills of tourism practitioners in poverty-stricken areas and improve the service quality of TAP.

b. Economic Values Center on Eliminating Poverty and Economic Stimulation

As an economic engine of China, tourism has become one of the most important ways to reduce absolute poverty throughout the country. Boosting the local economy of poverty-stricken areas represented the core specific values under the economic value dimension in TAPPs, aiming to help the poor population tackle income poverty. As shown in Table 4-4, the frequency of eliminating poverty and getting rich and economic stimulation broke 100, about twice that of the other economic value categories. The two economic value categories ranked first and third in 15 value categories respectively, dominating the value orientations of TAPPs. In order to realize these values, TAPPs initiated TAP projects in poor areas, especially in the central and western regions, ethnic minority areas, old revolutionary bases, and poor rural areas, to develop characteristic cultural tourism, leisure agriculture and rural tourism. These TAP projects aimed to play tourism's role in promoting industrial convergence and creating more employment opportunities so that the poverty population could remove economic poverty and gradually realize their moderately prosperous life.

These economic values were consistent with the socialist essential requirements of "eliminating poverty and achieving common prosperity" proposed by the Chinese CPC Central Committee. The overview of the Chinese anti-poverty initiative showed that the Chinese government has started to combat absolute poverty since the founding of the People's Republic of China in 1949. However, the national large-scale absolute poverty alleviation campaign didn't start until the launch of reform and opening-up in 1978 and mainly experienced five stages: poor region-targeted period (1978-1985), poor county-targeted period (1986- 2000), poor village-targeted period (2001-2012) and poor household-targeted period (2013-2020). China's tourism industry didn't kick off until reform and opening-up policy was implemented in 1978. TAP mainly fell in the last three stages of the absolute poverty reduction campaign. The common feature of the national poverty alleviation policies in these three stages focused on the endogenous development of poor areas and populations. Poverty alleviation through industry development was an important way to promote "blood-forming" 1 poverty alleviation. Assisting the poor to increase their income, which was the main indicator to measure absolute poverty, was the primary value goal of poverty alleviation through industrial development. As the main way of poverty alleviation through industrial development, TAPPs economic values echoed the mission of the country's absolute poverty alleviation program.

c. Social and Cultural Values Highlight Public Service and Participation

Participation and cooperation and public service were the top two value categories of social and cultural value dimension in TAPPs. Since the implementation of development-oriented poverty alleviation in 1980s, the government has been devoted to optimizing conditions for TAP mainly by guiding social participation, increasing policy and institutional supply and improving infrastructure and other public service system. Table 4-4 showed that the total frequencies of reference points for participation, cooperation, and public service were 106 and 91, respectively, ranking second and fourth among the 15 value categories.

Participation and cooperation value was exhibited in TAPPs by urging local governments to pay due attention to tourism planning for poor areas. The government encouraged the young officials, experts, university students, returning migrant workers, enterprises, research institutes, colleges and universities to participate in TAP development actively. The TAP model was innovated through targeted poverty alleviation measures such as collaboration between the central and western regions, regional tourism integration, designated assistance, and counterpart aid to construct a TAP multi-participation and coordination pattern. The public service value in TAPPs focused on improving infrastructure construction of transportation, communication, water and power, culture and education, medical and health care, disaster prevention and mitigation in poor areas. Tourism's public service capacity in public health, information services, public culture, public

1 "Blood forming" poverty alleviation is a term coined by the Chinese government. It refers to improving the impoverished population's capabilities and skills to overcome poverty (source:https://baike.baidu.com/item/%E9%80%A0%E8%A1%80%E5%BC%8F%E6%89%B6%E8%B4%AB/18459058).

safety and emergency rescue was enhanced to provide a good environment for tourism development in poor areas.

d. Environmental Values Stressing Environmental Protection and Improvement of Human Habitat

The poor population in most of the poverty-stricken areas in China suffered from fragile ecological environment and poor living conditions. It was an inevitable choice for TAPPs to emphasize ecological, environmental protection and improvement of human habitat to achieve TAP sustainable development. Table 4-4 shows that in the early exploration period, there were no reference points for environmental values in TAPPs. The environmental value reference points only emerged in the initial development period in the late 1990s. The value shift was closely related to the positioning of the national poverty alleviation strategy for constructing ecological civilization. The "National Eighth Seven Year Plan for Poverty Alleviation (1994-2000)" linked poverty alleviation with ecological environmental protection for the first time. In the 21st century, the "China Rural Poverty Alleviation and Development Program (2001-2010)" and the "China Rural Poverty Alleviation and Development Program (2011-2020)" both regarded the improvement of the ecological environment as the focus of poverty alleviation. The "China Rural Poverty Alleviation and Development Outline (2011-2020)" even proposed that China's poverty alleviation should put the ecological environment improvement on the top agenda.

The reference points of environmental values witnessed a leap-forward increase in TAPPs. Table 4-4 showed that environmental value reference points rose from six in the initial development period to 160 in the target and efficient period, an increase of 257%, accounting for 88% of the total environmental value reference points in the four periods. The total number of reference points for environmental protection leapt to 80, making it the fifth-ranked value category among the 15 value categories. The content of this value category extended from ecological construction, energy conservation, pollution prevention and control to the construction of laws and regulations for conserving tourism resources and protecting natural and cultural heritage. Improving the rural human habitat became important to constructing the rural tourism service system in the target and efficient period. This value emphasized improving the production and living conditions of poor villages, helping rural tourism operators upgrade tourism facilities and the surrounding environment, restoring villages and towns with characteristic tourism resources, famous historical and cultural villages and towns, and continuously optimizing the environment of leisure agriculture and rural tourism.

Results of Identifying TAPPs Targets

Whether PPT policies target tourism growth or poverty alleviation is one of the focuses that PPT policy scholars are concerned about. The two target orientations determine how much tourism's benefits could be channelled to the poor. Though few studies investigated the Chinese TAPPs goals, there are some researches on the evaluation of TAPPs' impacts on the poor (Qin et. al., 2019; Xie et. al., 2020), which aimed at measuring the effects of TAPPs targets.

TAPPs impact researchers commonly assessed economic, social, cultural and environmental indicators. Echoing the three sustainability value dimensions of TAPPs, these indicators reflected the dimensions of TAPPs targets but did not specify the major targets in different TAP stages. The formulation of TAPPs followed the national poverty alleviation and tourism development strategies to ensure tourism's contribution to the sustainable development of poor areas. Therefore, based on the TAPPs semantic network, TAPPs sustainability values, objectives of Chinese poverty alleviation strategies (Liu, 2018) and tourism development strategies (Tang, 2016) in different stages, the targets of TAPPs in this study were identified as exploring TAP model (1984-1996), promoting sustainable regional TAP (1997-2004), initiating sustainable rural TAP (2005-2012) and implementing sustainable TAP projects precisely (since 2013).

The target of exploring the TAP model in the early exploration period (1984-1996) centred on reforming government and market relationships in TAP, indicated by high-frequency keywords such as "reform", “system”, “government”, and "market" in Figure 4.1. This target followed the national poverty alleviation strategy's objectives of reforming the institutional system for promoting socioeconomic development and poverty relief in rural areas since 1978 and tourism's economic target of earning foreign exchange in the first 15 years after reform and opening up. Since tourism was still in its initial development stage, TAPPs in this stage targeted more at casting off the shackles of planned economic system for tourism growth than the sustainable development of poor areas. This policy goal fully reflected the TAPPs' value focus on exploring tourism's growth for social and economic development in tourist destinations without considering the environmental issues.

TAPPs' target of promoting sustainable regional TAP (1997-2004) in the preliminary development period (1997-2004) could be implied by the high-frequency keywords of "region", "poverty", "scenic area", "ecology", and "development" in the TAPPs document semantic network. Figure 4.3 and Table 4-4 show that the environmental value was added to the TAPPs value, making the TAPPs target in this period more environmental-friendly than the previous period. In response to the national poverty alleviation and mass tourism development strategies in this period, TAPPs strive to attract the middle class's tourism consumption in TAP pilot zones by improving public service and upgrading scenic areas to help the poor tackle food and clothing problem.

The target of initiating sustainable rural TAP in the rapid improvement period (2005-2012) could be reflected in the high-frequency words of "agriculture", "rural", "village", "tourism", "ecology", and "development" in the semantic network in Figure 4.1. This target echoed the national poverty alleviation strategy's attention to ecological environment improvement in the poor countryside and the tourism's objective of expanding the power of domestic tourism to rural areas. Rural tourism was even set as the theme of Chinese tourism by the Chinese National Tourism Administration in 2006. Since then, rural tourism has become a major tool for realizing the TAPPs sustainability values in poor rural areas.

The target of implementing sustainable TAP projects precisely in the targeted and efficient period (since 2013) could be exhibited through high-frequency words of "key issues", "tourism", "projects", "promoting", "social", "organization", and "enterprises". Under the guidance of the more balanced three dimensions of sustainability values of TAPPs, this target kept consistent with the poverty alleviation strategy's target of eliminating absolute poverty precisely and the tourism strategy's goal of improving people's livelihood. It pushed tourism to the central area of Chinese poverty alleviation program by attracting the wide participation of enterprises, organizations and other social forces to the key sustainable TAP projects planned by the government.

Results of Identifying Policy Instruments

As the linkage between policy formulation and implementation, policy instruments are used to realize policy values and achieve policy targets (Howlett, 2005; Ali, 2013; Guo, 2020). It provides a proper perspective to understand TAPPs' role in strengthening the tourism-poverty link and promoting sustainable development of poor areas in China. Capano, Priton and Vicentini (2019) argued that an instrument-based approach could better enlighten the nature of policy dynamics and help policymakers make more effective decisions. The understanding of instrument and mix dynamics over time needs to be deepened through more empirical studies (Capano & Howlett, 2020).

Classification of TAPPs Instruments

The classification of policy tools, which could assist policymakers in understanding the features of instruments and their application to the context, is typically where the selection of individual and mixtures of instruments from the "toolbox" begins (Howlett, 2005; Howlett & Ramesh, 1993). Among several popular instrument typologies by Salamon, Vedung, Schneider and Ingram, Hood and Rothwell, Rothwell's taxonomy of policy tools was considered applicable to this study as this typology emphasizes the policy impact on the practical work (Yue et. al., 2020) and has been widely used in the Chinese context (Lin et. al., 2017; Zhou et. al., 2020; Zhang et. al., 2019; Yue et. al., 2020).

Therefore, this study classified TAPPs tools into supply-side, demand-side, and environmental instruments (Table 4-5). Among them, supply-side instruments mainly refer to the government's input of tourism production factors such as capital, information, technology, talents and public service to push the smooth development of TAP sectors. Demand-side tools rely on the government to purchase TAP products and services, develop TAP resources and projects, organize enterprises, institutions and individuals and other social forces to purchase and consume TAP products and services to provide partner assistance to poor households and provide subsidy to reduce the uncertain market risks for TAP programs. Environmental tools mean that the government creates a good environment for TAP development by making scientific planning, reforming, innovating and issuing policies for tourism land use, tax reduction and exemption, financial assistance, and strategic measures. It can be seen from Figure 4.4 that these three categories of policy tools are combined to push, pull and influence the achievement of TAPPs targets.

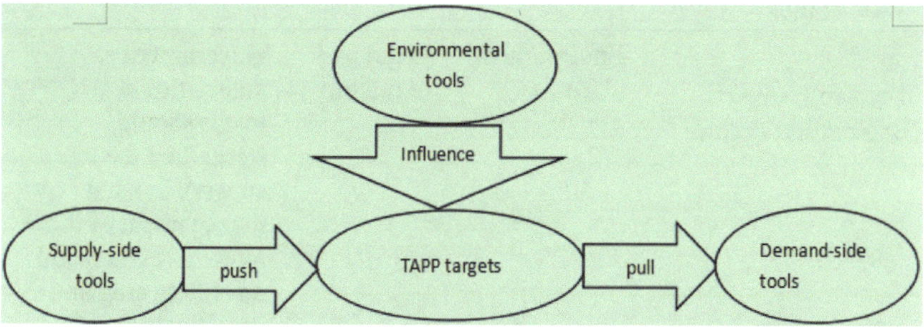

Figure 4-4 The role of TAPPs instruments in realizing TAPPs targets

Table 4-5 Classification of TAPPs instruments

Supply-side	**Environmental-side**	**Demand-side**
Funding	Land	Government purchase
Information	Taxation	Project development
Talent	Planning	Partner assistance
Technical support	Reform and innovation	Subsidy
Public service	Legal and regulatory	
	Strategic measures	
	Financial	

Source: Adapted from taxonomy of policy tools by Rothwell (1985)

TAPPs Texts Encoding for TAPPs Instruments Analysis

This section further mines these tools in the TAPPs documents with NVivo to understand what policy tools are used to realize TAPPs goals. First, import the previously selected 64 policy texts into NVivo. Then label supply-side, demand-side, and environmental tools as tree nodes and specific policy tools as sub-nodes. Next, code the imported texts semantically line by line and categorize words, sentences or paragraphs into the corresponding sub-nodes. Finally, form a coding level of "stage-tree node-sub node-reference point" (Table 4-6). Two coders worked on the coding independently. Through the coding comparison function in NVivo, it was found that the two coders' coding agreement percentage reached 96.15%, which indicated the high credibility of the coding results.

Table 4-6 Encoding process example

Texts in Different TAP Stages	**Tree Node**	**Sub-node**	**Reference Point**
Texts in Early Exploration Period	Environmental Tools	Legal and regulatory	Government authorities at all levels should strengthen the supervision and management of the tourism market, and resolutely stop and investigate fraud, forced sales and other actions that harm the interests of tourists
Texts in Initial Development Period	Supply-side Tools	Funding	The government increases financial investment in tourism infrastructure construction
Texts in Rapid Improvement Period	Environmental Tools	Strategic Measures	Promote the coordinated development of regional tourism. The central and western regions, the frontier and ethnic regions should make use of natural and cultural tourism resources to cultivate characteristic and advantageous TAP industries

Texts in Different TAP Stages	Tree Node	Sub-node	Reference Point
Texts in Targeted and Efficient Period	Demand-side Tools	Partner Assistance	Encourage every tourism awards winners and top tourism enterprise to select assistance targets across the country, and help not less than two key TAP rural villages.

In Nvivo, 1020 codes were classified according to the framework of policy tools, and the frequency distribution of each type of tool is shown in Figure 4.5. The TAP targeted and efficient period witnessed a peak of reference points of TAPPs instruments, hitting 859 of the total 1020 codes because 55 of the total 64 TAPPs samples were collected in this period (Table 4-1). In the first three stages, the reference points of policy instruments increased gradually though the number of TAPPs issued by the Chinese central government varied slightly. The increase of TAPPs documents and policy instrument reference points presented the trajectory of tourism moving from the edge to the center of China's anti-poverty strategy. The three types of tools were distributed unevenly from 1984-2020.

Throughout the four stages, environmental tools reached the highest total reference points of 497, with a frequency close to 49%. Demand-side tools were the least used, with 212 reference points and a frequency of only 21%. The proportion of supply-side tools was moderate, with reference points of 311 and a frequency of 30%. The government's heavy reliance on environmental policy tools showed that the development of TAP mainly followed the "market prioritized and government promoted development" model (Guo, 2020). The government utilized the environmental policy tools such as land allocation, financial, taxation and strategic measures to influence the participation and investment of market entities in the TAP initiative. Other environmental tools, including target planning, regulatory control, reform and innovation, were used to ensure the TAP market development under the government's rational TAP goals, scientific planning and supervision.

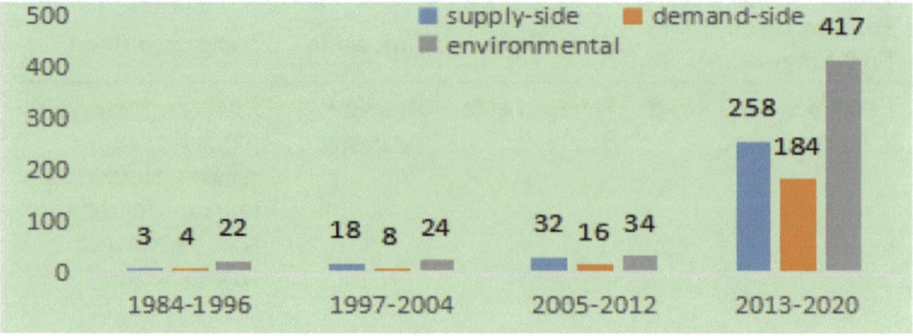

Figure 4-5 Distribution of three tool categories in TAP stages

Use of Policy Instruments for Policy Values and Targets in TAP Stages

The different distribution of policy tools indicates the choice of policy tool differs in achieving different TAPPs values and targets in four TAP stages.

a. More Environmental Tools for the Explorative TAP Model in 1984-1996

In the TAP early exploration period (1984-1996), the Chinese Central Government started to explore the new TAP model by reforming the self-closed tourism system under the original planned economic system. The "Notice on Strengthening Domestic Tourism Management" and the "Report on Several Issues in Current Tourism System Reform" issued by the National Tourism Administration in 1984 and 1985 initiated the domestic tourism market reform. The tourism industry was incorporated into "the National Economic and Social Development Plan" in 1986, stimulating the enthusiasm for tourism development in poor areas but rich in tourism resources, such as Western China's Guizhou Province. Since then, the contribution of tourism to poverty reduction has emerged in China. The TAP initiative in economically underdeveloped areas was further promoted by the National Tourism Administration's "Notice on Actively Developing Domestic Tourism Opinions" in 1993 and the "Ninth Five-Year Plan and 2010 Vision Goal Outline of China's Tourism Development" in 1995.

TAPPs of this stage mainly depended on environmental tools to adjust the relationship between the market and the government in TAP model. It could be seen from Figure 4.5 that among the 29 reference points for policy tools in the exploration period, there were 22 reference points for environmental tools and only three and four reference points for supply and demand tools, respectively. Figure 4.6 showed that reform and innovation and legal and regulatory were the most frequently-used environmental tools, focusing on gradually breaking the boundaries of tourism market factors such as tourism transportation, scenic spot construction, tourism product development, tourist source export and reception between departments and regions. Tourism industry service standards, management and supervision systems, and legal regulations were initially established to change the self-closed service system of the tourism industry. Owing to the use of these environmental tools, the original government-sponsored TAP model was transformed into a "market + government" dual-track TAP model.

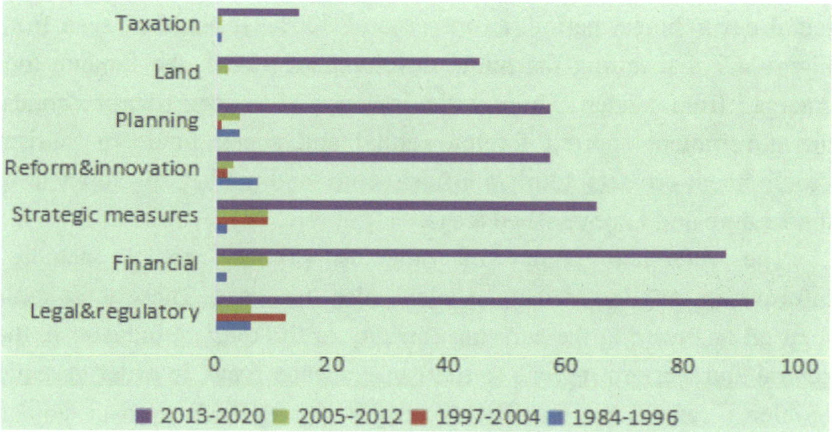

Figure 4-6 Structure and distribution of environmental tools in TAP stages

b. Supply-side Tools Increased for Regional TAP in 1997-2004

As TAP was included in the “China National Tourism Development Plan of the Ninth Five-Year Plan” and the national western development strategy, TAP entered its initial development period (1997-2004). In this period, tourism’s role in promoting social and cultural development in poor areas of central and western regions of China was more recognized in TAPPs values. Legal and regulatory tools were more frequently adopted to stimulate people’s tourism demands (Figure 4.6). The State Council, in 1999, issued “Measures on National Lunar New Year and Memorial Holidays” where “Spring Festival”, “May Day” and “National Day” were set as national week-long holidays. This policy successfully made these three holidays the “tourism golden weeks”. In order to satisfy the demands of holiday tourists, the National Tourism Administration and nine other departments jointly issued "Several Opinions on Further Development of Holiday Tourism" to increase the input of tourism factors. Thanks to the holiday tourism's contribution to income increase of local people, especially the poor and economic development in lag-behind central and western regions, the "Notice on Further Accelerating the Development of the Tourism Industry" issued by the State Council in 2001, clearly set out the task of constructing TAP pilot zones.

Improving tourism supply in pilot zones was critical to advance TAP development. Therefore, TAPPs for this stage increased the use of supply-side policy instruments. The reference points of supply-side tools in Figure 4.5 rose from three in the early exploration period to 18 in the initial development period, an increase of 500%. It could be seen from Figure 4.7 that during the initial development period, the funding tool emerged from scratch. Through the issuance of tourism treasury bonds, the government spurred foreign capital and social funds to tourism development projects, tourism infrastructure and market development in the western and impoverished areas.

The reference points of other supply-side tools, including information, public service and talent, also increased. These three tools focused on ensuring the carrying capacity of the tourism industry in the central and western regions as tourism demands grew. In order to avoid problems caused by insufficient supply during the” tourism golden weeks”, the government provided tourism information statistics, tourism product information and forecast services for tourists to arrange their routes and schedules properly. Besides, the supplies of public services such as transportation, post and telecommunications, and medical treatment were strengthened, and tourism service and management teams were established to ensure the quality of tourism services in poor areas. The implementation of these TAPPs instruments greatly expanded TAP effects. From 1978 to 2004, the number of poor people who directly benefited from tourism development was 60 to 80 million, accounting for one-quarter to one-third of the total number of poor people.

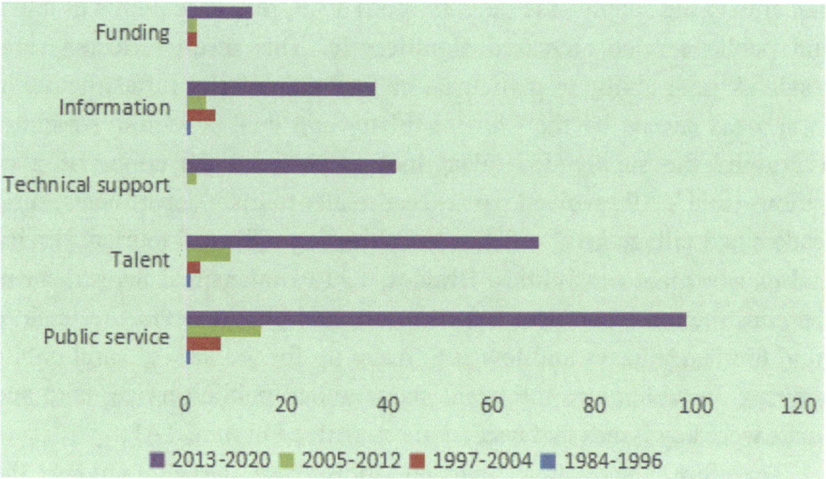

Figure 4-7 Structure and distribution of supply-side tools in TAP stages

c. Supply and Environmental Tools Balanced for Rural TAP in 2005-2012

During the rapid improvement period (2005-2012), the gap between the proportion of economic values and social and cultural values was significantly reduced (Figure 4.3). TAP target shifted from regional to rural areas to carry out the important historical task of building a new socialist countryside proposed by the Chinese Central Government. In 2006, the National Tourism Administration issued "Guiding Opinions on Promoting Rural Tourism Development" and other special policy documents on rural tourism and signed a cooperation agreement with the Ministry of Agriculture on promoting the construction of new socialist countryside and the development of rural tourism. The National Tourism Administration also designated 2006 "China Rural Tourism Year". After six years of rapid development, TAP was listed as one of the main methods in the national poverty alleviation program document in 2012. Based on the significant TAP effects produced by increasing supply-type tools during the initial development period, rural tourism development policies continued to strengthen the role of supply-type tools in promoting TAP. The frequency of supply-side tools became close to environmental tools with reference points 32 and 34, respectively (Figure 4.5).

The balanced use of supply-side and environmental TAPPs tools aimed to improve the weak foundation of rural tourism. Figure 4.7 shows that among the supply-side tools for rural TAP, reference points of talent and public service increased significantly. This result reflected rural residents' poor ability to participate in TAP and inferior infrastructure in rural areas caused by the Chinese urban-rural dual economic structure. Therefore, the supply-side talent tool emphasized the cooperation of various rural TAP involved parties, especially tourism departments, rural leaders and village-level officials in cultivating villagers' tourism service and management capabilities. Besides, TAPPs intensified investment in the construction of tourism infrastructure and public service systems in rural tourism villages and towns to make up for the lack of rural public services. In addition to the talent shortage and public service, land and funds were key issues that needed to be resolved in rural TAP.

Therefore, land and financial tools rose largely among the environmental tools shown in Figure 4.6. The government encouraged demolition and land reclamation to ensure the land use for rural tourism. The special fund for rural tourism was established to strengthen credit and guarantee support for rural TAP. Under the guidance of national TAPPs in the rapid improvement period, Guizhou Province took the lead in formulating the "Guizhou Province Rural Tourism Plan", which set rural tourism as the main poverty alleviation means.

d. Project Development Tool Pulling TAP Precise Effect in 2013-2020

Following the Chinese target poverty alleviation strategy proposed in 2013, TAP moved to the target and efficient development period. In this stage, the tourism industry matured with an established and consolidated industry system through more than 30 years of reform and opening-up. Tourism's capacity to drive the economic development in poverty-stricken areas was obviously enhanced, making it a major poverty alleviation tool in the targeted poverty alleviation stage since 2012. The implementation of precise policy measures such as the Rural Tourism Project and the Rural Tourism Maker Plan, TAP provides the poor with more opportunities for employment and entrepreneurship, speeding up the pace of poverty alleviation in poverty-stricken villages. Gradually, economic values become the leading value of TAPPs.

According to the "China Rural Poverty Alleviation and Development Program (2011-2020)", rural TAP was listed as one of the ten key tasks for poverty alleviation and development in the new period. The central government issued more than ten special TAPPs documents, such as the "Rural TAP Project Action Plan", listing rural TAP projects as the core pulling force of the TAPPs mix with three major types of tools working together to further promote poverty alleviation through rural tourism.

It could be seen from Figure 4.8 that among the demand-side tools, the frequency of project development approximates 140, which is nearly 7 times the sum of the reference points in the previous three periods, making it a specific tool with the most reference points among the three types of tools. In 2019, the China Ministry of Culture and Tourism (CMCT, the former National Tourism Administration) deepened the implementation of the rural TAP projects. It jointly launched the first batch of 320 national rural tourism key villages with the National Development and Reform Commission (NDRC). CMCT and NDRC also approved the construction of tourism infrastructure in deeply impoverished areas through 329 investment projects within the central government's budget.

The implementation of the project requires a standardized, orderly and innovative institutional environment as a strong guarantee. Therefore, supply and environmental tools in the third stage were broken. The proportion of environmental tools increased twice and four times that of supply-side tools and demand-side tools respectively (Figure 4.5). Among environmental tools, legal and regulatory and financial tools were specific tools with the most reference points (Figure 4.6). This fully illustrated that TAP projects were carried out under the regulatory control in the targeted and efficient stage. The source of project funds was wider than fiscal funds. Various financing methods, such as direct financing, indirect financing, project financing and non-project financing, were also comprehensively adopted, and financing channels were continuously expanded. Among the supply-side tools, the government's funding increased dramatically compared with the previous stages (Figure 4.7). The scope and scale of government fund in TAP was further expanded. The information tool was updated with dynamic monitoring, and the release of TAP project data was added.

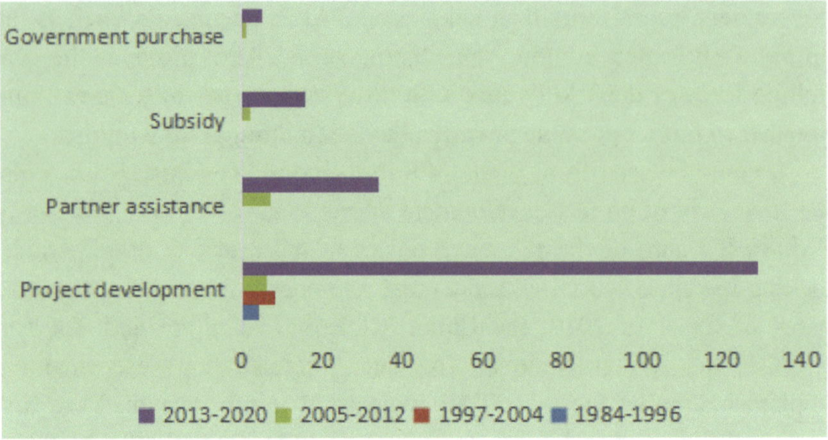

Figure 4.8: Structure and distribution of demand-side tools in TAP stages

The above analysis showed that TAPPs instruments mainly served the realization of economic, social and cultural values and targets of TAP. Though environmental values have become an integral part of TAPPs sustainability values since the TAP initial development period, they were subordinate to economic, social and cultural values (Figure 4.3) despite the steady increase from 12% in the TAP initial development period to 21% in the TAP targeted and efficient period. Ecological improvement was mentioned in TAPPs but not constituted the main part of the TAPPs targets. Therefore, no specific policy tools are used to realize environmental values though attention to environmental issues was given in TAPPs tools of public service and project development.

As China's fulfilment of SDG1 was mainly measured by the income poverty line, TAPPs sustainability values were dominated by the economic sustainability in the TAP targeted and efficient period with the implementation of sustainable TAP projects as the policy goal. The policy instrument of rural TAP project development was used as a leading policy instrument by the Chinese government to increase rural poor residents' income to get rid of poverty. Therefore, it's necessary to further explore how tourism development affects impoverished people's income by implementing TAPPs in the next section.

Results of Establishment of Chinese TAP CGE Model

Among the most popular academic methods of evaluating tourism's economic impacts on poverty alleviation listed in Table 2-2 of chapter two, CGE has the unique advantages of distinguishing tourism's impacts on outputs, incomes and employment from its net effects with the flow of tourism receipts within an economy. Under the modeller's assumptions about the government policy settings, the CGE model could incorporate a more realistic set of economy-wide constraints on the economy's supply side, allowing for general specifications of the behaviour of consumers, producers, and investors. In order to quantify the tourism-poverty link under TAPPs, this chapter explores how Chinese tourism development under TAPPs affects the distribution of income to the poor and the impact mechanism through CGE analysis.

A Brief Historical Overview of CGE Modeling

The theoretical foundation of CGE modelling is Walras' Law, proposed by Léon Walras (1874a, b). According to this Law, general equilibrium conditions exist among different markets in an economy at any set of prices. A Walrasian equilibrium is defined as an allocation of the available level of goods and a set of prices given by the demand functions at the equilibrium prices. Nevertheless, Walras did not provide formal proof of the solution for this system which he presupposed to be unique. Wald (1936) mathematically proved the existence of static equilibrium solutions in perfectly competitive and imperfectly competitive markets. However, each model he proved was only a special case of a general equilibrium system. Arrow (1951), Arrow and Debreu (1954) refined Walras' ideas with more abstract mathematical tools such as set theory and typology. They further proved that optimal equilibrium prices exist in finite economies with the Kakutani fixed point theorem.

Walrasian general equilibrium theory was transformed into the Arrow-Debreu framework by Arrow and Debreu (1954), Debreu (1959), and Arrow and Hahn (1971). In this framework, consumers with an endowment of components and commodities are expected to maximize utility; producers are assumed to maximize profits; the market demand and supply of any good are continuous, non-negative, homogeneous of degree zero, and subject to the condition that, for any given set of prices, the total value of consumer spending equals consumer income. This framework uses four different types of equations: (1) equations for equilibrium conditions for each market to guarantee that supply and demand for each good and service are equal; (2) equations for income-expenditure identities to guarantee the balance of each account; (3) equations for behavioural relationships to describe how economic agents respond to changes in prices and incomes; and (4) equations for production functions to calculate the output for each sector. The CGE modelling process is built on top of this framework.

The predecessors of CGE modelling are Input-output (I-O) analysis and social accounting matrices (SAMs) based on Walrasian general equilibrium theory. Leontief model, an approximation of Walrasian general equilibrium theory, was the first typical I-O analysis of US economy (Leontief 1936, 1941). I-O models depict the flows between businesses within an economy while accounting for all industry revenues and expenditures (Winters et. al., 2013). Developed from I-O Table, SAMs add more flows to other institutions, such as households, the government, and the rest of the world. Both approaches require that the income and spending flows within the mapped economy should add up to account for all economic activities.

Thanks to their abilities to estimate the aggregate and sectoral level economic impacts and to trace the linkages between industries, I–O analysis and SAMs became the two most basic models for mapping the economy-wide effects of tourism during the 1950s -1980s. However, one of the major drawbacks of these two approaches is that they do not include prices or wages. The fact is that tourists and other consumers will respond to pricing changes, and tourist enterprises and other firms will respond to changes in input prices and wages. The exclusion of price and wage changes in these two approaches restricts their capacity to estimate the impact of adjustments in tourism demand (Blake et. al., 2001).

The limitations of the I-O model and SAMs motivate the advent of the computable general equilibrium (CGE) model. Since Johansen (1960) created the first world-recognized CGE model, this approach has developed from early models built on the Arrow–Debreu framework under perfect competition conditions (e.g. Dixon et. al., 1982) to models incorporating imperfect competition (e.g. Harris et. al., 1985), industrial organization features (e.g. Harrison et. al., 1996; Adams & Parmenter,

1999; Lofgren et. al., 2001) and even dynamics (Dixon & Parmenter, 1996; Madsen & Sorensen, 2002). By the 1980s, the CGE model had developed into a fairly standard model. In the early 1990s, CGE analysis became one of the important areas of applied economics. Taking the SAMs as the basic data, CGE models incorporate behavioural presumptions and restrictions that reflect a view of the economy based on economic theories. CGE models could simulate how an economy works using theoretical models, parameters for these models derived using real-world data, and data on the economy contained in the SAMs. Similar to SAMs, CGE models could assess how tourism affects the economy if a tourist account and necessary model parameters are identified.

Since 1990, CGE modelling has replaced I-O modelling and has become a popular policy assessment tool. This technique has been employed as a crucial tool to assess the effects of shocks or changes in policies by some influential international organizations such as the World Bank, the International Food Policy Research Institute (IFPRI), the World Trade Organization (WTO) and the Organizations for Economic Cooperation and Development (OECD). It is also used in a wide range of fields, including trade analysis, macroeconomics, industry analysis, environmental analysis, natural resource analysis, tourism analysis and other sectors.

CGE modelling is a helpful technique for tourism studies, especially for impact analysis, because of the characteristics of tourism. It is generally recognized that tourists demand for travel is highly erratic, making tourism demand a crucial research and policy concern (Meng & Siriwardana, 2017). Tourists' likelihood and decisions to visit a destination depend on various factors, including their preferences, level of income and health, the marketing plan, tourism regulations, and sporting and cultural events in tourist destinations. These factors could be included in a CGE model to assess their effects on tourism demand.

On the other hand, tourists' spending on tourism activities could impact the overall economy. Products and services consumed by tourists are produced and supplied by a wide range of industries or from imports. Tourist consumption directly creates revenues and employment opportunities for tourism products and services manufacturers and suppliers, termed tourism's "direct effects". In order to satisfy tourists' demand, tourism products and services producers have to purchase or import inputs from other industries. This purchase affects the earnings and employment in the supply chain, termed tourism's "indirect effects". Residents and households could earn income from the employment opportunities from tourism products and services produced and their supply chain. They spend part of this income on domestically produced goods, termed tourism" induced effects". Tourism's employment linkage and inter-industry linkage could be easily measured using CGE modelling.

However, CGE is seldom used to quantify Chinese tourism's distributional effects on poor households' income. Therefore, it's necessary to build up a Chinese TAP CGE to assess Chinese TAPPs' impacts on the achievement of SDG1 to unpack the mechanism of how Chinese tourism benefits could reach the poor. Chinese TAP CGE simulation results will also be significant in guiding the Chinese government to improve the fairness of tourism income distribution impacts on households in rural revitalization.

Chinese TAP CGE Structure

There are different types of typical CGE models by categorization criteria. A CGE model may fall under one or more categories: static or dynamic, single-country or worldwide, single-region or multi-regional, top-down or bottom-up, single-household or multi-household, single-occupation group or multi-occupation group. A CGE model could also be categorized as environmental CGE model, energy CGE model, agricultural CGE model, tourism CGE model, CGE model on water, CGE model on land use, CGE model for trade, and so forth, depending on the research issues being addressed.

Considering the model reliability, applicability and data availability, this study chooses the static "standard" CGE model in GAMS by Hans Lofgren, Rebecca Lee Harris and Sherman Robinson (2002) as the basic model for Chinese TAP CGE modelling. This "standard" model features its applicability in developing countries through the research projects funded by the International Food Policy Research Institute (IFPRI). No matter what type a typical CGE is, they all comprise two major parts: the model structure and the database. The CGE model structure is a set of equations that simulates how different aspects of an economy are interconnected. All data that must be fed into the CGE model structure is contained in a CGE database to produce simulation results.

a. Basic CGE Structure

The basic structure of the Chinese TAP CGE model is modified from IFPIR's "standard" CGE model. According to Figure 4.9, this model explains all of the payments recorded in the social accounting matrix (SAM). The model therefore follows the SAM disaggregation of factors, activities, commodities, and institutions. Based on a required SAM database, the Chinese TAP CGE model consists of the following key structural components:

(1) Production and trade

Producers' profit-maximizing decisions and production activities (QA_a) subject to a production technology are described as a nested constant elasticity of substitution (CES) function of quantities of value-added (QVA_a) and aggregate intermediate input use $(QINTA_a)$ (equations 4.1-4.2). Each production activity's demand for value-added is a CES function of primary factors (equation 4.3) whereas the demand for disaggregated intermediate inputs $(QINT_{ca})$ for each activity is calculated through a Leontief function of the aggregate intermediate input consumption amount multiplied by a preset intermediate input coefficient (ica_{ca}) (equation 4.6). Value added taxes (VAT) are imposed on primary factor composites as is stated in equations 4.4-4.5.

The trade block mainly covers the allocation of domestic production output and aggregation of supply to the domestic market. The allocation of the domestic production output (QX_c) between exports (QE_c) and domestic demand (QDC_c) is defined by a CET (constant elasticity of transformation) function (equations 4.7-4.8). Composite commodities (QQ_c) for intermediate and final demands are made up of domestic supplies (QDC_c) and imports (QM_c) whose optimal mix is described by the Armington function (equations 4.9-4.10). Like many countries, export tariffs are seldom imposed in China to enhance the competition of exports while import tariffs are collected on most imported commodities (equation 4.22).

$$QA_a = a_a^q[\delta_a^q QVA_a^{\rho a} + (1-\delta_a^q)QINTA_a^{\rho a}]^{\frac{1}{\rho a}}, a \in A \quad (4.1)$$

$$\frac{PVA_a}{PINTA_a} = \frac{\delta_a^q}{1-\delta_a^q}(\frac{QINTA_a}{QVA_a})^{1-\rho a}, a \in A \quad (4.2)$$

$$QVA_a = \alpha_a^{va}\left[\delta_a^{va}QLD_a^{\rho a^{va}} + (1-\delta_a^{va})QKD_a^{\rho a^{va}}\right]^{\frac{1}{\rho a^{va}}}, a \in A \quad (4.3)$$

$$\frac{(1+tval)*WL}{(1+tvak)*WK} = \frac{\delta_a^{va}}{(1-\delta_a^{va})}(\frac{QKD_a}{QLD_a})^{1-\rho a^{va}}, a \in A \quad (4.4)$$

$$PVA_a * QVA_a = (1+tval)*WL*QLD_a + (1+tvak)*WK*QKD_a, a \in A \quad (4.5)$$

$$QINT_{ca} = ica_{ca} * QINTA_a, a \in A, c \in C \quad (4.6)$$

$$QX_c = a_c^t[(\delta_c^t QDC_c^{\rho c^t} + (1-\delta_c^t)QE_c^{\rho c^t}]^{\frac{1}{\rho c^t}}, \rho ct > 1, c \in C \quad (4.7)$$

$$\frac{PDC_c}{PE_c} = \frac{\delta_c^t}{1-\delta_c^t}\left(\frac{QE_c}{QDC_c}\right)^{1-\rho c^t}, c \in C \quad (4.8)$$

$$QQ_c = \alpha_c^q(\delta_c^q QDC_c^{\rho c^q} + (1-\delta_c^q)QM_c^{\rho c^q})^{\frac{1}{\rho c^q}}, c \in C \quad (4.9)$$

$$\frac{PDC_c}{PM_c} = \frac{\delta_c^q}{(1-\delta_c^q)}\left(\frac{QM_c}{QDC_c}\right)^{1-\rho c^q}, c \in C \quad (4.10)$$

Where

QA_a = quantity of activity,

QVA_a = quantity of aggregate value – added,

$QINTA_a$ = quantity of aggregate intermediate input,

PVA_a = price of aggregate value – added,

$PINTA_a$ = price of aggregate intermediate input,

QLD_a = quantity demanded of labor from activity a,

QKD_a = quantity demanded of capital from activity a,

WL = average price of labor

WK = average price of capital

$QINT_{ca}$= quantity of commodity c as intermediate input to activity a,

QX_c = aggregate marketed quantity of domestic output of commodity,

$QDC_c =$ quantity sold domestically of domestic output,
$QE_c =$ quantity of exports,
$PDC_c =$ demand price for commodity produced and sold domestically,
$PE_c =$ export price,
$QQ_c =$ quantity of goods supplied to domestic market (composite supply),
$QM_c =$ quantity of imports of commodity,
$PM_c =$ import price
$\alpha_a^q =$ efficiency parameter in the CES activity function,
$\delta_a^q =$ CES activity function share parameter,
$\rho^a =$ CES activity function exponent,
$\alpha_a^{va} =$ efficiency parameter in the CES value – added function,
$\delta_a^{va} =$ CES value – added function share parameter for labor in activity a,
$\rho_a^{va} =$ CES value – added function exponent,
$tval =$ labor value – added tax
$tvak =$ capital value – added tax
$ica_{ca} =$ quantity of c per unit of aggregate intermediate input a,
$\alpha_c^t =$ a CET function shift parameter,
$\delta_c^t =$ a CET function share parameter, and
$\rho_c^t =$ a CET function exponent.

(2) Institutions

The CGE model typically represents institutions by household groups, enterprises, the government and the rest of the world (ROW). The household groups earn income from production and transfers from enterprises, government and ROW (equation 4.11). Household consumption behaviour is depicted by the Cobb-Douglas function (equation 4.12). Their disposable income and savings are stated in equations 4.13 and 4.14. A series of equations represent enterprises' income from factor, government transfer and income allocation among taxes, savings and transfers to other institutions (equations 4.14-4.17, 4.11). Government's revenue from taxes, transfers and expenditure on consumption, transfers and savings are modelled in the same way as the payments to and from enterprises (equations 4.17-4.19). Foreign savings, transfer payments and commodity trade between the rest of the world and domestic institutions are expressed by equation 4.20.

$$YH_h = WL * QLSAGG * shif_{hl} + WK * QKSAGG * shif_{hk} + transfr_{hgov} + transfr_{hent} + transfr_{hrow} * EXR, h \in H \tag{4.11}$$

$$PQ_c * QH_{ch} = shrh_{ch} * mpc_h * (1 - ti_h) * YH_h, c \in C, h \in H \tag{4.12}$$

$$DIH_h = YH_h * (1 - ti_h), h \in H \tag{4.13}$$

$$HSAV_h = (1 - mpc_h) * (1 - ti_h) * YH_h, h \in H \tag{4.14}$$

$$YENT = shif_{entk} * WK * QKSAGG + transfr_{entgov} \tag{4.15}$$

$$ENTSAV = (1 - ti_{ent}) * YENT - \sum_h transfr_{hent} \tag{4.16}$$

$$YG = tval * WL * QLD_a + tvak * WK * QKD_a + \sum_h ti_h * YH_h + ta_a * (PINTA_a * QINTA_a + PVA_a * QVA_a)$$

$$+ ti_{ent} * YENT + tm_c * pwm_c * QM_c * EXR + transfr_{govrow} * \text{EXR}, \quad c \in C, a \in A, h \in H \tag{4.17}$$

$$EG = PQ_c * \overline{QG_c} + \sum_h transfr_{hgov} + transfr_{entgov} \tag{4.18}$$

$$GSAV = YG - EG \tag{4.19}$$

$$\sum_c pwm_c * QM_c = \sum_c pwe_c * QE_c + transfr_{govrow} + FSAV, c \in C \tag{4.20}$$

Where

YH_h = income of household h,

QLSAGG = aggregate quantity supplied of labor,

QKSAGG = aggregate quantity supplied of capital,

PQ_c = composite commodity price,

QH_{ch} = quantity consumed of commodity c by household h,

DIH_h = disposable income of household h,

$HSAV_h$ = savings of household h,

YENT = revenue of enterprises,

ENTSAV = savings of enterpries,

YG = revenue of government,

EG = expenditure of government,

QG_c = quantity consumed of commodity c by government,

GSAV = savings of government,

FSAV = foreign savings,

EXR = exchange rate,

$shif_{hl}$ = share parameter of labor for household h,
$shif_{hk}$ = share parameter of capital for household h,
$transfr_{hgov}$ = transfer from government to household h,
$transfr_{hent}$ = transfer from enterprises to household h,
$transfr_{hrow}$ = transfer from rest of the world to household h,
shr_{ch} = share parameter of household expenditure on commodity c,
mpc_{h} = household marginal propensity to consume
ti_{h} = income tax rate of household h,
$shif_{entk}$ = share parameter of capital for enterprises,
$transfr_{entgov}$ = transfer from government to enterprises,
ti_{ent} = direct tax rate of enterprises,
ta_{a} = tax rate of activity production,
tm_{c} = import tarrif rate
pwm_{c} = import price,
$transfr_{govrow}$ = transfer from rest of the world to government, and
pwe_{c} = export price.

(3) Price

Since there assume different qualities among composite commodities including imports, exports and domestically consumed outputs, the price block contains equations which link endogenous and exogenous prices of various variables such as export price (equation 4.21), import price (equation 4.22), aggregate price of commodities produced domestically (equation 4.23), aggregate intermediate input price (equation 4.24), activity revenue and costs (equation 4.25), demand price for commodity produced and sold domestically (derived from equations 4.8, 4.9), domestic marketed output value (equation 4.26), marketed output value (equation 4.27), price of aggregate value-added (derived from equation 4.4), and aggregate price of gross domestic product (GDP) (equation 4.28).

$$PE_c = pwe_c * EXR, c \in C \tag{4.21}$$

$$PM_c = pwm_c(1 + tm_c)EXR, c \in C \tag{4.22}$$

$$PX_c = \sum_a sax_{ac} * PA_a \tag{4.23}$$

$$PINTA_a = \sum_{c \in C} ica_{ca} * PQ_c, a \in A \tag{4.24}$$

$$PA_a * QA_a = (1 + ta_a)(PVA_a * QVA_a + PINTA_a * QINTA_a), a \in A \tag{4.25}$$

$$PQ_c * QQ_c = PDC_c * QDC_c + PM_c * QM_c, c \in C \tag{4.26}$$

$$PX_c * QX_c = PDC_c * QDC_c + PE_c * QE_c, c \in C \tag{4.27}$$

$$PGDP * GDP = \sum_{c \in C} PQc * (\sum_{h \in H} QH_{ch} + \overline{QINV_c} + \overline{QG_c}) + \sum_{c \in C} PE_c * QE_c - \sum_{c \in C} tm_c * pwm_c * EXR * QM_c \tag{4.28}$$

Where

PX_c − aggregate producer price for commodity,

PA_a = activity price,

PGDP = price of gross domestic product,

GDP = gross domestic product, and

$QINV_c$ = quantity of investment demand for commodity.

(4) Macroeconomic closure

Macroeconomic closures define exogenous and endogenous variables based on macroeconomic theories to reflect the functioning of the real-world economy. Taylor (1991) noted that closure, in essence, is a perception of the driving macroeconomic forces in the CGE system. The three most popular closures discussed in the literature are the savings-driven "neoclassical closure", investment-driven "Johansen closure", and "Keynesian closure", assuming flexible real wage in a setting with unemployment. The "standard" CGE model provides different closure rules for these styles. Under different closure styles, the effects and transmission mechanisms of the same policy shocks on the economy differ significantly, generating different simulation results. The macroeconomic balances included in the closure system are mainly the government balance (equation 4.19), the external balance or trade balance (equation 4.20) and the savings-Investment balance (equation 4.32) besides the commodity market balance (equation 4.29) and the factor markets balance (equations 4.30-4.31).

Based on the macroeconomic balances, the proper choice among various closure rules depends on the modellers' understanding of the analysis context, especially the macroeconomic background and transmission path of simulated policies. During 2017-2022, the average

Chinese national surveyed urban unemployment rate exceeds 4%, with even higher overall unemployment rate if rural employment is considered. The lingering pandemic deepens the contradiction between surplus supply and insufficient demand in China and the rest of the world. Therefore, the CGE model in this study adopts the “Keynesian closure”. In this closure, capital supply and wage variables are fixed (equations 4.33-4.34), while the labour supply and wage variables are flexible.

$$QQ_c = \sum_a QINT_{ca} + \sum_h QH_{ch} + \overline{QINV_c} + \overline{QG_c}, c \in C, a \in A, h \in H \quad (4.29)$$

$$\sum_a QLD_a = QLSAGG \quad (4.30)$$

$$\sum_a QKD_a = QKSAGG \quad (4.31)$$

$$EINV = \sum_h HSAV_h + ENTSAV + GSAV + EXR * FSAV + VBIS \quad (4.32)$$

$$QKSAGG = \overline{QKSAGG} \quad (4.33)$$

$$WK = \overline{WK} \quad (4.34)$$

Where

EINV = aggregate investment,

VBIS = dummy vairable to check the savings − investment balance.

b. Introducing Tourism into Basic CGE Structure

Introducing tourism into the general CGE model is a critical step in the process of tourism CGE modelling. In order to narrow the gap between the model and Chinese reality, this study introduces tourism into the basic CGE model by separating tourism expenditure from household consumption and exports. This modeling way is different from most typical tourism CGE models by Alavalapati & Adamowicz (2000), Gooroochurn & Milner (2004), Blake et. al. (2006), Wattanakuljarus & Coxhead (2008), Li et. al. (2011) and Li et. al. (2019). Their models capture the supply and demand of tourism activities by modelling the production and price of tourism products in production activities and tourists' demand for products in their tourism activities. In these tourism models, tourism supply was affected by the input of production factors and the intermediate input of the tourism production sector, etc. On the other hand, tourism demand is influenced by tourists' income, quantity, quality and market price of tourism products and services. Therefore, these models have to make a series of assumptions for tourism products to introduce the production equations of tourism products. These assumptions have widened the distance between the model and reality and increased the task of basic data collation for modelling.

Other CGE scholars, such as Meng and Siriwardana (2017), proposed that the entry point of tourism in a CGE model should be tourism expenditure. However, it's a challenge to model the tourism industry if tourism is not defined properly in the statistical standards. In China, tourism is defined as tourists' activities such as travel, accommodation, dining, sightseeing, shopping, entertainment, etc., in the Statistical Classification of National Tourism and Related Industries (2018) issued by the China National Bureau of Statistics. Domestic tourism expenditure is part of household consumption, and inbound tourism expenditure could be considered part of exports. Detailed tourism expenditure data could be obtained from the Chinese National Tourism Sampling Survey and China Statistical Yearbook. Based on these data, it's quite feasible for this study to model tourism and its related industries by splitting tourism expenditure from household consumption and exports, which could be closer to reality, as is shown in Table 4-11. Hence, household groups' domestic tourism consumption is a function of household groups' disposable income:

$$PQ_c * QHT_{ch} = \lambda_{ch} * A^h * DIH^{\alpha^h}, 0 < \lambda_{ch} < 1, \sum \lambda_{ch} = 1, c \in C \tag{4.35}$$

Where λ_{ch} is the share of composite commodity c consumed in household groups' tourism activities, A^h is the factor affecting household groups' tourism demand, α^h is the household groups' disposable income elasticity of tourism demand. Household groups' tourism demand could be directly separated from household consumption through the CET function:

$$QH_{ch} = QHT_{ch} + QHNT_{ch}, c \in C, h \in H \tag{4.36}$$

Where QH_{ch} is the quantity of household groups' consumption demand of composite commodity c. QHT_{ch} is the quantity of composite commodity c demanded in household groups' tourism activities and $QHNT_{ch}$ is the quantity of composite commodity c demanded in household groups' non-tourism activities. Inbound tourism consumption could be split from exports:

$$PE_c * QET_c = \lambda_{ce} * PE_c * QE_c, c \in C \quad (4.37)$$

Where PE_c is the export price of composite commodity c, QET_c is the quantity of composite commodity c consumed in the inbound tourism activities, λ_c^e and is the share of tourism consumed commodity QE_c which represents exports of composite commodity c. The inbound tourism demand could be expressed through the CET function:

$$PE_c * QE_c = PE_c * (QET_c + QENT_c), c \in C \quad (4.38)$$

The total export demand quantity is divided into the quantity of inbound tourism demand QET_c and the quantity of exports for non-tourism demand $QENT_c$. In this way, inbound tourism demand is separated from the total exports. These equations implicitly assume that for the same product, when it could satisfy all demands of tourism consumption, daily consumption and exports, the substitutability within the product is infinite.

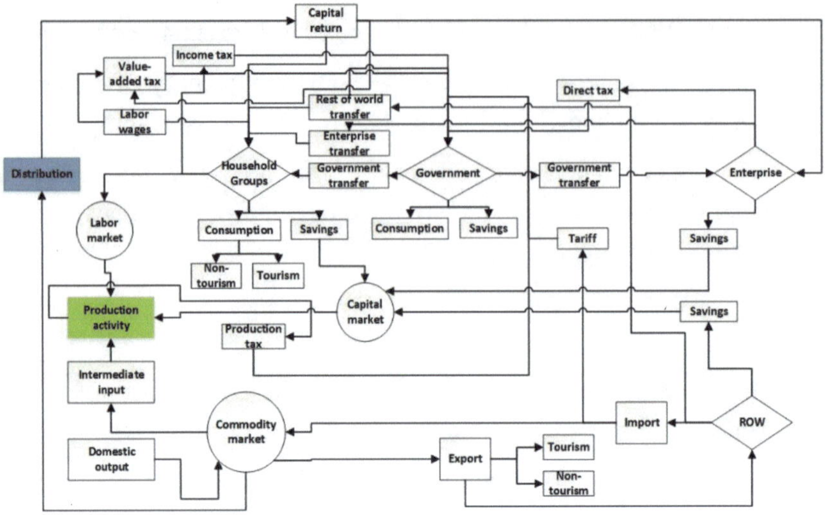

Figure 4-9 Basic structure of Chinese TAP CGE

Note: Adapted from Lofgren, H., Harris, R. L. & Robinson, S. 2002. A Standard Computable General Equilibrium (CGE) Model in GAMS. Vol. 5. Washington D.C.: International Food Policy Research Institute.

Results of Chinese TAP CGE Database and Parameters

As mentioned in the previous section, the Chinese TAP CGE modelling requires a consistent and coherent benchmark data set arranged as a Social Accounting Matrix (SAM). The SAM is used to estimate the parameters and exogenous variables in CGE equations that depict the economic behaviours of various social and economic agents and the conditions for the economy to reach an equilibrium state. According to the guidelines for the construction of a SAM (Keuning & Ruuter, 1988), the most important steps to construct a SAM are the overall design of the SAM framework, identification of data sources, the choice of a base year, defining classification, tabulation, data cleaning and re-tabulation. This section focuses on explaining the structure of Chinese SAM for Chinese TAP CGE modelling, choice of the base year, aggregation and disaggregation of SAM accounts, the data source and balancing the SAM, and parameters for CGE model implementation.

SAM Structure

A social accounting matrix (SAM) is an economic-wide framework, generally representing the function of the real economy of a country. Technically speaking, a SAM is a square matrix with a row and a column for each account. The payment from the account of its column to the account of its row is displayed in each cell. As a result, an account's income is displayed along its row, while its expenses are displayed along its column. According to the fundamental rule of double-entry accounting, total revenue (row total) should equal total expenditure for each account in the SAM (column total).

China started SAM development and application at the end of the 1980s when the Development Research Center of the China State Council constructed the first Chinese SAM in 1987. Since the 1990s, more and more Chinese scholars have been devoted to researching and improving Chinese SAM compilation. The most influential Chinese SAM scholars are Li et. al. (1996) and Fan et. al. (2010). Li et. al. (1996) first discussed the Chinese SAM framework while Fan et. al. (2010) updated the Chinese SAM structure based on the improvement of SAM research and the adjustment of the Chinese national economic accounting system and statistic calibre. The SAM for Chinese TAP CGE is compiled from the SAM for IFPIR's CGE modelling and the latest Chinese SAM framework by Fan et. al. (2010). Table 4-7 shows the basic structure of the SAM (with verbal explanations in place of numbers).

Table 4-7 Basic structure of the Chinese SAM

	Activities	Commodities	Labor	Capital	Households	Enterprises	Government	Labor value-added tax	Capital value-added tax	Production tax	Tariffs	Rest of World	Investment	Total
Activities		Domestic output												Activity income
Commodities (i=2)	Inter-mediate inputs				Household consumption		Government consumption					Exports	Fixed capital formation	Total demand
Labor	Labor remuneration													Labor earnings
Capital	Capital return													Capital earnings
Households			Labor income	Capital income		Transfers to households	Transfers to households					Transfers to Households		Household income
Enterprises				Capital income			Transfers to enterprises							Enterprise earnings
Government					Income tax	Indirect tax		Labor value-added tax	Capital value-added tax	Production tax	Tariffs		Transfers to government	Government income
Labor value-added tax	Labor value-added tax													Labor value-added tax
Capital value-added tax	Capital value-added tax													Capital value-added tax
Production tax	Production tax													Production tax
Tariffs		Tariffs												Tariffs
Rest of the World		Imports					transfers to rest of world							Foreign exchange outflow
Savings					Household savings	Enterprise savings	Government savings					Foreign savings		Total Savings
Total	Gross output	Total supply	Labor expenditure	Capital expenditure	Household expenditure	Enterprise expenditure	Government expenditure	Labor value-added tax	Capital value-added tax	Production tax	Tariffs	Foreign exchange inflow	Total Investment	

Source: Fan et. al., 2010

As required by the "standard" CGE modelling, this SAM makes a distinction between "activities" (i.e., the production-related entities) and "commodities" (representing markets for goods and non-factor services). SAM flows are valued at producers' prices in the activity accounts, whereas they are evaluated at market prices in the commodity accounts. The commodities include exports and domestic sales of activity outputs and imports. In the activity columns, payments are made to commodities (intermediate demand) and production factors (labour remuneration and capital return) and various activity taxes (value-added tax, production tax and production tax). In the commodities columns, payments are made to domestic output, the rest of the world (imports) and tariffs. The information needed to represent imports as perfect or insufficient substitutes for domestic production is provided by this treatment.

The government is disaggregated into a core government account and some tax accounts (value-added tax, production tax and tariffs). This disaggregation is frequently required because the economic meaning of some payments could otherwise be unclear. Payments made between the government and other non-government institutions in the SAM are used for transfers. Government consumption demand is a purchase of the output from the government services activity. Non-government institutions in the SAM are households, enterprises and the rest of the world. Both households and enterprises earn income from the production factors and transfers from other institutions. Households pay their income for their consumption of commodities, taxes and savings. Enterprises do not consume but allocate their income to direct taxes, transfers to other institutions and savings. The rest of the world accounts record the flow of foreign exchange through the commodity trade, transfers between domestic markets, institutions and the rest of the world, and foreign currency spending and receipts.

Choice of Base Year and SAM Accounts Disaggregation

Since SAM could be regarded as an extension of the Input-Output (I-O) matrix, the availability of the authoritative I-O Table is critical to the SAM construction. The Chinese government has released I-O Table every five years since 1987. The latest I-O Table was I-O Table 2017. As found in chapter four, most TAPPs were issued during the target and efficient TAP period (2013-2020) when tourism became a major pro-poor tool. Therefore, it's feasible and reasonable to choose 2017 as the base year for this SAM for the CGE analysis of TAPPs' impacts on poverty alleviation in China.

As this chapter strives to explore the distributional effects of Chinese tourism on income of the poor under TAPPs, 142 sectors from the IO Table 2017 are aggregated into tourism and non-tourism categories in line with the Statistical Classification of National Tourism and Related Industries (2018) and the Chinese National Tourism Sampling Survey 2018. The tourism category includes nine aggregated sectors (Table 4-8), while the non-tourism category includes 33 aggregated sectors from the IO Table. Besides, the household is disaggregated into urban household groups of three income levels and rural household groups of three income levels (Table 4-8) according to the China Statistical Yearbook 2018 to identify poor households. Household groups' expenditure on tourism and non-tourism activities is split into nine aggregated tourism sectors from IO Table based on the 2018 Chinese National Tourism Sampling Survey. After the disaggregation of activities, commodities and households accounts, the number of accounts increases from 14 in the basic structure of Chinese SAM to 21 in the disaggregated SAM for the Chinese TAP CGE model (Table 4-8).

Table 4-8 Aggregated tourism sectors and disaggregated household groups

Tourism Sectors	Wholesale and Retailing	Transport, Warehouse and Postal Services	Accommodation and Catering	Culture, Sports and Entertainment	Finance	
	Leasing and Business Services	Water Conservancy, Environment and Public Facilities Management	Resident Services, Repairs, and Other Services	Information Transmission, Software and Information Technology Services		
Household Groups	Urban Low Income Househo	Urban Medium Income Household	Urban High Income Household (HHU3,	Rural Low Income Household (HHR1,	Rural Medium Income Househo	Rural High Income Househo

ld (HHU1, 20%)	(HHU2, 60%)	20%)	20%)	ld (HHR2, 60%)	ld (HHR3, 20%)

Source: Chinese National Statistics Bureau. 2018. Statistical Classification of National Tourism and Related Industries, http://www.gov.cn/zhengce/zhengceku/2018-12/31/content_5427567.htm

SAM Data Source and Balancing

The quality of the SAM data depends on the uniformity of the data source. As the extended version of the I-O Table, Chinese SAM adds the information of institutions involving other diversified statistics sources, including the statistical yearbook, the capital flow statement, the balance of international payments, the tax yearbook, the finance yearbook and the customs statistics yearbook etc. For the components of each account, there are occasionally more than one data source. In this case, we tend to choose the source used most frequently during compilation. For example, when production tax data is available in the I-O Table and the tax yearbook, we prefer the former, which has the most sources for data in the SAM. The justification for this treatment is that the SAM could not be balanced due to the diversity of data sources differing in sampling, statistical calibre, etc. So this chapter relies on the most frequently-used data source for components with diversified data sources. Table 4-9 shows the main data sources for each account.

Table 4-9 Data source for the initial Chinese SAM 2017 compilation

Row	**Column**	**Account**	**Data source**	**Base amount (100 mln RMB)**
Activities	Commodity	Domestic output	I-O Table 2017	2257734
Commodities	Activities	Inter-mediate inputs	I-O Table 2017	1434518
	Households	Household consumption	I-O Table 2017	320427
	Government	Government	China Finance	130755

Row	Column	Account	Data source	Base amount (100 mln RMB)
		consumption	Yearbook 2018	
	Rest of World	Exports	I-O Table 2017	163846
	Investment	Fixed capital formation	I-O Table 2017	367459
Labor	Activities	Labor remuneration	I-O Table 2017	423268
Capital	Activities	Capital return	Capital Flow Statement, Balance of International Payments 2017	304969
Households	Labor	Labor income	I-O Table 2017	423268
	Capital	Capital income	Capital Flow Statement, Balance of International Payments 2017	29289
	Enterprises	Transfers to households	Balance of the Household Column	34265
	Government	Transfers to households	China Finance Yearbook 2018	28139
	Rest of the World	Transfers to households	Balance of International Payments 2017	64395
Enterprises	Capital	Capital income	Capital Flow Statement, Balance of International Payments 2017	275572

Row	Column	Account	Data source	Base amount (100 mln RMB)
	Government	Transfers to enterprises	China Finance Yearbook 2018	13870
Government	Households	Income tax	China Finance Yearbook 2018	11966
	Enterprises	Indirect tax	China Finance Yearbook 2018	38795
	Labor value-added tax	Labor value-added tax	China Tax Yearbook 2018	32768
	Capital value-added tax	Capital value-added tax	China Tax Yearbook 2018	23609
	Production tax	Production tax	I-O Table 2017	38600
	Tariffs	Tariffs	China Finance Yearbook 2018	2998
	Rest of world	Transfers to government	Balance of International Payments 2017	69605
Labor value-added tax	Activities	Labor value-added tax	China Tax Yearbook 2018	32768
Capital value-added tax	Activities	Capital value-added tax	China Tax Yearbook 2018	23609
Production tax	Activities	Production tax	I-O Table 2017	38600
Tariffs	Commodities	Tariffs	China Finance Yearbook 2018	2998
Rest of the World	Commodities	Imports	I-O Table 2017	149268

Row	**Column**	**Account**	**Data source**	**Base amount (100 mln RMB)**
	Government	transfers to rest of world	China Finance Yearbook 2018	204
Savings	Households	Household savings	Capital Flow Statement	178603
	Enterprises	Enterprise savings	Balance of the Enterprise Column	265991
	Government	Government savings	Balance of the Government Column	45374
	Rest of world	Foreign savings	Balance of the ROW Column	-122509

The data in Table 4-9 could be combined into an initial SAM after being summarized, as shown in Table 4-10 below, which is the foundation for the data of the disaggregated SAM for the Chinese TAP CGE model. Some accounts of the initial SAM are not balanced due to the diversity of data sources. The disaggregated SAM from the initial SAM will be inevitably unbalanced. As required by the CGE modelling, balancing the SAM is a crucial and challenging step in the process of SAM compilation. The RAS and cross-entropy (CE) methods are the most commonly used to balance the matrix.

Table 4-10 Results of unbalanced initial Chinese SAM 2017 compilation

	Activities	Commodities	Labor	Capital	Households	Enterprises	Government	Labor value-added tax	Capital value-added tax	Production tax	Tariffs	Rest of World	Investment	Total
Activities		2257734												2257734
Commodities (i=2)	1434518				320427		130755					163846	367459	2417005
Labor	423268													423268
Capital	304969													304969
Households			423268	29289		34265	28139					64395		579356
Enterprises				275672			13870							289442
Government					11966	38795		32768	23609	38600	2998		69605	218342
Labor value-added tax	32768													32768
Capital value-added tax	23609													23609
Production tax	38600													38600
Tariffs		2998												2998
Rest of the World		149268					204							149472
Savings					178603	265991	45374					-122509		367459
Total	2257734	2410000	423268	304861	510996	339051	218342	32768	23609	38600	2998	105732	437064	

The RAS or bi-proportional method, a well-known method for data reconciliation designed by Stone (1961), Stone and Brown (1962) and extensively tested by Bacharach (1970). This method updates or balances a single matrix, such as the I-O Table or SAM, to conform to new row and column totals. The RAS approach is extensively used in the SAM balancing or updating process. If the row and column sums of the new matrix A1 are known, the base matrix A0 is multiplied to the left and right by the row multiplier r and the column multiplier s, respectively, to generate the new matrix A1 with the same dimension (n*n) as A0. Under the constraints of 2n-1 independent row and column directions, the 2n-1 unknown row multipliers and column multipliers could be produced through a series of iterative adjustments. The method was devised in a period when powerful computers were not available. It is very easy to apply and to understand when a solution exists. However, it has a narrower scope of applicability due to its disadvantages: Mathematically, RAS is an iterative scaling method. Therefore, it's criticized for lacking theoretical foundations. Besides, this method could not, or could not easily, accommodate information other than row and column totals (for example, we could not set constraints on subtotals other than a row or column totals) (Lemelin et. al., 2013).

The cross-entropy method (CE) is a more flexible approach to balancing SAM than RAS. Entropy is a concept from mechanical physics that was reinterpreted by Shannon (1948) in the information theory and applied to the problem of estimation and statistical inference. Theil (1967) introduced the technique to economics. Golan, Judge and Miller (1996) further extended this technique in econometric research. CE measures the one-way divergence of a posterior probability distribution (the adjusted matrix) from a prior distribution (the unadjusted matrix). The base matrix is adjusted to its marginal totals (and, as applicable, to additional restrictions) to minimise that divergence as part of the least cross-entropy adjustment procedure. The minimal cross-entropy criterion is also known as the least information-gain principle because this method is interpreted in information theory as reducing the amount of unnecessary information imposed upon the a priori matrix to meet the marginal totals. Sherman Robinson and colleagues at the IFPRI created a cross-entropy SAM balancing approach (Robinson, Cattaneo, & El-Said, 1998; Robinson & El-Said, 2000). Chinese SAM and CGE scholars Wang, Li and Gao

(2008) complied with the CE codes for balancing the Chinese SAM in GAMS.

This study chooses the more flexible CE method to balance the disaggregated Chinese SAM 2017 to fit the Chinese TAP CGE model running in GAMS. Table 4-11 shows the balanced SAM for the Chinese TAP CGE model

Table 4-11 Balanced disaggregated Chinese SAM 2017 for Chinese TAP CGE model

	AT	ANT	CT	CNT	L	K	HHU1	HHU2	HHU3	HHR1	HHR2	HHR3	ENT	GOV	TVAL	TVAK	TA	TM	ROW	INSAV	TOT
AT			495340																		495340
ANT				1713468																	1713468
CT	52143	240337					5494	44123	32869	644	7751	6509		13868					23117	91029	517884
CNT	193420	891506					12490	100322	74733	2380	28620	24035		75193					132194	312027	1846919
L	122094	281567																			403661
K	94840	218714																			313553
HHU1					21321	1369							1513	919					2924		50735
HHU2					171249	10992							12152	7383					23485		407501
HHU3					127569	8188							9052	5500					17495		303562
HHR1					3614	231							256	156					495		8597
HHR2					43433	2788							3082	1872					5956		103352
HHR3					36475	2341							2588	1573					4002		86796
ENT						287644								10118							297762
GOV							991	7960	5930	171	2045	1718	51708		39352	28354	46481	3547	-46374		141882
TVAL	10918	28434																			39352
TVAK	7867	20487																			28354
TA	14049	32422																			46481
TM			412	3035																	3547
ROW			22032	130417										0							152449
INSAV							9071	72856	54272	1557	18717	15718	217410	25299					-11844		403056
TOT	495340	1713468	517884	1846919	403661	313553	457615	225261	167805	4752	57132	47979	297762	141882	39352	28354	46481	3547	152449	403056	

Notes: AT=tourism activities; ANT=Non-tourism activities; CT=tourism commodities; CNT=non-tourism commodities; L=labor; K=capital; HHU1=urban low income households; HHU2=urban medium income households; HHU3=urban high income households; HHR1=rural low income households; HHR2=rural medium households; HHR3=rural high income households; ENT=enterprises; GOV=government; TVAL=labor value-added tax; TVAK=capital value-added tax; TA= production tax; TM=import tax; ROW=rest of world; INSAV=investment-savings.

4.6.4 Parameters for Chinese Tourism-assisting the Poor (TAP) Computable General Equilibrium (CGE) Model

The parameters to implement the Chinese TAP CGE model are mainly share parameters and elasticity parameters. Share parameters could be calculated from SAM, such as share of household income in consumption expenditure on tourism and non-tourism commodities, the share of consumption expenditure on the commodities in government revenue, income tax rates of household and enterprise, production tax rate, import tax rate, household marginal propensity to consume, the share of inbound tourism in exports, the share of household labour supply, the share of household capital supply and share of enterprise capital supply etc. Elasticity parameters are obtained from some typical CGE studies with Chinese data. There are five groups of elasticity parameters in this model, including the elasticity of substitution between the value-added and intermediate inputs, the elasticity of substitution between primary factors, the Armington elasticity and the constant elasticity of transformation (CET) in import and export trade and the elasticity parameter of household disposable income for tourism demand (Table 4-12). They are available from Zhai and Hertel (2004), Tian (2020), Ye (2014) and Yuan (2010). A robustness check of the model will be made by adjusting some of these parameters.

Table 4-12 Main elasticity parameters for Chinese TAP CGE model implementation

Category	VA-INTA	K-L	Armington elasticity	CET elasticity	DIH-QHTA elasticity
AT	-0.56	0.40			
ANT	-0.67	0.02			
CT			0.47	1.20	
CNT			0.64	1.10	
HHU1					0.47
HHU2					0.47
HHU3					0.47
HHR1					1.76
HHR2					1.76
HHR3					1.76

Notes: AT=tourism activities; ANT=Non-tourism activities; CT=tourism commodities; CNT=non-tourism commodities; HHU1=urban low income households; HHU2=urban medium income households; HHU3=urban high income households; HHR1=rural low income households; HHR2=rural medium households; HHR3=rural high income households.

Simulations and Results

In the Chinese TAP targeted and efficient period (2013-2020) when tourism is one of main poverty alleviation means Chinese TAPPs intensify the construction of tourism projects, especially in rural areas, pulling TAP initiative's precise poverty alleviation effect (Guo, 2020). The development of rural tourism projects satisfies the diversified tourists' demands in the period of Chinese quality tourism (since 2011). According to the China Tourism Yearbook statistics, the year-on-year increase rates of tourism investment and Chinese domestic tourism annual revenue during 2013-2019 averaged more than 20% and about 14%, respectively, with only about 4% increase in inbound tourism. In the "14th Five-Year" Tourism Development Plan (2021-2024) issued by the China Ministry of Tourism and Culture, the government has decided to attract and channel more investments in tourism projects to improve the tourism supply system to expand mass tourist consumption.

This study simulates the effects of a 20% increase in domestic tourist consumption (scenario 1), a 5% increase in inbound tourist consumption (scenario 2) and a 20% increase in tourism investment (scenario 3). The macroeconomic and distributional results, as well as sectoral aggregates from these three simulations, will be analyzed and compared to find out how tourism channel net benefits to the poor under Chinese TAPPs.

Macroeconomic Results

The macroeconomic results of the three simulations clearly show that the increases in domestic tourism expenditure, inbound tourism expenditure and tourism investment are positive for the growth of China's GDP. However, their shocks on households, enterprise, government and the rest of the world are different, facing the challenge of excessive supply and shortage of demand by choice of "Keynesian closure".

An increase of 20% in domestic tourism expenditure induces GDP growth of 0.0430% and creates more benefits to enterprises than households. As is shown in Table 4-13, in scenario 1, households have to reduce their savings and expenditure on non-tourism commodities to meet their 20% increase in domestic tourism expenditure. Though tourism demand for labour increases by 0.1766% with the expansion of domestic tourism demand, the overall wage of labour declines by 0.0017% due to the reductions of household non-tourism expenditure by 0.0501% and household non-tourism demand for labour by 2.7367%. Therefore, household revenue drops by 0.1048% despite more employment opportunities in the tourism sector. The export and import inevitably decline with vast resources attracted to the tourism sector to satisfy the increasing demand of domestic tourists and the rise of tourism commodity prices. The decrease in household revenue and increase in domestic tourism expenditure further tighten outbound tourism expenditure.

However, the increase of household domestic tourism expenditure and lower production cost induces higher growth of enterprise revenue and saving. This indicates that enterprises are China's main tourism commodity producers and suppliers. Investment also rises by 0.2262% to satisfy the increase in tourism demand. In order to stimulate tourism consumption and investment, the government should implement preferential tax policies, increase transfers to households and enterprises or invest more in public services and infrastructure facilities. These measures result in a decrease in government revenue and government saving but an increase in government expenditure.

In scenario 2, a 5% of inbound tourism expenditure creates positive effects on GDP, households and investment but negatively affects enterprises, governments and imports. The expansion of inbound tourism, which contributes to 0.0168% growth of real GDP, directly generates a 0.0007% rise in tourism demand for labour and induces the rise of labour wage by 0.0034%. The increase in labour wage and employment opportunities bring about 0.0022% growth of household revenue, resulting in the rise of household tourism expenditure and household non-tourism expenditure by 0.0334% and 0.0077%, separately. However, enterprise revenue falls by 0.0225% due to the rise in labour costs, leading to a decrease in government revenue by 0.0108%. On the other hand, more investment to meet the increasing demand of inbound tourism is mainly provided by enterprise, government and households whose savings decline by 0.0247%, 0.0140% and 0.0222%. Non-tourism imports and export shrink mainly due to the higher labour cost, while the fall in outbound tourism expenditure could be attributed to the increase in household spending on tourism, non-tourism and investment.

In scenario 3, a 20% rise in tourism investment generates the highest growth rates in GDP and household revenue among the three simulations as it raises labour demand in both tourism and non-tourism sectors in spite of a relatively slight drop in labour wage. Households, enterprises, and government reduce their savings or expenditure to finance the investment demand. Household revenue increase stimulates household tourism and non-tourism expenditure growth by 0.0105% and 0.0374%. Enterprise revenue and savings see notable declines of 0.2346% and 0.0001% due to the relatively lower household consumption and higher investment growth rates. Government revenue and saving decreases by 0.1207% and 0.0143% due to less revenue from enterprises and more expenditure on investment. The drop in inbound tourism and non-tourism exports could be an additional factor for the revenue decline of government and enterprises. The imports and exports go down as households and enterprises spend more money on domestic tourism consumption and investment, which further lead to the rise of tourism and non-tourism commodity prices.

The macroeconomic analysis reveals that household revenue declines despite the growth of domestic tourism consumption, which raises tourism demand for labour, enterprise revenue and investment but lowers labour wage and labour demand in non-tourism sectors. Household income increases with the growth of inbound tourism and investment. An inbound tourism boost leads to an increase in labour wage and labour demand, while investment growth increases tourism and non-tourism labour demand through labour wage drops slightly. Nevertheless, the changes in aggregate household revenue couldn't reflect whether tourism growth or investment under Chinese TAPPs is pro-poor or not. Therefore, the next section further investigates how changes in tourism and non-tourism consumption, social benefits, income and saving are distributed across different household income groups.

Table 4-13 Changes of macroeconomic results

Macro-variables	**base amount (bln USD; %)**	**Scenario 1 (%)**	**Scenario 2 (%)**	**Scenario 3 (%)**
GDP	12646.6112	0.0430	0.0168	0.0692
household revenue	6846.5506	-0.1048	0.0022	0.0043
household tourism expenditure	691.3767	20	0.0334	0.0105
Household non tourism expenditure	4156.2329	-0.0501	0.0077	0.0374
household saving	2702.0121	-0.2496	-0.0222	-0.1860
enterprise revenue	1264.3268	0.3478	-0.0225	-0.2346
enterprise saving	4024.0696	0.3816	-0.0247	-0.0001
government revenue	1264.3278	-0.1553	-0.0108	-0.1207
government expenditure	1978.1392	0.0713	0.0062	-0.0619
government saving	632.9501	-0.1346	-0.0140	-0.0143
investment	5559.1377	0.2262	0.0216	20
tourism demand for labor	100	0.1766	0.0007	0.2012
Non-tourism demand for labor	100	-2.7367	-0.0042	0.0161
wage of labor	100	-0.0017	0.0034	-0.0199
Price of tourism commodities	100	0.3109	0.0003	0.1178
Price of non-tourism commodities	100	-0.3025	-0.0001	0.2394
Inbound tourism expenditure	126.2003	-1.1435	5	-1.0404
Non-tourism export	2352.5592	-1.0746	-0.0351	-2.2420
Outbound tourism expenditure	285	-0.1146	-0.0017	-0.0112
Non-tourism import	1973.2148	-0.0068	-1.9463	-0.0006

Sectoral Aggregates

As analyzed previously, a nation's economic system has direct and indirect linkages between tourism and other sectors. The change in one sector has direct and indirect impacts on other sectors. Figure 4.10 depicts the changes in supply, factor demand and imports induced by the growth of domestic tourism expenditure, inbound tourism expenditure and investment in three scenarios.

Figure 4.10 (a) reveals that tourism development boosts the growth of tourism and non-tourism commodity supplies, except for the drop in non-tourism commodity supplies in scenario 1. According to Figure 4.10 (b), the tourism sector generally takes the highest rise in labour demand (QLD) and capital demand (QKD). QLD and QKD in tourism sector of scenario 1 both witness a relatively higher rise by about 0.18%, producing the greatest growth of tourism commodity quantity by 10.48% in scenario 1. The non-tourism supplies in this scenario experience a drop of 14.46% due to the flow of labour and capital to the tourism sector. Both tourism and non-tourism commodity supplies in scenario 2 and scenario 3 enjoy increases. It's obvious that tourism investment growth in scenario 3 creates more job opportunities in the tourism sector and provides more funds for non-tourism commodity output, balancing the allocation of labour and capital between tourism and non-tourism sectors. Figure 4.10 (c) shows that imports in tourism or non-tourism sectors in three simulations fall, indicating that tourism development in China stimulates the expansion of domestic-oriented industries. The deduction of imports also facilitates the realization of trade surplus and economic recovery amid the economic recession by choice of "Keynesian closure".

Figure 4.10 (a) Figure 4.10 (b) Figure 4.10 (c)

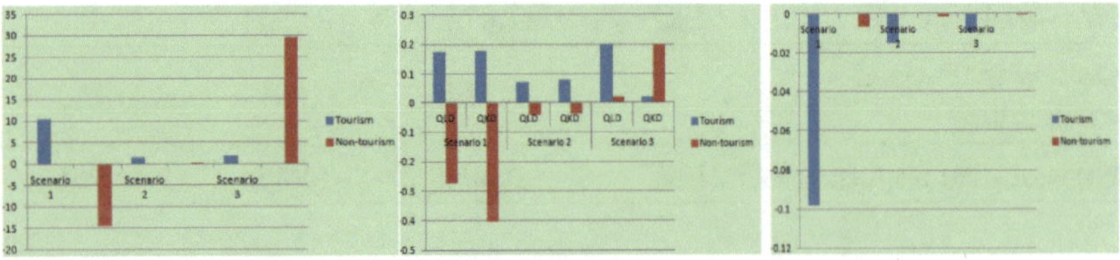

Figure 4-10 Changes of supply, factor demand and imports in tourism and non-tourism sectors

Distributional Results

Rural areas inhabit the largest poverty-stricken population in China because the rural–urban dualism has resulted in the large income gap between rural and urban households since the founding of the People's Republic of China. In 2020 when the Chinese government has eradicated absolute poverty nationwide; the income ratio between urban and rural residents was reduced to 2.56, still largely higher than that of the OECD (Organization for Economic Co-operation and Development) member countries such as the USA, whose average ratio is below 1.25. Considering the urban-rural income gap, this study identifies poor households as rural low-income households (HHR1). The distributional effects of tourism expenditure and investment growth under Chinese TAPPs are assessed in terms of whether they could contribute to a relatively greater increase rate of income, positive effects on social welfare for the poor households and a narrower urban-rural income gap.

The simulation results in Table 4-14 generally show that the poor households could benefit from both tourism growth and investment in China. The growth of domestic and inbound tourism in scenario 1 and scenario 2 generates positive social welfare for rural low-income households (HHR1) though reducing their income growth rate. The increase of tourism investment in scenario 3 induces the highest income growth rate in HHR1 but negatively affects poor households' social benefits. Among the three simulations, the urban-rural income gap ratio reaches the lowest level in scenario 3. The impacts of these three shocks on other indicators and income household groups are also different.

The aggregate domestic tourism expenditure increase in scenario 1 is not distributed evenly among households, leading to the household groups' different consumption demands for tourism and non-tourism commodities. It could be seen from Table 4-14 that the increase in tourism demand is mainly from urban households instead of rural households. In China, labour is the main source of rural households' income. The decrease in labour wages and non-tourism labour demand forces rural households to reduce their tourism demand and increase their non-tourism demand, especially for basic necessities, due to the rise of tourism demand in the recession of the economy. HHR1 achieves the highest increase in non-tourism consumption by 0.421% and enjoys a rise in social benefits by 0.0596%. The increased social welfare could be resulted from the reduction of non-tourism commodity prices by 0.3025%, as is shown in Table 4-13. On the contrary, the social welfare of urban households shrinks as they increase tourism demand at 0.3109% higher price and reduce their non-tourism consumption at 0.3025% lower price.

Despite the social welfare shrinks, urban household groups' income drop rate is much lower than rural household groups. Besides, HHU1 (urban low-income household) even realizes only a 0.0009% income increase among the six household groups. This increase might be generated from the tourism labour demand expansion, which indicates that HHU1 is more involved in the tourism industry than other groups, especially HHR1. The rise of HHU1 saving implies that urban low-income household relies more on labour rather than capital to increase their income as they spend less on investment than HHU2 and HHU3, whose savings are reduced significantly to meet investment demand growth. The decrease of rural household savings could be mainly attributed to the negative growth of their income and growing spending on non-tourism commodities.

The inbound tourism expansion in scenario 2 is effective in improving household groups' income except for HHR1, whose income growth drops by 2.617%, further echoing the conclusion that HHR1 could be the least involved in the tourism industry in scenario 1. It's also obvious that urban households' average income growth rate is much higher than rural households. This is the reason why the urban-rural income gap in this scenario hits the highest ratio of 7.38 among the three simulations. Since most household groups earn more revenue from inbound tourism growth, they could have extra spending on tourism demand. According to Table 4-14, all household groups but HHR1 increase their tourism consumption, causing the rise of tourism commodity prices by 0.003% (Table 4-13). As is the case in scenario 1, the changes in tourism and non-tourism commodity prices in relation to income growth and varied consumption demands affect household groups' social benefits. Because of the rising tourism commodity price and decreasing non-tourism commodity price, HHR1 obtain more benefits from their reduction in tourism demand and increase in non-tourism demand though their income growth declines. In addition, the rise of labour wages owing to the growing tourism demand for labour (Table 4-13) and the improvement of social benefits for the poor households bring positive growth of HHR1's saving while other household groups' savings see negative growth as they increase their spending on tourism consumption and investment.

Different from tourism expenditure simulation scenarios, investment growth in scenario 3 significantly increases rural household groups' income and savings but lowers income growth of urban household groups. This effect contributes directly to the narrowest urban-rural income gap at the ratio of 2.27, closest to the real income gap ratio of 2.56 in 2020. More earnings from investment growth stimulate rural households to increase expenditure on tourism and non-tourism consumption as well as savings, leading to the growth of aggregate household tourism and non-tourism spending by 0.0105% and 0.0374% (Table 4-13). However, the rise of tourism and non-tourism commodity prices due to the household consumption expansion reduces most household groups' social benefits, including all rural household groups.

Among all household groups, the poor HHR1 gains most from the investment shock with their income and saving scoring the highest growth rate by 0.1715% and 0.2640% despite the relatively low drop of social benefits by 0.081%. This result could more accurately prove TAPPs' significant positive impacts on the distributional benefits of the poor through tourism and its related investment growth. Since the initiation of target poverty alleviation in 2013, Chinese TAPPs have intensified tourism project investment and construction, especially in poverty-stricken rural areas. The "China Rural Poverty Alleviation and Development Program (2011-2020)" listed rural TAP as one of the ten key poverty alleviation and development tasks in the new period. The Chinese central government issued more than ten special TAPPs documents, such as the "Rural TAP Project Action Plan", where rural TAP project investment and construction were prioritized to improve the rural inhabitation environment and expand income channels for rural residents.

In 2019, the China Ministry of Culture and Tourism (CMCT) and the China National Development and Reform Commission (CNDRC) deepened the implementation of the rural TAP investments. They launched the first batch of 320 national rural tourism key villages and approved the construction of tourism infrastructure in deeply impoverished areas through 329 investment projects within the central government's budget. As the poor HHR1 are precisely identified and documented by local governments, they are privileged to get the job opportunities created by TAP investment projects. As many rural residents are migrant workers with rich experience in Chinese urban construction, they have stronger capabilities in participating in TAP project implementation. Besides the employment earnings, they could also benefit from other income channels such as land circulation revenue and TAP project operation bonus.

Table 4-14 Key distributional and income gap results (percentages)

Household indicators / **Household tourism consumption**	**Scenario 1**	**Scenario 2**	**Scenario 3**
HHU1	0.6447	0.3969	-0.0457
HHU2	0.6288	7.2291	-0.0366
HHU3	0.6362	5.1105	0.0582
HHR1	-5.3401	-0.2729	0.1335
HHR2	-3.6517	0.9894	0.0149
HHR3	-3.1054	1.0815	0.0199
Household non-tourism consumption			
HHU1	-0.0640	-0.0035	-0.0412
HHU2	-0.0368	0.4967	0.0703
HHU3	-0.0795	0.0062	0.0796
HHR1	0.4210	0.0233	0.4172
HHR2	0.3610	-0.1532	0.1215
HHR3	0.0330	-0.1000	0.1891
CV			
HHU1	-0.1735	-0.0020	0.0056
HHU2	-0.2031	-0.0025	-0.0073
HHU3	-0.2159	-0.0022	-0.0087
HHR1	0.0596	0.0031	-0.0810

Household indicators / **Household tourism consumption**	**Scenario 1**	**Scenario 2**	**Scenario 3**
HHR2	0.0753	-0.0010	-0.1257
HHR3	0.0484	-0.0013	-0.1070
Household income			
HHU1	0.0009	0.7145	-0.0273
HHU2	-0.0012	7.0700	-0.0026
HHU3	-0.0595	4.3532	-0.0391
HHR1	-0.0278	-2.6170	0.1715
HHR2	-0.0227	1.1048	0.1156
HHR3	-0.0207	0.4551	0.1022
Household saving			
HHU1	0.1723	-0.1955	-0.2287
HHU2	-0.2142	-0.2824	-0.2807
HHU3	-0.1524	-0.3196	-0.3139
HHR1	-3.4483	0.0014	0.2640
HHR2	-0.9003	-0.0004	0.1190
HHR3	-0.9679	-0.0001	0.0165
Urban-rural income gap	479	738	227

Notes: HHU1=urban low income households; HHU2=urban medium income households; HHU3=urban high income households; HHR1=rural low income households; HHR2=rural medium households; HHR3=rural high income households; CV=compensate variance.

Sensitivity Test

The robustness of the CGE model is the prerequisite for its accurate simulation results. One of the most commonly-used sensitivity test methods is to evaluate the robustness of the model by changing the exogenous parameters (Meng et. al., 2013, Tian, 2020). Implementing the Chinese TAP CGE model mainly uses share and elasticity parameters. Share parameters are calculated from SAM, while elasticity parameters are set exogenously based on some typical CGE studies with Chinese data. It's necessary to test whether changes in these elasticity parameters could affect the robustness of this model.

In this section, we choose to randomly change five groups of elasticity parameters in the test model. For example, the substitution elasticity parameters of the value-added and intermediate inputs are reset to 0.84 for the tourism sector and 0.8 for the non-tourism sector in the test model, 0.2 higher than those in the original model. The substitution elasticity parameters of primary factors change from 1.67 to 1.77 for tourism sector and from 1.02 to 1.12 for non-tourism sector. Table 4-15 shows the comparison between simulation results of the macroeconomic variables in the original and test models. The average deviation of macroeconomic results between the test model and the original model is below 0.0001, with many results in the two models almost the same such as GDP, household revenue, and household tourism expenditure. It's easily concluded that changing the exogenous parameters has little impact on the original model, proving the robustness of the Chinese TAP CGE model.

Table 4-15 Comparison of macroeconomic results between original model and sensitivity test model

Macro-variables	**Scenario 1**		**Scenario 2**		**Scenario 3**	
	Original Model	**Test model**	**Original model**	**Test model**	**Original model**	**Test model**
GDP	0.0430	0.0430	0.0168	0.0169	0.0692	0.0692
Household Revenue	-0.1048	-0.1048	0.0022	0.0022	0.0043	0.0043
Household Tourism Expenditure	20	20	0.0334	0.0334	0.0105	0.0105
Household Non Tourism Expenditure	-0.0501	-0.0501	0.0077	0.0302	0.0374	0.0374
Household Saving	-0.2496	-0.2496	-0.0222	-0.0222	-0.1860	-0.1860
Enterprise Revenue	0.3478	0.3478	-0.0225	-0.0223	-0.2346	-0.2346
Enterprise	0.3816	0.3816	-0.0247	-0.0244	-0.0001	-0.0001

Macro-variables	Scenario 1		Scenario 2		Scenario 3	
	Original Model	Test model	Original model	Test model	Original model	Test model
Saving						
Government Revenue	-0.1553	-0.1554	-0.0108	-0.0108	-0.1207	-0.1207
Government Expenditure	0.0713	0.0713	0.0062	0.0062	-0.0619	-0.0619
Government Saving	-0.1346	-0.1346	-0.0140	-0.0140	-0.0143	-0.0144
Investment	0.2262	0.2262	0.0216	0.0216	20	20
Tourism Demand for Labor	0.1766	0.1766	0.0007	0.0007	0.2012	0.2012
Non-Tourism Demand for Labor	-2.7367	-2.7367	-0.0042	-0.0043	0.0161	0.0161
Wage of Labor	-0.0017	-0.0017	0.0034	0.0034	-0.0199	-0.0199
Price of Tourism Commodities	0.3109	0.3109	0.0003	0.0001	0.1178	0.1178
Price of Non-Tourism Commodities	-0.3025	-0.3025	-0.0001	-0.0007	0.2394	0.2394
Inbound Tourism Expenditure	-1.1435	-1.1435	5	5	-1.0404	-1.0404
Non-Tourism Export	-1.0746	-1.0746	-0.0351	-0.0341	-2.2420	-2.2420
Outbound Tourism Expenditure	-0.1146	-0.0758	-0.0017	-0.0017	-0.0112	-0.0739
Non-Tourism Import	-0.0068	-0.0451	-1.9463	-1.9461	-0.0006	-0.0037

Conclusion

This chapter has reported the findings obtained from the content analysis of TAPPs documents and the CGE analysis of TAPPs' impacts on the income distribution to the poor through tourism development. The content analysis identified the sustainability values, policy targets and policy instruments contained in the TAPPs documents. TAPPs sustainability value orientations in different TAP stages are dominated by the economic values or social and cultural values. The environmental values remain their lowest proportion among the three value dimensions but experience a linear growth during the four TAP stages. Based on the number of reference points for value items under each value dimension, the study found a balanced distribution of social and cultural values and economic values. Economic values emphasize poverty eradication and economic stimulation, while social and cultural values highlight public service and participation. The growing environmental values stress environmental protection and the improvement of human habitat.

Different TAP stages have different TAP targets, including exploring the TAP model (1984-1996), promoting sustainable regional TAP (1997-2004), initiating sustainable rural TAP (2005-2012) and implementing sustainable TAP projects precisely (since 2013). Based on Rothwell's taxonomy of policy tools, this study classified policy tools contained in TAPPs as supply-side tools, demand-side tools and environmental tools. It's found that more environmental tools were used in the early exploration TAP stage; supply-side tools were increased in the TAP initial development period; the TAP rapid development stage saw the balanced use of supply and environmental tools; and project development tool was used to pull the precise effect of TAPPs in the targeted and efficient TAP stage.

As China's fulfillment of SDG1 is mainly measured by the income poverty line, TAPPs sustainability values are dominated by the economic sustainability in the TAP targeted and efficient period with the implementation of sustainable TAP projects as the policy goal. The policy instrument of rural TAP project development was used as a leading policy instrument by the Chinese government to increase rural poor residents' income to get rid of poverty. Therefore, the CGE method is used to investigate how Chinese tourism development under TAPPs affects income distribution to the poor.

The CGE investigation reveals that Chinese tourism development could contribute to poverty alleviation and equality improvement under the guidance of TAPPs. The CGE simulations show that the stimuli of tourism expenditure could improve the welfare of the poor households though their income growth rate decreases due to their less participation in tourism activities than the non-poor household groups. The TAP projects development-led investment expansion significantly increases the poor households' income as they are privileged to obtain more diversified employment opportunities within their capabilities channelled by the TAPPs. The investment expansion has also been proven to narrow the rural-urban income gap, thus playing a positive role in improving equality for poor households.

Besides these direct and secondary impacts of tourism development on poverty alleviation, all these TAPPs measures boost GDP growth from tourism development, promoting tourism's dynamic impacts on poverty relief. However, the CGE analysis in this chapter mainly focuses on tourism's impacts on the economic sustainability of poverty-stricken areas under TAPPs. As analyzed previously, poverty alleviation is a multi-dimensional issue, and TAPPs embraced sustainability values. It's necessary for the next chapter to further investigate TAPPs' contribution to multi-dimensional poverty reduction under the sustainable development paradigm and TAPPs' impacts on the sustainable development of TAP destinations perceived by TAP stakeholders.

Chapter 5
Chinese Tourism's Contribution to Sustainable Development

Introduction

This chapter further reports the results of the case study, which has made an in-depth investigation of Chinese tourism-assisting the poor policies' (TAPPs) impacts on the multi-dimensional poverty alleviation under the sustainable development paradigm and on the sustainable development of TAP destinations perceived by TAP stakeholders. As designed in the research methodology, the sustainable multi-dimensional poverty in Guizhou is evaluated through the quantitative Alkire-Frost Multi-dimensional Poverty Index (AF-MPI). Stakeholders' perceptions of TAPPs' effects on the sustainable development in a typical TAP destination-Zhaoxing Dong Ethnic Village in Guizhou are investigated with semi-structured interviews. Section one of this chapter overviews the measurement of tourism sustainability and multi-dimensional poverty. Section two reports the multi-dimensional poverty analysis under the sustainable development paradigm in Guizhou's TAP study area. Section three presents stakeholders' perceptions of TAPPs' impacts the sustainable development in Zhaoxing Dong Ethnic Village, Guizhou. The last section concludes the case study.

Results of Multi-Dimensional Poverty and Tourism Sustain ability Measurements

As this chapter aims to evaluate TAPPs' impacts on multi-dimensional poverty alleviation and sustainable development in TAP areas quantitatively and qualitatively, it's critical to identify what assessment approaches are most suitable. So this section must have an overview of multi-dimensional poverty and tourism sustainability measurement approaches.

Measurements of Multi-Dimensional Poverty

Sustainability is multi-dimensional and poor people's insufficiency of even basic needs is diversified but not limited to the sole indicator of income (Bourguignon & Chakravarty, 2003). Therefore, the concept and measurement of poverty under the sustainable development paradigm are necessarily multi-dimensional. Poverty was vividly introduced as a multi-faceted phenomenon in the 1997 Human Development Report, the 2000/1 World Development Report, and the Millennium Declaration and MDGs highlighting numerous facets of poverty. How poverty is quantified has a significant impact on the development of policies to address it (Alkire & Foster, 2011). Aligned with MDGs, the global multi-dimensional poverty index (MPI) was jointly developed by the Oxford Poverty and Human Development Initiative (OPHI) and the UNDP's Human Development Report Office (Alkire, Kanagaratnam, & Suppa, 2020). The global MPI explicitly reflects its mission to serve the achievement of various SDGs in 2030 (Table 5-1).

Table 5-1 Global MPI – Dimensions, Indicators and SDGs

Dimension of Poverty	**Indicator**	**SDG Area**
Health	Nutrition	SDG2: zero hunger
	Child mortality	SDG3: health and well-being
Education	Years of schooling	SDG4: quality education
	School attendance	SDG4: quality education
Living standards	Cooking fuel	SDG7: affordable clean energy
	Sanitation	SDG6: clean water and sanitation
	Drinking water	SDG6: clean water and sanitation
	Electricity	SDG7: affordable clean energy
	Housing	SDG11: sustainable cities and communities
	Assets	SDG1: no poverty

Source: Alkire, S., Kanagaratnam, U. & Suppa, N. 2020. The global Multidimensional Poverty Index (MPI): 2020 revision. OPHI MPI Methodological Note 49. Oxford Poverty and Human Development Initiative, University of Oxford.

The measurement of multi-dimensional poverty has been a growing research concern since the pioneering works of Bourguignon and Chakravarty (2003) and Tsui (2002). Sen (1976) proposed two steps of poverty measurement: identifying the poor and aggregating the characteristics of people experiencing poverty into an overall indicator. Following Sen's two general actions, Bourguignon and Chakravarty (2003) piloted the multi-dimensional poverty measurement by extending the Foster Greer and Thorbecke (FGT) class of indices and discussing interrelationships among dimensions. The other pioneer Tsui (2002) argued that counting measures should be more closely related to welfare economics by clicking the burgeoning axiomatic literature on multidimensional poverty measurements to the "counting" literature that had been put into practice in Europe.

After these two signal articles, there emerged various multi-dimensional poverty measurements methods such as Chakravarty, Deutsch, and Silber (2008), Deutsch and Silber (2005), Duclos, Sahn, and Younger (2006), Alkire and Foster (2007, 2011), Maasoumi and Lugo (2008), Alkire and Santos (2010) and Alkire et. al. (2014). Among them, the global Multidimensional Poverty Index (MPI) by Alkire and Santos (2010) based on Alkire-Foster Multi-Dimensional Poverty Measurement Methodology (AF methodology) gained wide popularity as it was included in the UNDP's Human Development Report 2010 for over 100 countries. The popularity of AF methodology worldwide stems from its broad framework for evaluating multidimensional poverty, with many critical decisions left to users. Users could choose from various dimensions, dimensional cut-offs, weights, and poverty cut-offs.

However, Masset and García-Hombrados (2021) argue that the global MPI should be used cautiously in assessing development programs. After comparing the use of MDG indicators and the global MPI in the evaluating-Northern Ghana Millennium Village Project (MVP), the authors found that the project had a limited impact on the MDGs indicators but a substantial impact on the global MPI. This divergence mainly lies in that the global MPI only includes the core indicators of MDGs indicators, making it more sensitive to small changes of deprivations, primarily through the flexible 'dual cut-off' method. However, this conclusion does not advocate avoiding using evaluation or policy analysis; rather, it recommends more testing to see if

MPI indicators could be improved. Vollmer and Alkire (2022) admit that it's a great challenge to design a comparable asset index for MPI when they surprisingly find that few items are available for 75 countries and 3.5 billion people.

Measurements of Tourism Sustainability and Its Policy Impacts

In response to the long-existing debate over measuring sustainability, the UNWTO's Working Group on Measuring Sustainable Tourism was established to implement the International Recommendations for Tourism Statistics that have been issued since 2008 (UNWTO, 2018). Besides, some international organisations or institutes carried out a series of Tourism Sustainability Assessment Initiatives (TSAIs), including UNWTO (Table 5-2).

As seen from Table 5-2, most of these international tourism sustainability assessment initiatives aim to facilitate sustainable tourism policy-making, planning and management by improving policymakers' capacity. The criteria of these initiatives seem to differ significantly, with their focuses evolving from a single dimension, such as the economic sustainability proposed by TSA (2008), IRTS (2008) and UNWTO (2016) and the environmental sustainability dimension by TOUERM (2016) to more complex dimensions including the destination competitiveness-based sustainability dimensions by OECD (2013) and protected area sustainability dimensions by ECST (2010), three pillars sustainability dimensions by ETIS (2016) and GSTC (2017) as well as a broader approach of sustainability dimensions by NECSTouR (2015) and dynamic adjustment of sustainability monitoring indicators to the specific destinations by UNWTI-INSTO (2018). It should also be noted that most of these proposed criteria target local levels, as sustainability is context-sensitive.

Table 5-2 Main Tourism Sustainability Assessment Initiatives (TSAI)

Organizations/ institutes	**Year**	**Target Groups**	**Criteria**	**Focuses**	**Spatial scale**
Tourism Satellite Account—TSA	2008	Policy Makers	(1) Visitors consumption National Data and Indicators (2) Production of	Economic sustainability	National

Organizations/ institutes	Year	Target Groups	Criteria	Focuses	Spatial scale
			goods and services (3) International trade of goods and services (4) Number of jobs		
International Recommendations for Tourism Statistics—IRTS	2008	Policy Makers	(1) Measuring Flows of Visitors National Indicators (2) Measuring the characteristics of visitors and tourism trips (3) Measuring Tourism Expenditure (4) Measuring the supply of services of tourism industries (4) Measuring Employment	Economic sustainability	National
European Charter for Sustainable Tourism in Protected Areas—ECST	2010	Managers of Protected Areas	(1) Partnership with local tourism stakeholders Local Indicators (2) Sustainable tourism strategy and action plan (3) Protecting natural and cultural heritage (4) Meeting visitor needs/quality of experience (4) Communication about the area (6) Tourism	Sustainable management of protected areas	Local

Organizations/ institutes	Year	Target Groups	Criteria	Focuses	Spatial scale
			products relating to the protected area (7) Training (8) Community involvement and maintaining local quality of life (9) Benefits to the local economy and local community (10) Managing visitor flows		
Organization for Economic Co-operation and Development—OECD	2013	Policy Makers	(1) Tourism performance and Impacts National Indicators (2) Ability of a destination to deliver quality and competitive tourism services (3) Attractiveness of a destination (4) Policy responses and economic opportunities	Destination competitiveness for sustainability	National
Network of European Regions for Sustainable and Competitive Tourism—NECSTouR	2015	Policy makers	(1) Limit the environmental impact of transport Local Indicators (2) Increase the quality of life of residents (3) Increase the quality of employment (4) Reduce the	A broader approach of sustainability to the EU Agenda for Sustainable and Competitive Tourism	Local

Organizations/ institutes	Year	Target Groups	Criteria	Focuses	Spatial scale
			seasonality of tourism flows (4) Protect the cultural heritage (6) Protect the environmental heritage (7) Protect the identity of destinations (8) Reduce and optimise the use of natural resources and water in particular (9) Reduce and optimise energy consumption (10) Reduce and manage waste		
European Tourism Indicators System—ETIS	2016	Policy Makers	(1) Destination management Local Indicators (2) Social and Cultural Impact (3) Environmental Impact	Three pillars of sustainability	Local
United Nations World Tourism Organisation—UNWTO	2016	Policy Makers	The most recent revision includes only indicators for Economy and Employment	Economic sustainability	National
Tourism and Environment Reporting Mechanism—TOUERM	2016	Policy Makers	(1) Driver indicators Various Data/ Indicators (2) Pressure indicators (3) State indicators (4) Impact indica-	Environmental sustainability	Various

Organizations/ institutes	Year	Target Groups	Criteria	Focuses	Spatial scale
			tors (4) Response indicators		
Global Sustainable Tourism Council—GSTC	2017	Policy Makers and Private Actors	(1) Sustainable management Local Indicators (2) Socioeconomic impacts (3) Cultural impacts (4) Environmental impacts	Three pillars of sustainability	Local
UNWTO International Network of Sustainable Tourism Observatories (INSTO)	2018	Policy Makers	Various criteria according to the observatory	Observation of mandatory tourism sustainability issues published in UNWTO's 'Indicators of Sustainable Development for Tourism Destinations: A Guidebook' and dynamic adjustment of destination-specific indicators	National/ Local

Source: Niavis et. al. 2019. Conceptualising Tourism Sustainability and Operationalising its Assessment: Evidence from a Mediterranean Community of Projects. Sustainability.11(15): 4042.

Balas and Abson (2022) found that more than half of tourism sustainability assessment publications apply existing indicator sets or frameworks to specific case studies or develop new indicator sets and assessment frameworks for local or regional tourism contexts. Nearly all publications (83%) used theoretical frameworks as sources for their indicator development process. The UNWTO indicator compilation

(UNWTO, 2004) was the primary source for indicator selection (30%), followed by the European Tourism Indicator System ETIS (7%).

Despite the wide applicability of the indicator systems developed by TSAIs in various spatial scales and types of destinations, there is little evidence of how effective the TSAIs were as manuals for carrying out sustainability evaluations. The most common challenges for researchers involve stakeholders and the dearth of pertinent data under the exhaustive indicator system (Agyeiwaah et. al., 2017). Most TSAIs are mainly conducted by organizations that have launched these initiatives or destinations where the sustainability assessments are carried out independently from the organizations (Niavis et. al., 2019). Besides the indicator system could be dynamic as the feedback from the destinations might result in the update of the original indicators (EC, 2022). These difficulties in implementing the TSAI indicators by researchers lead to their attempts to develop new tourism sustainability assessment approaches or indicators. That's why the recent years have witnessed the increase of the diversified indicators, assessment contexts and conceptual frameworks. These various new frameworks and indicators are criticized to be too subjective and even create an almost obscure choice overload.

TSAIs' efforts to evaluate tourism sustainability mainly aim to offer recommendations to policy makers (Table 5-2). As a result, tourism scholars have become increasingly interested in studying sustainable tourism policy in recent years. Though sustainability has been a recognized concept among the tourism policy makers, the continued negative impact of tourism on environment proves the failure of sustainable tourism policy (Hall, 2011). This failure is partly due to the unsuccessful development and implementation of sustainable policies. Guo (2019) revealed that the existing sustainable tourism policy researchers focus on the policy development and implementation.

As how to measure sustainability remains a debate, no uniform indicator system has been recognized for tourism sustainability assessment. Sustainable tourism policy is an important academic concern for tourism researchers. They have been focusing on the development and implementation of sustainable tourism policy. However, they haven't paid enough attention to evaluating the impacts of sustainable tourism policies. Since the UN Sustainable Development Goals 2030 were initiated in 2016, tourism in many countries like China has shifted its development paradigm from economic growth to sustainable development. The inadequate assessments on the impacts of sustainable tourism policies will hinder the improvement of sustainable tourism policy development, policy implementation and the realization of SDGs. Poverty as a prioritized goal among SGDs tend to be conceptualized and measured multi-dimensionally because sustainability is a multi-dimensional concept. The most popular multi-dimensional poverty measurement is the global MPI which aims to facilitate the achievement of various SDGs.

Since China's fulfillment of SDG1 is mainly measured by the economic poverty line, it remains doubtful whether tourism development under Chinese TAPPs promotes the sustainable development in TAP destinations. Therefore, it's worthwhile for the following sections to evaluate Chinese TAPPs' impacts on the sustainable multi-dimensional poverty alleviation in the TAP case study area Guizhou. As designed in the methodology chapter and the measurement overview of this section, the global MPI will be classified and adapted according to the three pillars sustainability dimensions to quantitatively assess the sustainable multi-dimensional poverty alleviation. Then a semi-structured interview is used to further explore TAP stakeholders' perception of TAPPs' impacts on the sustainable development of TAP destinations.

The Study Area: Guizhou

Guizhou initiated the concept of tourism-assisting the poor (TAP) at China's national tourism development conference, in 1991, based on some farmers' pioneers in increasing their income through tourism in backward areas. Since then, tourism as a poverty alleviation tool has gradually drawn the attention of the central government and some local governments. Guizhou removed absolute poverty in China in 2020 though it was once a province with the largest poor population in the country. Guizhou, which boasts diverse ethnic culture and abundant tourism resources, has explored a typical rural TAP model recognized by tourism organizations. Despite the outbreak of Covid-19 pandemic, Guizhou has been labelled as a safe destination without new cases from March 29, 2020, to May 2021. The Guizhou government has decided to promote the high-quality development of rural tourism in the Fourteenth

Five-year Plan for Guizhou Tourism Industry (2021-2025) to further enhance the achievements of absolute eradication and revitalize rural areas through tourism. Guizhou has thus been known as a representative TAP area in China.

Guizhou is a mountainous province located in the southwest of China. The province covers an area of 67,200 square miles or 174,000 square km with Guiyang its provincial capital. As part of Yunnan-Guizhou Plateau, Guizhou has the frontier character of other southwestern plateau lands: rough topography, difficult communication and consequent isolation, and many ethnic minority groups. It was long considered one of China's poorest and most disadvantaged provinces, as characterized by the folk poem: "The sky is not clear three days; the land is not level for three li (2,115 feet, or 645 metres); the people don't have three cents." This multi-ethnic province with the largest poor population eradicated its absolute poverty in 2020 under the guidance of the Chinese government's poverty relief strategies and policies including TAPPs.

Guizhou boasts abundant tourism resources owing to its mild temperature in all seasons, typical karst landscape, diverse natural forests and mysterious ethnic culture. It enjoys a mild climate with warm summers and mild winters. The provincial capital Guiyang has a mean July temperature of about 76 °F (24 °C), lower than that of all other cities to the east on the same latitude. This is due to its high altitude and the cloudiness of the summer months. In winter, cold air from Siberia could not easily reach Guizhou because of the barrier effect of the Qin (Tsinling) Mountains to the north of the Sichuan Basin. 62% of Guizhou's land is covered by karst landforms, representing the country's highest proportion of karst landform (Xinhua, 2020).

It is one area that features the most typical, complex, and diverse karst landscapes worldwide. The natural landscapes of karst landforms are more abundant than other mountainous areas in China. Guizhou is well-known as a province of natural forest parks. With plenty of rain and dense vegetation, the province's forest coverage rate has reached 62%, ranking the sixth in the country. More than 3,860 wild plants are in these forests, among which are highly valued herbs in traditional Chinese medicine. In addition, there are more than 1,000 species of wild animals, some three dozen of which are rare or endangered (Xinhua, 2020).

Besides these natural tourism resources, Guizhou attracts tourists worldwide with its diversified ethnic culture. More than 40 ethnic minorities inhabit Guizhou. The most minority groups with relatively large population are the Hmong (known in China as the Miao), the Buyi, the Yi (also known as the Lolo), the Dong, the Shui, the Mien (known as the Yao in China), and the Zhuang. The traditional ethnic villages in Guizhou, where these major ethnic minorities live, have developed into unique tourist destinations (Wikipedia, 2022).

Poverty in Guizhou: Basic Realities and Causes

The Chinese government identified Guizhou as one of the most backward and impoverished provinces in China. Poverty was the major chronic problem impeding Guizhou development. In 1993, about 10 million rural residents suffered from absolute poverty in Guizhou, representing a poverty ratio of 34.4% (Figure 5-1). With the implementation of series of development-driven poverty alleviation strategies by the government in more than 10 years, the poverty ratio in Guizhou reduced gradually to the lowest 6.5% in 2007. However, as the Chinese central government raised the income poverty line, in 2008, poverty ratio in Guizhou increased to 21.8%. It even hit the highest ratio of 50.93% after the poverty line was raised to 2300 yuan per year in 2011, 92% higher than the poverty line of 1196 yuan per year in 2009. Though Guizhou witnessed another continuous decline in the poverty ratio from 2011, Figure 5-2 clearly shows that the poverty ratio in Guizhou between 2011 and 2019 is more than double the national level. As previously noted in Table 3-2, the population of Guizhou's impoverished people ranks the first among the provinces whose poor population exceeds two million in 2014 and 2015 with Guizhou's poverty ratio listed among the top five.

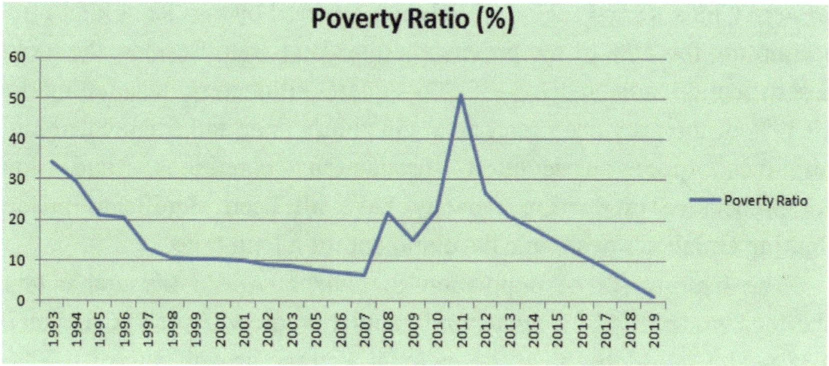

Figure 5-1 Poverty Ratio of Guizhou (1993-2019)
Source: Guizhou Staistical Yearbook 2020

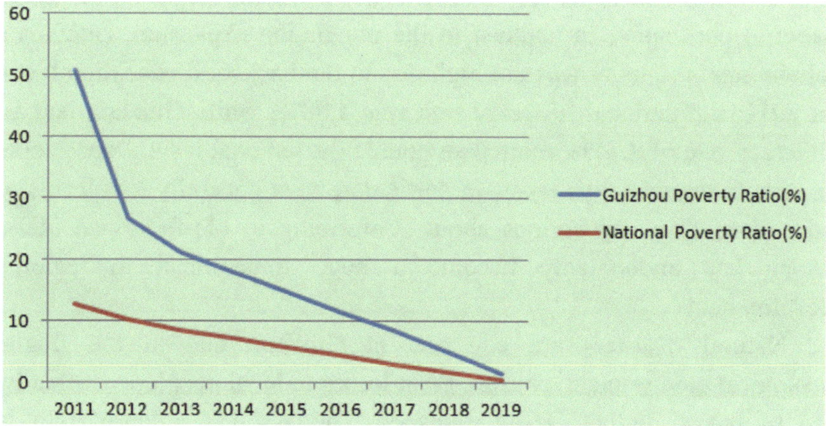

Figure 5-2 Comparison of National Poverty Ratio and
Guizhou Poverty Ratio (2011-2019)
Source: Guizhou Statistical Yearbook 2020

The difficulty in removing Guizhou's poverty has been recognized widely among academicians, government and other stakeholders as the causes for poverty or falling back to poverty are quite complicated (Hong & Li, 2012). Some major causes include the shortage of cultivated land, overgrowth of population, low-quality labour capital, frequent natural disasters, poor infrastructure and public services and weak foundation of industrial development. As part of the Yunnan-Guizhou Plateau, Guizhou Province is China's only inland province without plains for agricultural production. 93% of the province's land consists of hills and mountains with only 3% flat land. Located in the hinterland of south western China's karst region, Guizhou is covered by vast karst landforms, accounting for 71% of the province's total land area. Besides, the rocky desertification area reaches 35,900 square kilometers, accounting for 20.39% of the province's total area. Guizhou's poor and fragmented land resources, poor agricultural production conditions, and low comprehensive production capacity have all been significant factors limiting Guizhou's economic development for a long time.

The overgrowth of population in Guizhou made the arable land shortage worse. In 2011, the natural population growth rate in Guizhou is 6.38‰, 1.59‰ higher than the national average growth rate of 4.79‰. The per capital arable land area in the province was only 0.51 mu (about 0.034 hectare), far from the national average per capita area of 1.35 mu (0.9 hectare) and even less than the UN's benchmark 0.8 mu (0.053 hectare) per capita. In contrast to the population expansion, Guizhou's labour capital quality was not high due to the backward education level. In 2011, the national illiteracy rate was 4.08%, while Guizhou had an illiteracy rate of 8.74%, more than double the national level. Poor people in remote mountainous areas, in particular, have generally low levels of education. They are serious about conforming to old-fashioned ideas, which has undoubtedly become a huge impediment to regional development.

Natural disasters are common in Guizhou due to the fragile ecological environment, causing great losses to local people. Affected by the southwest Indian Ocean monsoon, Guizhou has a lot of rain in summer. Plentiful rain, poor terrain and landforms make the province more prone to natural disasters such as debris flows, especially in the deep mountainous areas where ethnic minorities live. Without strong disaster prevention capabilities, these ethnic minorities have to suffer large or small disasters almost every year, which results in serious economic losses and poverty. Table 5-3 shows that during 2012-2018, natural disasters affected an average of about 10 million people annually, incurring an annual direct economic loss of about 10 billion yuan.

Table 5-3 Losses from Natural Disasters in Guizhou (2012-2018)

Year	Affected population (mln)	Crop-affected area (thousand hectares)	Crop-failure are (thousand hectares)	Direct economic losses (bln yuan)
2012	12.28	552.7	67.42	6.62
2013	21.63	1578.05	362.84	14.01
2014	13.85	345.93	9.75	19.68
2014	5.81	217.06	31.65	7.38
2016	6.63	329.18	51.35	17.37
2017	5.32	257.29	40.79	6.03
2018	5.82	335	59	4.58

Source: Guizhou Statistics Bureau. 2019. Guizhou macroeconomic database

The poor infrastructure facilities and public services due to insufficient investment are another obstacle hindering Guizhou's social and economic development. Rural areas largely lag infrastructure construction, science, education, culture, healthcare and other public services. As of 2010, 22.36% of rural areas in Guizhou had no running water involving 12.998 million rural poor people facing drinking water safety threats; 13.4% of the poor population lacked access to wireless networks, and 8.7% had no televisions. The unequal improvement of infrastructure and public services enlarge the rural–urban gap and unbalanced regional development, further deepening poverty and inequality.

Booming industries and optimized industrial structure are the foundation for expanding the impoverished population's income channels. However, besides the shortage of arable land and poor agricultural production conditions, the secondary industry is not well-developed due to the constraints of the "Three High Thresholds" (high development threshold, high environmental protection threshold, and high capital investment threshold). Due to the weak industrial foundation, it's difficult to take conventional industrialization as engine of economic development and poverty alleviation in Guizhou. In 2011, the contribution rates of agriculture, industry and service to the Giuizhou's GDP are 12.7%, 38.5%, and 48.8% while in 2019, the three major industries' GDP contribution rates changed to 13.6%, 36.1% and 50.3%.

The tertiary industry including tourism has become an economic booster in Guizhou. Though the industrial structure has been improved significantly, the per capita income of households in Guizhou remains lower than the national average level. According to Table 5-4, from 2014 t0 2017, the per capita disposable income of both urban and rural households in Guizhou witnessed significant increase thanks to the implementation of the Chinese government's targeted poverty alleviation strategies. However, the ratios of urban and rural households' per capita disposable income and the national average level are about 0.80 and 0.60 respectively, clearly demonstrating the income gap between Guizhou and other parts of China. The larger gap between Guizhou rural households and the national average level indicates that rural residents remain relatively poor despite eliminating absolute poverty.

Table 5-4 Comparison of Per Capita Disposable Income Level in Guizhou and National Average Level

		2014	2016	2017	2018	2019
National Average Per Capital Disposable Income (Yuan)	Urban Households	31195	33616	36396	39251	42359
	Rural Households	5919	12363	13432	14617	16021
Guizhou Per Capital Disposable Income (Yuan)	Urban Households	24580	26743	29080	31592	34404
	Rural Households	7387	8098	8869	9716	10756
Ratio of Guizhou and National Average	Urban Households	0.78	0.80	0.80	0.81	0.81
	Rural Households	0.65	0.65	0.66	0.67	0.67

Source: Guizhou Statistics Bureau. 2019. Guizhou Macroeconomic Database

Tourism Development and Poverty Alleviation in Guizhou

The karst landforms obstruct agricultural production and industrial development. However, these unique and characteristic terrains and landforms combined with mild weather and diversified ethnic culture could be valuable tourism resources. In fact, as 1980's, tourism became the natural choice for the local government to promote economic growth and reduce poverty. Under the guidance of the central government's TAPPs, Guizhou's TAP experienced four stages: the pilot period (1980-1995), the initial expansion period (1996-2000), the upgrading and rapid period (2000-2012) and targeted development period (2013-2020), roughly echoing the Chinese TAP stages.

As overviewed in chapter four, tourism was formally incorporated into China's economic and social development plan in 1985. The country started to increase investment in tourism to play tourism's positive role in economic development. In response to the central government's recognition of tourism as an integral part of social and economic development, the Guizhou local government decided to unveil the period of piloting poverty alleviation through tourism development. Taking the advantage of the province's natural tourism resources, the government formulated a planning scheme on development the west and east tourist routes around the provincial capital Guiyang. The east route runs from the provincial capital Guiyang through Kaili and the ancient town of Zhenyuan to the Wuyang River. The west route starts from Guiyang, passing through the Red Maple Lake scenic area and Huangguoshu Waterfall to Zhijin Cave. When the government found that tourists were also curious about the local ethnic culture, the tourism departments of the two routes selected 8 typical ethnic minority villages for ethnic culture tourism development. Since then, the poverty alleviation in ethnic minority villages was officially launched.

The pilot TAP initiative (1980-1995) significantly promoted local economic development and poverty alleviation. Statistics shows that from 1980 to 1995, Guizhou received more than 600,000 overseas tourists from 52 countries (regions), realizing foreign exchange income of nearly 80 million US dollars. The number of domestic tourists reached 92.08 million, generating 2.26 billion yuan in tourism revenue. The more than 10 years' TAP pilot directly or indirectly lifted 95,475 poor households or 332,000 poor people out of poverty. These benefits from tourism development made residents firmly believe they could get rich through tourism. How to transform Guizhou's high-quality tourism resources into a "magic weapon" for people to get rid of poverty and become rich has become an important strategic issue for the government to consider. At the Chinese National Tourism Director Conference in

1991, the Guizhou Provincial Tourism Administration first proposed the Chinese pro-poor tourism concept of "tourism-assisting the poor" (TAP).

Following the success of TAP pilot, the Guizhou government unveiled the period of TAP initial expansion by extending the east and west routes to other parts of the province and neighborhood provinces. The expansion laid the foundation of the province's tourism planning framework. At the National Tourism Conference in 1996, the National Tourism Administration proposed TAP as an important topic. Guizhou's TAP experience was introduced and promoted among participants.

During the initial expansion period (1996-2000), Guizhou received 774,000 foreign tourists and earned a foreign exchange of about 240 million US dollars. 94 million domestic tourists created a tourism income of 19.4 billion yuan in Guizhou. In 2000, the number of domestic tourists was four times that of 1990 while the number of foreign tourists soared by nearly 10.3 times. The domestic tourism incomes increased by nearly 21 times while the foreign exchange income increased by 4.8 times. The development of tourism in some poor areas expanded the employment opportunities for residents, increased their incomes significantly, updated their development concepts, optimized and adjusted the regional industrial structure. Tourism has become a pillar industry in some places, such as Shibing County in the central north of Guizhou and Libo County in the south of Guizhou. By the end of 2000, 496,765 poor people in the province had been lifted out of poverty through TAP expansion, accounting for 3.6% of the total number of poor people.

The economic growth –driven "Western Development" strategy implemented by the state in 1999 led Guizhou's TAP to a new period of upgrading and rapid development (2001-2012). In 2002, the state launched the "Trial National TAP Zone" plan, which marked the official initiation of TAP at the national level. In the same year, Guizhou issued the "Opinions on Accelerating the Development of Tourism", aiming to upgrade TAP structure by developing "village tourism". In 2003, under the guidance of the World Tourism Organization and the China National Tourism Administration, "the Guizhou Overall Planning for Tourism Development" further clarified the important role of rural tourism in reducing poverty and getting people rich. A series of measures were taken to expand rural tourism products such as ethnic cultural experience, modern agriculture tour, homestay, ancient town sightseeing, suburban farmhouses. These new tourism products became very popular in the rural tourism market and strengthen rural tourism's contribution to poverty relief. The rural tourism-led upgrading efforts encouraged more than 130 ethnic minority villages in Guizhou to participate in tourism development.

Guizhou's rural TAP experience was also popularized abroad and aroused widespread concern. Tourism agencies and experts from Ireland, New Zealand, France, the United States, and other countries visited Guizhou for investigation and cooperation (CTRI, 2018). In 2004, the World Bank, in partnership with the World Tourism Organization and the New Zealand government implemented the "Bala River Rural Tourism" poverty alleviation demonstration project in southeast Guizhou Province. In order to promote Guizhou's achievement in rural TAP, the World Bank also provided special technology and financial supports in developing rural tourism infrastructure construction, landscape attractions and tourism service promotion etc. Thanks to these upgrading measures, during the "Tenth-five Year Plan (2001-2005), 69.904 million yuan was allocated from the government's poverty relief fund and bank loans to the TAP investment for village construction, personnel training and infrastructure improvement. In 2004, Guizhou received 31.27 million tourists from home and abroad with the total tourism revenue hitting 25.114 billion yuan. As of 2005, Guizhou drove 630,300 people out of poverty through tourism development (Guizhou Statistics Bureau, 2006).

Guizhou issued the first local rural tourism development plan in China in 2006 to further push the rapid development of upgraded TAP. Based on the systematic summary of the poverty alleviation effects of various TAP modes implemented in Guizhou, the plan proposed to strengthen the integrated development of tourism industry, ethnic culture, sightseeing agriculture and other industries, and jointly promote the transformation and upgrading of rural tourism. In 2009, the World Tourism Organization selected Guizhou as China's first province to implement the "sustainable tourism poverty alleviation" plan by initiating the "Guizhou Cultural and Natural Heritage Protection and Development Project" with an investment of 500,000 US dollars to collect and develop handicrafts scattered in various ethnic villages. In the six years from 2009 to 2014, the World Bank issued 60 million US dollars in loans to

Guizhou. With the support of various forces, rural tourism in Guizhou enjoyed fast growth and achieved remarkable results. According to the Guizhou Provincial Tourism Bureau statistics, 3000 natural villages in Guizhou carried out rural tourism in 2012.

Since the launch of the targeted poverty alleviation strategy by the Chinese Central Government in 2013, rural tourism became a targeted means for poverty alleviation as 80% of the poor population inhabited villages with abundant tourism resources. In order to play rural tourism's active role in targeted poverty alleviation, during the 12th Five-Year Plan period (2011-2015), Guizhou built 10 provincial-level, 20 prefecture-level and 100 county-level tourism poverty alleviation demonstration zones, and selected 300 poverty-stricken villages as pilot villages for the tourism poverty alleviation multiplication plan. In this period, 517 villages in Guizhou were listed as the national key villages for rural TAP. And four national leisure agriculture and rural tourism demonstration counties were developed, providing a total of 2.34 million job opportunities and benefiting more than 4.7 million people. Rural tourism's annual average gross income exceeded 2 billion yuan, and 20% of the per capita net income of farmers was from rural tourism. The "Guizhou model" of rural TAP was highly recognized by the United Nations World Tourism Organization (UNWTO).

In the 13th Five -Year Plan period (2016-2020), Guizhou took five major measures to intensify its efforts to eradicate poverty through tourism development. The first measure was to establish multi-benefits linkage between the scenic area and the poor locals by implementing the project of constructing top 100 tourist attractions in Guizhou. For example, through the general survey of resources and infrastructure in villages around the scenic spot, some poor villages suitable for rural tourism development will be included in the construction list. The poor villagers' housing, land, labor and other resources were quantified and invested as shares in tourism projects. In this way, these TAP projects created ticket dividends, employment and self-employment opportunities for the local poor.

Then, while implementing a series of rural TAP projects, efforts were made to develop characteristic industries in TAP villages by promoting the strategies of "One Featured Product in One Village", "One Skill by One Household" and "One Specialty from One Household".

Poor farmers could directly obtain employment opportunities or income by running small tourism enterprises, selling characteristic agricultural and sideline products, renting houses or investing capital to these rural TAP projects. Thirdly, focusing on the overall tourism images of "Colorful Guizhou" and "Mountain Park", a series of rural TAP brands marketing campaigns were carried out for some ethnic villages with profound historical background and distinctive regional characteristics and those featured TAP destinations. Fourthly, the training for the rural tourism employees was intensified to back up the TAP projects implementation.

Finally, with the government's fund for poverty relief as the stimulus, innovative financing channels were expanded for TAP enterprises and poor households to overcome their difficulty in obtaining loans and financing through the cooperation with the National Development Bank and Rural Commercial Bank. Further by implementing the "Three Year Action Plan for Guizhou Province to Eradicate Poverty through Tourism (2017-2019)", 1 million documented poor people had shaken off poverty through tourism by 2019 and more than 1/4 of the per capita net income was contributed by the tourism industry. 3,347 poverty-stricken villages, 510,000 poverty-stricken households and 1,722,400 poverty-stricken people in the province were registered in the TAP cloud system. Tourism professional training was carried out in 9,000 poor villages suitable for TAP.

The overview shows that based on regional and ethnic characteristics, Guizhou has creatively developed a unique path of TAP, which has significantly contributed to absolute poverty reduction. Up to now, there are thousands of ethnic village tourist attractions, large and small, scattering all over the province. Six of them were listed as the National TAP Demonstration Cases for Rural Revitalization by the China Ministry of Culture and Tourism in 2019 including Zhaoxing Dong Ethnic Village, Haohuahong Buyi Ethnic Village, Shepeng Li and Miao Ethnic Village, Xiaohewan Village, Longguan Village and Yunshe Tujia Ethnic Village (CMCT, 2021).

Zhaoxing Dong Ethnic Village: A Typical TAP Destination in Guizhou

Among the 9,000 poor villages identified as suitable TAP destinations by the Guizhou government, Zhaoxing Dong Ethnic village is selected as a representative TAP destination. Firstly, it is one of the poorest ethnic villages in the south of Liping County, a Chinese national-level poverty-stricken county of the Qiandongnan Miao and Dong Autonomous Prefecture in the southeast Guizhou Province. This county has the largest population of the Dong ethnic minority in China, while Zhaoxing Dong Ethnic Village is known as the largest Dong village in China. At the beginning of the Chinese targeted poverty alleviation strategy implementation in 2014, the absolute poverty rate in Liping County hit 28.56%, 10.56% higher than the poverty rate of 18% in Guizhou, inhabited by the largest impoverished population in China. The county was one of the last batches of 64 national-level impoverished counties in Guizhou that were finally lifted out of absolute poverty in 2020. Among 4395 residents of 1284 households in Zhaoxing Dong Village, 3484 of 817 households were documented as impoverished, accounting for 64% of the whole population in the village.

Zhaoxing Dong Ethnic Village earned its reputation as the "Chinese Village of Drum Tower and Dong Culture" in 1993 thanks to its abundant ethnic, cultural and natural tourism resources. In 2001, the Dong Village Drum Tower cluster in Zhaoxing was listed in the Guinness Book of World Records. The history of this ethnic village could be dated back to the Southern Song Dynasty (1127–1279). Since then, the Dong people have gradually developed their unique tradition of composing and teaching folk songs and dances, such as the "Dong Big Song", from generation to generation. The "Dong Big Song" features its chorus without conductors or accompaniment, complex musical forms, and varied vocal combinations.

In 1986, the "Dong Big Song" was first performed at the Paris Art Festival, astonishing the world audience with the characteristic chorus like sparkling water. In 2009, the "Dong Big Song" was included in the World Intangible Cultural Heritage list by UNESCO. Besides the Dong folk songs and dances, the Dong village is also known for its various ethnic festivals and customs, such as the "Lusheng (reed-pipe wind instrument) grand gathering" held from lunar August 13-15th every other year. This gathering is usually participated by dozens of Lusheng teams from neighbourhood villages.

In addition, the Dong traditional handicrafts, the "Dong Brocade" and the "Dong Cloth" in particular, have drawn wide attention from tourists. Dong brocade is a hand-made brocade belt made by Dong women. They create flowers, birds, worms, and fish with exquisite patterns and fine textures using five-colour silk threads. Dong's weaving and dyeing skills are represented by the bright cloth, whose manufacturing process is highly complicated. Nowadays, the "Dong cloth" has been used to make some beautiful and functional tourism commodities, such as Dong clothing and ethnic bags. The village attracts tourists with the Sasui Mounta, the Dong people's "Mecca of the Holy Land", and Pilin Cave, a typical "karst" mountain landform featuring a spectacular cave group and cliff stone carvings.

Despite the fames of a popular tourist destination since the 1990s (Table 5-5), absolute poverty has not been reduced significantly in Zhaoxing Dong Ethnic Village until the implementation of the targeted TAPPs. Taking the golden opportunities brought by the Guizhou expressway network construction, the Liping government has strived to help the impoverished villagers in Zhaoxing Dong Ethnic Village increase their income by speeding up tourism development. Efforts were devoted to fully exploring the Dong culture, improving tourism infrastructure construction and innovating tourism products and services. In order to channel more tourism benefits to people experiencing poverty, the village established a TAP model through a link mechanism for the protection, development, management, and distribution of tourism resources by enterprises, villagers and the government. This TAP model transforms villagers into stakeholders of tourism projects so that they could share tourism benefits through joint construction and management of the village with other stakeholders.

These targeted measures generated significant impacts on the TAP initiative in the village. In 2016, Zhaoxing Village received 1.1 million tourists, a year-on-year rise of 39.2% and earned a total tourism income of 880 million yuan, up by 58% yearly. Farmers' annual per capita net income reached 10,500 yuan, an increase of 16% yearly. By 2020, 3,484 poor villagers of 817 households had been lifted out of poverty by participating in tourism and related industries. Besides, more than 15,000 impoverished people in the neighbouring villages or towns enjoyed poverty relief by seizing job opportunities from the Zhaoxing tourism-driven industries.

Table 5-5 Main Honors of Zhaoxing Dong Ethnic Village as a Popular Ethnic TAP Destination

Year	**Honor**	**Year**	**Honor**
1993	Chinese Village of Drum Tower and Dong Culture	2001	World Guinness Records
2003	National ethnic and folk culture protection pilot village	2005	Listed among China six most beautiful rural towns
2007	Listed among 33 most attractive global destinations	2007	Famous Chinese Historical and Cultural Village
2008	Charming global Olympic tourism destination	2009	National civilized tourist destination
2010	National Culture protection and inheritance construction demonstration base	2012	Guizhou demonstration town
2014	Listed among national AAAA tourist attractions	2014	Chinese typical ethnic village
2015	Dong Dage included in the UN Intangible Cultural Heritage of Humanity	2017	China model habitat award
2018	CCTV Spring Festival Gala venue	2021	List of national "Village Spring Festival Gala" venue

Source: http://www.lp.gov.cn/

Results of Assessing the Multi-dimensional Poverty Relief in Guizhou

It was revealed from chapter one that tourism was a key to reducing absolute poverty in Guizhou under TAPPs. Since 80% of the poverty-stricken population was identified in villages with abundant tourism resources, the measurement of multi-dimensional poverty in the province could reflect tourism's contribution to multi-dimensional poverty relief. The overview of multi-dimensional poverty assessment showed that the global Multi-dimensional Poverty Index (MPI) calculated with Alkire and Foster multi-dimensional poverty measurement methodology (AF methodology) enjoys the widest popularity worldwide. The changes of China global MPI with AF methodology from 2012 to 2014 measured by Alkire and Sen (2017) is a good reference for the measurement of multi-dimensional poverty reduction under TAPPs in Guizhou.

Method

This study chooses AF methodology to calculate the global MPI in Guizhou. Suppose there are n individuals in Guizhou with each individual denoted by i with i=1,..., n. Their well-being is assessed by d indicators, each denoted by j with j=1,...,d. Let x_{ij} be the achievement of individual i in each indicator j. The study further denotes by wj the weight for dimension j and $\sum_{j=1}^{d} w_j = 1$. Let zj the deprivation cutoff for dimension j. If the achievement of any individual i in indicator j falls below zj, the individual i is considered to be deprived in that indicator. Finally, the study denotes k the "poverty cutoff", where $0 < k \leqslant 1$ identifies a household as multi-dimensionally poor. The M0 or MPI could thus be constructed in three steps (Alkire & Foster, 2007; 2011):

Firstly, calculate the deprivation status score g_{ij} assigned to denote each individual i's deprivation status in each indicator j based on z_j. If individual i is deprived in indicator j, g_{ij}=1; Otherwise, g_{ij} = 0. Collect the deprivation status values in an n by d deprivation matrix g0. Secondly, calculate the deprivation score of each person i and denoted by c_i where $c_i = \sum_j w_j g_{ij}$. If c_i is higher than or equal to k, then individual i is multi-dimensionally poor. Censor the matrix g0 by assigning the value zero to any deprivations experienced by individuals who are not considered to be poor, then designate it as g0 (k). The vector of deprivation scores should also be censored such that if a person is poor, $c_i(k) = c_i$ and if not, $c_i(k) = 0$. And finally compute the multidimensional poverty index MPI or the adjusted headcount ratio M_0. M_0 is the arithmetic mean of the censored deprivation score: $M_0 = MPI = \frac{1}{n}\sum_{i=1}^{d} c_i(k)$.

As stated previously, the MPI or M_0 has good properties for analysis with significant policy implications. This study draws particularly on the following three properties. The first property is that MPI could be a product of the incidence and intensity of multidimensional poverty. Assuming that q people in Guizhou are identified as multi-dimensionally poor using the dual-cutoff approach, we could rewrite the MPI as follows: $M_0 = MPI = \frac{q}{n} * [\frac{1}{q}\sum_{i=1}^{d} c_i(k)] = H * A$. Where H represents the proportion of people identified as multi-dimensionally poor or the headcount ratio (incidence) of multidimensional poverty. A is the intensity of multi-dimensional poverty denoting the average share of weighted indicators in which poor people are deprived. This involves adding up the poor's deprivation scores and dividing them by the total number of poor people.

Second, the adjusted headcount ratio could be dissected to demonstrate how each indicator affects overall poverty (dimensional breakdown). The censored headcount ratio statistic is incredibly helpful for observing changes over time. The percentage of the population that is simultaneously multi-dimensionally poor and deprived in that particular indicator is known as the censored headcount ratio. We use h_j to signify the censored headcount ratio of indicator j. The weighted total of the censored headcount ratios for each of the component indicators could be used to express the MPI or M_0 as:

$$M_0 = MPI = \sum_{j=1}^{d} w_j h_j = \sum_{j=1}^{d} w_j [\frac{1}{n}\sum_{i=1}^{n} g_{ij}(k)].$$

The statistic of "percentage contribution" enables us to evaluate the dimensional deprivations that contribute most to poverty for any specific group or overall poverty due to the weighting structure of M_0.

The study designates $\Phi_j$the indicator j's weighted contribution to M_0. The indicator j's percentage contribution to M_0 is thus expressed:

A third property crucial for both policy and the UN Sustainable Development Goals is disaggregation. Assume that there are m groups that are mutually exclusive and exhaustive in the entire population. A weighted average of the M_0 values of the m subgroups could then be used to express the overall M_0, where weights are the corresponding population proportions. Let the subscript l=1,...,m designate the subgroups of the population with $\sum_{l=1}^{m} n_l = n$ and denote the adjusted headcount ratio M_0 or MPI of subgroup l by $M_0(n_l)$. The overall M_0 could thus be expressed as:

$$M_0 = MPI = \sum_{l=1}^{m} \frac{n_l}{n} * M_0(n_l).$$

This subgroup decomposability could help us understand the poverty level of different subgroups and their contributions to the overall poverty level.

Data

The study uses the data of the China Family Panel Studies (CFPS) from the Institute of Social Science Survey (ISSS) at Peking University. The CFPS is a national longitudinal general social survey initiative launched in 2010, designed to shed light on the Chinese economic and non-economic well-being aspects. The survey was conducted in 25 provinces/cities/autonomous regions across Mainland China (excluding Xinjiang, Qinghai, Inner Mongolia, Ningxia, Tibet, and Hainan) and Hong Kong, Macao, and Taiwan). Up to now, there have been six waves: 2010, 2012, 2014, 2016, 2018 and 2020 with data of 2020 still in data cleaning. Instead of presenting all the results from the available data of the five waves, this study only chooses the CFPS data of 2016 and 2018 to calculate Guizhou's global MPI involving 1,832 people in 431 households and 1796 people in 423 households in Guizhou respectively.

There are three reasons for the choice of the data: firstly, as explained in the literature, Alkire and Shen (2017) computed China's MPI using the CFPS data of 2010, 2012 and 2014, which offers implications for the changes of MPI in Guizhou. However, these findings need to be updated with the latest available survey data in 2016 and 2018 when the Chinese targeted poverty alleviation initiative was implemented. Secondly, the main task of this chapter is to investigate Chinese TAPPs' impacts on the sustainable multi-dimensional poverty relief. The documentary analysis and CGE analysis in the previous chapters have already shown that tourism developed into a major poverty alleviation tool after the Chinese government issued the largest number of TAPPs in the targeted TAP period (2013-2020). The CFPS data in 2016 and 2018 could more precisely explain tourism's contribution to multi-dimensional poverty reduction under the TAPPs.

Finally, choosing CFPS data in 2016 and 2018 ensures the comparability of the some key MPI indicators. With the improvement of Chinese people's economic and non-economic well-being, some indicators in the CFPS questionnaires might be deleted, added or adjusted. For example， the MPI indicator of improved sanitation has been removed from the CFPS questionnaire since 2016. The insurance indicator has been included in the survey since 2016 as establishing a uniform urban-rural insurance system was used to guarantee the social benefits of the impoverished.

Global MPI Indicators for Guizhou

The global MPI indicators in this study are defined in Table 5-6. Three major differences exist between the indicators the study uses for Guizhou and the standard global MPI indicators (Alkire, Kanagaratnam, & Suppa, 2020). First, as this chapter aims to evaluate TAPPs' impacts on the multi-dimensional poverty reduction in Guizhou under the sustainable development paradigm, the global indicators used in this section are reclassified in terms of the three pillar sustainability dimensions: economic, social and cultural and environment dimensions. Due to the reclassification of indicators in sustainability dimensions, the weight of each indicator is adjusted accordingly. Second, the study removed the indicator sanitation but added basic insurance. The reason is that the data on household sanitation facilities has no longer been provided since 2016 mainly owing to the nationwide "toilet revolution" in tourist sites from 2015. However, the basic insurance as a social security guarantee to the impoverished in the targeted fight against absolute poverty began to be included in the CFPS questionnaire in 2016.

Third, the indicators for Guizhou are specifically defined below based on the indicator description for China by Alkire and Sen (2017) and the indicator description in the CFPS workbook and questionnaire.

Table 5-6 Guizhou MPI: Dimension, Indicator, Cut-Off, Weight and SDGs

Dimension	**Indicator**	**Deprived if**	**Relative Weight**	**SDGs**
Economic Dimension	Assets ownership	The household does not own more than one of the following: TV, mobile telephone, bike (motorized), motorbike, refrigerator, or computer and does not own a car or similar vehicle.	1/12	SDG 1: No Poverty
	Nutrition	Any person under 70 years of age is malnourished.	1/12	SDG 2: Zero Hunger
	Child mortality	Any child has died in the family.	1/12	SDG 3: Health and Well-being
	Housing	The household has "inadequate housing"	1/12	SDG 11: Sustainable Cities and Communities
Social and Cultural Dimension	Years of schooling	No eligible household member has completed six years of schooling.	1/9	SDG 4: Quality Education
	Child school attendance	Any child aged 7–14 is not attending school up until the age at which they would complete class 8.	1/9	SDG 4: Quality Education
	Basic insurance	The household has no basic insurance coverage	1/9	SDG 1: No Poverty
Environmental Dimension	Improved drinking water	The household does not have access to improved drinking	1/9	SDG 6: Clean Water and

Dimension	Indicator	Deprived if	Relative Weight	SDGs
		water, defined as tap water, or mineral/purified/filtere d water		Sanitation
	Cooking fuel	The household cooks with agricultural crop/shrubs/wood, charcoal/ coal	1/9	SDG 7: Affordable and Clean Energy
	Electricity	The household has no electricity.	1/9	SDG 7: Affordable and Clean Energy

Note: Adapted from Alkire, S., Kanagaratnam, U. & Suppa, N. 2020. The global Multidimensional Poverty Index (MPI): 2020 revision. OPHI MPI Methodological Note 49. Oxford Poverty and Human Development Initiative, University of Oxford.

a. Economic Dimension

(1) Assets ownership

A household is considered deprived if it does not own more than one of the following assets with a total value of more than 1,000 yuan: TV, mobile phone, bike (motorized), motorbike, refrigerator or computer. They are not deprived of assets if they own a car or similar vehicle. The assets indicator differs from the global MPI 2020 in that it does not include a radio or an animal cart, and it substitutes a motorized bicycle for a bicycle.

(2) Nutrition

The entire household is considered deprived, as in the global MPI 2020, if at least one eligible member is malnourished. The global MPI normally only considers women under 49 and men under 59, whereas the CFPS dataset includes nutrition data for all age groups. We use BMI (Body Mass Index) to measure whether a household member is malnourished as CFPS provides the height and weight information. The household is considered deprived if the value of BMI of any household member is below 18.5. This standard might not accurately capture the nutrition status of the people of more than 70 years old due to their bone density decline during this life cycle period. Therefore, we limit our consideration to those younger than 70. However, CFPS employs the recall procedure for collecting the nutrition data, inevitably increasing the non-sampling measurement errors in the self-reported nutrition results.

(3) Child mortality

A household is deemed deprived by the global MPI 2020 if any child has passed away in the previous five years. While CFPS does not specify a date of death, it just inquires "whether any of your children perished in your family." We include all child fatalities reported by women under the age of 49 and men under the age of 59, just like in prior instances.

(4) Housing

According to the global MPI 2020, a household is considered deprived if it has inadequate housing materials in the three components: floor, roof or walls. CFPS provides information of floor area instead of material. Therefore, some Chinese scholars use inadequate housing area as the cut-off for housing (eg. Han & Gao, 2017; Li, 2018). This study adopts the cut-off of inadequate housing area. The household is considered deprived if its housing area is less than 30 square meters.

b. Social and Cultural Dimension

(1) Years of schooling

This indicator, similar to the global MPI 2020, considers if no eligible household member has completed six years of education or primary school, the entire household is considered deprived. Household members aged 12 years and above are eligible as most Chinese people started primary school at 7 (Alkire & Shen, 2017).

(2) Child school attendance

As in the global MPI 2020, the entire household is considered deprived if any child aged 7–14 is not attending school until the age at which they would complete class 8. This is roughly in conformity with the Chinese Compulsory Education Law which stipulates that any child at the age of 6 or 7 should be enrolled in school to finish nine years of compulsory education.

(3) Basic insurance

This indicator is added in the Chinese global MPI system because the coverage of basic insurance among the impoverished is a critical measure for the Chinese government to fulfillment of the absolute poverty eradication goal. Since the targeted poverty alleviation period, the

Chinese government has vowed to guarantee the basic needs of food and clothing for those living in poverty and ensure that they have proper access to compulsory education, medical care, and safe housing, whilst working to raise their incomes above the poverty line. Among them, the inability to afford medical care is a major cause for a household to get stuck in poverty or fall back into poverty. In 2016, the Chinese State Council released the "Opinions on Integrating the Basic Medical Insurance System for Urban and Rural Residents" to eradicate disease-related poverty. Therefore, the basic insurance indicator considers a household deprived if any member has no medical insurance, such as the basic medical insurance for rural and urban residents.

c. Environmental Dimension

(1) Improved drinking water

According to the global MPI 2020, this indicator considers a household to be deprived if the household has no source of safe drinking water or the safe drinking water or the safe drinking water is too far away, for example, a 30-minute or longer walk from home, roundtrip. The CFPS provides the information of drinking water source, classified into river/lake water, well water, tap water, or mineral/purified/filtered water, rain water, cellar water and pond/spring water. Although the well-protected well water or pond/spring water is clearly defined as safe water by MDGs, CFPS does not distinguish whether these sources are well-protected. Therefore, this study follows Alkire and Shen (2017) that a household is deprived if river/lake water well water, rain water, cellar water or pond/spring water is used for drinking. However, this cutoff might overestimate the water deprivation from protected spring, well or pond area.

(2) Cooking fuel

According to the global MPI 2020, a household is deemed to be deprived if using solid fuel such as dung, agricultural crop, shrubs, wood, charcoal, or coal for cooking fuel. The CFPS questionnaire classifies cooking fuel into agricultural crop/shrubs/wood, charcoal/ coal, canned / liquefied gas, natural gas/pipeline, solar/ biogas, and electricity. Therefore, the study considers households deprived if they cook with agricultural crop/shrubs/wood or charcoal/coal.

(3) Electricity

The alternatives for electricity in the CFPS surveys are as follows: 1) no electricity, 2) frequent power outages, 3) infrequent, and 4) almost no power outages. Households are considered to be deprived if they choose the first option.

Guizhou's Global MPI Results

a. Basic Results

The targeted poverty alleviation policies such as TAPPs positively impact the multi-dimensional poverty reduction in Guizhou. Table 5-7 shows that Guizhou's global MPI decreased significantly from 0.085 in 2016 to 0.048 in 2018. The absolute annualized change of MPI value achieved 0.019 with statistical significance at α=0.05. The headcount ratio (H) declined from 21.02% in 2016 to 12.76% in 2018 which is statistically significant. However, the annualized change of 1.2% in the intensity (A) shows that the average weighted deprivations among the poor is not statistically significant. This result indicates that, on average, Guizhou's MPI poor people are generally deprived in one economic indicator, one or two social and cultural indicators and one environmental indicator. Besides, Guizhou's MPI is almost close to the province's absolute poverty rate. In 2016, Guizhou's MPI is 0.085, slightly lower than the absolute poverty rate of 0.106. In 2018, the province's MPI is 0.048, close to the absolute poverty rate of 0.043.

As for two subgroups of the MPI poor, the study explored those who experience severe poverty and destitution. According to Alkire and Shen (2017), the subgroup suffering from severe poverty are the poor people deprived in 50% or more of indicators (K>=50%) while the destitution group are identified as those deprived in at least one third of the MPI indicators (K>=40% in this study). It could be easily seen from Figure 5-3 that the rates of destitution and severe poverty are significantly lower than MPI. Similar to the change of MPI, headcount ratios of destitution and severe poverty witnessed declines from 14.74% in 2016 to 5.89% in 2018 and 2.75% in 2016 to 1.63% in 2018. Among them, the destitution and MPI headcount ratios from 2016 to 2018 see the largest reduction rates by 8.85% and 8.26% respectively.

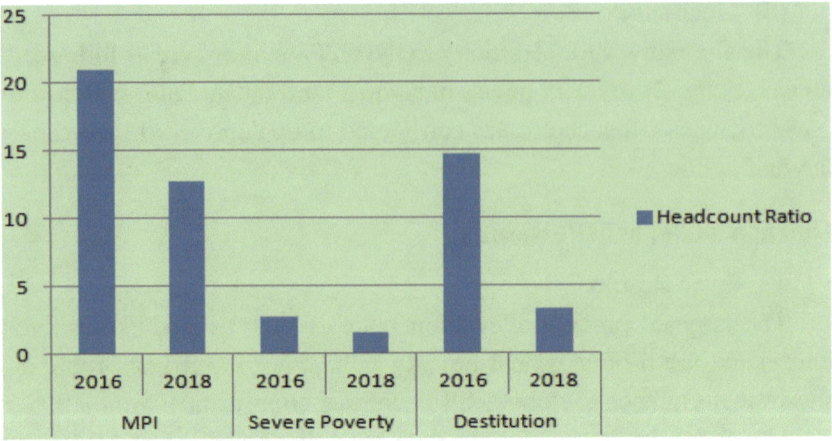

Figure 5-3 Multi-Dimensional Headcount Ratios (H)

Table 5-7 Guizhou's MPI Results: 2016, 2018

M0 Confidence Interval (%) (95%)	**H Confidence interval (%) (95%)**	**A Confidence Interval (%) (95%)**
	2016	
MPI 0.085[0.011, 0.159]	21.02 [3.11, 38.93]	40.35 [38.31, 42.39]
Severity 0.014 [0.003, 0.025]	2.75 [0.78,4.71]	52.24 [48.27, 56.21]
Destitution 0.064 [0.001, 0.127]	14.74 [0.04, 29.44]	43.68 [41.73, 45.63]
	2018	
MPI 0.048 [0.031, 0.066]	12.76[8.23,17.31]	37.9 [36.82,38.97]
Severity 0.015 [0.001, 0.032]	1.63 [0.52, 3.79]	48.37 [39.07, 57.68]
Destitution 0.025 [0.016, 0.034]	5.89 [3.77, 8.01]	43.29 [40.63, 45.95]

Note: Change is significant by 95%.

b. Indicator Analysis of MPI Composition under Sustainable Development Paradigm

The raw and censored headcount ratios are explored to understand each indicator's contribution to Guizhou's overall multi-dimensional poverty under sustainable development dimensions. The raw headcount ratio is the proportion of the population deprived in each indicator. The censored headcount ratio displays each indicator's impoverished and deprived population proportion. According to Figure 5-4, "years of schooling" indicator in social and cultural dimension has the highest raw headcount ratio followed by "cooking fuel" in environmental dimension and "insurance" in social and cultural dimension. However, regarding censored headcount ratio, "cooking fuel" in environmental dimension has the highest ratio followed by "years of schooling" and "insurance" in social and cultural dimension.

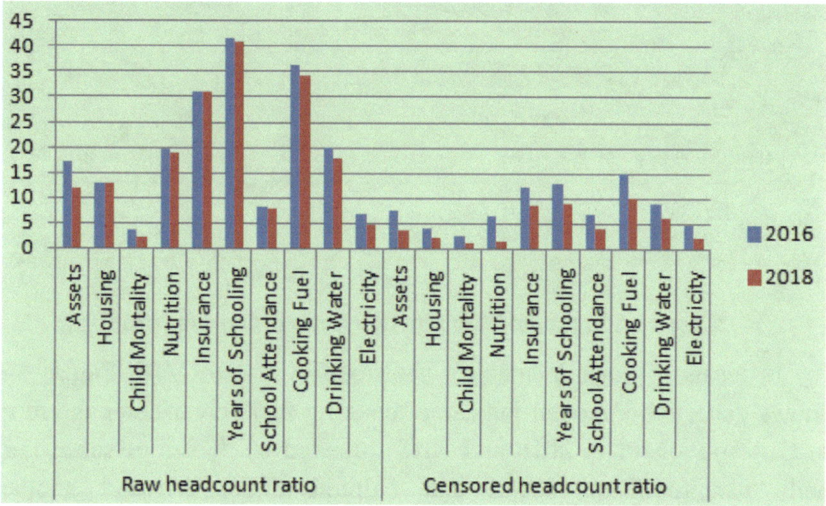

Figure 5-4 Raw Headcount Ratio and Censored Headcount Ratio of People Deprived in Each Indicator

Regarding the changes of censored headcount ratios over time (Figure 5-4), from 2016 to 2018, all indicators experienced a statistically significant decline, indicating that the MPI poor people in Guizhou have enjoyed economic, social, cultural and environmental improvements. "Cooking fuel" in environmental dimension, "nutrition" in economic dimension and "years of schooling" in social and cultural dimension are indicators with the largest decline percentage points by 4.91, 4.85 and 4.01. They are followed by "assets" in economic dimension and "insurance" in social and cultural dimension with reduction rates of 3.38% and 3.31%. The changes in the levels of the other indicators are less significant with the lowest decline rate of 1.31% in the economic indicator "child mortality". This is partly because the censored headcount ratios of these indicators are relatively low. For example, the deprivation ratios of "child mortality" are 2.55% in 2016 and 1.18% in 2018, the lowest among the ten indicators.

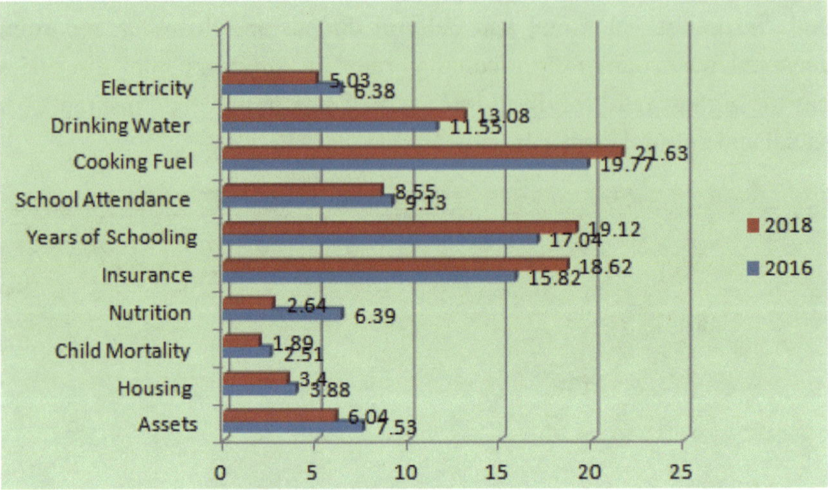

Figure 5-5 Indicators' Contribution Rates to Guizhou's MPI

In terms of each indicator's contribution rate to MPI, Figure 5-5 shows that environmental indicator "cooking fuel" contributes the most to Guizhou's MPI in 2016 and 2018 followed by "years of schooling" and "insurance" in social and cultural dimension and another environmental indicator "drinking water". Economic indicator "child mortality" contributed the lowest percentage points of 2.51 and 1.89 to the MPI, echoing the large decline of censored headcount ratio in nutrition and the least change of "child mortality" in economic dimension demonstrated in Figure 5-4. It could be further found that the indicators that have greater changes in the censored headcount ratio contributed more to the overall MPI such as environmental indicator "cooking fuel" and social and cultural indicators "years of schooling" and "insurance". Except for the added indicator of insurance in this study, the significant contribution rates of "cooking fuel", "years of schooling", and "drinking water" to the MPI in 2016 and 2018 were consistent with the results of indicator contribution rates to China's national MPI based on CFPS 2010, 2012 and 2014 by Alkire and Shen (2017). The consistency of these two results indicated that Guizhou's MPI realities reflect the typical characteristics of the whole country's multi-dimensional poverty.

Disaggregated Analysis of Guizhou's MPI under Sustainable Development Paradigm

Disaggregation is one of the AF global MPI's good properties for analysing poverty by various subgroups. CFPS for Guizhou Province provides information of different subgroups mainly by rural – urban areas, age, gender, marital status, education, household size and rural-urban hukous[2]. Since tourism's distributional effects on the income poverty of rural and urban household groups are quantified in the CGE analysis in chapter four, this section focuses on further investigating TAPPs' impacts on the multi-dimensional poverty of rural and urban households in Guizhou by observing the MPI changes in rural and urban areas as well as between rural and urban hukou households under the sustainable development paradigm.

a. MPI in Rural and Urban Areas

Like many countries and regions worldwide, China's national MPI in rural areas is higher than urban areas (Alkire & Shen, 2017; Alkire & Fang, 2018). Guizhou's MPI results in Table 5-9 further prove this statement. In 2016, 25.17% of the people in poor population in Guizhou rural areas are poor, 10.28% higher than that in urban areas. In 2018, the headcount ratio of the poor in rural areas declines to 17.12%, still 11.01% higher than urban areas. In both years, the intensity of multi-dimensional poverty in rural areas is either close or higher than in urban areas. As a result, the global MPI in rural areas reaches 0.102, 0.017 higher than the provincial MPI in Table 5-7 and 0.041 more than the MPI in urban areas. In 2018, the MPI in rural areas reduces to 0.066 but 0.018 and 0.044 higher than the provincial MPI and urban MPI respectively.

---

[2] Hukou is a system of household registration used in mainland China. It officially identifies a person as a permanent resident of an area and includes identifying information such as name, parents, spouse and date of birth. Due to its connection to social programs provided by the government, which assigns benefits based on agricultural and non-agricultural residency status (often referred to as rural and urban), the hukou system is sometimes likened to a form of caste system, which is considered the root cause of Chinese urban-rural dual structure. (source: Wikipedia, https://en.wikipedia.org/wiki/Hukou)

Table 5-8 MPI Results in Guizhou's Rural and Urban Areas

Area	Year	Pop share (%)	MPI	H (%)	A (%)
Rural	2016	54.49	0.102 [0.002, 0.196]	25.17[1.61,48.02]	40.67[38.47,41.77]
	2018	52.48	0.066 [0.042, 0.095]	17.12[10.05, 25.57]	38.33[35.62, 42.11]
Urban	2016	44.15	0.061[0.067, 0.185]	14.89[13.54, 44.64]	41.26[34.36, 51.04]
	2018	47.52	0.022[0.00, 0.051]	6.11[5.57, 14.38]	36.45[33.98, 42.51]

The intensified implementation of series of targeted TAP projects especially in rural areas during the 13th Five-Year Plan period (2016-2020) has brought decline of MPI in both rural and urban areas. Table 5-8 shows that from 2016 to 2018, the MPI, headcount ratio and intensity of multi-dimensional poverty in rural areas drop by 0.036, 8.05% and 2.34% separately only slightly lower than the decline rates of these three indexes by 0.039, 8.78% and 4.81% in urban areas. Despite a very low reduction of rural population share by 2.01% from 2016 to 2018 (Table 5-8), the annualized change of MPI in rural areas is 0.014, almost close to the urban MPI change of 0.019 while the annualized change of multi-dimensional poverty incidence in rural areas is even 1.97 percentage points higher than in urban areas (Table 5-9). The slight differences in change rates in MPI and headcount ratio between rural and urban areas prove that the TAP projects-led tourism growth could reduce the rural-urban gap and greatly benefit the rural poor simulated in the CGE analysis.

Table 5-9 Annualized MPI and Headcount Ratio Changes in Guizhou

	Absolute	t-statistics	P-value (two-tailored)
Rural （MPI）	0.014	-0.27**	0.804
Urban （MPI）	0.019	0.203**	0.842
Rural （H）	6.28	0.331**	0.762
Urban （H）	4.31	-0.016**	0.988

Note: ** statistically significant at $\alpha=0.05$.

Regarding the censored headcount ratio difference in three sustainable development dimensions, Table 5-10 reveals that the percentages of the MPI poor deprived in all dimensions in rural areas are significantly higher than in urban areas. In 2016, the total differences of deprivation levels in economic, social and cultural and environmental dimensions are 8.68%, 11.07% and 22.02% while in 2018 the differences in economic and environmental dimensions reduce to 4.19% and 19.32% except for the rise of social and cultural dimension to 16.02%. The increase of social and cultural dimension difference by 4.95% is mainly resulted from the large decrease of urban poor's deprivation level in insurance coverage from 10.64% in 2016 to 4.58% in 2018.

As for the differences of the censored headcount ratio in individual indicators between rural and urban areas, the rural poor's deprivation levels of all indicators are higher than that of the poor in urban area except for the economic indicator "housing". The percentage points of MPI poor deprived in housing in urban areas are 2.57 in 2016 and 0.86 in 2018 higher than in rural areas. The higher deprivation level of the poor population in urban areas is because housing cost is much lower in rural areas than in urban areas in China. Besides, when implementing targeted TAP projects under TAPPs, Guizhou invested the reconstruction and restoration of poor ethnic villages, which greatly improved the housing conditions of the poor in rural areas.

On the other hand, the three indicators that the rural poor are most deprived in are "cooking fuels", "years of schooling" and "drinking water", two of which are from environmental and one from social and cultural dimensions. In 2016, the deprivation levels in "cooking fuels", "years of schooling", and "drinking water" in rural areas are 20%, 15.51% and 11.03%, 15.04%, 7.71% and 6.07% higher than in urban areas. In 2018, the differences in deprivation levels of "cooking fuels" and "years of schooling" between rural areas and urban areas reduced to 10.31% and 6.38%. However, the rural-urban difference in "drinking water" deprivation levels widened to 6.69% despite that this indicator's deprivation level of the poor in rural areas decreased from 11.03% in 2016 to 8.22% in 2018.

The indicator analysis demonstrates that TAPPs contribute to the relief of rural MPI in all sustainability dimensions. From 2016 to 2018, the poor people in Guizhou rural areas enjoyed the decrease of all ten indicators with the largest reduction of deprivation level in the environmental indicator "cooking fuel" followed by social and cultural indicator "years of schooling" and economic indicator "assets". However, the deprivation levels of the poor in rural areas in these three indicators in 2018 remained higher than in urban areas though the gap became narrower. The proportions of the poor in urban areas deprived in most indicators didn't change as largely as in rural areas except for a reduction of deprivation level in basic insurance coverage in urban areas from 10.64% to 4.58%. Nevertheless, the impoverished people's deprivation level in basic insurance coverage in rural areas kept as high as 10.61% in 2018, partly explaining the higher child mortality rate in rural areas than urban areas.

Table 5-10 Censored Headcount Ratios and Differences in Urban and Rural Areas

Dimensions		**Economic dimension**				**Social and cultural dimension**			**Environmental dimension**		
Area	Year	A	H	CM	N	I	YS	SA	CF	DW	E
Rural	2016	8.62	3.1	4.96	8.27	13.1	15.51	7.8	20	11.03	5.17
		[-4.39, 21.56	[0.37,5.83]	[-11.57, 22.17]	[-6.01, 21.84]	[-2.98, 28.43]	[4.38, 25.92]	[-6.33, 22.65]	[-2.64, 42.56]	[0.13, 21.2]	[-0.91,11.3]
	2018	4.45	1.53	1.53	2.39	10.61	10.96	5.14	13.36	8.22	3.08
		[0.69, 9.6]	[-1.56, 4.98]	[-3.31, 6.34]	[0.31,4.48]	[1.29, 19.26]	[5.74, 14.81]	[-1.74, 11.33]	[2.48, 24.24]	[2.32, 14.12]	[-0.64, 6.8]
Urban	2016	5.67	5.67	1.38	3.55	10.64	7.8	6.9	4.96	4.96	4.26
		[-3.97, 15,72]	[0.18,11.39]	[-6.02,21.83]	[-3.44, 10.84]	[-15.54, 37.89]	[-3.53, 19.65]	[-9.66, 23.35]	[-6.16, 16.59]	[-8.61, 19.13]	[-0.66, 9.38]
	2018	2.29	2.39	1.03	0	4.58	4.58	1.53	3.05	1.53	0.76
		[-0.14, 2.38]	[-1.65, 3.17]	[-1.06,, 3.11]	[-1.65, 3.17]	[0.56, 10.19]	[-3.10,13.89]	[-3.41, 6.54]	[-2.58, 8.73]	[-0.14, 4.73]	[-1.65,3.17]
Rural-urban differences	2016	8.68				11.07			22.02		
	2018	4.19				16.02			19.32		

Notes: A represents "assets", H "housing", CM " child mortality", N "nutrition", I "basic insurance", YS "years of schooling", SA "school attendance", CF "cooking fuels", DW "drinking water" and E "electricity.

b. MPI in Rural and Urban Hukou Groups

A hukou is a record in China's legally mandated household registration system, dividing people into rural and non-rural population. The dual system is frequently viewed as a caste system in China (Chan & Zhang, 1999), and it caused problems with inequality, income poverty, and prejudice (Afridi et. al., 2015). In 2014, the Chinese government initiated the hukou system reform, which prevented migrants from equal access to pensions, education, and healthcare services. Many cities relaxed requirements for migrant registration. According to the China Ministry of Public Security (MPS), China has helped at least 100 million rural people settle in towns and cities, elevating the nation's urbanization rate of registered households from 35.9 percent in 2013 to 44.4 percent in 2019 (CMPS, 2020).

Hukou has significant impacts on the multi-dimensional poverty. The CFPS 2010, 2012 and 2014 proved that, in China, residents of rural hukou families are more likely to be poor. From 2010 to 2014, the multi-dimensional poverty changes in rural hukou groups were significant while urban hukou groups improved very little (Alkire & Shen, 2017). CFPS 2016 and 2018 for Guizhou tells a slightly different story. Although the rural hukou groups were multi-dimensionally poorer than urban hukou groups in Guizhou, the poverty changes of the both groups were significant.

As shown in Table 5-11, the MPI of the two groups was very close in 2016 as many impoverished rural hukou groups living in harsh natural conditions were relocated to habitable small towns since 2016. This was taken as a targeted poverty alleviation measure known as "poverty alleviation through relocation" under the hukou system reform. The relocation of the impoverished with rural hukou could explain the similar MPI of the rural and urban hukou groups in Guizhou. However, the MPI of urban hukou groups decreased by 0.034 from 2016 to 2018, almost double the reduction rate of MPI of rural hukou groups by 0.018.

Table 5-12 further revealed that the annualized change of MPI in urban hukou households was 0.001 higher than in rural Hukou households. In addition, the reduction of headcount ratios of multi-dimensional poverty in urban hukou households was also more significant than in rural hukou households. Similarly, the annualized change of multi-dimensional poverty headcount ratio of urban hukou households was 3.31% higher than that of rural hukou households. The differences in multi-dimensional poverty intensity were not as obvious as headcount ratio. The MPI and headcount ratio changes in rural and urban hukou groups also differed from those in rural and urban areas.

Compared with the censored headcount ratios in rural and urban areas, the impoverished with rural hukou were less deprived in economic and environmental indicators but more destitute of social and cultural indicators represented by "years of schooling" and "insurance". The deprivation levels of rural hukou households in "years of schooling" and "insurance" were 20% and 17.5% respectively in 2016, 4.49% and 4.4% higher than in rural areas (Table 5-10). In 2018, the destitute levels of rural hukou groups in the two social and cultural indicators reduced significantly. Still, they remained the most deprived indicators and higher than the levels of urban hukou groups (Table 5-13). The deprivation levels in most economic indicators in rural hukou groups were lower than in rural areas represented by "assets", "child mortality" and "nutrition".

However, in both years, the destitute levels of rural hukou households in housing were higher than in rural areas. This result could be explained by the migration of some impoverished rural residents who left their rural hometown for urban areas for survival. Unfortunately, they couldn't afford the adequate housing in the urban areas for years. Meanwhile, they strived to make a living in urban areas and were not willing to return the backward rural areas. Therefore, they gave up improving their housing conditions in rural hometown, causing the relatively higher deprivation level in housing in rural household groups and urban areas (Table 5-10). On the other hand, the Guizhou government's initiative in relocating the impoverished living in severe rural conditions led to the lower deprivation level of rural hukou groups in environmental indicators such as "cooking fuel" and "drinking water" than in rural areas but the higher destitute level of urban hukou groups in these indicators than in urban areas (Table 5-13).

Table 5-11 MPI Results of Rural and Urban Hukou Groups

Area	Year	MPI	H (%)	A (%)
Rural	2016	0.087 [-0.010, 0.183]	21.39 [-1.9,44.68]	40.69 [37.03,43.39]
	2018	0.069[-0.001,0.11]	17.54[4.09, 31.24]	39.72 [8.02, 56.89]
Urban	2016	0.083[0.046, 0.119]	21.05[8.28, 36.46]	39.42[27.29, 51.4]
	2018	0.049 [0.042, 0.095]	13.51 [10.05, 25.57]	36.26[35.62, 42.11]

Table 5-12 Annualized Change of MPI and Headcount Ratio of Rural and Urban Hukou Households

	Absolute	t-statistics	P-value(two-tailored)
Rural （MPI）	0.016	0.469**	0.671
Urban （MPI）	0.017	-0.026**	0.981
Rural （H） (%)	1.6	-0.079**	0.942
Urban （H） (%)	4.91	0.018**	0.987

Note: ** statistically significant at α=0.05

Table 5-13 Censored Headcount Ratios of Rural and Urban Hukou Groups

Hukou	Year	A	H	CM	N	I	YS	SA	CF	DW	E
Rural	2016	8.56	5.26	2.67	7.02	17.5	20	8.77	15.78	10	5.35
		[-2.86, 19.94]	[-3.28,11.02]	[-5.68, 10.89]	[5.67 8.53]	[4.16, 30.02]	[-1.82,41.57]	[-9.59, 28.75]	[-3.42, 35.07]	[-4.19, 24.84]	[-3.23, 13.97]
	2018	3.66	2.61	1.31	1.47	11.76	13.37	4	10.42	4.74	2.87
		[-0.66, 7.89]	[-1.96, 6.57]	[-1.75, 4.27]	[0.58,2.47]	[-3.15, 26.6]	[0.82, 25.94]	[10.9, 20.9]	[-3.87, 24.14]	[1.72, 9.8]	[-0.26, 5.97]
Urban	2016	7.5	3.74	1.75	6.42	14.04	10.53	6.68	15	9.36	1.75
		[-0.47, 15.01]	[-1.19, 8.66]	[-4.55, 8.71]	[-6.28, 19.18]	[-1.21, 30.25]	[-0.83, 22.17]	[-5.99, 19.3]	[5.37, 24.83]	[-2.85, 21.57]	[-3.89, 7.47]
	2018	1.75	0	0	2.5	8.09	8.09	3.91	9.92	5.26	0
		[-3.89, 7.47]	[0, 0]	[0, 0]	[-5.5, 10.5]	[1.22, 13.9]	[3.61, 12.04]	[-1.47, 9.38]	[2.11, 17.31]	[-6.69, 18.37]	[0, 0]
Rural-urban hukou differ-ences	2016	4.1				15.02			5.02		
	2018	4.9				10.04			3.95		

Notes: A represents "assets", H "housing", CM " child mortality", N "nutrition", I "basic insurance", YS "years of schooling", SA "school attendance", CF "cooking fuels", DW "drinking water" and E "electricity".

Robustness and Stability Analysis

This study chooses to change weighting structures to check the MPI's robustness to various weights. Based on Alkire and Fang (2018), the study selects four additional weighting structures besides the benchmark nested structure, giving equal weights to three dimensions and indicators within each dimension. The first three alternative weighting structures assign 50% of the relative weight to one of the three dimensions and 25% to the other two dimensions. In a fourth weighting vector, the study uses a specific frequency weighting structure to calculate the weight of each indicator j as follows:

$$w_{jt} = \ln\left(\frac{1}{h_{jt}}\right) / \sum_{j=1}^{d} \ln\left(\frac{1}{h_{jt}}\right) = \ln h_{jt} / \sum_{j=1}^{d} \ln\left(h_{jt}\right)$$

where h_{jt} denotes the raw headcount ratio of indicator j. This frequency weight gives more weight to indicators with a lower deprived proportion. The frequency weighting structure, unlike the other data-driven weighting structures, has its own economic implications. It implies that if a person is deprived in some universally used indicator, this deprivation is considered very serious. As a result, there are five different weighting structures for economic, social and cultural and environmental dimensions: nested weights for each dimension with 10 indicators; 50%, 25%, 25%; 25%, 50%, 25%; 25%, 25%, 50% and frequency weights, respectively. As a result, we refer to these as weights 1 through 5 (Table 5-14).

Table 5-14 Different MPI Weighting Structures

Weight 1	Weight 2	Weight 3	Weight 4	Weight 5
Nested	50% economic dimension	50% social and cultural dimension	50% environmental dimension	Frequency weights

First, the study computed MPI's Kendall -b rank correlations with different weighting structures. Then the adjusted first-order stochastic dominance method was used to test MPI stability for weighting changes.

Table 5-15 Kendall's T-B Rank Correlation Coefficients for MPI with Different Weights

	Weight 1	Weight 2	Weight 3	Weight 4	Weight 5
Weight 1	1.000	0.556*	0.644**	0.556*	0.378*
Weight 2	0.556*	1.000	0.733**	0.556*	0.644**
Weight 3	0.644**	0.733**	1.000	0.378*	0.556*
Weight 4	0.556*	0.446*	0.378*	1.000	0.644**
Weight 5	0.378*	0.644*	0.556*	0.644**	1.000

Notes: * and ** stand for correlation coefficients that are statistically significant at levels of 5% and 1% or lower respectively. Weight 1 denotes MPI with nested weight for each dimension with 10 indicators; weight2 denotes MPI with the weight structure 50% for economic dimension, 25% for social and cultural dimension and 25% for environmental dimension; weight3 refers to MPI with the weight structure 25% for economic dimension, 50% for social and cultural dimension, 25% for environmental dimension; weight4 refers to MPI with the weight structure 25% for economic dimension, 25% for social and cultural dimension, 50% for environmental dimension and weight5 refers to MPI with the frequency weight.

a. MPI Correlation with Various Weighting Structures

Table 5-15 presents the Kendall's τ-b rank correlation coefficients among MPIs with different weights. The computation is performed based on the pooled data. The scale of the correlation coefficients varies despite all being statistically significant at the 5% or 1% levels. The largest correlation coefficient is 0.733 between MPI under weight 2 and MPI under weight 3. The lowest correlation efficient of 0.378 is found between MPI under weight 3 and MPI under weight 4, MPI under weight 1 and MPI under weight 5. As set previously, 50% is assigned to the social and cultural dimension in weight 3 while the weight of this dimension reduces to 25% in weight 2 and weight 4. The significant differences in correlations between MPIs under weights 2, 3 and 4 indicate that the changes of social and cultural dimension weight are important to Guizhou MPI under the same indicators. The correlation of MPIs weight 1 and weight 3 is 0.644, only slightly higher than the coefficients of MPIs under weight 1 and weight 2, weight 1 and weight 3, both of which are 0.556. The relatively high and stable correlation of MPIs between weight 1 and the other three normative weights proves the robustness of MPI under normative weights. However, the lowest correlation between MPIs under weight 1 and weight 5 reflects that the MPI is sensitive to the switch from nested weights to frequency weights since weight 1 gives equal weight to each dimension and weight 5 is frequency weight which affects the MPI through the restriction between indicator poverty and indicator's weight.

b. First-Order Stochastic Dominance (FOSD) Analysis

The study further tests the variation of multi-dimensional poverty status of different income groups under five different weights. The horizontal axis of the first-order stochastic dominance (FOSD) is replaced with the income cumulative proportion. The construction steps are as follows: To begin, sort the deprivation scores by ascending income and compute the cumulative proportion of income, which the study could label with p; then define F (p) as the cumulative function of individual deprivation scores multiplied by p as is shown in the following function:

$$F(p_l) = \sum_{i \le l} \frac{p_i}{nm_0}.$$

The FOSD is defined as follows: Given two different cumulative distribution functions F1 (p) and F2 (p), F1 (p) first-order stochastically dominates F2 (p) if and only if F1 (p) < F2 (p). If there is FOSD relation between two distribution functions, namely F1 (p) and F2 (p), it could be stated that, in the case of the second distribution, most of the multidimensional poor people are much more concentrated in the low-income group, implying that its identified targets tend to overlap with the income poor. On the other hand, if the two cumulative distribution functions don't have the FOSD relations, it indicates that there is no great difference between the levels of multidimensional poverty under different weights. Besides, if the distributions fall on the diagonal line, it means that multidimensional poverty is distributed uniformly across income groups, and there is no difference in multidimensional poverty status among all income groups.

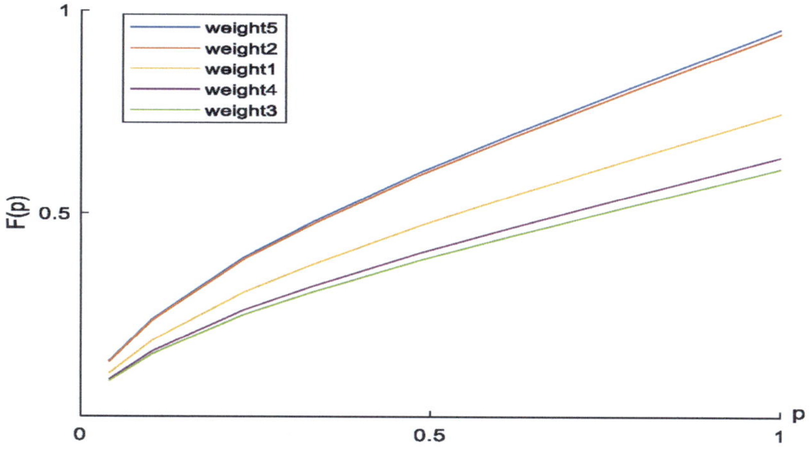

Figure 5-6 FOSD Analysis of MPIs under Different Weights in 2016

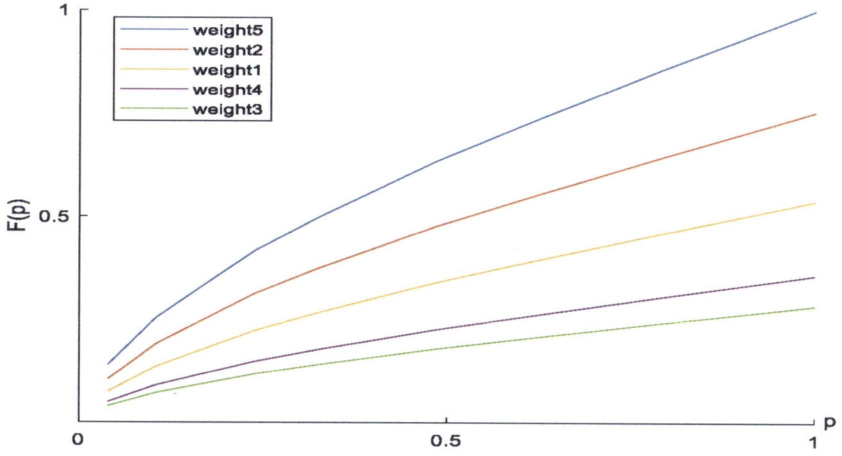

Figure 5-7 FOSD Analysis of MPIs under Different Weights in 2018

Figure 5-6 and Figure 5-7 show three levels of FOSD relations among Guizhou's MPIs under different weights: MPI under weight 5 and weight 2, MPI under weight 1 and MPI under weight 4 and 3. The dominance relations are as follows: the MPI under weight 4 and weight 2 dominates the MPI under weight1 and the MPI under weight 1 dominates the MPI under weight 4 and weight 3. In 2016 and 2018, the MPI under frequency weights dominates the MPIs under all normative weights. This echoes the conclusion of correlation analysis that there are differences between the MPI under frequency weights and the MPIs under normative weights especially the nested weights. It's also obvious that multi-dimensional poverty measurement under frequency weights is more concentrated on the low-income groups especially in 2018.

Among the measures under four normative weights, the MPI under weight 2 dominates the measurements under the other three normative weights in both years. This dominance relationship shows that the multi-dimensional poverty tend to be distributed among lower income groups if more weights are given to economic indicators, indicating the indicators under the economic dimension are highly related to the income level of households. The MPI under the nested weights dominate weight 4 and 3, proving that the multidimensional poverty measurement under nested weights also overlap the income poverty rate in Guizhou. This explains why Guizhou MPI results are similar to its absolute poverty rates in 2016 and 2018.

After the correlation analysis has proved the robustness of the MPI under normative weights in the previous section, the FOSD analysis in this section further reveals that the weighting structure is critical in measuring multidimensional poverty. The distribution of multidimensional poverty is affected by weight changes. The multidimensional poverty measured under frequency weights, weight 2 with greater weights to economic indicators and nested weights with equal weights to all dimensions are distributed among low income groups, making MPI results similar to income poverty rates. However, MPI could differ from absolute poverty rate if more weights are given to environmental, social, and cultural dimensions, as in weight 3 and weight 4. The reason is that they are less concentrated on low income groups than the MPIs under the other 3 weights. Therefore, it's a balanced and reliable choice for this study to choose equal weights for assessing TAPPs' impacts on Guizhou's global MPI under the sustainable development paradigm.

Results of Stakeholders' Perceptions of TAPPs' Impacts on the Sustainable Development at TAP Destination

The AF-MPI assessment results have proved that TAPPs impacted the multi-dimensional poverty reduction. However, AF-MPI assessment under sustainability dimensions using CFPS data provides a limited understanding of TAPPs' impacts on the sustainable development in

TAP destinations as the sustainability indicators reflected in the TAPPs are far more than global MPI related to SDGs. Therefore, in order to have a holistic understanding of TAPPs' impacts on the sustainable development in TAP destinations, this section focuses on investigating TAP stakeholders' perceptions of TAPPs' impacts on the sustainable development at Zhaoxing Dong Ethnic Village in Guizhou through the semi-structured interview.

Method

The data used in the CGE analysis and AFMPI analysis are both from government statistics or standard surveys, which could not provide sufficient evidence for holistic understanding TAPPs' impacts on the sustainable development in TAP destinations. Based on the documentary analysis of the sustainability of TAPPs, this section adopts the semi-structured interview to explore TAP stakeholders' perceptions of TAPPs' impacts on the sustainable development in a typical TAP destination in Guizhou to complement the findings of the CGE analysis and AFMPI analysis.

The interview guide was formulated mainly based on the AF-MPI indicators, and the core sustainability indicators developed by GSTC (2017) and ETIS (2016) under the three pillars of sustainability. The interview guide consists of open-ended and possible follow-up questions (Bernard, 2006; Hanna et. al., 2016) , focusing on TAP stakeholders' perception of TAPPs' impacts on economic, social, and cultural sustainability as environmental sustainability at Zhaoxing Dong Ethnic Village.

As Zhaoxing TAP projects in the targeted and efficient TAP period were jointly developed by the local government, enterprises and villagers, the semi-structured interview targeted local government officials, enterprise employers, documented poor villagers and non poor villagers. During the interview, enterprise owners were not specifically asked about TAPPs' contribution to the multidimensional poverty relief as they might not be familiar with details of these facts. Besides, the interview questions were phrased to elicit the changes of sustainable development at Zhaoxing Dong Ethnic Village and benefits brought by TAPPs that interviewees perceived.

A pilot study was conducted using the field-testing technique to ensure the intelligibility and effectiveness of the interview guide (Chenail, 2011; Kallio et. al., 2016). This technique is the most commonly used type of testing in developing a semi-structured interview process (Barriball & While, 1994; Krauss et. al., 2009; Turner, 2010). Field testing simulates the real interview situation and provides critical information about how the interviews are implemented and whether they elicit the participants' diverse perceptions and experiences (Barriball & While, 1994; Chenail, 2011). After the pilot interview with potential interviewees (n=4) on March 8, 2022, the order and form of some questions were reformulated to make them more practical and further improved the design.

With the help of head of the village CPC committee, the research team interviewed government officials responsible for TAP project development in the village and tourism related enterprise employers. Using opportunistic and snow-ball sampling, the researchers conducted semi-structured interviews with documented poor and non-poor villagers engaged in tourism or related industries. Another three interviews were made when the theoretical saturation was achieved in the 40th interview to verify the conjectures. The interviews stopped after the 43th interview. Table 5-16 shows the demographic information of the 43 interviewees. Interviews ranged from 20 minutes to one hour and a half with an average length of about 40 minutes. The researchers recorded the interviews primarily through photography and other recording methods, supplemented by written records of the key contents kept by the researchers. At the end of each day, the researchers kept a research diary. In addition to classifying and naming the photos and images, the researchers also structured and numbered the interview materials and other textual information.

Table 5-16 Demographic Features of Interviewees

	Number	
Gender	Male	26
	Female	17
Age	20-40	16
	41-60	20

	61 or above	7
Education	Primary School or No Schooling	18
	Junior School	8
	High School	13
	Bachelor or above	4
Occupation	Government Officials	5
	Enterprises Staff	10
	Farmers	28

Finally, the audio and video data were converted into text for coding and analysis. According to Table 5-17, there are three levels of codes: dimension, main codes and sub-codes. The main codes are from the TAPPs' sustainability values and core sustainability indicators under the three pillars of sustainability dimensions. The sub-codes are mainly from the Guizhou global MPI and the converted text. This study used two researchers with prior knowledge of tourism management to code text data separately to avoid human coding errors caused by errors in judgment. A binary data coding rule (yes or no) was used. In order to calculate coding consistency, we used the most common method (Gery and Russel, 2000): coding consistency =2M/(N1 + N2), where M represents the number of fully consistent codes, N1 represents the number of codes by the first coder, and N2 represents the number of codes by the second coder. Inter-coder reliability was 97.3% in the end.

Table 5-17 TAPPs' Impacts on Sustainable Development of TAP Destinations Perceived by Stakeholders

Dimension	**Codes**	**Sub-codes**	**Evidences**
Economic sustainability	economic stimulation	Government financial aid	"Our local government provides subsidies and funding to attract social investment for the village TAP projects."
		Free loan	"The bank grants me a three-year free

Dimension	Codes	Sub-codes	Evidences
			loan as my star-up capital."
		Investment promotion	"Our village TAP projects attracted more than 0.4 billion yuan through investment promotion."
		Industry revitalization	"Tourism boom has driven the revitalization of related industries."
	Employment and income	Expansion of job positions for the poor	"Poor villagers like me have the priorities to get the job positions offered by TAP projects."
		Income channel expansion for the poor	"Besides the wage from ethnic culture performance and local guide, I could get land rent and annual ticket dividend."
		Per capita income increase	"The annual per capita income of the village has increased greatly since 2013."
	Improved living conditions	Renovation of dilapidated rural houses	"With government's aid, the 110-year old wooden house of my family has been renovated for safety."
		Increase of assets ownership	"In the past, most of households in our village had no electrical appliances. But now many even own cars."
		More diversified diet	"While entertaining tourists, our own diets are more diversified than

Dimension	**Codes**	**Sub-codes**	**Evidences**
			before."
	Promotion of product and services	Marketing strategies to be intensified	"Our government should spend more marketing our village as the fast developing Xijiang Miao Village does."
	Income gap	Tourism participants-non participants' Income gap enlarged	"I could earn only a monthly salary of 600-800 yuan as a cleaning worker, less than the daily revenue of my neighbor, an ethnic homestay owner."
	Rising expenditure	Rise in prices	"The prices of necessities are much higher than before."
		High cost input	"I earned little from my plum garden for tourists as the input cost is too high."
Social and cultural sustainability	Education and health	Adults' years of schooling	"My wife and I had only three years of education."
		Skill training	"There are some irregular skill trainings held by the government or my company. But trainings are far from enough."
		Children's education quality	"As running a rural inn at home leaves more time with my sons, they are studying harder than before."
		Medical insurance	"The government subsidized me the medical insurance, greatly alleviating

Dimension	Codes	Sub-codes	Evidences
			the family's burden of my chronic disease."
	Professional service	Tourist complaints and satisfaction	"Most tourists enjoy their stay in our village but some complained about toilets and traffic jam in the scenic spots."
	Residents involvement, participation	Return of rural elites	"I worked as an art teacher in Shenzhen after college graduation.
		Return of migrant workers	In 2013, I was called for returning home to lead our villagers to get rich."
		Willingness to participate and cooperate	"My husband and I once worked in a factory in Guangdong. In 2014, We restored home and began to run this souvenir store." "I have a good relationship with my neighbors. We usually help one another to entertain our tourists better."
	Marginalization pressure relief	Self confidence improvement	"I'm more talkative after my living condition improved."
		Involvement in village management	"As villagers are shareholders of the scenic are, we have the voting right on important decisions.
		Family status improvement	"After getting a stable job in the tourism company, I

Dimension	Codes	Sub-codes	Evidences
			gain more respects from my family."
	Infrastructure	Transport network	"It's very convenient to get to our village from all over the country."
		Electricity, water and telecommunication improved	"Every household is accessible to electricity, tapped water and telecommunication services."
	Ethnic culture preservation	Actions and events taken to promote indigenous culture	"My family always actively participates in the cultural activities in the village."
		Maintenance of cultural sites	"There is a special fund for cultural sites maintenance."
		Retention of local customs and language	"I required my children to speak Dong language at home."
Environment sustainability	Scenic area upgrading	Tourism resources exploitation	"There is abundant tourism resource to be exploited."
		Renovation of tourist sites	"The government and enterprises are jointly responsible for the renovation of tourist sites."
		Improvement of tourism facilities	"Some tourism facilities such as the parking lots should be improved."
	Pollution curb	Air pollution curb	"We are not allowed to use firewood for cooking fuel."
		Water pollution curb	"Waste water restaurants and hotels is not allowed to

Dimension	Codes	Sub-codes	Evidences
			discharged into river directly”
		Solid waste discharge and management	“Solid wastes are reused in a garbage power plant.”
		Household sewage discharge	“Every household has indoor flush toilets.”
	Environmental protection awareness	Regulations on environmental protection	“The local government issued specific regulations on environmental protection in our village.”
		Residents’ environmental protection awareness	“We remind one another of not littering anywhere and would punish bad behaviors.”

The General Coding Results

Table 5-17 shows that in the process of three-level coding, the study identified 40 concrete impacts of 15 main impact items that constitute the stakeholders’ perception of TAPPs’ impacts on the sustainable development of Zhaoxing Dong Ethnic Village. Based on the three pillars sustainability framework for TAPPs documentary analysis (Purvis et. al., 2018; Guo, 2022), the data was coded into three sustainability dimensions: economic, social, cultural, and environmental sustainability.

It’s obvious that among the 15 main perceived impacts, 12 are related to economic sustainability and social and cultural sustainability while only three impacts are recognized under environmental sustainability. Besides, the perceived economic, social, and cultural sustainability impacts are almost the same. These results indicate that TAPPs have impacted economic, social, and cultural sustainability more than environmental sustainability at the TAP destination. This is consistent with the TAPPs’ sustainability value structure dominated by balanced economic, social, and cultural values.

It's easily found that tourism could contribute to the achievement of many interconnected SDGs not just limited to SDG1. The previous TAPPs documentary analysis and the quantitative assessment of TAPPs' impacts on poverty alleviation also revealed that the Chinese government's efforts to achieve SDG1 through TAP also facilitated the realization of other SDGs. Thus the perceived impacts of TAPPs on the sustainable development of TAP destinations were further classified into the impacts on the attainment of different SDGs. This classification was refined into economic, social-cultural, and environmental sustainability as shown in Table 5-18.

According to Table 5-18, Chinese TAPPs' impacts on the sustainable development at TAP destination involved 13 of the total 17 SDGs. Among them, five goals were most affected by TAPPs as they have the highest frequency. The five goals were SDG 1 (no poverty), SDG 17 (partnership for the goals), SDG 8 (decent work and economic growth), SDG 10 (reduced inequalities) and SDG 11 (sustainable cities and communities). Despite the diversified SDGs involved, stakeholders considered that SDG 1 and SDG 17 were the central goals impacted by TAPPs, indicating that the Chinese government strived to mobilize all relevant TAP stakeholders and different social forces to cooperate on eradicating absolute poverty and achieving other SDGs. SDG 17 is the only goal related to the perceived impacts under the three sustainability dimensions. These impacts reflected the effective implementation of TAPPs' sustainability values and targets through appropriate policy tools as analyzed in chapter four.

The consistency between the TAPPs' impacts and TAPPs' values revealed that Chinese TAPPs impacted the sustainable development at TAP destinations in terms of SDGs through the proper policy formulation and implementation. Most interviewees were satisfied with the TAPPs and are very optimistic about tourism's contribution to the sustainable development at the TAP destination.

Table 5-18 Perceived TAPPs' Impacts on the Attainment of SDGs at TAP Destination

Dimension	Perceived Impacts	SDGs
Economic sustainability	economic stimulation	SDG 1 and SDG 8
	Employment and income	SDG 1 and SDG 8
	Improved living conditions	SDG 1
	Promotion of product and services	SDG 8 and SDG 17
	Income gap	SDG 1 and SDG 10
	Rising expenditure	SDG 10
Social and cultural sustainability	Education and health	SDG 3 and SDG 4
	Professional service	SDG 17
	Residents involvement, participation	SDG 17
	Marginalization pressure relief	SDG 5
	Infrastructure	SDG 11
	Ethnic culture preservation	SDG 11
Environment sustainability	Scenic area upgrading	SDG 9
	Pollution curb	SDG 6, SDG 7 and SDG 12
	Environmental protection awareness	SDG 17

Stakeholders' Perceived Impacts of TAPPs on the Sustainable Development of TAP Destinations

Based on the general coding results of the semi-structured interview, this section further analyze TAP stakeholders' different perceptions of TAPPs' impacts on SDGs at the case study area under sustainability dimensions.

a. TAPPs' Impacts on Economic Sustainability

As found in chapter four, poverty alleviation and economic stimulation were the main focuses of the Chinese TAPPs' economic values in all TAP stages. The realization of TAPPs' economic values directly affected the government's fulfillment of SDGs especially SDG 1 (no poverty). Figure 5-8 shows that all stakeholder groups highly recognized the TAPPs' positive impacts on the economic sustainability. However, the poor and non-poor villagers also expressed their major concerns on the income gap between tourism and non-tourism residents and the increase of living costs due to the local tourism development under the TAPPs.

The TAPPs' positive impacts on the economic sustainability concentrate on TAP projects' contributions to SDG 1 (no poverty) and SDG 8 (decent work and economic growth). During the targeted and efficient TAP stage, TAPPs set the precise implementation of sustainable TAP projects as the main policy target. In order to ensure economic sustainability, the Guizhou local government used a mix of policy tools such as planning, funding, land, reform, innovation, and strategic measures (Table 4-5) when implementing TAP projects. For example, Guizhou first proposed and piloted "the Three-Pronged Reform Model for Rural Areas" in 2015 to revitalize poor rural residents' assets. This reform turns rural farmers' into shareholders, their resources into assets and their funds into shares in implementing pro-poor projects. Under the guidance of this policy reform and innovation, the Zhaoxing local government formulated a plan for the joint development of Zhaoxing Dong Ethnic Village with different stakeholders in 2015. An interviewee introduced:

"My family was once a documented poor household. In 2015, our local government encouraged us to participate in the development of the Dong village. The government offered me a three-year free loan and some subsidies to help me renovate my old shabby house into a Dong-ethnic homestay inn for renting to tourism companies. I earn rents and wages from the inn."

This innovated cooperative model under TAPPs facilitates the rapid development of TAP projects, expanding their income channels and maximizing the utilization of their resources. Two government officials further introduced that this model does not change the public ownership of land, nor crosses the red line of arable land. The reform highlights the mobilization of government resources which further leverages private sector resources. Three enterprise staffs believed this model has fostered and revitalized several tourism-related industries with local strengths. The boom of local tourism and its related industries created more job opportunities for the poor, increasing their income, improving their living conditions and the local economic growth. The head of Zhaoxing Township stated:

"Since 2015, our government has attracted more than 500 million yuan for TAP projects construction under the guidance of TAPPs. Despite the pandemic, the annual tourism revenue of the village maintains a year-on-year increase of about 50% during 2016-2021. Tourism-related sectors such as agriculture, livestock farming, cultural and creative industry witnessed fast development. The industrial revitalization created thousands of jobs for poor and non-poor residents. All poor households removed poverty by the end of 2020."

Despite TAPPs' positive impacts on economic sustainability, eight poor and non-poor villagers who were not directly involved in tourism sector were worried about the income gap between residents engaged in tourism and non –tourism positions. A second major concern is the rising expenditure which results in the rise of basic necessity prices and input cost. These two concerns reflect that TAPPs have no effective policy tools to curb tourism's most discussed negative impacts on equality, which may cause a detriment to SDG 1 (no poverty) at TAP destinations. A fifty-five-year-old orchard farmer told his story:

"My wife and I don't have the skills for entertaining tourists. In order to help my family eliminate poverty, the village officials suggested contracting an orchard with an area of 100 mu (about 6.67 hectares). However, we earned much less than our neighbors who work as tourist guides or run souvenir shops. As prices of most products have risen largely in recent years including pesticides and fertilizers, I have to input more to the orchard for the same harvest. Besides, the sale of my fruits is also a burden for me. My earnings are only enough to cover the expenditure of the orchard and my family's daily life."

The only controversy on TAPPs' impacts on economic sustainability lies in the inadequate efforts to promote tourism products and services of the TAP destination. As TAP projects are government-led, private tourism enterprises are unwilling to pay for the destination promotion campaign which might not generate immediate profits. Both enterprise staff and residents thought that it was the government's responsibility to expand TAP market through efforts to advertise uniqueness and image of the TAP destinations. However, the government officials revealed that the government alone couldn't afford the enough costs and efforts for promotion activities. This controversy is essentially a problem of ineffectively using the policy tool of strategic measures to the facts of TAP destinations. If not properly resolved, this problem may harm the achievement of SDG 8 and SDG 17 because the limited market expansion due to the lack of partnership could hinder the creation of jobs. As a non-poor villager who runs a supermarket in the scenic area suggested:

"The development of our village lags behind the Xijiang Miao Ethnic Village I once traveled to in another county in our province. I went there as I found something interesting in an advertisement of that village. I found various channels through which tourists get to know that place. I estimated that the number of tourists they receive triple that of ours. I hope our government could follow the Xijiang government and step up the measures for market expansion."

b. TAPPs' Impacts on Social and Cultural Sustainability

The interview results proved that SDG17 (partnership for the goals) is the only central goal involved in three sustainability dimensions, consistent with values of cooperation and participation and public service highlighted by TAPPs in its social and cultural value dimension. The involvement of SDG17 perceived by stakeholders in all dimensions indicates that TAPPs' impacts on achievement of social and cultural sustainability underpins the realization of SDGs under economic and environmental dimensions in the precise implementation of TAP projects. According to Figure 5-8, stakeholders perceived more positive impacts of TAPPs than negative ones on social and cultural sustainability.

However, they also expressed that TAPPs have little impact on improving adult education and professional service.

TAPPs mainly positively affected the attainment of SDG3 (good health and well-being), SDG4 (quality education), SDG5 (gender equality) and SDG11 (sustainable cities and communities) and SDG17 (partnership for the goals) under the social and cultural sustainability dimension. The government utilized policy tools such as talent, information, technical support, public service and partnership to reach social and cultural sustainability under these values. The TAPPs increased efforts to improve medical services, conditions and insurance. A government official introduced that Guizhou sent medical experts and encouraged medical graduates to TAP destinations to screen and cure the diseases of residents and tourists. The recent years also witness the popularity of heath tourism in Guizhou which features its superior natural environment for health enhancement and the technical advantage as the big data center of China. A seventy-year –old grandma stated:

"In these five years, old people at my age or above in my village have received regular medical check every year and enjoyed timely medical treatment funded by the medical insurance. Many of us stay in such good health that we could work as a 'Dong Big Song' teacher in tourism companies".

TAPPs impacted the realization of SDG4 mainly in the quality of children's education at the TAP destination. The interview found that the education of left-behind children was once a big problem in the village as their parents were migrant workers in faraway cities. Most of them were taken care of by their grandparents. With little or even no schooling, grandparents could only guarantee the basic life of their grandchildren. However, they didn't know how to help their grandchildren finish their homework or develop a good habit of living and learning. Many grandparents even spoiled their grandchildren. With the implementation of TAP projects, more and more villagers choose to take the jobs offered by TAP projects in the village. Thus, they could educate and accompany their children at home during non-working hours. Besides, the government sent volunteer teachers to improve the education quality in the village. A mother said,

"I once had to work for a living in Guangdong leaving my two children at home. The kids were very naughty and had no interest in schooling. They often skipped classes but their grandparents didn't know. Now I run a homestay inn and have time to help them solve problems. A new volunteer teacher also arouses their interest in learning. Their performance at school has improved a lot."

TAPPs are perceived to have empowered women and contributed to gender equality (SDG5). Almost all female respondents complained that women's status in Guizhou was generally lower than that of women in central and eastern provinces in China. As a marginalized group, they often suffer violence if they did not obey their bread-winner husbands who were the family's authority. Women usually have a narrow horizon as they are limited to raising children and housework at home. Girls usually have less schooling than boys as parents think girls will be daughters-in-law of other families when they grow up. However, the local tourism boom under TAPPs has liberated women from the shackles of the family. Tourism creates positions suitable for women such as tourist guide, hotel waitress, cleaning workers, embroidery artisan etc. The communications with tourists outside the village also broaden their horizon. Their tourism participation has earned more respect from the family and their social status has been improved significantly. A woman stated:

"My husband was very rude to me in the past. We fought frequently. Since I could obtain income from ethnic performances in the tourism company, he has respected me more and more and we seldom fight now. I will work hard to earn more to fund my daughter's schooling so that she will support herself in the future."

TAP development is conducive to the sustainable communities in terms of infrastructure improvement and ethnic cultural heritage preservation at TAP destinations (SDG11). Before the precise implementation of TAP projects, the village was isolated from the outside world due to the poor infrastructure. Most TAP destinations, including the village, are listed in Guizhou's expressway network construction planning to assist the TAP projects implementation. The

TAP destination has convenient connections with major airports in the province. The highways in the neighborhood of the village have been improved greatly. Besides the great progress of the transport network, electricity, tapped water and telecommunication services have reached every household. Thanks to the reputation as China's largest ethnic Dong Village, the government has put ethnic culture protection on the top agenda. A special program has been launched to restore the village's tangible and intangible cultural heritage. In addition, five villagers said they are encouraged to participate in various cultural activities and retain the ethnic Dong language and customs in their daily life. A villager said,

"Our children are required to speak the Dong language at home though they are taught to speak standard Chinese at school. They are told they must retain our language and culture which is our pride and resource of living."

TAPPs have stimulated residents' involvement, participation and cooperation in TAP projects (SDG17). The local government surveyed the rural elites to ensure the reserve of high-quality human resources for TAP projects. Since 2013, rural elites working outside the village have been invited and persuaded to return home for hometown development. They have made great contribution to TAP projects' construction and operation. Led by the rural elites, more and more migrant workers returned home to get employed in the village. Besides, eight respondents agreed they have developed good relationship with their neighbors and are willing to cooperate to provide best services for tourists and exhibit the good image of their village.

"All residents in our village share the same surname "Lu". Our village is like a big family. In the past, we occasionally quarreled over something tiny. With tourism development, we are busy entertaining tourists collaboratively and becoming more tolerant."

Nevertheless, TAPPs haven't solved the problems in adult education and professional services. Many adults in the village born before 1990's have no or less than six years of schooling. Poor households in particular took their children as labor force to struggle for a living. Their lack of education directly weakens their capabilities to participate in TAP projects. TAPPs propose professional training to improve the poor's competence in TAP participation. However, three residents criticized that such trainings are neither scheduled nor targeted. Most residents found it boring and unhelpful to attend these trainings. A rabbit keeper said:

"I have only two years of schooling. I dare not talk with tourists. So I raise rabbits and sell them to the restaurants in the scenic area. I have no experience in rabbit breeding. I attended a training lecture on animal breeding but got nothing useful. Thirty rabbits died for unknown reasons this May. I felt very depressed."

On the other hand, though TAPPs have made significant achievements in establishing partnership for sustainable TAP goals, the cooperation in enhancing the professional service of tackling tourists' complaints must be intensified. Two enterprise staffs reflected that the complaints from tourists focus on the difficulty in finding toilets and the traffic jam in the core scenic area. These complaints need to be resolved with the collaboration of different stakeholders, whereas there has been little progress.

"My guests told me that the signs of tourism toilets are not obvious. It's said the consultant of our village suggested that the change of the signs will affect the overall image of the ancient buildings. I think it ridiculous."

c. TAPPs' Impacts on Environmental Sustainability

Ecological construction was put on the top agenda of the Chinese poverty alleviation program in the targeted period. The TAPPs in TAP targeted and efficient stage, though still dominated by economic, social and cultural values, have significantly increased their attention to the environmental values. TAPPs emphasizing the environmental protection and improvement of human habitat in the environmental value have facilitated the environmental sustainability in TAP destinations. Figure 5-8 shows that enterprise staffs and government officials mentioned very little on the negative impacts of TAPPs on achieving environmental sustainability in TAP destination. At the same time, poor and non-poor villagers were not satisfied with the scenic area upgrading.

TAPPs were recognized to have played an active role in realizing SDG7 (affordable and clean energy), SDG6 (clean water and sanitation), SDG12 (responsible consumption and production) and SDG17 (partnership for the goals). Taking regulation, technical support and information as the main policy tools, the local government has made achievements in preventing air pollution (SDG7), water pollution (SDG6) and managing discharge of solid waste (SDG12) and raising residents' environmental protection awareness (SDG17).

Five interviewees mentioned that the local government issued a special environmental protection regulation. By the special regulation, households are not allowed to cut trees for firewood but take natural gas or marsh gas as cooking fuel instead of firewood. The sewage from different sources such as hotels, restaurants, and households must be treated in a sewage plant instead of being discharged directly into the river. With the support from experts invited by the local government, a garbage power plant was set up to recycle solid discharge from the village and the neighbourhood areas. The government environmental protection department releases environmental monitoring information regularly and anyone that violates the regulation will be fined or punished. The environmental protection awareness of the residents has thus been raised significantly. Besides, the improved living conditions under the economic sustainability, particularly the renovation of dilapidated houses of the poor villagers subsidized by the government and enterprises, also actively respond to the TAPPs' environmental value of human habitat improvement.

"In the past, we were immersed in the smoke from kitchen chimneys. Now we use clean gas. The sky is brighter without smoke and the water tastes sweeter without sewage. Littering is very rare. Our village has become safer and more charming with renovated houses of ethnic architecture style."

Despite the government's achievements in environmental protection, TAPPs need to improve its impacts on SDG 9 (industry, innovation and infrastructure) regarding scenic area upgrading under TAPPs' environmental value dimension. The scenic area upgrading could help improve TAP destination image and optimize tourists' experience. Two poor residents and three non-poor residents noted that though the government and enterprises jointly restored and renovated some cultural tourist sites, there's abundant natural tourism resource to be exploited for expanding the scenic area and increasing the stay of tourists. Besides, some tourism facilities such as the parking lots couldn't satisfy the increase the self-driving tourists, which is also the major cause of tourists' complaints about the traffic jam in the village.

"There are few parking lots in our village. Many tourists drive here. It's very difficult for them to find a parking space. In the peak season, they have to park their cars in parking lots in the county, which is 41 kilometers away from our village at a very high expense."

d. Stakeholders' Different Perceptions of TAPPs' Positive and Negative Impacts on TAP Destination Sustainable Development

Based on various TAP stakeholders' perceptions of TAPPs' impacts on attaining SDGs under three sustainability dimensions, this section further reviews the TAPPs' positive and negative impacts on TAP destination sustainable development perceived by main TAP stakeholders. The percentage of perceived impact items mentioned by different stakeholders is shown in Figure 5-8. In general, different stakeholders have different perspectives on the positive and negative impacts of the TAPPs. Local government officials, enterprise staffs and poor villagers paid more attention to the positive impacts than negative impacts in all dimensions. However, non-poor villagers attached almost equal attention to positive and negative impacts of TAPPs on sustainable development at TAP destinations. Besides, government officials and enterprise staffs expressed less on TAPPs' negative environmental sustainability impacts than poor and non-poor villagers.

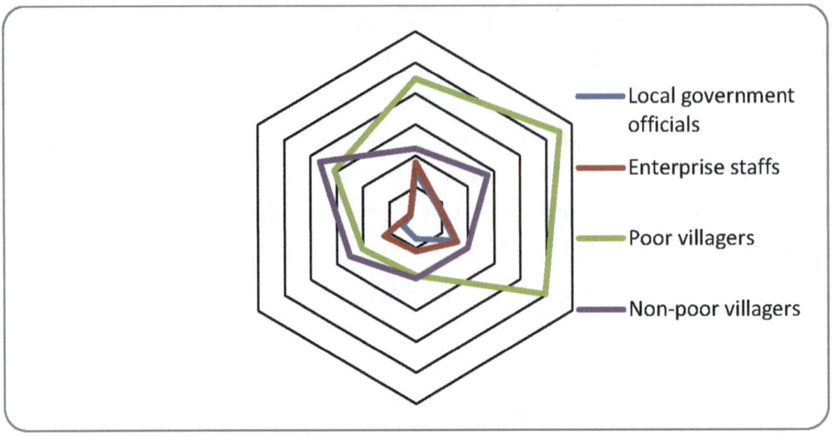

Figure 5-8 Percentage of Perceived Impact Items Mentioned by Main TAP Stakeholders

Notes: 1. Positive impacts I are " positive economic sustainability impacts"; Positive impacts II are " positive social and cultural sustainability impacts"; Positive impacts III are " positive environmental sustainability impacts"; Negative impacts I are " negative economic sustainability impacts"; Negative impacts II are " negative social and cultural sustainability impacts"; Negative impacts II are " negative environmental sustainability impacts".

Conclusion

As poverty targeted in SDG1 is a multi-dimensional problem, this chapter has reported MPI results under the sustainable development paradigm. In order to understand TAPPs' impacts on sustainable multi-dimensional poverty reduction through tourism, the study chose a typical TAP province Guizhou as the instrumental case study area. The Alkire-Frost methodology was used to compute TAPPs' impacts on Guizhou's multi-dimensional poverty reduction adapted from the global MPI 2020. After the global MPI analysis under the sustainable development paradigm, this chapter used a semi-structured interview to further investigate stakeholders' perceptions of TAPPs' impacts on the SDG1–led sustainable development at TAP destinations.

It's concluded from AF-MPI analysis that TAPPs facilitated the alleviation of multi-dimensional poverty in the study area. Using the latest China Family Panel Studies (CFPS) in 2016 and 2018, the study found that Guizhou's global MPI values and absolute poverty rates were very close in these two years. The province's MPI values also witnessed similar reduction rates to its absolute poverty rates. The Guizhou poor has a very high deprivation level in the social and cultural indicator "years of schooling", which has been identified as the major cause for their incapability in TAP participation analyzed in the CGE analysis. The disaggregation analysis of two sub-groups rural-urban area group and rural-urban hukou group shows that the TAPPs have reduced the rural-urban gap in the multi-dimensional poverty.

Despite the similar decline rates of the MPI and the narrowed overall censored headcount ratio differences in economic and environmental indicators between rural-urban area groups, the gap in the deprivation level of the social and cultural indicators between the two groups was widened due to the urban area's faster improvements in these indicators. On the other hand, rural-urban hukou groups' MPI values got closer owing to the hukou reform from 2014 and the relocation of some impoverished rural hukou groups under TAPPs. However, the MPI reduction rate of urban hukou group doubled that of the rural hukou group because the latter is more deprived in the social and cultural indicators "years of schooling" and "insurance" even than the rural area group. The higher social and cultural indicator deprivation weakened their ability to overcome multi-dimensional poverty.

Following the quantitative AF-MPI analysis, the qualitative semi-structured interview investigated the TAP stakeholders' perceptions of TAPPs' impacts on the sustainable development at a typical TAP destination in the case study area. It's found that the four main stakeholder groups at the TAP destination are satisfied with TAPPs' positive impacts. However, non-poor and poor residents expressed more concerns than enterprise staffs and government officials. Besides, they perceived TAPPs' more impacts on the economic, social, and cultural sustainability than environmental sustainability at the TAP destination, consistent with TAPPs' value orientations dominated by economic, social, and cultural values. SDG1 (no poverty) and SDG17 (partnerships for the goals) were perceived as the central goals impacted by the TAPPs, appropriately reflecting the Chinese government's efforts to fight against poverty through cooperation with different stakeholders.

Among the identified 40 concrete impacts of 15 impact items, TAPPs' positive impacts on economic sustainability focus on their contributions to achieving SDG1 and SDG8 represented by all concrete impacts of economic stimulation, increasing employment and income, improved living conditions. Nevertheless, the stakeholders also expressed their worries about the income gap, expenditure rise and the lack of partnership for TAP destination marketing, which might obstacle poverty elimination (SDG1) and inequality reduction (SDG10). TAPPs are perceived to have promoted the social and cultural sustainability involving SDG3 (good health ensured by improved medical insurance coverage), SDG4 (improved children education quality), SDG5 (marginalization pressure relief), SDG11 (infrastructure) and SDG17 (residents involvement and participation and environmental protection awareness). However, there are concerns about adult education quality (SDG4) and partnership in professional services (SDG17). Despite the least impacts on environmental sustainability, TAPPs are considered to have promoted the attainment of SDG6 (water pollution curb), SDG7 (air pollution curb) and SDG12 (solid waste discharge and management, household sewage discharge). However, TAPPs need to be improved for TAP destination upgrading involved in SDG9. The findings in chapters four and five will be integrated and discussed in the next chapter.

Chapter 6
Impact Mechanism and Model for Sustainable Development

Introduction

This chapter summarizes and integrates the main findings that have been presented in previous chapters. The chapter consists of four sections. The study's main results are recapitulated and discussed in the first section. Then the implications of the research are presented in section two. The third section introduces limitations and future research directions. Finally, the chapter ends with the conclusion of the overall study. The results are discussed in relation to the literature in chapter two. The discussions revolve around the five research objectives, which are:

1. To identify sustainability value orientations and policy targets of TAPPs in different TAP stages;
2. To investigate the combinations of policy tools used to realize TAPPs sustainability values and targets;
3. To examine consumption-driven and investment-led tourism growth's impacts on the economic sustainability of the poor under the guidance of TAPPs;
4. To investigate TAPPs' contribution to reducing multi-dimensional poverty under the sustainable development paradigm;
5. To explore TAP stakeholders' perceptions of TAPPs' impacts on the sustainable development of TAP destinations.

Discussions of the Main Results of the Study

This section first summarizes the main results of the study. The discussions of these results are presented in response to the research objectives and literature review.

Discussion on the Identified TAPPs Sustainability Values and Targets in TAP Stages

The results from the content analysis of the TAPPs documents showed that TAPPs contained economic, social and cultural and environmental sustainability values throughout the four TAP stages. The TAPPs were dominated by the social and cultural values of "reform and innovation" in the early exploration TAP stage (1984-1996) as well as "public service" and "governance under regulation and law" in the initial TAP stage (1997-2004). In consistency with these values, the government set "the exploration of TAP model" as the TAPPs target for the first TAP stage and "implementation of sustainable regional TAP" for the second stage. The economic values "economic stimulation", "eliminating poverty and getting rich" became almost parallel values to the dominant social and cultural values in the rapid improvement TAP stage (2005-2012) and dominated the sustainability values of TAPPs in the targeted and efficient TAP stage (2013-2020). In the last two stages, TAPPs increasingly highlighted economic values, which promoted tourism as a major means for China's poverty alleviation initiative by setting "sustainable rural TAP" and "sustainable TAP projects" as the policy targets. As the Chinese government focused on absolute poverty alleviation under the reform and opening-up strategy, the TAPPs attached the least importance to environmental values in all TAP stages. These findings reflect the sustainability policy values pair proposed by Stewart (2009), Chinese TAP connotation (Zeng & Ryan, 2012) and the typical three sustainability intersecting circles model (Purvis et. al. 2018).

The evolution of sustainability values and targets of TAPPs indicated that the Chinese government strived to ensure tourism pro-poor through policy formulation. Social and cultural values were optimized to improve the capabilities of the poor. TAPPs strived to establish a multi-participatory TAP model through the optimization of social and cultural values to improve the poor population's abilities to shake off poverty. In the early exploration and initial development periods, TAPPs mainly provided public services in areas of tourism traffic safety, market information, medical and health, and emergency rescue through cooperation between various government departments and regions. The training of TAP practitioners' professional and ethical qualities was emphasized to ensure the smooth operation of the tourism market and the quality of tourism services. During the rapid improvement period, TAPPs further expanded the TAP model, participated by more stakeholders varying from government departments, market entities, universities, and social organizations to individuals from all walks of life. In order to give full play to the advantages of labour resources in poverty-stricken areas, TAPPs organized officials, experts, and skilled workers to help impoverished people improve their skills and qualifications for participating in TAP. The multi-participatory TAP model advocated by the social and cultural values elaborated the distinctive characteristics of PPT defined by Ashley et. al. (2001). Their study noted that PPT focuses on strategies that enhance benefits to the poor, involving a range of stakeholders such as government, poor people, the private sector, and civil society, which the government-led multi-participatory TAP model highlighted.

In the targeted and efficient TAP period, Chinese President Xi proposed new guidelines on poverty alleviation with the stress on helping the poor increase their ambitions and intelligence to tackle poverty (Li et. al., 2021). In response to these guidelines, TAPPs required local governments to improve TAP implementation strategies and interest linkage mechanisms, especially in rural tourism. A series of key TAP projects were carried out in rural areas to improve TAP infrastructure facilities in impoverished villages. In order to stimulate the initiative and enthusiasm of the poor to participate in TAP initiative and consolidate their lasting endogenous motivations, TAPPs introduced a series of precise "enabling" measures. Tourism graduates, professional volunteers and cultural workers were sent to villages to help poverty-stricken villagers enhance rural tourism skills, provide consulting services for their entrepreneurship and enhance rural residents' interests and capabilities in rural TAP participation. These results highlight the Chinese government's efforts to build up the poor's capacity and abilities to catch TAP opportunities (Rao & Chen, 2018) as Knight (2018) noted that pro-poor tourism is both an opportunity-dependent and an opportunity-generating process. Poor people's lack of capabilities and skills in participating in the pro-poor tourism projects is one of the main barriers to draw the maximum benefits from tourism (Ondicho, 2017).

The economic values of TAPPs focused on promoting the development of backward regions and poor rural areas through tourism in different TAP stages. TAPPs gradually established the "government + market" TAP model in its early exploration and initial development periods. The "TAP pilot zone" was set up to promote the socio-economic development in old revolutionary areas and border areas. In TAP's rapid development period, TAPPs began to emphasize the expansion of tourism in the central and western regions and the rural areas. The tourism industry became a connection between the eastern region and the central and western regions. TAPPs were devoted to promoting the fair distribution of social resources, civilization achievements and wealth between urban and rural areas through tourism. This was in line with regional coordination and urban-rural coordinated development proposed by the western development strategy and the scientific development concept (Xi, 2017). In this way, TAP was expected to help under-developed central and western regions and rural areas achieve economic growth. In TAP targeted and efficient period, TAPPs tended to fulfill the absolute poverty elimination task by implementing rural tourism projects, backing up key scenic areas in their roles in stimulating social-economic development of poor areas in the neighborhood. These efforts aimed to ensure that poor areas and poor rural people would not stay caught up on their way to get rid of poverty and become rich.

These findings are different from the neoliberalism-dominated pro-poor tourism policies in six countries in Sub-Saharan African (SSA) countries (Folarin & Adeniyi, 2020), Laos (Harrison & Schipani, 2007), Vietnam (Truong, 2013) and South Asia (Lemma, 2014). As tourism growth is the core of pro-poor tourism policies in these countries rather than poverty alleviation, the pro-poor tourism policies' impacts on the economic improvements of the impoverished are either potential, limited or inexplicit. Suppose the development of poverty-stricken areas and the impoverished population is not the major target of the pro-poor tourism policies. In that case, tourism's benefits might not reach the poor who have no entrepreneurial skills or capital to directly participate in the highly competitive tourism industry (Farrell & Twining-Ward, 2005; Spenceley & Goodwin, 2007; King & Dinkoksung, 2014; Truong, Hall, & Garry, 2014; Xi & Zhang, 2016; Lo et. al., 2018). However, the Chinese government has always focused on pursuing common prosperity and a well-off society ideology (Xin, 2018). Under the guidance of the strategic concepts of common prosperity and a well-off society, TAPPs as the major part of the Chinese government's poverty alleviation strategy naturally put poverty elimination on the top agenda. Thus, Chinese TAPPs guaranteed tourism's economic benefits to the poor and reduced tourism leakages in TAP areas.

In line with the sustainable development strategy (Zhang & Wen, 2008; Wang & Chang, 2014), TAPPs environmental values focused on constructing infrastructure and ecological protection facilities of scenic areas in central and western regions. In the comprehensive poverty alleviation stage, ecological environment construction was listed as the focus of China's national poverty alleviation strategy (Xiaoming & Qi, 2017; Guo & Liu, 2022). Therefore, TAPPs in the rapid development period put forward a specific guideline for resource protection, energy conservation and emission reduction of TAP. During the period of targeted and efficient period, "green poverty reduction" became an important model for targeted poverty alleviation. The main goal of "green poverty reduction" was to achieve ecological civilization and a win-win situation for poverty elimination and prosperity.

Under the "green poverty reduction" model, environmental values of TAPPs focused on comprehensive improvement of rural habitat, washroom renovation and treatment of garbage and sewage in key TAP villages. Special rectifications are taken to restore traditional villages, dwellings, and historical villages and preserve the local and rural features, making them more ecological and livable. The environmental values identified in Chinese TAPPs indicated that the government-led pro-poor tourism could possibly reduce the doubts whether tourism is one of the best choices for poverty alleviation in some impoverished areas with abundant tourism resources but lack of supportive assets such as infrastructure (Suntikul et. al., 2009). These findings also indicated that tourism's environmental damage in the impoverished host communities (Gascón, 2015) could be curbed and even reversed with government interventions.

Discussion on Combinations of Policy Tools Used to Realize TAPPs Sustainability Values and Targets

Following the typical policy analysis framework of "policy value-policy target-policy instrument mix", the results of chapter four revealed that TAPPs instruments were selected and used to realize TAPPs values and targets throughout TAP stages. In the TAP early exploration period (1984-1996), the TAPPs were led by social and cultural values such as reform and innovation. Environmental tools were relied on to explore the TAP model by adjusting the relationship between the tourism market and the government. In the TAP initial development period (1997-2004), the government set the sustainable regional TAP as TAPPs target under the guidance of the dominant social and cultural values such as public service, governance under regulation and law. In order to implement the TAP initiative in the poor western areas targeted by TAPPs, the government increased supply-side tools such as funds, information, public service and talent to stimulate TAP demands and guarantee TAP supplies.

During the rapid improvement period (2005-2012), the government balanced the economic values and social - cultural values in the TAPPs while implementing sustainable rural TAP. The supply-side and environmental TAPPs tools were almost evenly used to improve the weak foundation of rural tourism, aiming to promote the economic, social and cultural development in fulfilling the historical task of building the new socialist countryside proposed by the Chinese Central Government. In the TAP targeted and efficient period (2013-2020), in response to the national targeted poverty alleviation strategy, the economic values became the top value dimension of the TAPPs. In addition, the maturity of the tourism industry enhanced tourism's capacity to drive economic development in poverty-stricken areas, making tourism a leading means of targeted poverty alleviation in rural areas. The demand-side project development tool was taken as a core force pulling the joint force of three categories of TAPP instruments to generate the targeted effect of TAPPs implementation. As environmental issues have yet to occupy the dominant position in TAPPs sustainability values and targets in all TAP stages, TAPPs instruments paid the least attention to realizing environmental values. The government's least attention to environmental values and instruments could best explain why tourism growth in some Chinese regions is still criticized for causing environmental degradation (Yu et. al., 2021).

These findings reflected that policy tools are governance techniques through which governments pursue their policy values and targets (Howlett, 2005; Ali, 2013; Guo, 2020; Capano & Howlett, 2020). The TAPPs instruments classified according to Rothwell (1985) are properly selected to realize TAPPs values and targets in different TAP stages as this typology emphasizes the policy impact on the practical work (Yue et. al., 2020). The different mix of TAPPs instruments in different TAP stages indicated that the selection and implementation of TAPPs tools are not only determined by their characteristics but also affected by the environment and background, as agreed by many scholars who analyzed public policies in different areas with Rothwell's policy instrument typology (e.g. Bergek & Norrman, 2014; Lin et. al., 2017; Zhou et. al., 2020; Zhang et. al., 2019; Yue et. al., 2020). The results also indicated that the evolution of TAPPs sustainability values and targets in different TAP stages are consistent with Chinese economic and social development strategies such as the reform and opening up strategy, the national poverty alleviation strategies, and tourism development strategies, which underpinned the choice of TAPPs instruments. The match of TAPPs values, targets and instruments in different TAP stages provided empirical analysis that has deepened the understanding of instrument and mix dynamics over time (Capano & Howlett, 2020).

Discussion on Consumption-driven and Investment-led Tourism Growth's impacts on the Economic Sustainability of the Poor under TAPPs

The Computable General Equilibrium (CGE) simulation results in chapter four showed TAPPs could help Chinese tourism development contribute to reducing poverty and promoting equality. While poor households' income growth rates declined as a result of their lower engagement in tourism activities than non-poor household groups, the stimulation of tourism consumption could still increase their welfare. The income of disadvantaged households was greatly increased by the TAP project's development-led investment expansion as they were privileged to access more varied work alternatives that are within their capabilities and are channelled via the TAPPs. The study also found a reduction in the rural-urban income gap, which improved equality for low-income rural households. In addition to these primary and secondary effects of tourism development on reducing poverty, all of these TAPPs measurements promoted GDP growth from tourism development, highlighting the dynamic effects of tourism on reducing poverty.

The Chinese TAP CGE analysis echoes most studies' agreements that tourism development is a booster of GDP growth and is conducive to poverty alleviation in China (Donaldson, 2007; Li et. al., 2018; Qin et. al., 2019; Zhao & Xu, 2020). In order to improve tourism's persistent contribution to the sustainable development of rural areas and poverty-alleviated areas, it is necessary to unpack what mechanism ensures tourism's benefits are channelled to the poor. This section explored the Chinese TAPPs' pro-poor mechanism (Figure 6-1) based on the tourism-poverty link-related theories in chapter two and the analysis of simulation results in chapter four.

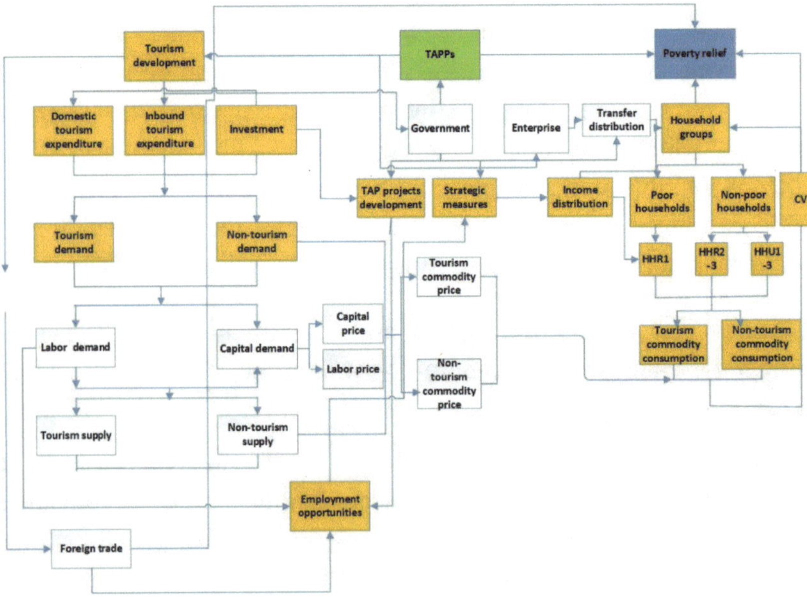

Figure 6.1: The Mechanism of TAPPs' Impacts on Tourism's Economic Contribution to Poverty Alleviation

Notes: HHU1=urban low income households; HHU2=urban medium income households; HHU3=urban high income households; HHR1=rural low income households; HHR2=rural medium households; HHR3=rural high income households.

According to Mitchell and Ashley (2010), the key economic impacts of tourism on poverty relief are mainly direct, secondary, and dynamic impacts. Direct impacts of tourism on poverty alleviation come from tourists' expenditure on goods and services, which could increase employment and income for the poor, especially if they participate in serving tourists. Secondary impacts highlight tourism's inter-sectoral linkages with non-tourism industries. The dynamic impacts are the tourism-led growth's effects on the investment, capital formation and development of other tourism-related industries of the local economy in tourist destinations. Long-term effects could help reduce poverty if the poor could share the benefits of local economic improvement led by tourism development. As shown in Figure 6-1, tourism development under the guidance of TAPPs issued by the government could reduce poverty by providing more employment opportunities to poor households, increasing their income, improving their welfare measured by compensate variance (CV) or boosting GDP growth. The stimuli of tourism consumption and investment were the main measures the government could take to accelerate tourism development.

The stimulus of domestic and inbound tourism consumption resulted in the growth of tourism demand but the reduction of demand for non-tourism commodities. The rising tourism demand triggered the labour and capital demand expansion in the tourism sector and the rise of tourism commodities. As tourism demand created employment opportunities, poor households could earn more income if they were highly engaged in tourism activities. The TAPPs document analysis in chapter four showed that since the targeted and efficient TAP period (2013-2020), the Chinese government has implemented some "enabling" measures to improve poor households' capabilities in tourism participation. However, the CGE analysis based on the 2017 SAM showed that non-poor household groups enjoyed a higher income growth rate than poor households. This result indicated that the "enabling measures" in the TAPPs were far from enough to improve the participation of the impoverished people in tourism activities, hindering the reach of tourism's direct benefits to the poor (Farrell & Twining-Ward, 2005; Dinkoksung,2014; Adiyia & Vanneste, 2018).

According to the CGE results in chapter four, non-poor household groups rather than poor households tended to increase their tourism expenditure. The growth of both domestic and inbound tourism demand leads to the rise of tourism commodity prices but the reduction of non-commodity prices, labour wages and demand in the non-tourism sector. As labour is the main source of poor households in China, the poor face a negative income growth rate due to their least participation in tourism activities and the labour wage drop. It would be wise for them to reduce their tourism commodity consumption but increase non-tourism commodity consumption, especially the basic necessities. This choice surely raised the poor households' utility or welfare. Besides, under the TAPPs, the government and enterprises could increase their transfers to the poor households if their revenues were multiplied by tourism boom. The improved utility or welfare and increased transfers from other institutions were tourism's positive secondary impacts on the poor households.

Furthermore, they could also share the benefits of GDP growth led by the tourism boom, which was tourism's dynamic impact on poverty alleviation. These findings reflected that, despite the relatively few direct impacts of tourism on the impoverished from the increase of tourism expenditure, the welfare of the poor measured by compensation variance could be improved owing to the changes in tourism and non-tourism commodity prices with the shock of tourism expenditure stimulus (Blake et. al., 2008).

The dominant TAPPs measure during the targeted and efficient TAP period (2013-2020) was investment expansion in TAP project development, particularly in rural areas where the largest poor population in China was inhabited. The CGE simulations proved that this measure was the most effective effort to help the poor households overcome income poverty. According to Figure 6-1, the TAP projects development-led tourism investment boosted tourism and non-tourism demand, further stimulating labour demand. TAP projects implementation provided more diversified employment opportunities poor households have the capabilities to seize, such as tourism infrastructure construction. Besides, since the poor households were precisely documented, these employment opportunities could be privileges to the capable impoverished through the strategic measures under TAPPs. The closer involvement in TAP project construction made it more possible for the poor to raise their income level. Furthermore, these employment opportunities could activate and cultivate the impoverished people's awareness of TAP participation and enhance their self-confidence in poverty alleviation.

Investment expansion could play a bigger role in driving higher GDP growth and narrowing the urban-rural income gap than the tourism expenditure stimulus. The poor households' welfare decreased slightly due to the price rises of tourism and non-tourism commodities. Nevertheless, the poor still benefited most from investment-led tourism development with the higher income growth, greater shared benefits from GDP growth and transfers of other institutions as well as improved fairness from narrower urban-rural income gap. The bigger pro-poor role of investment – led tourism development under TAPPs offered a new scenario for the academic community to understand tourism-poverty link as most scholars (e.g. Blake et. al., 2008; Wattanakuljarus & Coxhead, 2008; Mahadevan et. al., 2016; Pang, 2019) focused on exploring whether tourist consumption increase contributes to poverty alleviation.

Discussion on TAPPs' Impacts on the MPI Reduction under Sustainable Development Paradigm

a. Discussion on Basic Results of MPI Evaluation

The primary results of the global MPI evaluation in chapter five suggested that TAPPs facilitated the reduction of multi-dimensional poverty in Guizhou in the targeted and efficient TAP stage. The calculation of the province's MPI with the latest CFPS data showed that, from 2016 to 2018, a significant decrease in Guizhou's MPI from 0.085 to 0.048, similar to the reduction of province's absolute poverty rate from 0.106 to 0.043. Besides the parallel change, the closeness of MPI and absolute poverty rates in both years indicates that Guizhou's MPI closely matched its monetary poverty rate. Besides, the rates of destitution ($0.33<=K<0.5$) and severity ($0.5<=K<1$) were lower than MPI, and the headcount ratios of deprivation and severe poverty witnessed apparent declines.

The closeness and similar change of Guizhou's MPI and its income poverty rate are different from the mismatch of China's MPI and income poverty ratio identified by Shen (2013), Alkire and Shen (2017) and Alkire and Fang (2018). The similarity of Guizhou's MPI and the income poverty ratio indicated that the multi-dimensional poor people in Guizhou were more concentrated in income-poor groups. This finding was consistent with Yu (2013), who found that Guizhou's MPI and income poverty ratio were almost similar in 2010. The relative change in Guizhou's MPI and income poverty ratio proved that, from 2016 to 2018, TAPPs developed tourism into a pillar industry that helped the province's largest poor population overcome absolute and multi-dimensional poverty. The lower levels of destitution and severity than MPI and their significant declines in Guizhou were consistent with the results in China and most developing countries worldwide (Alkire et. al., 2022).

b. Discussion on MPI Indicator Analysis

The findings of indicators' contribution to Guizhou's MPI composition in this study also revealed that social and cultural indicators "years of schooling" and environmental indicator "cooking fuels" were mostly deprived among the Guizhou people raw headcount ratio and censored headcount ratio. These findings in Guizhou are consistent with high deprivation levels of the two indicators in China reported by Alkire and Shen (2017) and Alkire and Fang (2018) and other developing countries such as Iran (Torabi Kahlan et. al., 2022). The social and cultural indicator "years of schooling" had the highest raw headcount ratio among indicators in all dimensions. This could explain why the increase in tourism consumption growth in the CGE analysis did not lead to the income growth rate of poor households. Due to the high deprivation level in "years of schooling", people experiencing poverty had fewer qualifications and abilities to participate in tourism activities than non-poor households with relatively low deprivation levels in this indicator. The poor's incapability from education shortage hindered them from seizing more job opportunities offered by tourism growth, thus leading to their lower income growth rate than the more competent non-poor. The impoverished rural residents' lack of environmental protection awareness and limited income growth capacity due to their deprivation of education resulted in the highest censored headcount ratio in the environmental indicator "cooking fuels".

The statistical decline of censored headcount ratios in all indicators proved that the MPI poor in Guizhou experienced economic, social, cultural, and environmental improvements with the implementation TAPPs. The more significant decreases in censored headcount ratios were found in economic indicators "nutrition", "assets", social and cultural indicators "years of schooling", "insurance", and environmental indicator "cooking fuels". The deprivation levels in economic indicators have resulted from the poor households' income growth from TAP projects identified by CGE analysis. The income-growth-driven multi-dimensional poverty reduction in Guizhou explained that asset deprivations correspond to the trend of income poverty in China (Alkire & Fang, 2018; Yu, 2013). In line with these authors, the decline of Guizhou's destitute levels in economic indicators "nutrition" and "assets" improved their affordability to the environmental indicator "cooking fuels" and social and cultural indicator "insurance", which could also be subsidised by the government's tax revenue rise from tourism growth. The more job opportunities provided by the TAP projects for residents reduced the number of "left-behind" children, which thus resulted in the reduction of "years of schooling".

c. Discussion on MPI Analysis of Disaggregated Groups

The MPI results of households classified by rural-urban areas and rural-urban hukous showed that TAPPs had reduced the overall rural-urban gap in multi-dimensional poverty. From 2016 to 2018, the MPI, headcount ratio and intensity of the multi-dimensional poverty in rural areas witnessed similar decline rates to those in urban areas owing to the precise implementation of rural TAP projects during the 13th-Five Year Plan period (2015-2020). One of the most effective measures is to list poor villages suitable for rural tourism in constructing Guizhou's top 100 tourist attractions. The implementation of these construction projects narrowed the overall censored headcount ratio differences from 2016 to 2018 in economic and environmental indicators between rural areas and urban areas. However, the gap in the overall deprivation level of social and cultural indicators was enlarged because the urban areas still enjoyed faster social and cultural improvements from China's significant progress in urbanisation in recent years. This finding indicated that even though the Chinese migrant rural poor might be able to escape income poverty, they could not enjoy the same social benefits as the urban groups. These findings are similar to most countries and regions worldwide (Alkire & Shen, 2017; Alkire et. al., 2022; Saifullah, 2022).

The deprivation levels of almost all indicators in rural areas stayed higher than those in urban areas except for the economic indicator "housing". This exception reflected two facts: one was that the housing cost in urban areas was much higher than in rural areas; the other was that rural TAP projects improved the housing condition of the poor in rural areas through subsidised restoration and renovation. The three indicators in which the poor in rural areas were most deprived were environmental indicators “cooking fuels”, “drinking water”, and social and cultural indicators “years of schooling”. Along with the economic indicator "assets", the environmental indicator “cooking fuels”, and the social and cultural indicator “years of schooling" experienced the most considerable reduction in their deprivation level differences between the rural areas and urban areas. This result implied that the high deprivation of "years of schooling" in Guizhou was mainly attributed to rural areas, consistent with a similar phenomenon in China (Yu, 2013).

The indicator analysis of rural and urban areas also revealed that the gap was widened in destitute levels of the environmental indicator “drinking water” and the social and cultural indicator "insurance" between the rural and urban areas. This partly indicated that Guizhou people in rural areas prefer to drink water from shallow wells, ponds, or rivers due to history, customs, local resources and lower costs. This could explain why the deprivation level of the “drinking water" gap was enlarged. Alkire and Fang (2018) also identified similar findings in China. Nevertheless, Guizhou witnessed the reduction of "cooking fuels", which is different from the Chinese farmers' tradition of cooking with wood, agricultural waste and coal. This difference reflected the government's intervention in environmental protection to implement TAP projects as identified in TAPPs.

The disaggregated rural-urban hukou analysis findings showed that the MPI values were quite close between rural and urban hukou groups in 2016. This MPI closeness resulted from the reform of the hukou system started in 2014 in China, which relaxed the household registration requirements for rural migrants. This reform has allowed the poor to relocate from their inhospitable villages to habitable towns under the government’s targeted poverty strategy to change their hukou status from rural to urban. The relocation measure also significantly reduced the deprivation levels of rural hukou groups in environmental indicators such as “cooking fuels” and "drinking water" and economic indicators "assets", "nutrition", and "child mortality". The inflow of poor rural hukou groups into the urban hukou groups could balance the MPI gap between the two groups for a period. However, from 2016 to 2018, the reduction rate of MPI in urban hukou groups doubled that in rural hukou groups, also different from the similar MPI decrease rate in rural-urban areas. This difference indicates that the rural hukou groups are more deprived of social and cultural indicators of “years of schooling” and “insurance” than even rural area groups with the least competence in overcoming poverty through tourism. The rural hukou group's higher destitute level in housing than the rural area group further proved that it's challenging for the migrant rural hukou group to afford high housing costs in urban areas if they are less competent. In response to China's household registration reform, these results updated the findings of Alkire and Shen (2017), focusing on China's rural migration impacts on rural-urban MPI levels.

Discussion on TAPPs’ Impacts on TAP Destination Sustainable Development Perceived by Stakeholders

The results of TAPPs’ impacts on sustainable development at TAP destinations showed that stakeholders perceived TAPPs’ more implications on economic, social, and cultural sustainability than environmental sustainability at TAP destinations. This conclusion is consistent with TAPPs' sustainability value orientations dominated by economic and social, and cultural values. 13 of 17 goals in the SDGs were involved in TAPPs’ impacts on the typical TAP destination in the case study area. Five of them were the most affected SDGs, including SDG1 (no poverty), SDG17 (partnership for the goals), SDG8 (decent work and economic growth), SDG10 (reduced inequalities) and SDG11 (sustainable cities and communities). SDG1 and SDG17 were considered the core goals impacted by the TAPPs, as interviewees most frequently mentioned them. TAPPs’ core goal of realising SDG1 is intermingled with other related SDGs, as Birendra (2021) found that the SDG agenda highlights tourism’s role in advancing SDGs inter-connected with one another.

a. Discussion on TAPPs' Impacts on SDGs under Economic Sustainability

The semi-structured interview in chapter five found that the positive impacts of TAPPs on economic sustainability lay in its contributions to SDG1 (no poverty) and SDG8 (decent work and economic growth). This finding aligns with tourism's contributions to economic sustainability revealed by Trupp and Dolezal (2020) and Rasoolimanesh et. al. (2020). The construction of TAP projects under TAPPs helped the rural poor overcome income poverty by providing more specific positions and expanding income channels, thus increasing their per capita income. Thanks to their income increase and government subsidy, the rural poor's living conditions were also improved with the renovation of dilapidated rural houses, increased asset ownership, and more diversified diets. Besides, TAPPs also stimulated local economic growth by attracting investment with the government's preferential policies such as government financial aid, bank free loan for entrepreneurship and investment promotion activities. The tourism boom under the TAPPs drove the development of tourism-related industries, creating more decent work for the residents.

However, stakeholders expressed concerns about the increased income gap between tourism and non-tourism participants and the increased expenditure due to the rise of commodity prices. The consequences might harm poverty eradication (SDG1) and reduce inequality (SDG10). These two concerns were also reported by Qin (2019). Additionally, the interviewees suggested that the local government should optimise the partnership (SDG 17) in marketing the TAP destination image, products and services to increase the popularity of the TAP destinations. Movono and Hughes (2020) also highlighted the collaboration of stakeholders for SDGs

b. Discussion on TAPPs' Impacts on SDGs under Social-Cultural Sustainability

TAPPs' impacts on social-cultural sustainability were believed to have improved good health and well-being (SDG3), quality education (SDG4), partnership for the goals (SDG17) and sustainable cities and communities (SDG11). The improvement of residents' health and well-being was also reported in the MPI analysis, in which "insurance" was one of the most deprived social and cultural indicators but witnessed a significant decrease from 2016 to 2018. Similar to the findings of Knight and Cottrell (2016) and Qin (2019), children's education quality (SDG4) was better as they could have better family education accompanied by their parents, who could earn income at home from TAP projects.

Residents' involvement in TAP projects (SDG17) was enhanced by encouraging the return of rural elites and migrant workers and stimulating residents' willingness to cooperate. The collaborative measures to strengthen residents' involvement in TAP projects (SDG17) were quite characteristic. The increasing participation of migrant elites and workers in TAP projects is owing to the abundant entrepreneurial and job opportunities from these projects under the strong leadership of the Chinese government (Yang et. al., 2021). Considering the multi-dimensional nature of SDG1, Scheyvens and Hughes (2019) suggested that tourism players should empower marginalised people such as the poorer and women. Without careful planning, women's personal, social, economic, and environmental conditions may be materially harmed by tourism developments in their communities (Boluk, 2019). TAPPs have empowered women and the poor in their self-confidence, involvement in village management and their family status, also echoing the findings of Anker (1998), Scheyvens (2002) and Knight and Cottrell (2016). The ethnic and cultural preservation (SDG 11) was improved as the local government has taken actions to promote indigenous culture, maintain cultural sites and inherit local customs and language, similar to what the Nepal government did (Birendra, 2021).

Despite these positive social and cultural impacts, residents expressed concerns about improving the quality of adult education and partnership in professional services. TAPPs' ineffective measure on adult education further explained the high deprivation level of "years of schooling" in the MPI analysis and low-income households' less participation in tourism service supplies in the CGE analysis. This finding suggested targeted and regular training as a possible way to improve the capability of the poor's participation in TAP projects. These results supported the Chinese government's persistent efforts to improve the poor's capabilities to seize PPT opportunities (Rao & Chen, 2018).

Liu (2020) noted that the central and local governments play different roles in rural tourism development in China. The central government steers rural tourism in the desired direction, while the local government serves by directly managing tourism development and coordinating with businesses and residents to provide services and solve problems. Interviewees' concerns about the partnership between the government and other stakeholders in dealing with tourists' complaints indicated that it's challenging for the local governments in TAP destinations to optimise their management efficiency and cooperation with other stakeholders.

c. Discussion on TAPPs' Impacts on SDGs under Environmental Sustainability

TAPPs were perceived to have the most negligible impact on environmental sustainability, with no SDGs involved drawing the most attention from the stakeholders as SDG1 and SDG17 under the other two sustainability dimensions. The active roles of TAPPs in promoting environmental sustainability focused on curbing air pollution by using clean and affordable energy (SDG7), preventing water pollution (SDG6) by treating wastewater before it was discharged into the river, managing the discharge of solid waste (SDG12) by using it for power generation and raising residents' environmental protection awareness by implementing targeted local environmental protection regulations.

Despite these positive roles, some residents also suggested that the government and enterprises should jointly intensify efforts to upgrade TAP destinations (SDG9) as abundant tourism resources can be exploited. Some tourism facilities must be improved to facilitate sustainable infrastructure development in the TAP destinations. There is a difference between the environmental sustainability results from the interview data and the CFPS data. The former found the improvement in using clean and affordable energy (SDG7), whereas the latter still reported the poor households' high deprivation level in the environmental indicator "cooking fuels". The difference may have resulted from the different years for the data collection, indicating the possible improvement of SDG7 as the government has increasingly valued environmental sustainability. The government's regulations on curbing various pollutions were also noted in the study on the Nepal government's efforts to realise SDGs through tourism by Birendra (2021).

d. Discussion on Stakeholders' Different Perceptions of TAPPs' Impacts on TAP Destination Sustainable Development

The study also analysed the perceived impacts of different stakeholders in the implementation of TAPPs. As identified previously, SDG17 (partnership for the goals) is a central goal parallel to SDG1 that TAPPs impacted most. The two goals appropriately reflected that the Chinese government strived to eradicate poverty through tourism by cooperating with different TAP stakeholders. The cooperative relationship between TAP stakeholders was a critical factor that has affected the Chinese government's achievement of SDG1 and other related SDGs. These findings reflected that the cooperation between stakeholders is a vital force in maximising tourism's potential for SDGs (WTO & UNDP, 2017; NPC, 2017; Hall, 2019; Guo et. al., 2019; Movono & Hughes, 2020).

The government, enterprises, and poor and non-poor villagers were identified as the main stakeholders in TAP projects. This study clarified how these main TAP stakeholders perceived the positive and negative impacts of TAPPs on the sustainable development of the TAP destination. The government officials, the policymakers and executors mainly focused on TAPPs' positive impacts through their appropriate policy formulation and implementation. Enterprises which are the primary implementers of TAP projects under TAPPs also paid more attention to the promotion of positive impacts of the policy. The poor villagers who are the target beneficiaries of the policy recognised more positive implications than their concerns about the procedure. However, the non-poor villagers who did not enjoy the privileged benefits from the TAPPs tended to be more critical of the policy impacts than the other stakeholder groups. Besides, both poor and non-poor residents expressed more negative effects of TAPPs on environmental sustainability than government officials and enterprise staff, reflecting the tensions and distortions caused by the Chinese top-down TAP approach (Dai et. al., 2012).

e. The Conceptual Model of TAPPs' Impacts on TAP Destination Sustainable Development

Based on the discussions of content analysis, CGE analysis and case study results, this section finally summarised a conceptual model (Figure 6-2) for how TAPPs affected the sustainable development of TAP destinations regarding SDGs in the government-led model. Decision-makers, especially in some developing countries, recognised tourism's role in poverty alleviation, which is the top goal of the UN Sustainable Development Goals 2030. However, most policy makers regarded poverty reduction as secondary to tourism development (Harrison & Schipani, 2007; Truong et. al., 2014). Although Qin (2019) investigated stakeholders' perceived impacts of TAPPs, her model focuses on the policy and tourism-related effects only on the poor rather than on the holistic, sustainable development of TAP destinations in line with SDGs. Our conceptual model clearly shows how TAPPs impact sustainable development regarding SDGs at TAP destinations through policy formulation and implementation.

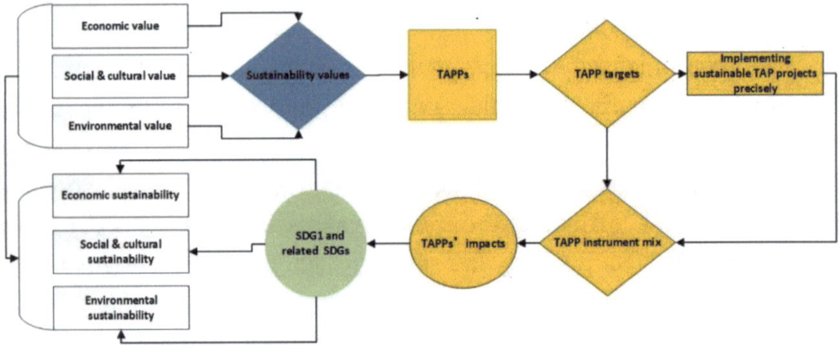

Figure 6-2 Conceptual Model of TAPPs' Impacts on the Sustainable Development of TAP Destination

Besides, tourism is considered to have great potential to accelerate the achievement of SDGs (Scheyvens, 2018). Chinese TAPPs, which made tourism a major tool to realise SDG1, actually contained economic, social and cultural and environmental sustainability values facilitating the achievement of various SDGs not limited to SDG1. However, TAP decision-makers often focus on the contribution of tourism to poverty reduction while ignoring TAPPs' impacts on the SDGs intermingled with SDG1 in practice. These impacts may undermine the sustainable development of TAP destinations if not planned and managed properly (Boluk, 2019).

Therefore, policymakers must improve interventions and tourism development management at TAP destinations. Previous studies discussed the government's pivotal role in controlling, planning, and directing tourism growth (Mowforth & Munt, 2015). Nevertheless, government strategies for poverty alleviation through tourism do not occupy a central position in many countries' national tourism policies (Lemma, 2014; Folarin & Adeniyi, 2020). On the other hand, sustainable tourism policies are criticised for overemphasising economic growth (Mai & Smiths, 2015; Anderson et. al., 2018). There needs to be an in-depth study of the impact of tourism on poverty alleviation under the sustainable development paradigm and of the mechanism underlying these impacts.

In the context of how the government-led TAP initiative works, this study explored stakeholders' perceived impacts of TAPPs on the sustainable development at TAP destinations in terms of SDGs and the impact conceptual model under the guidance of the policy formulation and implementation analysis framework "TAPP sustainability values-TAPP targets- TAPP instrument mix". In response to the UN Sustainable Development Goals 2030 and the China targeted poverty alleviation strategy, the Chinese government tried to embrace the three pillars of sustainability values in formulating TAPPs. Under the guidance of sustainability values, the government set the precise implementation of sustainable TAP projects as the TAPP target. In order to realise the sustainability values and TAPP targets, the government utilised a mix of policy instruments, which impacted the economic, social, cultural, and environmental sustainability of TAP destinations. These impacts under the three sustainability dimensions perceived by the stakeholders are connected with SDGs. The TAPPs' perceived impacts on sustainable development at TAP destinations are thus observed and could be optimized in terms of maximizing tourism's roles in advancing SDGs led by SDG1.

Implications of the Findings

Based on the summary of findings in the previous section, this section elaborates on the theoretical and practical implications of this research.

Theoretical Implications

This study contributes to the knowledge of the government's approach to guiding pro-poor tourism to advance SDG1-led SDGs through policy formulation and implementation. As analysed in the literature review in chapter two, academic doubts exist on the limited tourism-poverty link due to the need for more empirical evidence and theoretical underpinnings. The pro-poor tourism in most countries is criticised for tourism's limited applicability in poverty reduction and accessibility of few benefits to the poor under the neo-liberal orthodoxy. Neo-liberalism was regarded as an approach that could increase inequality and widen the gap between developing and developed countries. Therefore, the "new poverty" agenda was proposed, which focused on enhancing the role of the state and on the importance of strong institutions, governance, and more effectively targeting poverty and vulnerability. Some developing countries represented by Vietnam, Laos and some African countries implemented government strategies for pro-poor tourism. However, the pro-poor tourism policies in these countries still followed the neo-liberal approach by putting tourism development on the top agenda rather than poverty alleviation. The poor population could hardly benefit from tourism growth as they have fewer opportunities for participating in tourism activities.

This study has expanded the literature on the government's approach to strengthening the tourism-poverty relationship by playing a leading role of the government in directing tourism to the reduction of poverty and vulnerability. The content analysis of TAPPs documents revealed that, different from the dominant neo-liberal approach to pro-poor tourism in most countries, Chinese TAPPs listed poverty alleviation as the core part of tourism development in poverty-stricken areas. The identification of policy values, targets and tools of TAPPs revealed the government's strategies for guaranteeing tourism's benefits to the poor and sustainable development of the impoverished areas.

This study added empirical evidence to the tourism-poverty link by finding that the growth of tourist consumption and tourism investment under the Chinese TAPPs could increase social benefits or generate a higher income growth rate for the poor. The TAPPs' impact mechanism on tourism's economic contribution to poverty eradication increased the theoretical underpinnings of the tourism-poverty link. The mechanism noted that the investment-led tourism development under TAPPs could lead to a higher income growth rate for low-income groups than for consumption-led tourism growth. This conclusion has provided a new scenario for scholars to understand the tourism-poverty link.

This research has also made a theoretical contribution to development theories by proposing a conceptual model of TAPPs' impacts on sustainable development at TAP destinations. As reviewed previously, most tourism-poverty link researches center on their economic relationship. However, sustainable development and poverty are multi-dimensional issues. As the top goal of the UN Sustainable Development Agenda, SDG1 should be interconnected with other SDGs. Tourism's contribution to the achievement of SDG1 should not be limited to economic sustainability, as Scheyvens (2018) suggested. However, tourism policies in most countries are criticised for overemphasising economic growth without due attention to sustainable development. This problem could result from stakeholders' different understandings of tourism sustainability, usually contextualised but not universally conceptualised.

The conceptual model in this study further contributed to the pro-poor tourism theory by proposing the government-led pro-poor tourism framework of advancing SDG1 and related SDGs through policy formulation and implementation. Unlike the neo-liberalism - based pro-poor tourism framework, this model suggests that the government is the leading stakeholder in promoting the achievement of SDGs in TAP destinations. Governments at different levels play different roles in advancing SDGs through tourism in China and other countries worldwide. Therefore, the model implies that stakeholder partnership and allocation of power, resources and capacities could be integral parts of TAPPs formulation and implementation to maximise tourism's potential to achieve SDGs. Following the framework of "TAPP sustainability values- TAPP targets- TAPP instrument mix", the model highlights the shift of exploring the tourism-poverty link from the existing focus on economic sustainability to the holistic and balanced attention to advancing SDGs under economic, social-cultural and environmental sustainability at TAP destinations. The model demonstrates that the tourism-poverty link could be extended through government policy formulation and implementation under the three pillars of the sustainability framework. The extension of the tourism-poverty link could be an important milestone for conceptualising tourism sustainability in the government-led pro-poor tourism framework.

Practical Implications

Tourism has been identified as an advantageous means for achieving SDG1 in many developing countries. Regarding practical contribution, the conceptual model of policy impacts on the SDG1-led sustainable development of TAP destinations proposed in this study could offer insights to developing-country governments in formulating strategies and policies to increase tourism's contribution to poverty alleviation. This study suggested that government could prioritise poverty alleviation over tourism growth as a primary pro-poor tourism policy goal, with due consideration given to destination sustainability.

Furthermore, since the Chinese government has maintained its efforts to reduce relative poverty by launching a rural revitalisation strategy, this study has provided a reference for the Chinese governments at all levels to improve the sustainability of tourism policies in order to promote and consolidate the sustainable development of rural areas in accordance with the SDGs. The CGE analysis shows that low-income households benefit less from consumption-led tourism growth due to less participation in tourism service supplies. The AF-MPI analysis identified that poor households have a higher deprivation level in the social and cultural indicator "years of schooling," which has weakened the impoverished residents' capabilities to seize job opportunities created by tourism consumption growth. The Chinese government has worked on realizing TAPPs' social and cultural sustainability values that emphasize enhancing the poor's capabilities through a mix of policy instruments such as talent tools, public service and partner assistance. However, the semi-structured interview found that the professional training for poor households is not regular or effective as many training seminars are too general rather than targeted. These findings imply that the government could make a more specific plan and strategy for improving the efficiency in enhancing the poor's professional skills and capabilities for tourism participation which is a principal obstacle to achieving SDG1 and SDG10.

Additionally, the Chinese government could pay more attention to environmental sustainability in its rural revitalisation through tourism.

Though the main stakeholders at the TAP destination of Zhaoxing Dong Ethnic village perceived the improvement of SDG7 (clean and affordable energy), they mentioned their dissatisfaction with another environmental item, TAP destination upgrading, especially the sustainable infrastructure development (SDG9). The environmental sustainability problems are far more than the complaints reported in the semi-structured interview in this study. As analysed in previous chapters, poor Chinese people live in rural areas with a highly degraded ecology, like many countries. Facing the fragile ecological environment, the Chinese TAPPs should shift their focus on economic, social and cultural sustainability to balanced attention to economic, social and cultural and environmental sustainability. Finally, the Chinese government has made remarkable achievements in achieving SDG1 through close partnerships with various stakeholders. The semi-structured interview reported the ineffective partnership for TAP destination marketing and professional services, indicating that the local governments could further optimise stakeholder partnership in rural revitalisation through tourism.

Limitations and Future Research Directions

There is one limitation of this study, which future researchers should mention. The limitation of this study is the generalisation of the findings. Tourism was criticised for being difficult or even financially risky for the poor to participate in the business of tourism without adequate support and knowledge transfer. By putting poverty alleviation on the top agenda of TAPPs, the Chinese government ensured tourism's benefits to the poor through policy formulation and implementation. This study mainly followed the policy analysis framework of "policy values-policy targets-policy instruments" for the content analysis of TAPPs documents and the semi-structured interview analysis in the case study area. This research has strived to realise the transferability of qualitative research by offering a detailed description of how TAPPs evolved in different TAP stages, the historical overview of TAP development in the case study area, the demographic information and setting of all participants as well as saturation point. This description could help the reader judge the transferability of the study in but non-identical setting (Parron, 1990). However, policy formulation and implementation is a complicated process involving inter-jurisdictional coordination, power resources, and capacities distribution in a multilevel governance system (Daniell, Coombes & White, 2014; Bisaro, Hinkel & Kranz, 2010; Barbosa & Brusca, 2015; Marquardt, 2017).

Therefore, future research could investigate how coordination and distribution of power resources and capacities between the Chinese central government and local governments affect tourism's contribution to the sustainable development of rural revitalisation through policy formulation and implementation. The multilevel governance perspective could help world scholars and policymakers understand how government-led tourism development would benefit the relatively poor rural residents and contribute to the attainment of SDGs. This future research could also help the Chinese government understand how to optimise partnerships with other stakeholders in rural revitalisation through tourism.

Besides, the CGE analysis of tourism's economic contribution to poverty elimination in this study is based on the latest Chinese Input-Output Table 2017. The China Family Panel Studies data used for the Multi-dimensional Poverty Index analysis has its latest version, 2018. These two data sources should have included information on the impacts of the Covid-19 outbreak since 2020. These available data could sufficiently explain TAPPs' impacts on both income poverty relief and multi-dimensional poverty reduction in the targeted and efficient TAP stage when tourism was taken as a major poverty alleviation tool. However, this study could not provide implications for how government should help the rural TAP destinations recover from the pandemic. It's thus suggested pandemic factor could be included in future research, which would be of great significance to guide governments to promote sustainable tourism worldwide following the unprecedented pandemic change.

Conclusion

The study followed the research objectives and fully answered the research questions. Some suggestions could be made to the Chinese government and governments in some developing countries for their references based on the findings of this study. The content analysis of

TAPPs documents suggested the government could guarantee tourism's benefits to the poor if poverty alleviation was taken as the core part of the pro-poor tourism policy formulation and implementation. The CGE analysis recommended that if the poor have fewer competencies in participating in tourism activities, the government should stimulate investment-driven tourism development, which could create more diversified opportunities for the poor than consumption-led tourism growth. On the other hand, the government should step up measures to enhance the poor's capabilities and skills for tourism participation so that they could share benefits from consumption-led tourism growth.

The MPI analysis under the sustainable development paradigm suggested that targeted pro-poor tourism projects could effectively reduce the overall MPI and the deprivation levels of various indicators under the sustainability dimensions. The government could also use these targeted pro-poor projects to reduce the rural and urban gap. The semi-structured interview with government officials, poor and non-poor residents and enterprise staff revealed that different stakeholders had different perspectives on these impacts. Government officials and enterprise staff tended to promote the positive impacts of TAPPs as they were the policymakers and main implementers of TAP projects under TAPPs. However, residents were more critical about the TAPPs' impacts as there might be tensions and distortions in implementing TAPPs following the top-down approach. The tensions and distortions should be lessened through the optimised partnership of different stakeholders.

Finally, the semi-structured interview investigated stakeholders' perceptions of TAPPs' impacts on sustainable development at TAP destinations. TAPPs were perceived to have impacted 13 of the 17 SDGs, among which SDG1 (no poverty) and SDG17 (partnership for the goals) were identified as the core goals as the stakeholders most frequently mentioned them. The two goals indicated that the Chinese government accomplished TAP by cooperating with various stakeholders. Consistent with the sustainability value structure of TAPPs, the stakeholders perceived more economic, social, and cultural impacts of TAPPs than environmental ones. The TAPPs' impacts on eight of the 13 involved SDGs were perceived as positive. However, stakeholders also expressed concerns about tourism's detriments on SDG1 (no poverty) and SDG10 (reduced inequality) from the income gap between tourism participants and non-tourism participants and rising expenditure. These negative impacts could be solved if irregular and untargeted resident training (SDG4) could be improved under the government's intervention. The SDG17 (partnership for the goals) between various stakeholders should be improved in marketing the TAP destination image, products and services, and TAP professional service in spite of TAPPs' conducive impacts on attaining SDG17 in other aspects such as residents' more involvement in TAP projects. Stakeholders' complaints on SDG17 indicated that the partnership of stakeholders as the critical factor for attaining SDGs through tourism remains a great challenge for the Chinese governments at different levels. Residents also suggested that the government and enterprises should jointly intensify efforts to upgrade TAP destinations (SDG9), indicating that TAPPs should increase attention to environmental sustainability.

References

Abate, G. Y. (2022). Stakeholder Collaboration for Sustainable Pro Poor Tourism Development: The Case of Hawassa City, Sidama Regional State. Hawassa, Ethiopia: Hawassa University.

Abbasi, M., Majdzadeh, R., Zali, A., Karimi, A., & Akrami, F. (2018). The Evolution of Public Health Ethics Frameworks: Systematic Review of Moral Values and Norms in Public Health Policy. Medicine, Health Care and Philosophy. 21:387-402.

Abdelhakim, A. S. (2021). Adopted Research Designs by Tourism and Hospitality Postgraduates in the Light of Research Onion. International Journal of Tourism and Hospitality Management. 4(2): 98-124.

Acciai, C. & Capano, G. (2021). Policy Instruments at Work: A Meta - Analysis of their Applications. Public Administration. 99(1): 118-136.

Adams, B., & Parmenter, B. (1999). General Equilibrium Models. In Kristine Corcoran (eds.). Valuing Tourism: Methods and Techniques, pp. 110-121. Canberra: Bureau of Tourism Research.

Adiyia, B. & Vanneste, D. (2018). Local Tourism Value Chain Linkages as Pro-Poor Tools for Regional Development in Western Uganda. Development Southern Africa. 35(2): 210-224.

Afridi, F., Li, S. X., & Ren, Y. (2015). Social identity and inequality: The impact of China's hukou system. Journal of Public Economics. 123: 17-29.

Agyeiwaah, E., McKercher, B. & Suntikul, W. (2017). Identifying Core Indicators of Sustainable Tourism: A Path Forward? Tourism Management Perspectives. 24: 26-33.

Ajakaiye, D.O. & Adeyeye, V.A. (2001). Concepts, Measurement and Causes of Poverty. CBN Economic and Financial Review. 39(4): 5-36.

Akama, J. S. (1996). Western Environmental Values and Nature-Based Tourism in Kenya. Tourism Management. 17(8): 567-574.

Akama, J. S. (2004). Neocolonialism, Dependency and External Control of Kenya's Tourism Industry: A Case Study of Wildlife Safari Tourism in Kenya. In C.M. Hall and H. Tucker (eds.). Tourism and Postcolonialism: Contested Discourses, Identities and Representations, pp. 140-152. London: Routledge.

Akindola, R. B. (2009). Towards A Definition of Poverty: Poor People's Perspectives and Implications for Poverty Reduction. Journal of Developing Societies. 25(2): 121-150.

Alavalapati, J. R. & Adamowicz, W. L. (2000). Tourism Impact Modeling for Resource Extraction Regions. Annals of Tourism Research. 27(1): 188-202.

Ali, M. (2013). Assessment of Policy Instruments. Amsterdam: Elsevier Inc.

Alkire, S. & J. Foster. (2007). Counting and Multidimensional Poverty Measurement. OPHI Working Papers Nro. 7. Oxford, Oxford University.

Alkire, S., & Shen, Y. (2017). Exploring Multidimensional Poverty in China: 2010 to 2014. In Sanghamitra B. and Juan G. R. (eds.). Research on Economic Inequality: Poverty, Inequality and Welfare, pp. 161-228. Bingley: Emerald Publishing Limited.

Alkire, S. & Fang, Y. (2019). Dynamics of Multidimensional Poverty and Uni-Dimensional Income Poverty: An Evidence of Stability Analysis from China. Social Indicators Research. 142: 25-64.

Alkire, S. & Foster, J. (2011). Counting and Multidimensional Poverty Measurement. Journal of Public Economics. 95(7-8): 476-487.

Alkire, S. & Foster, J. (2011). Understandings and Misunderstandings of Multidimensional Poverty Measurement. The Journal of Economic Inequality. 9: 289-314.

Alkire, S., Kanagaratnam, U., Nogales, R. & Suppa, N. (2022a). Revising the Global Multidimensional Poverty Index: Empirical Insights and Robustness. Review of Income and Wealth. 68: S347-S384.

Alkire, S., Kanagaratnam, U., & Suppa, N. (2022b). The Global Multidimensional Poverty Index (MPI) 2022 Country Results and Methodological Note. OPHI MPI Methodological Note 52, Oxford Poverty and Human Development Initiative, University of Oxford.

Alkire, S., Kanagaratnam, U., & Suppa, N. (2022c). The Global Multidimensional Poverty Index (MPI) 2022 Disaggregation Results and Methodological Note. OPHI MPI Methodological Note 53, Oxford Poverty and Human Development Initiative, University of Oxford.

Alkire, S., & Seth, S. (2015). Multidimensional poverty reduction in India between 1999 and 2006: Where and how? World Development. 72: 93-108.

Alkire, S., Roche, J. M., & Vaz, A. (2017). Changes over Time in Multidimensional Poverty: Methodology and Results for 34 Countries. World Development. 94: 232-249.

Alkire, S., Kovesdi, F., Scharlin-Pettee, S., & Pinilla Roncancio, M. (2020). Changes over Time in the Global Multidimensional Poverty Index and Other Measures: Towards National Poverty Reports. OPHI Research in Progress 57a, Oxford Poverty and Human Development Initiative. University of Oxford.

Alkire, S., & Kovesdi, F. (2020). Multidimensional Poverty across Ethnic Groups: Disaggregating the Global MPI. OPHI Briefing 55. Oxford Poverty and Human Development Initiative (OPHI). University of Oxford.

Alkire, S., Kanagaratnam, U. & Suppa, N. (2020). The Global Multidimensional Poverty Index (MPI): 2020 Revision. OPHI MPI Methodological Note 49. Oxford Poverty and Human Development Initiative. University of Oxford.

Alkire, S. & Santos, M. E. (2010). Acute Multidimensional Poverty: A New Index for Developing Countries, https://dx.doi.org/10.2139/ssrn.1815243.

Alkire, S., Chatterje, M., Conconi, A., Seth, S. & Vaz, A. (2014). Poverty in Rural and Urban Areas: Direct Comparisons Using the Global MPI 2014. OPHI Briefing 24. University of Oxford.

Amir, A. F. , Ghapar, A. A. , Jamal, S. A. & Ahmad, K. N. (2015). Sustainable Tourism Development: A Study on Community Resilience for Rural Tourism in Malaysia. Procedia Social and Behavioral Sciences. 168(9): 116-122.

Amalia, R. R. & Kadir, K. (2016). Multidimensional Poverty Index (MPI) in Agricultural

Household in Indonesia, https://mpra.ub.uni-muenchen.de/95114/1/MPRA_paper_95114.pdf.

Amankwah-Amoah, J., Khan, Z. & Wood, G. (2021). COVID-19 and Business Failures: The Paradoxes of Experience, Scale, and Scope for Theory and Practice. European Management Journal. 39(2): 179-184.

Anker, R. (1998). Gender and Jobs: Sex Segregation of Occupations in the World. Geneva: International Labour Organization.

Anand, S. & Sen, A. (1997). Concepts of Human Development and Poverty: A Multidimensional Perspective in United Nations Development Programme. Poverty and Human Development: Human Development Papers 1997. United Nations. 1-20.

Andersen, I. M. V., Blichfeldt, B. S. & Liburd, J. J. (2018). Sustainability in Coastal Tourism Development: An Example From Denmark. Current Issues in Tourism. 21(12): 1329-1336.

Appleton, S., Song, L. & Xia, Q. (2010). Growing Out of Poverty: Trends and Patterns of Urban Poverty in China 1988–2002. World Development. 38(5): 665-678.

Arrow, K. J. (1951). Alternative Approaches to the Theory of Choice in Risk-Taking Situations. Econometrica: Journal of the Econometric Society. 19(4): 404-437.

Arrow, K. J. & Debreu, G. (1954). Existence of an Equilibrium for a Competitive Economy. Econometrica: Journal of the Econometric Society. 22(3): 265-290.

Arrow K. & Hahn F.H. (1971). General Competitive Analysis. Amsterdam: North Holland.

Asmelash, A. G. & Kumar, S. (2019). Assessing Progress of Tourism Sustainability: Developing and Validating Sustainability Indicators. Tourism Management. 71: 67-83.

Ashley, C., Roe, D. & Goodwin, H. (2001). Pro-Poor Tourism Strategies: Making Tourism Work for the Poor – A Review of Experience. London. April 2001.

Ashley, C. & Roe, D. (2003). Working with the Private Sector on Pro-Poor Tourism: Opinions and Experience from Two Development Practitioners. Pro-Poor Tourism Working Paper. Overseas Development Institute. London.

Ashley, C. & Roe, D. (2017). Enhancing Pro-Poor Tourism Impacts: Strategies for Achieving Success. London: Routledge.

Ashley, C., Boyd, C. & Goodwin, H. (2000). Pro-poor Tourism: Putting Poverty at the Heart of the Tourism Agenda. Natural Resource Perspectives. 51(3): 1–6.

Ashley, C., & Mitchell, J. (2007). Assessing How Tourism Revenues Reach The Poor. ODI Briefing Paper No. 21. Overseas Development Institute. London.

Atkinson, A. B. (2003). Multidimensional Deprivation: Contrasting Social Welfare and Counting Approaches. Journal of Economic Inequality. 1(1): 51-65.

Axelsson, R., Angelstam, P., Elbakidze, M., Stryamets, N. & Johansson, K. E.(2011). Sustainable Development and Sustainability: Landscape Approach as a Practical Interpretation of Principles and Implementation Concepts. Journal of Landscape Ecology. 4(3): 5-30.

Awangku, H., & Hao, L. (2011). Research in Ecotourism Success: Unraveling the Complexity. Proceedings of 2nd Regional Conference on Tourism Research, Venturing into New Tourism Research. Sustainable Tourism Research Cluster, Penang, Malaysia. 133-144.

Balas, M. & Abson, D. J. (2022). Characterising and Identifying Gaps in Sustainability Assessments of Tourism-a Review. Tourism Management Perspectives. 43: 101004.

Bacharach, M. (1970). Biproportional Matrices and Input-Output Change. Vol. 16. Cambridge: Cambridge University Press Archive.

Banerjee, O., Cicowiez, M. & Moreda, A. (2019). Evaluating the Economic Viability of Public Investments in Tourism. Journal of Benefit-Cost Analysis. 11(1): 101-130.

Bartik, A. W., Bertrand, M., Cullen, Z., Glaeser, E. L., Luca, M. and Stanton, C. (2020). The Impact of COVID-19 on Small Business Outcomes and Expectations. Proceedings of the National Academy of Sciences. 117(30): 17656-17666.

Barriball, K. L. & While, A. (1994). Collecting Data Using a Semi-Structured Interview: A Discussion Paper. Journal of Advanced Nursing-Institutional Subscription. 19(2): 328-335.

Baran, P. (1963). On the Political Economy of Backwardness. In A. Agarwala and S. Singh (eds.). The Economics of Underdevelopment. pp. 75–92. Oxford: Oxford University Press.

Baum, T. (2018). Sustainable Human Resource Management as a Driver in Tourism Policy and Planning: a Serious Sin of Omission? Journal of Sustainable Tourism. 26(6): 873-889.

Beeton, S. (2005). The Case Study in Tourism Research: A Multi-Method Case Study Approach. In Ritchie, B. W., Burns, P. M., & Palmer, C. A. (eds.).Tourism Research Methods: Integrating Theory with Practice. 37- 48.

Beckerman, W. (1994). “Sustainable development”: Is it a useful concept? Environmental Values, 3(3), 191–209.

Begovic, B., Matkovic, G., Mijatovic, B. & Popovic, B. (2007). From Poverty to Prosperity: Free Market Based Solution. Belgrade, Serbia: Centre for Liberal-Democratic Studies.

Belisle, F. J. (1984). Tourism and Food Imports: The Case of Jamaica. Economic Development and Cultural Change. 32(4): 819-842.

Bergek, A. & Norrman, C. (2015). Integrating the Supply and Demand Sides of Public Support to New Technology-Based Firms. Science and Public Policy. 42(4): 514-529.

Berrittella, M., Bigano, A., Roson, R. & Tol, R. S. (2006). A General Equilibrium Analysis of Climate Change Impacts on Tourism. Tourism Management. 27(5): 913-924.

Berelson, B. (1952). Content analysis in Communication Research. New York: The Free Press.

Bigano, A., Bosello, F., Roson, R. & Tol, R. S. (2008). Economy-Wide Impacts of Climate Change: A Joint Analysis for Sea Level Rise and Tourism. Mitigation and Adaptation Strategies for Global Change. 13: 765-791.

Birendra, K. C., Dhungana, A. & Dangi, T. B. (2021). Tourism and the Sustainable Development Goals: Stakeholders' Perspectives from Nepal. Tourism Management Perspectives. 38(4): 100822.

Blackstock, K. (2005). A Critical Look at Community Based Tourism. Community Development Journal. 40(1): 39-49.

Blake, A., Durbarry, R., Sinclair, M. T. & Sugiyarto, G. (2001). Modelling Tourism and Travel Using Tourism Satellite Accounts and Tourism Policy and Forecasting Models. Tourism and Travel Research Institute Discussion Paper. 4: 2001-2004.

Blake, A. & Sinclair, M. T. (2003). Managing Tourism Shocks: CGE Analysis of September 11. International Conference on Tourism and Sustainable Economic Development. Policy Press.1-29.

Blake A. (2008). Tourism and Income Distribution in East Africa. International Journal of Tourism Research. 10(6): 511–524.

Blake A., Arbache J.S., Sinclair M.T. & Teles V. (2008). Tourism and Poverty Relief. Annals of Tourism Research. 35(1): 107–126.

Blank, R. M. (2003). Selecting Among Anti-Poverty Policies: Can an Economist Be Both Critical and Caring? Review of Social Economy. 61(4): 447-469.

Blancas, F. J., González, M., Lozano-Oyola, M. & Pérez, F. (2010). The Assessment of Sustainable Tourism: Application to Spanish Coastal Destinations. Ecological Indicators. 10(2): 484-492.

Blancas, F. J., Lozano-Oyola, M., Gonzalez, M., Guerrero, F. M., & Caballero, R. (2011). How to Use Sustainability Indicators for Tourism Planning: The Case of Rural Tourism in Andalusia (Spain). Science of the Total Environment. 412: 28-45.

Bloomberg, L. D. & Volpe, M. (2012). Completing Your Qualitative Dissertation: A Road Map from Beginning to End. Thousand Oaks, CA: Sage.

Boer, R. & Boer, R. (2021). Seeking a Xiaokang Society, or, Socialist Modernisation. In Boer, R. (eds.). Socialism with Chinese Characteristics: A Guide for Foreigners, pp.139-163. Singapore: Springer.

Boluk, K. A., Cavaliere, C. T. & Higgins-Desbiolles, F. (2019). A Critical Framework for Interrogating the United Nations Sustainable Development Goals Agenda (2030 Agenda) in Tourism. Journal of Sustainable Tourism. 27(7): 847-864.

Bourguignon, F. & Chakravarty, S. R. (2003). The Measurement of Multidimensional Poverty. Journal of Economic Inequality. 1(1): 25-49.

Bossert, W., D'ambrosio, C., & Peragine, V. (2007). Deprivation and Social Exclusion. Economica. 74(296): 777-803.

Bossert, W., Chakravarty, S. R., & d'Ambrosio, C. (2019). Poverty and Time. Singapore :Springer.

Bramwell, B. & Lane, B. (2011). Critical Research on the Governance of Tourism and Sustainability. Journal of Sustainable Tourism. 19(4-5): 411-421.

Bramwell, B. & Lane, B. (1993). Sustainable Tourism: An Evolving Global Approach. Journal of Sustainable Tourism. 1(1)： 1-5.

Bramwell, B. (ed.). (2004). Coastal Mass Tourism: Diversification and Sustainable Development in Southern Europe. Bristol: Channel View Publications.

Bramwell, B., Higham, J., Lane, B. & Miller, G. (2017). Twenty Five Years of Sustainable Tourism and the Journal Of Sustainable Tourism: Looking Back and Moving Forward. Journal of Sustainable Tourism. 25(1): 1–9.

Bramwell, B. , Lane, B., McCabe, S., Mosedale, J. & Scarles, C. (2008). Research Perspectives on Responsible Tourism. Journal of Sustainable Tourism. 16(3): 253-257.

Bramwell, B. (2010). Participative Planning and Governance for Sustainable Tourism. Tourism Recreation Research. 35(3): 239–249.

Bradshaw, J., Williams, J., Levitas, R., Pantazis, C., Patsios, D., Townsend, P., ... & Middleton, S. (2000). The Relationship between Poverty and Social Exclusion in Britain. The 26th General Conference of the International Association for Research in Income and Wealth Cracow. Poland.

Brendehaug, E., Aall, C. & Dodds, R. (2017). Environmental Policy Integration as a Strategy for Sustainable Tourism Planning: Issues in Implementation. Journal of Sustainable Tourism. 25(9): 1257-1274.

Britton, S. (1982). The Political Economy of Tourism in the Third World. Annals of Tourism Research. 9(3): 331–358.

Brokaj, R. (2014). Local Governments Role in the Sustainable Tourism Development of a Destination. European Scientific Journal. 10(31): 103-117.

Bryman, A. (2006). Integrating Quantitative And Qualitative Research: How is tt Done? Qualitative Research. 6(1): 97-113.

Bryman, A. (2012). Social Research Methods. (5th edition). Oxford: Oxford University Press.

Brohman, J. (1996). New Directions in Tourism for Third World Development. Annals of Tourism Research. 23(1): 48–70.

Burrell, G. & Morgan, G. (2017). Sociological Paradigms and Organisational Analysis: Elements of the Sociology of Corporate Life. Abingdon: Routledge.

Butler, R. W. (1990). Alternative Tourism: Pious Hope or Trojan Horse? Journal of Travel Research. 28(3): 40-45.

Burchardt, T., Le Grand, J. & Piachaud, D. (1999). Social Exclusion in Britain 1991—1995. Social Policy and Administration. 33(3): 227-244.

Burns, P. & Holden A. (1995). Tourism: A New Perspective. London: Prentice Hall.

Burns, P. M. (2004). Tourism Planning: A Third Way? Annals of Tourism Research. 31(1): 24-43.

Budowski, G. (1976). Tourism and Environmental Conservation: Conflict, Coexistence or Symbiosis? Environmental Conservation. 3 (1): 27–31.

Burkard, A.W. & Knox, S. (2014). Qualitative Research Interviews: An Update, epublications.marquette.edu/cgi/viewcontent.

Butler, R. & Clark, G. (1992). Tourism in rural areas: Canada and United Kingdom. In I. Bowler, C. Bryant, & M. Nellis (eds.). Contemporary Rural Systems in Transition, Economy and Society, pp. 166–186. Wallingford: CAB International.

Butler, R., Curran, R. W., & Ogorman, K. D. (2013). Pro - Poor Tourism in a First World Urban Setting: Case Study of Glasgow Govan. International Journal of Tourism Research. 15(5): 443-457.

Cavanagh, David, Mark Hoey, Andrew Clark, Michael Small, Paul Bailey & Jon Watson. (2020). West Australian Pandemic Response: The Black Swan of Black Swans, https://arxiv.org/pdf/2008.08918.pdf.

Capano, G., Pritoni, A. & Vicentini, G. (2020). Do Policy Instruments Matter? Governments' Choice of Policy Mix and Higher Education Performance in Western Europe. Journal of Public Policy. 40(3): 375-401.

Capano, G. &Howlett, M. (2020). The Knowns and Unknowns of Policy Instrument Analysis: Policy Tools and the Current Research Agenda on Policy Mixes. SAGE Open. 10 (3):1-13.

Cao, X. (2015). Challenges and Potential Improvements in the Policy and Regulatory Framework for Sustainable Tourism Planning in China: The Case of Shanxi Province. Journal of Sustainable Tourism. 23(3): 455-476.

Castellani, V. & Sala, S. (2010). Sustainable Performance Index for Tourism Policy Development. Tourism Management. 31(6): 871-880.

Cater, E. (1993). Ecotourism in the Third World: Problems For Sustainable Tourism Development. Tourism Management. 14(2): 85-90.

Ceballos-Lascurain, H. (1988). Tourism, Ecotourism, and Protected Areas. Ecotourism and Resources Conservation: A Collection of Papers. Mandison.

Chan, J. K. (2010). Building Sustainable Tourism Destination and Developing Responsible Tourism: Conceptual Framework, Key Issues and Challenges. Tourism Development Journal–An International Research Journal. 8(1): 24–32.

Chan, K. W., & Zhang, L. (1999). The Hukou System and Rural-Urban Migration in China: Processes and Changes. The China Quarterly. 160: 818-855.

Chakravarty, S. R., Deutsch, J. & Silber, J. (2008). On the Watts Multidimensional Poverty Index and its Decomposition. World Development. 36(6): 1067-1077.

Chenail, R. J. (2011). Interviewing the Investigator: Strategies for Addressing Instrumentation and Researcher Bias Concerns in Qualitative Research. Qualitative Report. 16(1): 255-262.

Chen, L. (2019). Evaluation of TAP Effects in Wuling Mountain Concentrated Contiguous Destitute Area. Journal of Agricultural Resources and Regional Planning. 7: 246-250.

Chen, K. H., & Yang, H. Y. (2010). Appraising the Economic Impact of the "Opening Up to Mainland Chinese Tourist Arrivals" Policy on Taiwan with A Tourism-CGE Model. Asia Pacific Journal of Tourism Research. 15(2): 155-175.

Chen Y., Yang Y., Cheng D. D. & Liu Z. (2020). Review and Prospect of China's Tourism Development. East China Economic Management. 34(3): 1-9.

Chen, S. & Ravallion, M. (2013). More Relatively - Poor People in a Less Absolutely - Poor World. Review of Income and Wealth. 59(1), 1-28.

Chok, S., Macbeth, J., & Warren, C. (2007). Tourism as a Tool for Poverty Alleviation: a Critical Analysis of "Pro-Poor Tourism" and Implications for Sustainability. In C.M. Hall (eds.). Pro-poor tourism: Who benefits? pp. 34–55. Clevedon: Channel View Publications.

Choi, H. C. & Murray, I. (2010). Resident Attitudes toward Sustainable Community Tourism. Journal of Sustainable Tourism. 18(4): 575–594

Chirisa, I., Mutambisi, T., Chivenge, M., Mbasera, M., Sidambe, M., Muchenje, B., … and Zengeni, D. (2020). Scope for Virtual Tourism in the Times of COVID-19 in Select African Destinations. Journal of Social Sciences. 64(1-3):1-13.

China Ministry of Culture and Tourism (CMCT). (2021). National Tourism-Assisting the Poor Demonstration Cases for Rural Revitalization,
https://www.mct.gov.cn/whzx/whyw/202110/t20211028_928591.htm.

Chipfuva, T. (2021). Developing a pro-poor tourism framework for Zimbabwe. Potchefstroom,Vanderbijlpark, South Africa: North-West University.

Church, A., & Coles, T. (ed.). (2007). Tourism, Power, and Space. pp. 1-46. London: Routledge.

Clancy, M. J. (1999). Tourism and Development Evidence from Mexico. Annals of Tourism Research. 26(1): 1-20.

Colebatch, H. (2002). Policy. (2nd edition). Buckingham: Open University Press.

Conway, D., & Timms, B. F. (2010). Re-branding alternative tourism in the Caribbean: The case for "slow tourism." Tourism and Hospitality Research, 10(4), 329–344.

Council of the European Communities. (1975). Council Decision of 22 July 1975 Concerning A Programme of Pilot Schemes and Studies to Combat Poverty. Brussels.

Cox, J. W., & Hassard, J. (2010). Triangulation. Encyclopedia of Case Study Research.1: 944-947.

Croes, R. (2014). The Role of Tourism in Poverty Reduction: an Empirical Assessment. Tourism Economics. 20(2): 207–226.

Croes, R. & Vanegas S. M. (2008). Cointegration and Causality between Tourism and Poverty Reduction. Journal of Travel Research. 47(1): 94–103.

Crotty, M. (1998). The Foundations of Social Research: Meaning and Perspective in the Research Process. (1st edition). London: Sage.

Crotty, M. (1998). The Foundations of Social Research. London: Sage.

Coccossis, H. & Mexa, A. (2004). The Challenge of Tourism Carrying Capacity Assessment: Theory and Practice. Aldershot: Ashgate.

Cutler, P. (1984). The Measurement Of Poverty: A Review of Attempts to Quantify the Poor, With Special Reference To India. World Development. 12(11-12): 1119-1130.

Cukier, J. (2002). Tourism Employment Issues in Developing Countries: Examples from Indonesia. Tourism and Development: Concepts and Issues. 7(4): 165-201.

Dai, Sh., Xu, H., Scott, N., Ding, P. & Laws, E. (2012). Distortions in Tourism Development in the Dali Autonomous Region, China. Asia Pacific Journal of Tourism Research. 17(2):146–163.

Da Silva'Farias, K. S., & Figueiredo, S. L. (2021). Public Tourism Policies in the Brazilian Amazon: Participation and Networks. Journal of Multidisciplinary Academic Tourism. (Special Issue 1), 53-67.

Dadwal, S. S. (2018). Developing Tourism Sector with Neoliberalism Orientated Strategies in Countries with Scarce Financial Resources in Neoliberalism in the Tourism and Hospitality Sector. London: IGI Global.

Daly, M. (2010). Lisbon and Beyond: The EU Approach to Combating Poverty and Social Exclusion in the Last Decade. Poverty and Social Exclusion PSE Working Papers. PSE UK.

D'Anna, G., Fernández, T. V., Pipitone, C., Garofalo, G. & Badalamenti, F. (2016). Governance Analysis in the Egadi Islands Marine

Protected Area: A Mediterranean Case Study. Marine Policy. 71, 301-309.
Debreu, G. (1959). Theory of Value: An Axiomatic Analysis of Economic Equilibrium. Vol. 17. New Haven, Connecticutz: Yale University Press.
Defourny, J. & Thorbecke, E. (1984). Structural Path Analysis and Multiplier Decomposition within a Social Accounting Matrix Framework. The Economic Journal. 94(373): 111-136.
Dehury, B., & Mohanty, S. K. (2017). Multidimensional Poverty, Household Environment and Short-Term Morbidity in India. Genus. 73(1): 1-23.
De Kadt, E. (1979). Tourism: Passport to Development. Perspectives on the Social and Cultural Effects of Tourism in Developing Countries. New York: Oxford University Press.
Deller, S. (2010). Rural Poverty, Tourism and Spatial Heterogeneity. Annals of Tourism Research. 37(1): 180-205.
Deng X. H. (2015). Targeted Tourism-assisting the Poor Initiative in China. Yunnan: Yunnan University.
Denzin, N. K., & Lincoln, Y. S. (ed.). (2011). The Sage Handbook of Qualitative Research. London: Sage.
Dernoi, L. A. (1981). Alternative Tourism: Towards a New Style in North-South Relations. International Journal of Tourism Management. 2(4): 253-264.
Deriu, S., Cassar, I. P., Pretaroli, R. & Socci, C. (2022). The Economic Impact of Covid-19 Pandemic in Sardinia. Research in Transportation Economics. 93(6): 101090.
Deutsch, J. & Silber, J. (2004). Measuring the Impact of Various Income Sources on the Link Between Inequality and Development: Implications for the Kuznets Curve. Review of Development Economics. 8(1): 110-127.
Dieke, P. (1995). Tourism and Structural Adjustment Programmes in the African Economy. Tourism Economics. 1 (1): 71–93.
Dixon, P. B., Parmenter, B. R., Sutton, J. & Vincent, D. P. (1982). ORANI: A Multisectoral Model of the Australian Economy. Amsterdam: North-Holland.
Dixon, P. B. & Parmenter, B. R. (1996). Computable General Equilibrium Modelling for Policy Analysis and Forecasting. In

Amman, H. M., Tesfatsion, L., Kendrick, D. A., Rust, J., Judd, K. L., Schmedders, K., ... & LeBaron, B. D. (eds.). Handbook of Computational Economics: Agent-based Computational Economics, pp. 3-85. Amsterdam: Elsevier.

Ding, J., j. & Zhou, S., Y. (2018). Analysis on the Heterogeneity of TAP Effect in Wuling Mountain Area. Journal of Xiangtan University. 42(2):83-88.

Doern B & Phidd R. (1983). Canadian Public Policy: Ideas, Structure, Process. Toronto: Macmillan.

Donaldson, J. A. (2007). Tourism, Development and Poverty Reduction in Guizhou and Yunnan. The China Quarterly. 190: 333-351.

Dos Santos, T. (1970). The Structure of Dependency. American Economic Review. 60 (2): 231–236.

Dovers, S. & Handmer, J. (1992). Uncertainty, Sustainability and Change. Global Environment Change. 2: 262-276.

Dredge, D. & Jenkins, J. M. (2007). Tourism Planning and Policy. Milton: John Wiley.

Duménil, G. & Lévy, D. (2005). The Neoliberal (Counter-) Revolution. In E de Kadt (eds.). Tourism: Passport to Development? New York: Oxford University Press.

Duffy, K. (1995). Social Exclusion and Human Dignity in Europe: Background Report for the Proposed Initiative by the Council of Europe. Council of Europe. Strasbourg, France.

Duclos, J. Y., Sahn, D. E. & Younger, S. D. (2006). Robust Multidimensional Poverty Comparisons. The Economic Journal. 116(514):943-968.

Dwyer, L., Forsyth, P., Spurr, R. & VanHo, T. (2003). Tourism's Contribution to a State Economy: a Multi-Regional General Equilibrium Analysis. Tourism Economics. 9(4): 431-448.

Dwyer, L., Forsyth, P., & Spurr, R. (2005). Estimating the Impacts of Special Events on An Economy. Journal of Travel Research. 43(4): 351-359.

Dwyer, L., Forsyth, P. & Spurr, R. (2006). Assessing the Economic Impacts of Events: a Computable General Equilibrium Approach. Journal of Travel Research. 45(1): 59-66.

Dwyer, L., Forsyth, P. & Spurr, R. (2012). Wither Australian Tourism? Implications of the Carbon Tax. Journal of Hospitality and Tourism Management. 19(1): 15-30.

Dwyer, L., Pham, T., Jago, L., Bailey, G. & Marshall, J. (2016). Modeling the Impact of Australia's Mining Boom on Tourism: A Classic Case of Dutch Disease. Journal of Travel Research. 55(2): 233-245.

Dye, R. T. (2005). Understanding Public Policy. New Jersey: Person Education Inc.

Easton, D. (1965). A Framework for Political Analysis. New Jersey: Prentice Hall, Inc.

Eliadis, F. P., Hill, M. M., & Howlett, M. (ed.). (2005). Designing Government: from Instruments to Governance. Kingston. Canada: McGill-Queen's University Press.

Everingham, P. & Chassagne, N. (2020). Post COVID-19 Ecological and Social Reset: Moving Away from Capitalist Growth Models towards Tourism As Buen Vivir. Tourism Geographies. 22(3): 555-566.

European Commission (EC). (2022). Presentations from the ETIS and Accessible Tourism, Conference, http://ec.europa.eu/DocsRoom/documents/15362/attachments/1/translations/en/renditions/native.

Ezeuduji, I. O. (2015). Strategic Event-Based Rural Tourism Development for Sub-Saharan Africa. Current Issues in Tourism. 18(3): 212-228.

Fan, j; Yang, Z. W. & Zhao, T. (2010). Compilation of China's Macro Social Accounting Matrix. World Economic Papers. 8(4): 103-119.

Farrell, B. & McLellan, R. (1987). Tourism and Physical Environment Research. Annals of Tourism Research. 14 (1): 1–16.

Farrell, B. & Twining-Ward, L. (2005). Seven Steps Towards Sustainability: Tourism in the Context of New Knowledge. Journal of Sustainable Tourism. 13(2): 109-122.

Fayissa, B., Nsiah, C. & Tedesse, B. (2008). Impact of Tourism on Economic Growth an Development in Africa. Tourism Economics. 14(4): 807-18.

Fayissa, B.; Nsiah, C. & Tedesse, B. (2009). Tourism and Economic Growth in Latin American Countries: Further Empirical Evidence.

Department of Economics and Finance Working Paper Series. Murfreesboro: Middle Tennessee State University.

Featherston, C. R. & O'Sullivan, E. (2017). Enabling Technologies, Lifecycle Transitions, and Industrial Systems in Technology Foresight: Insights from Advanced Materials FTA. Technological Forecasting and Social Change. 115: 261-277.

Fernández-Tabales, A., Foronda-Robles, C., Galindo-Pérez-de-Azpillaga, L. & García-López, A. (2017). Developing a System of Territorial Governance Indicators for Tourism Destinations. Journal of Sustainable Tourism. 25(9): 1275-1305.

Fennell, D. A. (2020). Ecotourism (5th ed.). London UK: Routledge.

Fink, C. (1970). Die Massentourismus (Mass Tourism). Verlag Paul Haupt und Stuttgart.

Fischer, A. M. (2019). Bringing Development Back into Development Studies. Development and Change. 50(2): 426-444.

Flanagan, K., Uyarra, E. & Laranja, M. (2011). Reconceptualising the 'Policy Mix' for Innovation. Research Policy. 40(5): 702-713.

Flik, J., & Van Praag, B. (1991). Subjective Poverty Line Definitions. De Economist. 139(3): 311-330.

Folarin, O. & Adeniyi, O. (2020). Does Tourism Reduce Poverty in Sub-Saharan African Countries? Journal of Travel Research. 59(1), 140-155.

Forsyth, P., Dwyer, L., Seetaram, N. & King, B. (2012). Measuring the Economic Impact of Migration-Induced Tourism. Tourism Analysis. 17(5): 559-571.

Forsyth, P., Dwyer, L. & Spurr, R. (2014). Is Australian Tourism Suffering Dutch Disease? Annals of Tourism Research. 46: 1-15.

Foster, J. E. (1998). Absolute Versus Relative Poverty. The American Economic Review. 88(2): 335-341.

Francis, J. J., Johnston, M., Robertson, C., Glidewell, L., Entwistle, V., Eccles, M. P. & Grimshaw, J. M. (2010). What is an Adequate Sample Size? Operationalising Data Saturation for Theory-Based Interview Studies. Psychology and Health. 25(10): 1229-1245.

Freeman, R. E., Harrison, J. S., & Zyglidopoulos, S. (2018). Stakeholder theory: Concepts and strategies. Cambridge UK: Cambridge University Press.

Garrod, B., & Fyall, A. (ed.). (2018). Beyond the rural-urban divide: Cross-continental perspectives on the differentiated countryside and its regulation. Bingley UK: Emerald Group Publishing Limited.

Garau-Vadell, J. B., Gutierrez-Taño, D., & Diaz-Armas, R. (2018). Economic crisis and residents' perception of the impacts of tourism in mass tourism destinations. Journal of Destination Marketing & Management, 7, 68–75.

Gascón, J. (2015). Pro-Poor Tourism as a Strategy to Fight Rural Poverty: A Critique. Journal of Agrarian Change. 15(4): 499–518.

Geoffrey Deladem, T., Xiao, Z., Siueia, T. T., Doku, S., & Tettey, I. (2021). Developing sustainable tourism through public-private partnership to alleviate poverty in Ghana. Tourist Studies. 21(2): 317-343.

Gery, R., & Russel, B. H. (2000). Data Management and Analysis Methods. Handbook of Qualitative Research. 32(3): 125–139.

Giampiccoli, A. & Saayman, M. (2016). Community-Based Tourism: From a Local to A Global Push. Acta Commercii. 16(1): 1-10.

Giampiccoli, A. & Saayman, M. (2017). Community-Based Tourism, Responsible Tourism, and Infrastructure Development and Poverty. African Journal of Hospitality, Tourism and Leisure. 6(2): 1-28.

Gilliland, T. E., Sanchirico, J. N. & Taylor, J. E. (2020). Market-Driven Bioeconomic General Equilibrium Impacts of Tourism on Resource-Dependent Local Economies: A Case from the Western Philippines. Journal of Environmental Management. 271: 1-30.

Goh, C. C., Xubei, L. U. O. & Nong, Z. H. U. (2009). Income Growth, Inequality and Poverty Reduction: A Case Study of Eight Provinces in China. China Economic Review. 20(3): 485-496.

Golan, A., Judge G. G. & Miller. D. (1996). Maximum Entropy Econometrics: Robust Estimation with Limited Data. Chichester, UK: Wiley.

Golan, A. & Vogel, S. J. (2000). Estimation of Non-Stationary Social Accounting Matrix Coefficients with Supply-Side Information. Economic Systems Research. 12(4): 447-471.

Gonzo, F. C. (2023). Pro-poor tourism and poverty alleviation. In Nadda, V., Gonzo, F., Batta, R., & Sharma, A. (ed.). Inclusive Community

Development Through Tourism and Hospitality Practices. pp. 125-159. Pennsylvania: IGI Global.
Gordon, D., Davey Smith, G., Dorling, D. &Shaw, M. (ed.). (1999). Inequalities in health: The evidence presented to the Independent Inquiry into Inequalities in Health. Bristol: The Policy Press.
Goodwin, H. (2007). Measuring and Reporting the Impact of Tourism on Poverty. In Airey, D. & Tribe, J. (eds.). Developments in Tourism Research. pp. 79-92. Abingdon :Routledge.
Goodwin, H. (2008). Tourism, Local Economic Development and Poverty Reduction. Applied Research in Economic Development. 5(3): 55–64.
Goodwin, H. & Santilli, R. (2009). Community-Based Tourism: A Success. ICRT Occasional Paper. 11(1): 37.
Gooroochurn, N., & Milner, C. (2004). Efficiency Effects of Tourism Taxes: A Computable General Equilibrium Analysis. University of Nottingham, Christel DeHaan Tourism and Travel Research Institute.
Gooroochurn, N. & Sinclair, M. T. (2005). Economics of Tourism Taxation: Evidence from Mauritius. Annals of Tourism Research. 32(2): 478-498.
Gordon, D. (2006). The Concept and Measurement of Poverty. In R. Levitas (eds.). Poverty and Social Exclusion in Britain, pp. 29-70. Bristol: Policy Press.
Gore, C., & Figueiredo, J. (1997). Resources for Debate. Social Exclusion and Anti-poverty Poverty: A Debate. Research Series. 110: 7-34.
Gössling, S., Scott, D., Hall, C. M., Ceron, J. P. & Dubois, G. (2012). Consumer Behaviour and Demand Response of Tourists to Climate Change. Annals of Tourism Research. 39(1): 36-58.
Greener, S. (2008). Business Research Methods. London: BookBoon.
Griggs, D., Stafford-Smith, M., Gaffney, O., Rockström, J., Öhman, M.C., Shyamsundar, P., Steffen, W., Glaser, G., Kanie, N., Nobel, I.O. (2013). Policy: Sustainable Development Goals for People and Planet. Nature. 495(7441): 305–307.
Gul, H. (2015). Effects of Foreign Demand Increase in the Tourism Industry: A CGE Approach to Turkey. Anatolia. 26(4): 598-611.

Guo, Y., Jiang, J. & Li, S. (2019). A Sustainable Tourism Policy Research Review. Sustainability. 11(11): 3187.

Guo, Y. (2020). How China's Tourism Assisting The Poor Policies Strengthen Tourism-Poverty Link. BIMP-EAGA Journal for Sustainable Tourism Development. 9(1):20-38.

Guo, Y. & Liu, Y. (2022). Sustainable Poverty Alleviation and Green Development in China's Underdeveloped Areas. Journal of Geographical Sciences. 32(1): 23-43.

Haibo, C., Ayamba, E. C., Udimal, T. B., Agyemang, A. O. & Ruth, A. (2020). Tourism and Sustainable Development in China: A Review. Environmental Science and Pollution Research. 27: 39077-39093.

Hall, C. M. (1994). Tourism and Politics: Policy, Power and Place. London: Wiley.

Hall, M. (2007). Editorial: Pro-Poor Tourism: Do "Tourism Exchanges Benefit Primarily the Countries of the South?" In M. Hall (eds.). Pro-poor Tourism: Who Benefits? Perspectives on Tourism and Poverty Reduction. pp. 1–8. Clevedon: Channel View Publications.

Hall, D. & Brown, F. (ed.). (2006). Tourism and Welfare: Ethics, Responsibility and Sustained Well-Being. Wallingford: CABI.

Hall, C. M. (ed.). (2008). Tourism Planning: Policies, Processes and Relationships. New York: Prentice Hall.

Hall, C. M. (ed.). (2011). Researching the Political in Tourism: Where Knowledge Meets Power in Fieldwork in Tourism: Methods, Issues and Reflections. pp. 39–54. London: Routledge.

Hall, C. M. (2011). A Typology of Governance and its Implications for Tourism Policy Analysis. Journal of Sustainable Tourism. 19(4-5):437-457.

Hall, C. M. (2019). Constructing Sustainable Tourism Development: The Agenda (2030 Agenda) and the Managerial Ecology of Sustainable Tourism. Journal of Sustainable Tourism. 27(7): 1044-1060.

Hall, C. Michael, Scott Daniel & Stefan Gössling. (2020). Pandemics, Transformations and Tourism: Be Careful What You Wish for. Tourism Geographies. 22(3): 577-598.

Han, H. W., & Gao Q. (2017). Research on the protection effect of China's rural basic living allowance system: empirical evidence from the China Family Panel Studies (CFPS). Public Administration Journal. (2): 81-96.

Harris Jr, C. C. & Nadji, M. (1985). The Spatial Content of the Arrow - Debreu General Equilibrium System. Journal of Regional Science. 25(1): 1-10.

Harrison, B., Kelley, M. R., & Gant, J. (1996). Innovative Firm Behavior and Local Milieu: Exploring the Intersection of Agglomeration, Firm Effects, and Technological Change. Economic Geography. 72(3): 233-258.

Harrison, D. & Schipani, S. (2007). Lao Tourism and Poverty Alleviation: Community-Based Tourism and the Private Sector. Current Issues in Tourism. 10 (23): 194–230.

Harrison, D. (2008). Pro-poor Tourism: A Critique. Third World Quarterly. 29(5): 851–868.

Häusler, N. (2008). Community-based Tourism (CBT)–What Works and What Does Not Work? Drawing on Experiences in South America and Asia, International Conference on Responsible Tourism. 21–24 March, 2008. Kerala, India.

Haywood, M. K. (2020). A Post COVID-19 Future – Tourism Re-Imagined and Re-Enabled. Tourism Geographies. 22(3): 599–609.

He, W.S., Du, X.L. & Ren, P.L. (2018). Evolution Characteristics of China's Policy of Rural Poverty Alleviation in New Century and its Value Orientation: On the Basis of the Analysis of the Policy Texts of Gansu Province. Beijing Adm. Inst. 6: 42–50.

He Y. & Lou C. W. (2020). Governance of Poverty in the Post-Poverty Era: a Predictive Analysis. Qinghai Journal of Social Sciences. 1:109-117.

Hettne, B. (1990). Development Theory and the Three Worlds. Harlow: Longman.

Herrera-Cano, C. & Herrera-Cano, A. (2016). Maldivian Disaster Risk Management and Climate Change Action in Tourism Sector: Lessons For The Sustainable Development Agenda. Advances in Sustainability and Environmental Justice. 19:113-131.

Higgins-Desbiolles, F. (2006). More Than an "Industry": the Forgotten Power of Tourism as a Social Force. Tourism Management. 27(6): 1192-1208.

Höhler, S. (2015). Spaceship earth in the environmental age, 1960–1990. London UK: Routledge.

Holden, P. (ed.). (1984). Alternative Tourism, with a Focus on Asia. Bangkok: Ecumenical Coalition on Third World Tourism.

Holden, A., Sonne, J. & Novelli, M. (2011). Tourism and Poverty Reduction: An Interpretation by the Poor of Elmina, Ghana. Tourism Planning and Development. 8(3): 317-334.

Holden, A. (2013). Tourism, Poverty, and Development. New York: Routledge.

Holton, J. A. (2007). The Coding Process and its Challenges. In Bryant, A., and Charmaz, K. (eds.). 2007. The Sage Handbook of Grounded Theory, pp.265-289. Thousand Oaks, CA: Sage.

Hoque, M. A. (2020). Community-Based Indigenous Tourism, NGOs and Indigenous Poverty in Bangladesh. Dunedin: University of Otago.

Howlett, M. & Ramesh, M. (1993). Patterns of Policy Instrument Choice: Policy Styles, Policy Learning and the Privatization Experience. Review of Policy Research. 12(1-2): 3-24.

Howlett, M. (2000). Managing the 'Hollow State': Procedural Policy Instruments and Modern Governance. Canadian Public Administration. 43(4): 412–431.

Howlett, M., Mukherjee, I., & Woo, J. J. (2018). Thirty Years of Research on Policy Instruments. In Colebatch, H. K. (eds.). Handbook on Policy, Process and Governing, pp. 147-168. Cheltenham: Edward Elgar Publishing.

Howlett, M. (2020). Policy instruments: definitions and approaches. In Capano, G. and Howlett, M. (eds.). A Modern Guide to Public Policy, pp.165-177. Cheltenham: Edward Elgar Publishing.

Hu, B. M. & Huang, J. (2019). Policy Evolution and Prospect of China's Tourism Development in the Past 70 Years. Journal of Sichuan Normal University. 46(6):63-72.

Huang, C., Yang, C. & Su, J. (2018). Policy Change Analysis based on "Policy Target–Policy Instrument" Patterns: A Case Study of China's Nuclear Energy Policy. Scientometrics. 117: 1081-1114.

Hummel, J. & Rene, V. (2012). Tourism and Development at Work: 15 Years of Tourism and Poverty Reduction within the SNV Netherlands Development Organization. Journal of Sustainable Tourism. 20(3), 319-338.

Huynh, Da Van, Long Hai Duong, Nhan Trong Nguyen & Thuy Thi Kim Truong. (2022). Tourism Vulnerability amid the Pandemic Crisis: Impacts and Implications for Rebuilding Resilience of a Local Tourism System in Vietnam. Social Sciences. 11(10): 441.

Hunter, C., & Green, H. (1995). Tourism and the environment. A sustainable relationship? London UK: Routledge.

Ihalanayake, R. (2012). Economic Effects of Tourism Tax Changes in Australia: Empirical Evidence from a Computable General Equilibrium Model. Tourism Economics. 18(1): 181-202.

Ihalanayake, R. (2013). Tourism Taxes and Negative Externalities in Tourism in Australia: A CGE Approach. Corporate Ownership and Control. 10(4): 200-214.

Imon, S. S. (2017). Cultural Heritage Management Under Tourism Pressure. Worldwide Hospitality and Tourism Themes. 9(3): 335-348.

Ingham, B. (1995). Economics and Development. Maidenhead: McGraw Hill.

Inskeep, E. (1991). Tourism planning: An integrated and sustainable development approach. London UK: Routledge.

International Union for Conservation of Nature (IUCN). (1980). World Conservation Strategy. Paris: IUCN-UNEP-WWF.

Inchausti-Sintes, F. (2015). Tourism: Economic Growth, Employment and Dutch Disease. Annals of Tourism Research. 54:172-189.

Inchausti-Sintes, F. (2020). The Macroeconomic Consequences of Quality Improvement Policies in Advanced Tourism-Led Economies. Current Issues in Tourism. 23(24): 3073-3092.

Inchausti-Sintes, F., Voltes-Dorta, A. & Suau-Sánchez, P. (2021). The Income Elasticity Gap and its Implications for Economic Growth and Tourism Development: The Balearic Vs the Canary Islands. Current Issues in Tourism. 24(1): 98-116.

Ivanov, S. & Webster, C. (2007). Measuring the Impact of Tourism on Economic Growth. Tourism Economics. 13(3): 379-388.

Jackie Ong, L. T. & Smith, R. A. (2014). Perception and Reality of Managing Sustainable Coastal Tourism in Emerging Destinations: The Case of Sihanoukville, Cambodia. Journal of Sustainable Tourism. 22(2): 256-278.

Jamal, T. B. & Getz, D. (1995). Collaboration Theory and Community Tourism Planning. Annals of Tourism Research. 22(1): 186-204.

Jamieson, W., Goodwin, H. & Edmunds, C. (2004). Contribution of Tourism to Poverty Alleviation. Transport and Tourism Division. United Nations Economic and Social Commission for Asia and Pacific. Bangkok.

Jiang, Y. (2009). Evaluating Eco-Sustainability and its Spatial Variability in Tourism Areas: A Case Study in Lijiang County, China. International Journal of Sustainable Development and World Ecology. 16(2): 117-126.

Jiang H. M., Zhang Y. X., Ji Y. Q. & Gu L. L. (2019). Research on the Transformation of Poverty Alleviation and Development Policy after 2020. Taxation and Economy. 227(6):48-54.

Job, H. & Paesler, F. (2013). Links Between Nature-Based Tourism, Protected Areas, Poverty Alleviation and Crises—the Example of Wasini Island (Kenya). Journal of Outdoor Recreation and Tourism. 1(2): 18-28.

Johnson, H.G. (1960). The Costs of Protection and the Scientific Tariff. Journal of Political Economy. 68(8): 327-345.

Jovicic, D. Z. (2014). Key Issues in the Implementation of Sustainable Tourism. Current Issues in Tourism. 17(4): 297-302.

Kallio, H., Pietilä, A. M., Johnson, M. & Kangasniemi, M. (2016). Systematic Methodological Review: Developing a Framework for a Qualitative Semi-Structured Interview Guide. Journal of Advanced Nursing. 72(12): 2954-2965.

Kanungo, S. , Nath, D. , Mazumder, G. , Mukherjee, S. & Roychowdhuri, D. (2019). Measuring Poverty in Eastern India through Multi-Dimensional Poverty Index (MPI): Tool to Focus Where to Invest in Public Health. National Journal of Community Medicine. 10(2): 55-61.

Karnani, A. (2007.) The Mirage of Marketing to the Bottom of the Pyramid: How the Private Sector Can Help Alleviate Poverty. California Management Review. 49(4): 90-111.

Kates, R. W., Clark, W. C., Corell, R., Hall, J. M., Jaeger, C. C., Lowe, I., ... & Svedin, U. (2001). Sustainability Science. Science. 292(5517): 641-642.

Kennedy, B.L. and Thornberg, R. (2018). Deduction, induction, and abduction. In Flick, U. (eds.). The SAGE Handbook of Qualitative Data Collection, pp. 49-64. London: Sage Publications.

Keuning, S. J. & de Ruuter, W. A. (1988). Guidelines to the Construction of a Social Accounting Matrix. Review of Income and Wealth. 34(1): 71-100.

Khan, M. R., Khan, H. U. R., Lim, C. K., Tan, K. L. & Ahmed, M. F. (2021). Sustainable Tourism Policy, Destination Management and Sustainable Tourism Development: A Moderated-Mediation Model. Sustainability. 13(21): 12156.

Kibicho, W. (2008). Community-Based Tourism: A Factor-Cluster Segmentation Approach. Journal of Sustainable Tourism. 16(2): 211-231.

Kim, N. , Song, H. J. & Ju, H. P. (2016). The Relationship among Tourism, Poverty, and Economic Development in Developing Countries A Panel Data Regression Analysis. Tourism Economics. 22(6): 1174-1190.

King, V. T. (2018). Tourism and Erik Cohen in Thailand: Comparisons, Impacts, Mobilities and Encounters. International Journal of Asia-Pacific Studies. 14(2): 1-38.

King, R. & Dinkoksung, S. (2014). Ban Pa-Ao, Pro-Poor Tourism and Uneven Development. Tourism Geographies. 16(4): 687–703.

Klasen, S. (2002). Social Exclusion and Children in OECD Countries: Some Conceptual Issues.The School Field. 13: 9–25.

Knight, D. W. & Cottrell, S. P. (2016). Evaluating Tourism-Linked Empowerment in Cuzco, Peru. Annals of Tourism Research. 56: 32–47.

Knight, D. W. (2018). An Institutional Analysis of Local Strategies for Enhancing Pro-Poor Tourism Outcomes in Cuzco, Peru. Journal of Sustainable Tourism. 26(4): 631-648.

Konan, D. E. (2011). Limits To Growth: Tourism and Regional Labor Migration. Economic Modelling. 28(1-2): 473-481.

Kotler, P., Roberto, N. & Leisner, T. (2006). Alleviating Poverty: A Macro/Micro Marketing Perspective. Journal of Macromarketing. 26(2): 233-239.

Krippendorff, K. (2012). Content Analysis: An Introduction to its Methodology. Thousand Oaks, CA: Sage.

Krauss S. E., Hamzah A., Omar Z., Suandi T., Ismail I. A. & Zahari M. Z. (2009). Preliminary Investigation and Interview Guide Development for Studying How Malaysian Farmers Form their Mental Models of Farming. The Qualitative Report. 14(2): 245-260.

Laderchi, C. R., Saith, R. & Stewart, F. (2003). Does It Matter That We Do Not Agree on The Definition of Poverty? A Comparison of Four Approaches. Oxford Development Studies. 31(3): 243-274.

Lansing, P. & Vries, P. D. (2007). Sustainable Tourism: Ethical Alternative or Marketing Ploy? Journal of Business Ethics. 72:77-85.

Lasswell, H. D. (1948). The Structure and Function of Communication in Society. The Communication of Ideas. 37(1): 136-139.

Lea, J. (2006). Tourism and Development in the Third World. London: Routledge.

Lemma, A. (2014). Tourism for Poverty Reduction in South Asia, EPS-PEAKS services, http://partnerplatform.org/eps-peaks.

Lemelin, A., Fofana, I. & Cockburn, J. (2013). Balancing a Social Accounting Matrix: Theory and Application. Revised Edition. Nairobi, Kenya: Partnership for Economic Policy (PEP).

Lenzen, M., Sun, Y. Y., Faturay, F., Ting, Y. P., Geschke, A., & Malik, A. (2018). The carbon footprint of global tourism. Nature Climate Change, 8(6), 522–528.

Lenoir, R. (1989). Les Exclus: Un Français Sur Dix. 1974. Paris: Éditions du Seuil.

Leontief, W. W. (1936). Quantitative Input and Output Relations in the Economic Systems of the United States. The Review of Economic Statistics. 18(3):105-125.

Leontief, W. W. (1941). The Structure of American Economy, 1919–1929. An Empirical Application of Equilibrium Analysis. Cambridge: Harvard University Press.

Levine, S., Muwonge, J. & Batana, Y. M. (2014). A Robust Multi-Dimensional Poverty Profile for Uganda. Journal of Human Development and Capabilities. 15(4): 369-390.

Li, F., Luo L.Q., Pan, L.L. (2018). An exploration of multidimensional poverty indicators and weights: an analysis based on CFPS data.

Journal of Jiangxi University of Finance and Economics. 120(6),82-93.

Li, S. T.; Li Q.; Qi, S. C. & Zhai, F. (1996). Social Accounting Matrix of Chinese Economy. The Journal of Quantitative and Technical Economics. 1:42-48.

Li, S., Liu, G. & Yu, Y. (2021). Analysis of the Implementation Process of Targeted Poverty Alleviation Policy. 2021 4th International Conference on Humanities Education and Social Sciences (ICHESS 2021). Atlantis Press. 2467-2473.

Li, S., Blake, A., & Cooper, C. (2010). China's Tourism in a Global Financial Crisis: a Computable General Equilibrium Approach. Current Issues in Tourism. 13(5): 435-453.

Li, S., Blake, A., & Cooper, C. (2011). Modelling the Economic Impact of International Tourism on the Chinese Economy: A CGE Analysis of the Beijing 2008 Olympics. Tourism Economics. 17(2): 279-303.

Li, Y., & Hunter, C. (2015). Community Involvement for Sustainable Heritage Tourism: A Conceptual Model. Journal of Cultural Heritage Management and Sustainable Development. 5(3): 248-262.

Li X.Y. & Xu H. Y. (2018). Some Thoughts on Poverty Alleviation after 2020. Journal of CAG. 112(1):62-66.

Li, S., Liu, A. & Song, H. (2019). Does Tourism Support Supply-Side Structural Reform in China? Tourism Management. 71: 305-314.

Li, W., Qi, J., Huang, S., Fu, W., Zhong, L. & He, B. J. (2021). A Pressure-State-Response Framework for the Sustainability Analysis of Water National Parks in China. Ecological Indicators. 131: 108127.

Liang, Z. & Bao, J. (2018). Targeted Poverty Alleviation in China: Segmenting Small Tourism Entrepreneurs and Effectively Supporting them. Journal of Sustainable Tourism. 26(11): 1984-2001.

Lin, K. C., Shyu, J. Z. & Ding, K. (2017). A Cross-Strait Comparison of Innovation Policy Under Industry 4.0 and Sustainability Development Transition. Sustainability. 9(5):786.

Liu, Z. (2003). Sustainable Tourism Development: A Critique. Journal of Sustainable Tourism. 11(6): 459-475.

Liu, W. (2014). Application of Content Analysis in Public Management Research. Chinese Public Administration. 6: 93-98.

Liu, A. & Wall, G. (2006). Planning Tourism Employment: A Developing Country Perspective. Tourism Management. 27 (1): 159–170.

Liu, H. M. & Ji C.W. (2017). The Evolution of China's Tourism Policies. Journal of Seeking. 4:137-143.

Liu, Y. , Guo, Y. , Zhou, Y. , Xin, X. & Xin, X. (2018). Poverty Alleviation in Rural China: Policy Changes, Future Challenges and Policy Implications. China Agricultural Economic Review. 10(2): 241-259.

Liu, C., Dou, X., Li, J. & Cai, L. A. (2020). Analyzing Government Role in Rural Tourism Development: An Empirical Investigation from China. Journal of Rural Studies. 79: 177-188.

Lofgren, H. (2001). External Shocks and Domestic Poverty Alleviation: Simulation with a CGE Model of Malawi. 1043 TMD Discussion Paper 71. International Food Policy Research Institute. Washington D.C.

Lofgren, H., Harris, R. L. & Robinson, S. (2002). A Standard Computable General Equilibrium (CGE) Model in GAMS. Vol. 5. Washington D.C.: International Food Policy Research Institute.

Lok-Dessallien, R. (1999). Review of Poverty Concepts and Indicators, www. undp. orgpovertypublicationspovReview pdf,21.

Lo, K., Li, J., Wang, M., Li, C., Li, S. & Li, Y. (2019). A Comparative Analysis of Participating and Non-Participating Households in Pro-Poor Tourism in Southern Shaanxi, China. Tourism Planning and Development. 16(3): 318-333.

Lor, J. J., Kwa, S., & Donaldson, J. A. (2019). Making ethnic tourism good for the poor. Annals of Tourism Research. 76: 140-152.

Maasoumi, E. & Lugo, M. A. (2008). The Information Basis of Multivariate Poverty Assessments. London Borough of Camden: Palgrave Macmillan UK.

Madsen, A. D. & Sorensen, M. L. (2002). Effects of Trade and Market Integration in A Small Open Economy–Dynamic CGE Approach, Danish Rational Economic Agents Model (DREAM). Danish Ministry of Finance. Denmark

Madill, A. (2011). Interaction in the Semi-Structured Interview: A Comparative Analysis of the Use of and Response to Indirect Complaints. Qualitative Research in Psychology. 8(4): 333-353.

Manzoor, F. , Wei, L. , Asif, M. , Haq, M. & Rehman, H. U. (2019). The Contribution of Sustainable Tourism to Economic Growth and Employment in Pakistan. International Journal of Environmental Research and Public Health. 16(19): 3785.

Mansur, K. M., Bagul, A. H. B. P. P., Yusof, R., Liew-Tsonis, J., Husin, R., Mail, R., ... & Sung, T. P. (2013). A Study on Poverty Concepts and Perspectives: Conceptual Paper. BIMP-EAGA Journal for Sustainable Tourism Development. 2(1): 42-46.

Manyara, G. & Jones, E. (2007). Community-based Tourism Enterprises Development in Kenya: An Exploration of Their Potential as Avenues of Poverty Reduction. Journal of Sustainable Tourism. 15(6): 628-644.

Mauri, C. (2020). What Comes to Mind When You Think of Sustainability? Qualitative Research with ZMET. Worldwide Hospitality and Tourism Themes. 12(4): 459-470.

Maxwell, S. (1999). International Targets for Poverty Reduction and Food Security: A Mildly Sceptical But Resolutely Pragmatic View With a Call for Greater Subsidiarity 1. IDS Bulletin. 30(2): 92-105.

May, P. J. (2012). Policy Design and Implementation. In Peters BG & Pierre J (eds.). The Sage Handbook of Public Administration, pp. 279-291. London: Sage.

Mahadevan, R. , Amir, H. & Nugroho, A. (2017). Regional Impacts Of Tourism-Led Growth on Poverty and Income Inequality: A Dynamic General Equilibrium Analysis for Indonesia. Tourism Economics the Business and Finance of Tourism and Recreation. 23(3): 614-631.

Mahadevan, R., Amir, H., & Nugroho, A. (2017). How Pro-Poor and Income Equitable are Tourism Taxation Policies in A Developing Country? Evidence from a Computable General Equilibrium Model. Journal of Travel Research. 56(3): 334-346.

Mai, T. & Smith, C. (2015). Addressing the Threats to Tourism Sustainability Using Systems Thinking: A Case Study of Cat Ba Island, Vietnam. Journal of Sustainable Tourism. 23(10): 1504-1528.

Marx, S. (2011). Community-Based and Pro-Poor Tourism. International Trade Forum. International Trade Centre, Geneva.

Marson, D. (2011). From Mass Tourism to Niche Tourism. In Robinson, P., Heitmann, S., & Dieke, P. (eds.). Research Themes for Tourism, pp. 1-15. Wallingford: CABI.

Masset, E. & García-Hombrados, J. (2021). Sensitivity Matters. Comparing the Use of Multiple Indicators and of a Multidimensional Poverty Index in the Evaluation of a Poverty Eradication Program. World Development. 137: 105162.

Matilainen, A., Keskinarkaus, S. & Törmä, H. (2016). The Economic Significance of Hunting Tourism in East Lapland, Finland. Human Dimensions of Wildlife. 21(3): 203-222.

Mbaiwa, J. E. & Darkoh, M. (2009). The Socio-Economic Impacts of Tourism in the Okavango Delta, Botswana. In J.Saarinen, F. Becker, H.Manwa & D. Wilson (eds.). Sustainable Tourism in Journal of Sustainable Tourism 315 Southern Africa: Local Communities and Natural Resources in Transition, pp.210-230. Clevedon: Channel View Publications.

McKercher, B. (1993a). Some fundamental truths about tourism: Understanding tourism's social and environmental impacts, Journal of Sustainable Tourism, 1(1), 6–16.

McKercher, B. (1993b). The unrecognized threat to tourism: Can tourism survive "sustainability"? Tourism Management, 14(2), 131–136.

McLaren, D. (2003). Rethinking Tourism and Ecotravel. West Hartford: Kumarian Press.

Meadows, D. H., Meadows, D. L., Randers, J., & Behrens, W. W. (2018). The limits to growth. In Green planet blues (pp. 25-29). Routledge.

Medina-Muñoz, D. R., Medina-Muñoz, R. D. & Gutiérrez-Pérez, F. J. (2016). The Impacts of Tourism on Poverty Alleviation: An Integrated Research Framework. Journal of Sustainable Tourism. 24(2): 270-298.

Meng, X., Gregory, R. & Wang, Y. (2005). Poverty, Inequality, and Growth in Urban China, 1986–2000. Journal of Comparative Economics. 33(4): 710-729.

Meng, S., & Siriwardana, M. (2017). Assessing the Economic Impact of Tourism: A Computable General Equilibrium Modelling Approach.

London Borough of Camden: Palgrave-Macmillan Publisher Limited.
Meng, X., Siriwardana, M. & Pham, T. (2013). A CGE Assessment of Singapore's Tourism Policies. Tourism Management. 34: 25-36.
Meng, S. (2014). The Role of Inbound Tourism in the Singaporean Economy: A Computable General Equilibrium (CGE) Assessment. Journal of Travel and Tourism Marketing. 31(8): 1071-1089.
Meng, S., & Pham, T. (2017). The Impact of the Australian Carbon Tax on the Tourism Industry. Tourism Economics. 23(3): 506-522.
Mestrum, F. (2006). Global Poverty Reduction: A New Social Paradigm? Development. 49(2): 62-66.
Meyer, D. (2007). Pro-Poor Tourism: From Leakages To Linkages. A Conceptual Framework for Creating Linkages between the Accommodation Sector and 'Poor' Neighbouring Communities. Current Issues in Tourism. 10(6): 558-583.
Miller, G. (2001). The Development of Indicators for Sustainable Tourism: Results of A Delphi Survey of Tourism Researchers. Tourism Management. 22(4): 351-362.
Milne, S. & Ateljevic, I. (2001). Tourism, Economic Development and the Global-Local Nexus: Theory Embracing Complexity. Tourism Geographies. 3(4): 369-393.
Mitchell, J., & C. Ashley. (2007). Can Tourism Offer Pro-Poor Pathways to Prosperity? London: Overseas Development Institute.
Mitchell, J. & Ashley, C. (2010). Tourism and Poverty Reduction: Pathways to Prosperity. London: Earthscan.
Misturelli, F. & Heffernan, C. (2010). The Concept of Poverty: A Synchronic Perspective. Progress in Development Studies. 10(1): 35–58.
Mishra, P. K., Rout, H. B. & Mohapatra, S. S. (2011). Causality Between Tourism and Economic Growth: Empirical Evidence from India. European Journal of Social Sciences. 18(4): 518-527.
Mitra, S. K. (2017). Politics in India: Structure, Process and Policy. London: Routledge.
Mori, K. & Christodoulou, A. (2012). Review of Sustainability Indices and Indicators: Towards a New City Sustainability Index (CSI). Environmental Impact Assessment Review. 32(1): 94-106.

Mosley, P. & Toye, J. (1988). The Design of Structural Adjustment Programmes. Development Policy Review. 6 (4): 395–413.

Movono, A. & Hughes, E. (2022). Tourism Partnerships: Localizing the SDG Agenda in Fiji. Journal of Sustainable Tourism. 30(10), 2318-2332.

Mowafi, M. (2004). The Meaning and Measurement of Poverty: A Look into the Global Debate. Development Gateway Foundation. 8(5): 1-53.

Mowforth, M., Charlton, C. & Munt, I. (2008). Tourism and Responsibility Perspectives from Latin America and the Caribbean. London: Routledge.

Mowforth, M. & Munt, I. (2009). Tourism and Sustainability: Development, Globalization and New Tourism in the Third World. London: Routledge.

Mowforth, M. & Munt, I. (2015). Tourism and Sustainability: Development, Globalization and New Tourism in the Third World. (4th edition). Abingdon: Routledge.

Moyle, B. D., McLennan, C. L. J., Ruhanen, L. & Weiler, B. (2014). Tracking the Concept of Sustainability in Australian Tourism Policy and Planning Documents. Journal of Sustainable Tourism. 22(7): 1037-1051.

Narayan, P. K. (2004). Economic Impact of Tourism on Fiji's Economy: Empirical Evidence from the Computable General Equilibrium Model. Tourism Economics. 10(4):419-433.

Narayan, P. K., Narayan, S., Prasad, A. & Prasad, B. C. (2010). Tourism and Economic Growth: A Panel Data Analysis for Pacific Island Countries. Tourism Economics. 16(1): 169-83.

Neto, F. (2003). A New Approach to Sustainable Tourism Development: Moving Beyond Environmental Protection. Natural Resources Forum. 27(3): 212-222.

Niavis, S., Papatheochari, T., Psycharis, Y., Rodriguez, J., Font, X. & Martinez Codina, A. (2019). Conceptualising Tourism Sustainability and Operationalising its Assessment: Evidence from a Mediterranean Community of Projects. Sustainability. 11(15): 4042.

Njoya, E. T. & Seetaram, N. (2018). Tourism Contribution to Poverty Alleviation in Kenya: A Dynamic Computable General Equilibrium Analysis. Journal of Travel Research. 57(4): 513-524.

Norton, B. G. (2005). Sustainability: A Philosophy of Adaptive Ecosystem Management. Chicago: University of Chicago Press.

Novak, T. (1995). Rethinking Poverty. Critical Social Policy. 15(44-45): 58-74.

Olawumi, T. O. & Chan, D. W. M. (2018). A Scientometric Review of Global Research on Sustainability and Sustainable Development. Journal of Cleaner Production. 183: 231-250.

Oppenheim C, Harker L. (1996). Poverty: The Facts. London: Child Poverty Action Group.

Oppermann, M. & Chon, K.S. (1997). Tourism in Developing Countries. London: International Thompson Business Press.

Oppong, S. H. (2013). The Problem of Sampling in Qualitative Research. Asian Journal of Management Sciences and Education. 2: 202-210.

Orams, M. B. (1995). Towards A More Desirable Form of Ecotourism. Tourism Management. 16(1): 3-8.

Page, S. (1999). Tourism and Development: The Evidence from Mauritius, South Africa, and Zimbabwe. London: Overseas Development Institute.

Pang, W, H. (2019). Grey Correlation Analysis of Rural Tourism Poverty Alleviation and Tourism Income in Longnan City. Journal of Longdong University. 30(4): 104-108.

Paugam, S. & Russell, H. (2000). The Effects of Employment Precarity and Unemployment on Social Isolation. In D. Gallie & S. Paugam (eds.). Welfare Regimes and the Experience of Unemployment in Europe, pp. 243–64. Oxford: Oxford University Press.

Park, A. & Wang, S. (2001). China's Poverty Statistics. China Economic Review. 12(4): 384-398.

Park, D.-B., Lee, K.-W., Choi, H.-S. & Yoon, Y. (2012). Factors Influencing Social Capital in Rural Tourism Communities in South Korea. Tourism Management. 33(6): 1511–1520.

Park, N. & Ondicho, T. G. (2017). Contribution Of Tourism on Poverty Reduction: A Case of Communities Living Adjacent to Amboseli Nation Park. The International Journal of Development Dialogue. 2(1): 34-53.

Parrotta, J., Agnoletti, M. & Johan, E. (2006). Cultural Heritage and Sustainable Forest Management: The Role of Traditional Knowledge. Ministerial Conference on the Protection of Forests in Europe. Liaison Unit Warsaw.

Patrick, M. (2019). Poverty Alleviation Through Tourism Activities: A Case of Amani and Uluguru Mountain Nature Reserves. International Conference on the Future of Tourism. OUT. April 2019.

Patton, M. Q. (1990). Qualitative Evaluation and Research Methods. Thousand Oaks, CA: Sage.

Patton, M. Q. (1999). Enhancing the Quality and Credibility of Qualitative Analysis. Health Services Research. 34(2-5): 1189.

Peeters, P. (2012). A clear path towards sustainable mass tourism? Rejoinder to the paper "Organic, incremental and induced paths to sustainable mass tourism convergence" by David B. Weaver. Tourism Management, 33(5), 1038–1041.

Petrevska, B., Terzić, A. & Andreeski, C. (2020). More Or Less Sustainable? Assessment from A Policy Perspective. Sustainability. 12(8): 3491.

Perroux, F. (1955). Note on the Concept of Growth Poles. In I. Livingstone (eds.). Economic Policy for Development: Selected Readings. Harmondsworth: Penguin.

Pham, T. P. T., Cho, C. W. & Yun, Y. S. (2010). Environmental Fate and Toxicity of Ionic Liquids: A Review. Water Research. 44(2): 352-372.

Pham, T., Jago, L., Spurr, R. & Marshall, J. (2015). The Dutch Disease Effects on Tourism–The Case of Australia. Tourism Management. 46: 610-622.

Phi, G. T., Whitford, M. & Reid, S. (2018). What's in the Black Box? Evaluating Anti-Poverty Tourism Interventions Utilizing Theory Of Change. Current Issues in Tourism. 21(17): 1930-1945.

Phommavong, S. & Sorensson, E. (2014). Ethnic Tourism in Lao PDR: Gendered Divisions of labor in Community-Based Tourism for Poverty Reduction. Current Issues in Tourism. 17(4): 350-362.

Polukhina, A., Sheresheva, M., Efremova, M., Suranova, O., Agalakova, O. & Antonov-Ovseenko, A. (2021). The Concept of Sustainable Rural Tourism Development in the Face of COVID-19 Crisis:

Evidence From Russia. Journal of Risk and Financial Management. 14(1): 38.

Poon, A. (1993). Tourism, Technology and Competitive Strategies. Wallingford: CAB International.

Potter, R. (1993). Basic Needs and Development in the Small Island States of the Eastern Caribbean. In D.G. Lockhart, D. Drakakis-Smith & J. Schembri (eds.). The Development Process in Small Island States, pp. 92 – 116. London: Routledge.

Pratt, S. (2015). The Economic Impact of Tourism in SIDS. Annals of Tourism Research. 52: 148-160.

Prideaux, B., Thompson, M. & Pabel, A. (2020). Lessons From COVID-19 Can Prepare Global Tourism for the Economic Transformation Needed to Combat Climate Change. Tourism Geographies. 22(3): 667–678.

Purvis, B., Mao, Y. & Robinson, D. (2019). Three Pillars Of Sustainability: In Search Of Conceptual Origins. Sustainability Science. 14: 681-695.

Pyatt, G. & Round, J. I. (1979). Accounting and Fixed Price Multipliers in a Social Accounting Matrix Framework. The Economic Journal. 89(356): 850-873.

Qin, D., Xu, H. & Chung, Y. (2019). Perceived Impacts of the Poverty Alleviation Tourism Policy on the Poor in China. Journal of Hospitality and Tourism Management. 41:41-50.

Qin, C. & Zhang, W. (2022). Green, Poverty Reduction and Spatial Spillover: An Analysis from 21 Provinces of China. Environment, Development and Sustainability. 24: 13610–13629.

Qiu Zhang, H., Fan, D. X., Tse, T. S. & King, B. (2017). Creating a Scale for Assessing Socially Sustainable Tourism. Journal of Sustainable Tourism. 25(1): 61-78.

Rao, Y. & Chen, S. (2018). Cross-Group Knowledge Transfer and Capacity-Building for the Poor: A Case Study of Tourism Targeted Poverty Alleviation in Guangdong Province, China. Advances in Applied Sociology. 8(7): 495-516.

Rasoolimanesh, S. M., Ramakrishna, S., Hall, C. M., Esfandiar, K. & Seyfi, S. (2020). A Systematic Scoping Review of Sustainable Tourism Indicators in Relation to the Sustainable Development Goals. Journal of Sustainable Tourism. 7:1-21.

Redclift, M. (1987). Sustainable Development: Exploring the Contradictions. London: Routledge.

Rein, M. & Schön, D. (1996). Frame-Critical Policy Analysis and Frame-Reflective Policy Practice. Knowledge and Policy. 9(1): 85-104.

Ren, W., & Han, F. (2018). Indicators for Assessing the Sustainability of Built Heritage Attractions: An Anglo-Chinese Study. Sustainability. 10(7): 2504.

Renwick, N. (2016). The Global Pursuit of Human Dignity. In Chathapuram S Ramanathan, Srilatha Juvva, Subhabrata Dutta, and Khadija Khaja (eds.). Spirituality, Culture, and Development: Implications for Social Work, pp. 55-77. New York: Lexington Books.

Richards, G. & Hall, D. (2003). Tourism and Sustainable Community Development. London: Routledge.

Richards, G. (2019). Tourism and Poverty Reduction: Principles and Impacts in Developing Countries. London: Routledge.

Rivera, J. P. R., & Tuazon, G. P. (2019). A conceptual and empirical framework on pro-poor tourism. Review of Integrative Business and Economics Research. 8(3): 66.

Robinson, S., Cattaneo, A. & El-Said, M. (1998). Estimating a Social Accounting Matrix Using Cross Entropy Methods. Trade and Macroeconomics Division Discussion Paper No. 33. Washington: International Food Policy Research Institute.

Robinson S. & El-Said, M. (2000). GAMS Code for Estimating A Social Accounting Matrix (SAM) Using Cross-Entropy Methods. Discussion Paper No. 64. Washington: International Food Policy Research Institute.

Roe, D., Goodwin, H. & Ashley, C. (2004). Pro-Poor Tourism: Benefiting the Poor. In Singh, T. V. (eds). New Horizons in Tourism: Strange Experiences and Stranger Practices, pp.147-161. Wallingford: CABI Publishing.

Rogan, M. (2016). Gender and Multidimensional Poverty in South Africa: Applying the Global Multidimensional Poverty Index (MPI). Social Indicators Research. 126: 987-1006.

Rossouw, R. & Saayman, M. (2011). Assimilation of Tourism Satellite Accounts and Applied General Equilibrium Models to Inform Tourism Policy Analysis. Tourism Economics. 17(4): 753-783.

Roson, R. & Sartori, M. (2014). Climate Change, Tourism and Water Resources in the Mediterranean: A General Equilibrium Analysis. International Journal of Climate Change Strategies and Management. 6(2): 212-228.

Rostow, W. (1960). The Stages of Economic Growth: A Non-Communist Manifesto. Cambridge: Cambridge University Press.

Rothwell, R. (1985). Reindustrialization and Technology: Towards a National Policy Framework. Science and Public Policy. 12(3): 113-130.

Room, G. (ed.). (1995). Beyond the Threshold: the Measurement and Analysis of Social Exclusion. Bristol: Policy Press.

Round, J. I. (1991). A SAM for Europe: Problems and Perspectives. Economic Systems Research. 3(3): 249-268.

Rowntree, S. (1901). Poverty: A Study of Town Life. London: Macmillan.

Rutty, M., Gössling, S., Scott, D., & Hall, C. M. (2015). The global effects and impacts of tourism: An Overview. In C. M. Hall , S. Gössling & D. Scott (Eds.). The Routledge Handbook of Tourism and Sustainability, pp.36–63. Abingdon: Routledge.

Ryel, R. & Grasse, T. (1991). Marketing Ecotourism: Attracting the Elusive Ecotourist. In T. Whelan (eds.). Nature Tourism: Managing for the Environment, pp. 164-186. Washington, DC: Island Press.

Saayman, M., Rossouw, R. & Krugell, W. (2012). The Impact of Tourism on Poverty in South Africa. Development Southern Africa. 29(3): 462-487.

Saayman, M. & Giampiccoli, A. (2015). Community-Based Tourism and Pro-Poor Tourism: Dissimilar Positioning in Relation to Community Development. Journal for New Generation Sciences. 13 (3): 163-181.

Saayman, M. & Giampiccoli, A. (2016). Community-Based and Pro-Poor Tourism: Initial Assessment of Their Relation to Community Development. European Journal of Tourism Research. 12: 145-190.

Saarinen, J., Becker, F. O., Manwa, H., & Wilson, D. (ed.). (2009). Sustainable Tourism in Southern Africa: Local Communities and Natural Resources in Transition. Bristol: Channel View Publications.

Sachs, J. D. (2005). Can Extreme Poverty Be Eliminated? Scientific American. 293(3): 56-65.

Saffu, K., Obeng Apori, S., Elijah-Mensah, A. & Ahumatah, J. (2008). The Contribution of Human Capital and Resource-Based View to Small-and Medium-Sized Tourism Venture Performance in Ghana. International Journal of Emerging Markets. 3(3): 268–284.

Saigaran, N. G., Karupiah, P. & Gopal, P. S. (2015). The Capability Approach: Comparing Amartya Sen and Martha Nussbaum. Proceedings of Universiti Sains Malaysia. USM. 1.

Saifullah, M. K. (2022). Well-Being Index of Indigenous People of Peninsular Malaysia: An Application of the Multidimensional Poverty Index (MPI). AlterNative: An International Journal of Indigenous Peoples. 18(3): 424-435.

Salamon, L. M. (2000). The New Governance and the Tools of Public Action: An Introduction. Fordham Urban Law Journal. 28(5): 1611-1674.

Salamon, L. M. (2002). The Tools of Government: A Guide to the New Governance. Oxford: Oxford University Press.

Sartori, S., Latronico, F. & Campos, L. M. S. (2014). Sustainability and Sustainable Development: A Taxonomy in the Field of Literature. Ambiente Sociedade. 17: 01-22.

Saunders, M., Lewis, P. & Thornhill, A. (2016). Research Methods for Business Students. (6th edition). New York:Pearson Education Limited.

Saunders, M., Lewis, P., &Thornhill, A. (2019). Research Methods for Business Students. (8th edition). New York: Pearson Education Limited.

Scheyvens, R. (2007). Exploring the Tourism-Poverty Nexus. Current Issues in Tourism. 10(2–3):231–254.

Scheyvens, R. & Momsen, J. H. (2008). Tourism and Poverty Reduction: Issues for Small Island States. Tourism Geographies. 10(1): 22-41.

Scheyvens, R. (2009). Pro-Poor Tourism: Is there Value Beyond the Rhetoric? Tourism Recreation Research. 34(2): 191-196.

Scheyvens, R. (2011). The Challenge of Sustainable Tourism Development in the Maldives: Understanding the Social and Political Dimensions of Sustainability. Asia Pacific Viewpoint. 52(2): 148-164.

Scheyvens, R. (2018). Linking Tourism to the Sustainable Development Goals: A Geographical Perspective. Tourism Geographies. 20(2): 341-342.

Scheyvens, R. & Hughes, E. (2019). Can Tourism Help to "End Poverty In All Its Forms Everywhere"? the Challenge of Tourism Addressing SDG1. Journal of Sustainable Tourism. 27(9): 1061-1079.

Scheyvens, R., & Momsen, J. (2019). Tourism and Gender: Embodiment, Sensuality and Experience. Bristol: Channel View Publications.

Scheyvens, R. (2002). Tourism for Development: Empowering Communities. New York: Pearson Education.

Scheyvens, R. (1999). Ecotourism and the Empowerment of Local Communities. Tourism Management. 20(2):245-249.

Schneider, A. & Ingram, H. (1990). Behavioral Assumptions of Policy Tools. The Journal of Politics. 52(2): 510-529.

Schilcher, D. (2007). Growth Versus Equity: The Continuum of Pro-Poor Tourism and Neoliberal Governance. Current Issues in Tourism. 10(2-3): 166-193.

Schram T. H. (2003). Conceptualizing Qualitative Inquiry: Mindwork for Fieldwork in Education and the Social Sciences. Upper Saddle River, New Jersey: Merrill Prentice Hall.

Scott, D., Hall, C. M. & Gössling, S. (2016). A Review of the IPCC 5th Assessment and Implications for Tourism Sector Climate Resilience and Decarbonization. Journal of Sustainable Tourism. 24(1): 8-30.

Scott, D., Gössling, S., Hall, C. M., & Peeters, P. (2016). Can Tourism Be Part of the Decarbonized Global Economy? The Costs and Risks of Carbon Reduction Pathways. Journal of Sustainable Tourism. 24(1): 52-72.

Schumacher, E. (1974). Small is Beautiful: A Study of Economics as if People Mattered. London: Abacus.

Sen, A. (1976). Poverty: An Ordinal Approach to Measurement. Econometrica: Journal of the Econometric Society. 44 (2): 219-231.

Sen, A. (1983). Poor, Relatively Speaking. Oxford Economic Papers. 35(2): 153-169.

Sen, A. (2000). Social Exclusion: Concept, Application, and Scrutiny. Manila: Asian Development Bank.

Seers, D. (1969). The Meaning of Development, www.ids.ac.uk.

Seraphin, H. & F Dosquet. (2020). Mountain Tourism and Second Home Tourism As Post Covid-19 Lockdown Placebo? Worldwide Hospitality and Tourism Themes. 12(4): 485-500.

Shannon, C. E. (1948). A Mathematical Theory of Communication. The Bell System Technical Journal. 27(3): 379-423.

Sharpley, R. (2000). Tourism and Sustainable Development: Exploring the Theoretical Divide. Journal of Sustainable Tourism. 8(1):1-19.

Sharpley, R. & Telfer, D. J. (2015). Tourism and Development in the Developing World. London: Routledge.

Sher, K., Bagul, A. & Din, S. (2015). The Influence of Community Attachment and Community Involvement towards Resident's Support on Sustainable Tourism Development by Mediating Perceived Benefits and Perceived Costs. Agricultural and Environmental Science. 15: 133-138.

Silva, L. (2022). The Impact of the COVID-19 Pandemic on Rural Tourism: A Case Study from Portugal. Anatolia. 33(1): 157-159.

Silverman, D. (2013). A Very Short, Fairly Interesting and Reasonably Cheap Book about Qualitative Research. London: Sage.

Simão, J. N. & Partidario, M. D. R. (2012). How Does Tourism Planning Contribute to Sustainable Development? Sustainable Development. 20(6): 372-385.

Sinclair, M. (1998). Tourism and Economic Development: a Survey. Journal of Development Studies. 34(5):1–51.

Slimane, M. (2012). Role and Relationship Between Leadership and Sustainable Development to Release Social, Human, and Cultural Dimension. Procedia-Social and Behavioral Sciences. 41: 92-99.

Slocum, S. L. & Backman, K. (2011). Understanding Government Capacity in Tourism Development as a Poverty Alleviation Tool: A Case Study of Tanzanian Policy-Makers. Tourism Planning and Development. 8(3):281-296.

Smith, V. L., & Eadington, W. R. (ed.). (1992). Tourism Alternatives: Potentials and Problems in the Development of Tourism. Pennsylvania: University of Pennsylvania Press.

Sofield, T. H. (ed.). (2003). Empowerment for Sustainable Tourism Development. Bingley: Emerald Group Publishing.

Spenceley, A. & Meyer, D. (2012). Tourism and Poverty Reduction: Theory and Practice in Less Economically Developed Countries. Journal of Sustainable Tourism. 20(3): 297-317.

Spenceley, A. & Goodwin, H. (2007). Nature-Based Tourism and Poverty Alleviation: Impacts of Private Sector and Parastatal Enterprises in and around Kruger National Park, South Africa. Current Issues in Tourism. 10(2-3): 255-277.

Spenceley, A. (2008). Tourism and Poverty Alleviation: Lessons from Southern Africa. In McCool, S. F. & Moisey, R. N. (eds.). Tourism, Recreation and Sustainability: Linking Culture and the Environment, pp. 197-219. Wallingford: CABI.

Stastna, M., Vaishar, A., Ryglová, K., Rasovska, I. & Zamecnik, S. (2020). Cultural Tourism as a Possible Driver of Rural Development in Czechia. Wine Tourism in Moravia as a Case Study. European Countryside. 12(3): 292-311.

Stewart, J. (2009). Public Policy Values. Berlin: Springer.

Stone, L. S. & Stone, T. M. (2011). Community-Based Tourism Enterprises: Challenges and Prospects for Community Participation; Khama Rhino Sanctuary Trust, Botswana. Journal of Sustainable Tourism. 19(1): 97-114.

Stone, R. (1961). Input-Output and National Accounts. Paris: OECD.

Stone, R. &Brown, A. (1962). A Programme for Growth: A Computable Model of Economic Growth. Cambridge, MA: The MIT Press.

Streeten, P. (1977). The basic Features of a Basic Needs Approach to Development. International Development Review. 3: 8-16.

Streeten, P. (1984). Basic Needs: Some Unsettled Questions. World Development. 12(9): 973-978.

Stronza, A. & Gordillo, J. (2008). Community Views of Ecotourism. Annals of Tourism Research. 35(2): 448-468.

Sugiyarto, G., Blake, A. & Sinclair, M. T. (2003). Tourism and Globalization: Economic Impact in Indonesia. Annals of Tourism Research. 30(3): 683-701.

Sumner, A. (2007). Meaning Versus Measurement: Why Do 'Economic' Indicators Of Poverty Still Predominate? Development in Practice. 17(1):4-13.

Sun J. W. & Li X. (2019). Research on Tackling Deep Poverty and Post-2020 Poverty Alleviation Strategy. Academic Journal of Zhongzhou. 273(9):67-73.

Sun, Y. Y. & Pratt, S. (2014). The Economic, Carbon Emission, and Water Impacts of Chinese Visitors to Taiwan: Eco-Efficiency and Impact Evaluation. Journal of Travel Research. 53(6): 733-746.

Suntikul, W., Bauer, T. & Song, H. (2009). Pro-Poor Tourism Development in Viengxay, Laos: Current State and Future Prospects. Asia Pacific Journal of Tourism Research. 14(2): 153–168.

Su, J.Q. & Zhang, L.L. (2015). Normative Assessment of the Theoretical Construction——Comparative Study Based on Content Analysis. Management Review. 27(8), 223-233.

Swarbrooke, J. (1998). Sustainable Tourism Management. Oxon: Cabi Publishing.

Tang, X. (2017). The Historical Evolution of China's Tourism Development Policies (1949–2013)- A Quantitative Research Approach. Tourism Management. 58: 259-269.

Tanguay, G. A., Rajaonson, J. & Therrien, M. C. (2013). Sustainable Tourism Indicators: Selection Criteria for Policy Implementation and Scientific Recognition. Journal of Sustainable Tourism. 21(6): 862-879.

Taylor, J. E.; Yúnez-Naude, A.; Dyer, G.; Ardila, S. & Stewart, M. (2003). The Economics of Eco-Tourism: A Galapagos Island Economy-wide Perspective. Economic Development and Cultural Change. 51(4): 977-97.

Taylor, J. E., Hardner, J. & Stewart, M. (2009). Ecotourism and Economic Growth in the Galapagos: An Island Economy-wide Analysis. Environment and Development Economics. 14: 139-62.

Tashakkori A, Teddle C. (2003). Handbook of Mixed Methods in Social and Behavioral Research. Thousand Oaks, CA: Sage.

Teng, Y., Cox, A., & Chatziantoniou, I. (2021). Environmental Degradation, Economic Growth and Tourism Development in

Chinese Regions. Environmental Science and Pollution Research. 28, 33781-33793.
Teo, P. & Li, L. H. (2003). Global and Local Interactions in Tourism. Annals of Tourism Research. 30(2): 287-306.
Thacher, D. & Rein, M. (2004). Managing Value Conflict in Public Policy. Governance. 17(4), 457-486.
Theil, H. & Uribe, P. (1967). The Information Approach to the Aggregation of Input-Output Tables. The Review of Economics and Statistics. 49:451-462.
Tian, S. D. (2020). The Impact of Covid-10 on China Macroeconomics: a Computable General Equilibrium Analysis. Consumer Economics. 36(3): 42-52.
Tian, C., Peng, J., Zhang, W., Zhang, S. & Wang, J. (2020). Tourism Environmental Impact Assessment Based on Improved AHP And Picture Fuzzy PROMETHEE II Methods. Technological and Economic Development of Economy. 26(2): 355-378.
Todaro, M. & Smith, S. (2011). Economic Development. (11th edition). Addison: Wesley.
Toh, R. S., Khan, H., & Ng, F. T. C. (1997). Prospects for the Tourism and Hotel Industry in Singapore: a Regression Model. Cornell Hotel and Restaurant Administration Quarterly. 38(5): 80-87.
Torabi Kahlan, P., Navvabpour, H., & Bidarbakht Nia, A. (2022). Missing Aspects of Poverty: The Case of Multidimensional Poverty in Iran. Journal of Poverty. 26(5): 424-437.
Torres, R. (2002). Toward A Better Understanding of Tourism and Agriculture Linkages in the Yucatan: Tourist Food Consumption and Preferences. Tourism Geographies. 4(3): 282-306.
Torres, R. (2003). Linkages between Tourism and Agriculture in Mexico. Annals of Tourism Research. 30(3): 546-566.
Torres-Delgado, A., & Palomeque, F. L. (2012). The Growth and Spread of the Concept of Sustainable Tourism: the Contribution of Institutional Initiatives to Tourism Policy. Tourism Management Perspectives. 4: 1-10.
Torres-Delgado, A. & Saarinen, J. (2014). Using Indicators to Assess Sustainable Tourism Development: A Review. Tourism Geographies. 16(1): 31-47.

Torres, R. & Momsen, J. H. (2004). Challenges and Potential for Linking Tourism and Agriculture to Achieve Pro-Poor Tourism Objectives. Progress in Development Studies. 4(4): 294-318.

Tourism Concern. (2004). Holidays from Hell, http://mailhost.tssa.org.uk/article=78.php3?id_article=630.

Townsend, P. (1979). Poverty in the United Kingdom: A Survey of Household Resources and Standards of Living. California: University of California Press.

Trejos, B. & Chiang, L. H. N. (2009). Local Economic Linkages to Community-Based Tourism in Rural Costa Rica. Singapore Journal of Tropical Geography. 30(3): 373-387.

Trupp, A. & Dolezal, C. (2020). Tourism and the Sustainable Development Goals in Southeast Asia. Austrian Journal of South-East Asian Studies. 13(1): 1-16.

Truong, V. D.(2013). Tourism Policy Development in Vietnam: A Pro-Poor Perspective. Journal of Policy Research in Tourism, Leisure and Events. 5(1): 28-45.

Truong, V. D., Hall, C. M., & Garry, T. (2014). Tourism and Poverty Alleviation: Perceptions and Experiences of Poor People in Sapa, Vietnam. Journal of Sustainable Tourism. 22(5): 1071-1089.

Tsakloglou, P., & Papadopoulos, F. (2002). Aggregate Level and Determining Factors of Social Exclusion in Twelve European Countries. Journal of European Social Policy. 12(3): 211-225.

Tsui, K. Y. (2002). Multidimensional Poverty Indices. Social Choice and Welfare. 19(1): 69-93.

Turner D. W. (2010). Qualitative Interview Design: A Practical Guide for Novice Researcher. The Qualitative Report. 15(3): 754-760.

Twining - Ward, L. & Butler, R. (2002). Implementing STD on a Small Island: Development and Use of Sustainable Tourism Development Indicators in Samoa. Journal of Sustainable Tourism. 10(5): 363 - 387.

United Nations World Tourism Organization (UNWTO) & United Nations Conference on Trade and Development (UNCTAD). (2001). Tourism in the Least Developed Countries. Madrid: UNWTO.

United Nations (UN). (1995). The Copenhagen Declaration and Programme of Action: World Summit for Social Development 6-12 March 1995. New York: United Nations Department of Publications.

United Nations World Tourism Organization (UNWTO). (2002). Tourism and Poverty Alleviation. Madrid: UNWTO.

United Nations World Tourism Organization (UNWTO). (2005). Making Tourism More Sustainable - A Guide for Policy Makers, https://wedocs.unep.org/20.500.11822/8741.

United Nations World Tourism Organization (UNWTO). (2004). Tourism and Poverty Alleviation: Recommendations for Action. Madrid: UNWTO.

United Nations World Tourism Organization (UNWTO). (2020). UNWTO world tourism barometer. United Nations World Tourism Organization.

United Nations World Tourism Organization (UNWTO). (2022). Tourism Grows 4% in 2021 but Remains Far Below Pre-Pandemic Levels, www.unwto.org/news/tourism-grows-4-in-2021-but-remains-far-below-pre-pandemic-levels.

United Nations World Tourism Organization (UNWTO). (2024). Sustainable development, https://www.unwto.org/sustainable-development.

United Nations Conference on Trade & Development (UNCTAD). (2017). Economic Development in Africa: Tourism for Transformative and Inclusive Growth. New York: UNCTAD.

United Nations Conference on Trade & Development (UNCTAD). (2013). Sustainable Tourism: Contribution To Economic Growth And Sustainable Development. UNCTAD Trade and Development Board. March 2013.

UNDP. 1990–2004. Human Development Report. New York, NY: Oxford University Press.

United Nations Development Program (UNDP). (2010). Human Development Report 2010 the Real Wealth of Nations: Pathways To Human Development. New York: UNDP.

United Nations World Tourism Organization (UNWTO) & United Nations Development Program (UNDP). (2017). Tourism and the

Sustainable Development Goals – Journey to 2030. Madrid: UNWTO.

United Nations (UN). (2014). The Road to Dignity by 2030: Ending Poverty, Transforming All Lives and Protecting the Planet. Synthesis Report of the Secretary-General on the Post-2015 Agenda, www.un.org/ga/search/view_doc.asp?symbol=A/69/700and Lang=E.

Van Dijk, T. A. (ed). (1997). Discourse as Structure and Process. Thousand Oaks, CA: Sage.

Vedung, E. (1998). Policy instruments: Typologies and theories. In M.-L. Bemelmans-Videc, R. C. Rist, & E. Vedung (eds.). Carrots, Sticks, and Sermons: Policy Instruments and their Evaluation, pp. 21–58. New Jersey: Transaction Publishers.

Vellecco, I. & Mancino, A. (2010). Sustainability and Tourism Development in Three Italian Destinations: Stakeholders' Opinions and Behaviours. The Service Industries Journal. 30(13): 2201-2223.

Vinodan, A., Sethumadhavan, M., & Manalel, J. (2022). Exploring sustainability facets of pro-poor tourism programs in India. Enlightening Tourism. A Pathmaking Journal. 12(2): 732-766.

Voltes-Dorta, A. & Inchausti-Sintes, F. (2021). The Spatial and Quality Dimensions of Airbnb Markets. Tourism Economics. 27(4): 688-702.

Vollmer, F. & Alkire, S. (2022). Consolidating and Improving the Assets Indicator in the Global Multidimensional Poverty Index. World Development. 158: 105997.

Vukadin, I. M., Zovko, M. & Krešić, D. (2020). Review and Evaluation of Existing International Systems of Tourism Sustainability Indicators. Croatian Geographical Bulletin. 82(1):85-110.

Wagle, U. (2002). Rethinking Poverty: Definition and Measurement. International Social Science Journal. 54(171):155-165.

Wagle, U. (2008). Multidimensional Poverty: An Alternative Measurement Approach for the United States? Social Science Research. 37(2): 559-580.

Wald, A. (1936). ÜBer Einige Gleichungssysteme Der Mathematischen Ökonomie. Journal of Economics. 7: 637-670.

Walras L. (1874a). Principes D'Une ThÉOrie MathÉMatique De L'ÉChange. Journal Des Economists. 34(100):5–21.

Walras L. (1874b). ÉLÉMents D'ÉConomie Politique Pure, Ou ThÉOrie De La Richesse Sociale, Fi Rst Instalment, Lausanne: L.Corbaz; Paris: Guillaumin; Basel: H. Georg.

Wang Q. W.; Li, S. T. & Gao, Y. (2008). Social Accounting Matrix: Principles, Methodology and Application. Beijing: Tsinghua University Press.

Wang, N. & Chang, Y. C. (2014). The Evolution of Low-Carbon Development Strategies in China. Energy. 68: 61-70.

Wang, H., Zhao, Q., Bai, Y., Zhang, L. & Yu, X. (2020). Poverty and Subjective Poverty in Rural China. Social Indicators Research. 150: 219-242.

Wattanakuljarus, A. (2006). The Nationwide Economic and Environmental Impacts of Tourism: A Computable General Equilibrium Approach for Thailand. Madison: University of Wisconsin Press.

Wattanakuljarus, A. & Coxhead, I. (2008). Is Tourism-based Development Good for the Poor?: A general equilibrium analysis for Thailand. Journal of Policy Modeling. 30(6): 29-55.

WCED. (1987). Our Common Future. In World Commission on Environment and Development. Brundtland Report, pp. 1-300. Brundtland: Oxford University Press.

Wearing, S. & McDonald, M. (2002). The Development of Community-Based Tourism: Re-Thinking the Relationship between Tour Operators and Development Agents as Intermediaries in Rural and Isolated Area Communities. Journal of Sustainable Tourism. 10(3): 191-206.

Weeden, C. (2002). Ethical Tourism: An Opportunity for Competitive Advantage? Journal of Vacation Marketing. 8(2): 141-153.

Wei, X. A. & Zeng B. W. (2018). Forty Years of Chinese Tourism Dialogue. Beijing: China Tourism Press.

Wesley, A. & Pforr, C. (2010). The Governance of Coastal Tourism: Unravelling the Layers of Complexity at Smiths Beach. Western Australia. Journal of Sustainable Tourism. 18(6): 773-792.

Weng, L., He, B. J., Liu, L., Li, C.& Zhang, X. (2019). Sustainability Assessment of Cultural Heritage Tourism: Case Study of Pingyao Ancient City in China. Sustainability. 11(5): 1392.

Werdiningtyas, R., Wei, Y. & Western, A. W. (2020). The Evolution of Policy Instruments Used in Water, Land and Environmental Governances in Victoria, Australia from 1860–2016. Environmental Science and Policy. 112: 348-360.

Wheller, B. (1992). Alternative Tourism – A Deceptive Ploy. Progress in Tourism and Hospitality Research. 4:140-145.

Wickramasinghe, K. & Naranpanawa, A. (2022). Systematic Literature Review on Computable General Equilibrium Applications in Tourism. Tourism Economics. 28(6): 1647-1668.

Willis, K. (2011). Theories and Practices of Development. London: Routledge.

Wilkinson, P. F. & Pratiwi, W. (1995). Gender and Tourism in an Indonesian Village. Annals of Tourism Research. 22(2): 283-299.

Winters, P., Corral, L. & Mora, A. M. (2013). Assessing the Role of Tourism in Poverty Alleviation: A Research Agenda. Development Policy Review. 31(2): 177–202.

WWF (World Wildlife Fund). (2001). Guidelines for Community-Based Ecotourism Development. Gland, Switzerland: WWF International.

World Travel & Tourism Council. (1998). Agenda 21 for the Travel and Tourism Industry: Towards Environmentally Sustainable Development, www.unep.fr/shared/publications/pdf/3207-TourismAgenda.pdf.

World Bank. (1980). World Development Report 1980. Washington, DC: The World Bank.

World Bank. (2016). Poverty and Shared Prosperity 2016: Taking on Inequality. Washingtong D C: The World Bank.

World Bank. (2020). COVID-19 to Add as Many as 150 Million Extreme Poor by2021,www.worldbank.org/en/news/press-release/2020/10/07/covid-19-to-add-as-many-as-150-million-extreme-poor-by-2021.

World Bank. (2022). Poverty and Shared Prosperity 2022: Correcting Course. Washington, DC: The World Bank.

Wu, G. (1995). Documentary Politics: Hypotheses, Process, and Case Studies. In C. L. Hamrin, & S. Zhao (eds.). Decision-Making in

Deng's China: Perspectives from Insiders, pp. 24–38. New York: M. E. Sharpe Incorporated.

Wulandari, N. & Firdausy, C. M. (2020). Effectiveness of Policies and Programs in Optimising Tourism Resource Potentials in Indonesia: A Research Note. International Journal of Tourism Policy. 10(2): 202-213.

Xi J.P. (2017). Secure a Decisive Victory in Building a Moderately Prosperous Society in All Respects and Strive for the Great Success of Socialism with Chinese Characteristics for a New Era. The 19th National Congress of the Communist Party of China. Beijing, China. October.

Xi, J. & Zhang, N. (2016). An Analysis of the Sustainable Livelihood of Tourism Households: A Case Study in Gougezhuang Village, Yesanpo Tourism Area. Tourism Tribune. 31(7): 65-75.

Xie,S.Y., Li L. &Feng, J. (2020). A Study on the Differences between Poor and Non-poor Households' Perception on Tourism Poverty Alleviation Policy Performance in Enshi. Tourism Tribune. 35(2): 80-92.

Xigen, W. (2019). China's Theoretical Innovation and Practical Contribution to the Right to Development: In Commemoration of the Thirtieth Anniversary of the United Nations Declaration on the Right to Development. Leiden: Brill Nijhoff.

Xin, M. (2018). Strategic Goal: Building a Well-off Society in an All-around Way. In Xin, M. (eds.). China's New Strategic Layout, pp. 21-44. Singapore: Springer.

Xinhua. (2020). China's Poverty Alleviation, a Success But Not a Full Stop, www.chinadaily.com.cn/a/202011/27/WS5fc06536a31024ad0ba96dad.html.

Xu, H. (2016). A Panel Quantile Regression Analysis of Tourism Effects on Poverty Alleviation. Proceedings of the International Conference on Poverty and Sustainable Development. Colombo, Sri Lanka. 54-65.

Yang, L. (2015). Rural Tourism and Poverty Alleviation: The Case of Nujiang, Yunnan, China. International Journal of Tourism Anthropology. 4(4): 343–366.

Yang, L. (2015). Tourism Development and Poverty Alleviation, https://scholarworks.umass.edu/cgi/viewcontent.cgi?article=1144a nd context=ttra.

Yang, H. Y., & Chen, K. H. (2009). A General Equilibrium Analysis of the Economic Impact of a Tourism Crisis: A Case Study of the SARS Epidemic in Taiwan. Journal of Policy Research in Tourism, Leisure and Events. 1(1): 37-60.

Yang, J., Zhu, B., & Han, Y. (2021). Research on the Influencing Factors and Entrepreneurship Supporting Strategies of Chinese Migrant Workers Returning Home. Proceedings of the Second International Conference on Modern Education Management, Innovation and Entrepreneurship and Social Science. Kuala Lumpur. 58-61.

Yanow, D. (1996). How does a Policy Mean?: Interpreting Policy and Organizational Actions. Washington D. C.: Georgetown University Press.

Ye W. Q. (2014). Chinese Computable General Equilibrium Micro-simulation Model: Construction and Application. Wuhan, China: Huazhong University of Science and Technology. School of Business Administration

Yin, R. K. (2014). Case Study Research: Design and Methods. Los Angeles: Sage.

Yu, J. (2013). Multidimensional Poverty in China: Findings Based on the CHNS. Social Indicators Research. 112: 315-336.

Yu, Y. (2022). AHP Evaluation of Chongqing Rural Tourism Poverty Alleviation and E-Commerce Poverty Alleviation Integration Development Strategy. Forest Chemicals Review. 1306-1316.

Yuan, Y. J. (2010). Tourism CGE System Development and Application. Shanghai, China: East China Normal University. School of Resources and Environmental Sciences.

Yue, X., Mu, K. & Liu, L. (2020). Selection of Policy Instruments on Integrated Care in China: Based on Documents Content Analysis. International Journal of Environmental Research and Public Health. 17(7): 2327.

Yüksel, A., Yüksel, F. & Culha, O. (2012). Ministers' Statements: A Policy Implementation Instrument for Sustainable Tourism? Journal of Sustainable Tourism. 20(4): 513-532.

Zandi, E. (2020). A Critical Approach to Pro-Poor. Tourism.Tourism of Culture. 1(2): 21-32.

Zeng, B. & Ryan, C. (2012). Assisting the Poor in China through Tourism Development: A Review of Research. Tourism Management. 33(2): 239-248.

Zhai, F., & Hertel, T. (2005). Impacts of the Doha Development Agenda on People's Republic of China: The Role of Complementary Education Reforms. World Bank Policy Research Working Paper No. 3702, https://ssrn.com/abstract=803626.

Zhang, Q. (2016). Research on Tourism Poverty Alleviation Model and Poverty Alleviation Effect - Analysis of survey data based on poor areas in Hainan Province. Technical Economics and Management Research. 11:124-128.

Zhang, C., Xu, Q., Zhou, X., Zhang, X. & Xie, Y. (2014). Are Poverty Rates Underestimated in China? New Evidence from Four Recent Surveys. China Economic Review. 31: 410-425.

Zhang, J. & Zhang, Y. (2018). Carbon Tax, Tourism CO2 Emissions and Economic Welfare. Annals of Tourism Research. 69: 18-30.

Zhang, J., & Zhang, Y. (2019). Exploring the Impacts of Carbon Tax on Tourism-Related Energy Consumption in China. Sustainable Development. 27(3): 296-303.

Zhang, H., Deng, T., Wang, M. and Chen, X. (2019). Content Analysis of Talent Policy on Promoting Sustainable Development of Talent: Taking Sichuan Province as an Example. Sustainability. 11(9): 2508.

Zhang, K. M. & Wen, Z. G. (2008). Review and Challenges of Policies of Environmental Protection and Sustainable Development in China. Journal of Environmental Management. 88(4): 1249-1261.

Zhao, W. & Ritchie, J. R. (2007). Tourism and Poverty Alleviation: An Integrative Research Framework. Current Issues in Tourism. 16(5):119-143.

Zhao, W., Ritchie, J. B. & Echtner, C. M. (2011). Social Capital and Tourism Entrepreneurship. Annals of Tourism Research. 38(4): 1570–1593.

Zhao, W., Yin, C., Hua, T., Meadows, M. E., Li, Y., Liu, Y., ... & Fu, B. (2022). Achieving the Sustainable Development Goals in the Post-Pandemic Era. Humanities and Social Sciences Communications. 9(1): 1-7.

Zhou, D., Chong, Z. & Wang, Q. (2020). What is the Future Policy for Photovoltaic Power Applications in China? Lessons from the Past. Resources Policy. 65:101575.

Zhou, D., Yanagida, J. F., Chakravorty, U., & Leung, P. (1997). Estimating Economic Impacts from Tourism. Annals of Tourism Research. 24(1): 76-89.

Ziffer K. (1989). Ecotourism: the Uneasy Alliance. Washington: Conservation International and Ernest and Young.

Index

V

W

Z

Afterword

As I conclude this work, Tourism and Sustainable Development in China, I am reminded of the significant journey that began with a curiosity about the complex intersection between tourism, poverty, and sustainability. The research presented in this book reflects not only the outcome of rigorous academic inquiry but also my personal experiences and reflections gained from working alongside rural communities, policymakers, and tourism practitioners in China. What I have come to understand, and what this book seeks to convey, is that tourism has the potential to be a powerful tool for sustainable development. However, this potential can only be realized when the policies supporting it are carefully crafted, inclusive, and capable of addressing the needs of marginalized communities.

This book has explored the intricate relationships between tourism policies, poverty alleviation, and sustainable development, particularly in the context of China's Tourism-Assisting the Poor Policies (TAPPs). Through these efforts, it is clear that while TAPPs have made strides in reducing poverty and stimulating local economies, there remains a great deal of work to be done. The implementation of tourism policies must move beyond economic growth and focus on a more holistic and inclusive model of development—one that nurtures the social, cultural, and environmental sustainability of communities.

As we move forward, I believe it is imperative for future research to continue probing the effectiveness of government interventions in tourism, especially in developing countries where the challenges are most pronounced. In China's case, TAPPs have laid a foundation, but their long-term success will depend on how well these policies adapt to the evolving realities of rural communities, environmental concerns, and global trends in tourism.

One of the key insights I hope readers take from this book is the importance of viewing tourism not as a singular, isolated sector but as part of a broader, interconnected system of sustainable development. Tourism must be seen as one piece of a larger puzzle—one that involves cooperation between governments, communities, businesses, and international organizations. Only by embracing this collaborative, multifaceted approach can tourism truly contribute to poverty reduction and sustainable development in a meaningful way.

This work is also a reminder of the need for greater empirical evidence and theoretical advancements to bridge the gaps in our understanding of tourism's role in development. There is still much to be learned, particularly in understanding how tourism can be leveraged to achieve not just economic prosperity, but also social justice and environmental stewardship.

As I reflect on the future, I remain optimistic about the potential for tourism to continue its transformative role in sustainable development, especially in regions that have traditionally been underserved. However, the key to success lies in our ability to design policies that are not only evidence-based but also culturally sensitive, context-specific, and mindful of the broader impacts on communities and the environment.

In conclusion, this book is both a culmination of my doctoral journey and a call to action. I hope it will serve as a source of inspiration for those seeking to create a more just, inclusive, and sustainable world through tourism. It is my belief that when done right, tourism can be more than just an economic engine—it can be a powerful force for positive change, helping to shape a more equitable future for all.

Thank you for joining me on this journey. The path ahead is one of continued exploration and learning, and I look forward to the conversations and discoveries that will undoubtedly follow.

Made in the USA
Monee, IL
05 November 2026

67812663R00199